DATE

ALSO BY CHRISTINE LEIGH HEYRMAN

*Commerce and Culture: The Maritime Communities of
Colonial Massachusetts, 1690–1750*

*Southern Cross: The Beginnings of the Bible Belt*

# AMERICAN APOSTLES

# AMERICAN APOSTLES

When Evangelicals Entered

the World of

Islam

CHRISTINE LEIGH HEYRMAN

Hill and Wang  A division of Farrar, Straus and Giroux  New York

Hill and Wang
A division of Farrar, Straus and Giroux
18 West 18th Street, New York 10011

Library of Congress Cataloging-in-Publication Data
Heyrman, Christine Leigh.
    American apostles : when evangelicals entered the world of Islam / Christine
Heyrman. — First edition.
        pages   cm
    Includes bibliographical references and index.
    ISBN 978-0-8090-2398-1 (hardcover) — ISBN 978-0-8090-2399-8 (e-book)
    1. Missions—Middle East—History—19th century.    2. Protestant churches—
Missions—History—19th century.    3. Missions, American—Middle East—History—
19th century.    4. Missionaries—United States—Biography.    I. Title.

BV3160 .H48 2015
266.0092'313056—dc23

                                                                2014047049

Designed by Abby Kagan

Hill and Wang books may be purchased for educational, business, or promotional use.
For information on bulk purchases, please contact the Macmillan Corporate and
Premium Sales Department at 1-800-221-7945, extension 5442, or write to
specialmarkets@macmillan.com.

www.fsgbooks.com
www.twitter.com/fsgbooks • www.facebook.com/fsgbooks

1  3  5  7  9  10  8  6  4  2

*For*

THOMAS CALVIN CARTER,

*as always*

# CONTENTS

# AMERICAN
# APOSTLES

# INTRODUCTION

They were the first Americans to explore the Middle East—"western Asia," they called it. They sailed up the Nile and island-hopped in Greece, but it was the Levant, an arc of land lining the eastern Mediterranean, where they spent the most time. For much of the 1820s, they sojourned in the great cities of Smyrna (Izmir), Alexandria and Cairo, Aleppo and Damascus, Jerusalem and Beirut. They made their way between them in caravans crossing the desert and in vessels plying the sea. They tried to master languages—French and Italian to converse in cosmopolitan merchant circles and then Turkish or Greek or Arabic to talk with everyone else. They made their first acquaintances with the few other Westerners who passed through or stayed on, most of them British and American naval officers and consuls, merchants and sea captains. Thereafter, they came to meet a wide circle of people native to the region—Muslims, Eastern Christians, and Jews. Of all those encounters, they kept careful records, making daily entries in journals dispatched back to the United States every few months. Newspapers and magazines there printed long excerpts, installments designed to bring many more Americans, if only in the mind's eye, to that part of the world.

Whisked over the Atlantic, through the Strait of Gibraltar, and across the Mediterranean, readers might set down anywhere in the Ottoman sultan's dominions. It could be on an island off the coast of Turkey, a high range of mountains ridging its length like a great limestone spine, the lowlands fragrant with orange and lemon trees, the mosques ablaze with light, and the cannons booming at sunset to break the Muslims' Ramadan fast. It could be on the slopes of Mount Lebanon, which, as they found out, was not a single peak "but a multitude of mountains thrown together," and at the foot of one rose the famous cedars, hundreds of them, the largest some forty feet around. Or it could be on the shores of the Dead Sea, its water so bitter that a sip turned the stomach, which made it easy to believe the Bedouins' stories about the "Apples of Sodom," local fruits that looked luscious but, once split open, crumbled to dust and smoke. What a thrill it was for readers to imagine themselves in such spots, seeing even greater wonders—the ruins of the ancient Egyptians, Greeks, and Romans, the settings of the Bible, the castles of the crusaders. To feature themselves riding donkeys along the coast between Beirut and Jerusalem, sailing a canal boat from Alexandria to Cairo, even crossing the Sinai on camels. To feel almost worldly in the knowledge that this great biblical desert was not so barren after all, because nearly everywhere thistles, grasses, and flowers sprouted from the sand.

The customs of these parts held even more fascination. A clash of cymbals heralded the entry of a Jewish bride to her wedding in Cairo. Mount Lebanon's Druze matrons seemed sprung from a race of unicorns, the silver horns of *tantours* sprouting from their heads, shimmering veils flowing from the tips. Muslim women were harder to spot, but "Mussulmen" turned up often. One was the spitting image of the Turks depicted in American geography books, this landlord of a village coffeehouse in Asia Minor, lounging on a sofa, "with a pipe in his hand and a sword and pistols behind him." More unexpected were the Arab sheikhs of Ottoman Syria who saluted male friends by grasping hands, then "put their foreheads together, and smacked their lips but without bringing their faces into contact." Stranger still, scarcely a stone's throw from Memphis, the city of the Pharaohs, an "idiot" man walked about "perfectly naked," neither taunted nor molested because Egypt's Muslims viewed such people as marabouts or saints who had "some peculiar connexion with the Deity." With every turn of the page, more curiosities, delights, and surprises tumbled out of the adventurers' dispatches. For many Americans, those reports made up the whole stock of their knowledge of western Asia and for many more, the fodder for dreams and fantasies.[1]

Not even half a century old in the 1820s, the United States had little in the way of profit or power at stake in the Middle East. If many in the West were predicting the collapse of the Ottoman Empire, which encompassed most of the region except for Persia and part of the Arabian Peninsula, its fate chiefly concerned the French, the British, and the

Russians. For the United States, strategic and economic investments lay many decades in the future. Petroleum hid deep in desert sands, its presence as unsuspected as its uses. The biggest American business in Ottoman domains was the opium trade, a commerce conducted by expatriate merchants who dispatched the drug from Turkey to China. The piracy practiced by the Barbary States of North Africa prompted occasional flurries of protest between 1785 and 1815, and the fledgling U.S. Navy retaliated with brief campaigns against Tripoli and Algiers. The Greek war for independence from the Ottomans fixed all eyes in the West on the eastern Mediterranean during the 1820s, but Americans did not stand to gain or lose by that conflict's outcome. The United States had no official diplomatic or military presence anywhere in western Asia until the 1830s, and only a few consuls. The Holy Land did not become a popular tourist destination for the affluent and the adventurous until the middle of the nineteenth century.[2]

Insignificant as the early United States' material concerns in the Middle East were, spiritual interests in the region ran high. That is what brought the first American explorers and reporters to the Ottoman Empire in the 1820s. They were Protestant missionaries—Yankee evangelicals—and, by the estimate of many in the early republic, nothing less than a new generation of apostles, successors to the disciples of Jesus. These "Palestine missionaries" would restore this stronghold of Islam to true Christianity, the faithful believed, and their accounts of converting the Muslim world, like latter-day epistles, would inspire piety and national pride at home.

Events quickly confounded those great expectations. The missionaries won no converts of any faith but instead learned the unsettling truth that the power to win hearts and minds—even among Western Christians in the Levant—belonged entirely to Islam. But if these explorer missionaries left little impress on the Middle East, they made a profound impact on their vast American audience. By both their words and their silences, by what they did and left undone, the Palestine missionaries shaped the ways in which many in the United States imagined Islam and its adherents. In turn, that invention played a key role in the ways in which evangelicals would come to define the character of their own religious movement. More broadly, this first, fateful encounter between evangelicals and the Islamic world heightened the tension between cosmopolitan and crusading impulses in American Christianity and culture. It is a contest that continues to the present, a legacy of the historical paradox that the nineteenth-century evangelical Protestants who sought religious hegemony at home and abroad also took the lead in introducing Americans to a wider world of many spiritual alternatives.

The number of God-fearing men and women in the new United States was growing fast after 1800, and the God whom many feared was one who showed special favor to evangelical Christians. Their common religious identity was still a work in progress. Disputes raged over theology and ritual practices; denominational rivalries and class antagonisms also cleaved their ranks, along with divisions over slavery and women's rights. But all evangelicals shared the signature conviction that a dramatic inward transformation—a "second birth" that regenerated the corrupt heart through saving faith in Jesus—defined what it meant to be a true Christian. Between the American Revolution and the Civil War, a growing number of converts promoted that message both at home and abroad, striving to gather as many people as possible into the evangelical fold. They aimed at nothing less than what they called "the conversion of the world."[3]

Evangelicals in the early republic aimed not only to persuade the world's peoples that their kind of Christianity was superior to all other faiths but also to convince their fellow Americans that it was indispensable to the success of the new nation. Their first discouragement was discovering that the eminences of the Revolutionary generation—many of whom were not Trinitarian Christians, let alone evangelicals— disagreed. In their private correspondence, the Unitarians John Adams and Thomas Jefferson disparaged all believers in the Trinity as "Athanasians," a reference to the fourth-century bishop who had guided church councils toward defining as Christian orthodoxy the doctrine of three persons in one God. For Jefferson, embracing that mystery convicted its believers of "the gullibility which they call faith." More gullible still were the evangelical Protestants in their ranks: he condemned their enthusiasm for missions as "a threatening cloud of fanaticism" and their missionary magazines as "satellites of religious inquisition." The nation's founders did hold one belief in common with evangelicals: both were convinced that everyone else in the world needed and, once properly informed, would desire the same thing. But for evangelicals, what the world's people would want was their kind of religion, whereas for the founders it was republican liberty.[4]

It dismayed evangelicals to discover how many men and women followed the founders and inclined toward a liberal religious outlook. By 1800, only a few Americans were radical deists, scorning convictions based on faith as superstition, but a goodly number were Christians of a non-evangelical sort—Episcopalians and Quakers, along with some Congregationalists, Presbyterians, and a great many others with no formal church affiliation. Their numbers were not growing at the brisk clip of evangelical ranks, but the Enlightenment's influence continued to draw many people toward some form of liberal Christianity. Believers of this stripe relied more on reason than revelation in forming their religious principles, regarded doing good to mankind rather than experiencing a "second birth" as evidence of being a true Christian, and often understood scripture as poetic rather than literal truth. Some among them were also coming to suspect, even to affirm publicly, that all of the world's religions taught something of value and that any religion had worth if it encouraged moral behavior.

A chorus of evangelicals told these liberals—in thunder—how wrong they were. One of the loudest voices belonged to the Reverend Asa McFarland, a formidable alloy of Scots ancestry and Calvinist conviction, who denounced the view "that it is not of material consequence what men believe, provided they maintain an upright character." On the contrary, as he assured his congregation in Concord, New Hampshire, "our domestic felicity is to be imputed to the influence of Gospel principles." It was a refrain that resounded in evangelical churches and publications: without the proper sort of Christianity, there would be no American republic—at least, not one worthy of that name. Only the right kind of religion, meaning evangelical Protestantism, could make for the right kind of state and society, providing the foundations of family harmony, social order, and political stability. It was a powerful argument in a well-stocked evangelical arsenal, and one often marshaled in the course of their long, bitter struggle to prevail over their Christian rivals—first religious liberals and then Roman Catholics.

Intent on proving their faith's power to promote order, evangelical leaders mounted the countless revivals that swelled the membership of their churches and distributed the millions of Bibles and tracts that reached people throughout the United States during the first half of the nineteenth century. They impressed their views and values on an ever wider constituency by controlling the opinion-making institutions of the new civil society taking shape in the early republic—schools and churches, voluntary societies and fraternal organizations, and the print media. They enlisted their converts in organizations to curb dueling and swearing, to close down all businesses on the Sabbath, and to re- form drunkards and prostitutes. The purpose common to all those campaigns was showing evangelical Protestantism's capacity to in- still the virtues of self-mastery essential to citizens in a republic. And those efforts met with considerable success. For a growing number of Americans, being an evangelical was coming to define what it meant to be much more—republican, respectable, and, in some sense still dimly understood in a nation so newly independent, patriotic. Once granted that evangelical Protestants made the best republicans, they hoped, it would prove a short step to concluding that all true republicans should be evangelical Protestants.[5]

The impact of this protean religious movement registered in every realm of American life during the nineteenth century, inflecting ideals of womanhood and the family, promoting respectability and reform, forging defenses and attacks on slavery and capitalism. Less familiar is the profound influence evangelicals exerted on how Americans un- derstood the world—and how that influence strengthened their reli- gious movement in its contest for ascendancy. Thanks to their mastery of the latest print technology, evangelicals reached an expanding audi- ence throughout the United States, and thanks to the information pro- duced by their foreign missionaries, they could describe distant peoples and cultures more authoritatively than any other group in the early republic. Installments from missionaries' journals became a staple of cheap, widely circulated religious periodicals and even some secular newspapers. Their pages became a primary resource—for some people, the most trusted resource—of information about the rest of the world, endowing evangelicals with the cultural authority that would empower their movement to mold public opinion on matters of foreign policy. No newspaper in the United States stationed a full-time foreign correspondent anywhere in the world until the mid-1840s, and most travel books were too expensive for readers of modest means to purchase. But for less than a dollar a month, religious periodicals took their readers around the globe. And, as one of their pious editors asked, who better than missionaries could "lay open the secrets" of the world? Here were Americans abroad who "associate with the people" and "wind themselves into their confidence," producing reports that "go into a minuteness of detail that can be found in no other accounts."

Put another way, what *National Geographic* offered the pre-Internet twentieth century—vivid, often intimate, glimpses of faraway places and peoples—missionary chronicles did for the pre-photography early nineteenth century. Week after week and month upon month, missionaries weighed in from western Asia, India, Ceylon (Sri Lanka), and the Sandwich Islands (Hawai'i), conjuring indelible images with words alone. Interspersed with those portrayals were accounts of native conversions, exchanges with rabbis and mullahs, priests and monks, and explanations of the differences among the many sects of Eastern Christians, Jews, Hindus, Muslims, and a riotous assortment of pagans. Through their missionary publications, evangelicals became the leading purveyors of a kind of popular cosmopolitanism. Although they did not celebrate the world's diverse cultures in general—and their diverse religions in particular—they were deeply interested in learning about all those differences, sharing their findings with a wide audience, and urging the duty of a globe-spanning benevolence.[6]

Missionary reports found a ready readership. Consumed as whites in the early republic were with domestic matters—buying and selling, pulling up stakes and moving, politicking and drinking, slaving and Indian fighting—they were newly eager for knowledge about the places and peoples beyond their borders. Americans of this era tore through print like termites and created new settings to read, meet, and talk. By 1820, there were scores of magazines and at least five hundred newspapers circulating in the United States, many more than in Britain, which had at least double the population. Even a country town like the Reverend McFarland's Concord—with some three thousand souls in 1820, not much bigger or smaller than most places in the United States—supported two newspapers and a library of a few hundred volumes. Some farmsteads and cider mills still dotted its main street, yet Concord boasted new gathering spots like the post office, the Phoenix

Hotel, and the Blazing Star Masonic Lodge. Under those influences and in those new venues, a fuller awareness of what lay beyond their localities expanded rapidly even among ordinary Americans. They were gestating first impressions and then forming fixed attitudes about the rest of the world.[7]

Evangelicals meant to play an important role in making up their minds. They believed that the eyewitness expertise of their missionaries would lend weight to evangelical judgments about the world's cultures, as well as informing the ways that Americans understood the importance of religion to the future of their republic. Ultimately, evangelicals were certain, the success of their foreign missions would settle the matter of their kind of Protestantism's superiority by bringing about the conversion of the world. But well before that happy event, their missionaries would confirm that false religious beliefs and practices explained why other countries failed to thrive. Missionaries would serve as unimpeachable observers and trusted commentators whose first-hand testimony would show that the wrong kind of religion fostered gross inequalities, despotic regimes, and despicable customs. As Mc-Farland summed up that strategy, even though some liberal thinkers might suggest "that the condition of society is as happy in heathen as in christian countries," missionary reports about the "religious rites and moral habits of the heathen" would loudly "contradict such an impious assertion."

Americans would also draw a crucial corollary: that evangelical influences alone kept towns like Concord from turning into Cairo. By delivering that message, missionaries abroad would become apostles to Americans at home. Decades before the foreign missions movement made American evangelicals formidable abroad, the campaign to convert the world powered their drive to dominate civil society within the United States.

It was the Islamic world that held the greatest challenge for evangelicals in the decades around 1800. For centuries before, Western traders and explorers, soldiers and diplomats, clergy and scholars, had fashioned diverse representations of Muslim cultures, constructing an Islam to serve their interests and to satisfy the requirements of their imaginations. Evangelicals now embarked on the same enterprise, even before initiating their foreign missions movement, inventing their version of Muhammad's life, their explanation for the spread of Islam, their propositions about that faith's purported impact on society and politics. Not least among the reasons that Islam riveted their attention was that it claimed a revelation superseding that of the New Testament. Muslims believed that the angel Gabriel had dictated their holy book, the Qur'an, directly to Muhammad, whose way had been prepared by other, lesser prophets before him—Abraham, Moses, and Jesus. By way of rejoinder, evangelicals pumped new life into a very old caricature of Muhammad as a bloody-minded impostor driven by ambition and lust. That particular invention had first seized Christendom's imagination in the Middle Ages, and, more than any other group, evangelicals kept it alive into the nineteenth century. They also took on board the opinions of those Enlightenment thinkers who contended that Islam encouraged the despotism of Ottoman rulers, the subjugation of Ottoman women, and the rejection of Western learning and technology by Ottoman scholars and bureaucrats. Such weaknesses spelled the ultimate doom of the sultan's empire and of Islam itself, they predicted, and evangelicals agreed, finding that outcome foretold in biblical prophecies.

Evangelicals promoted this understanding of Islam—a mix of medieval Christian polemic, selective borrowings from the Enlightenment, and apocalyptic speculation—in countless sermons, books, and religious periodicals. The energy and urgency with which they did so at first seems odd: after all, Muslims, for all their success elsewhere in the world, were not spreading their religious message in the West, and the Ottoman Empire, for centuries Islam's citadel, was fraying at its edges. But reading over the shoulders of people in the early republic— paging through the newspapers, leafing through the magazines, and checking out the libraries—turns up some clues. To enter that realm is to discover that Americans in the decades around 1800 were curious about Muhammad and his faith and that they were becoming acquainted with surprisingly diverse depictions of Islamic history and cultures. Less polemical and even positive estimates of Muhammad and his faith, the work of other Enlightenment thinkers, circulated widely in the United States, and some readers accepted them as more accurate than the Islam described by evangelicals. With his meetinghouse seating twelve hundred and his two weekly sermons, the Reverend McFarland still had prime opportunities to mold the opinions of his congregation, but he had plenty of competition, too.[8]

The outcome of this lively, even combative conversation about Islam mattered a great deal to evangelicals. They understood its importance for upholding their own faith's singularity, its truth claims, and its superiority to all other religious outlooks. To prevail in the court of public opinion, they counted, first and foremost, on their missionaries to the Ottoman Empire. Within the empire's bounds were all those places sacred to followers of Jesus, and few fixed upon that part of the world more fervidly than evangelicals, steeped as they were in the Bible. From these sacred sites, their Palestine missionaries would serve as informed, experienced experts, establishing beyond any doubt the falsity of Muhammad's creed, the fatuity of its claims to supersede the New Testament, and its poisonous effects on the sultan's dominions. Their reports from the field would amplify the images of Islam that earlier evangelicals had done so much to keep alive, enabling the foreign missions movement to extend its operations throughout the Middle East. Hopes ran just as high that the information provided by their men in western Asia would cultivate unity within evangelical ranks, enabling them to rout religious liberals and Roman Catholics back in the United States. What lay beyond the wildest imagining was that missionary encounters might offer challenges to the evangelical worldview or promote changes within their movement.

First came Levi Parsons and Pliny Fisk and, a few years later, Jonas King. Theirs were the names intoned from pulpits during missionary sermons, litanied during the monthly "Concert of Prayer" for missions, and whispered by believers during their private devotions. These founding members of the Palestine mission did not preach to large crowds or gather schools or organize churches or dispense medicine. Their primary purpose was to travel and collect information, particularly about the many religions in the sultan's domains. To that end, they moved about almost constantly, an unsettled and sometimes risky existence that ruled out marriage: bachelors they arrived and remained. No matter where travels took them, the three set down their findings in official journals nearly every day, forwarding them every few months to their sponsoring organization in Boston, the American Board of Commissioners for Foreign Missions. So earnestly did they compile information that they even charted the daily temperature during their first months in a new place. In short, these three Americans aimed to produce knowledge about the Middle East. Knowledge was power, they and their sponsors believed, and every page of these official journals attests to their determination to gain spiritual dominion over Ottoman Jews, Christians, and Muslims.

But acquiring all that information had unintended consequences. It astonished the missionaries to discover how little they actually knew about the beliefs and practices of Ottoman peoples—and how little what they had thought they knew was accurate. Even more of a shock than sounding the depth of their ignorance was discovering that Jews and Eastern Christians, even Roman Catholics and Muslims, found meaning and purpose, wisdom and comfort, in their faiths. From their earliest youth, they had cherished a certainty about the spiritual bankruptcy of these religions, never doubting that ignorance or fear or sheer stubbornness kept men and women within their folds. Now experience taught otherwise: western Asia, like their own New England, abounded in true believers. None were truer, it often seemed, than Muslims, who made up the overwhelming majority of the sultan's subjects and who succeeded at what the missionaries so signally failed—attracting converts to their faith. Here was knowledge and plenty of it, but of the sort that, instead of conferring power, sowed confusion and doubt within the ranks of these would-be apostles.

It was Pliny Fisk who proved most intent on reckoning with this dangerous knowledge about Islam. His first name—a classical ringer among so many biblical Levis and Jonases, Isaacs and Daniels—suggests that an independent streak ran in the Fisk family. There were two celebrated Plinys of Roman antiquity, uncle and nephew, both magistrates and men of letters, and most likely it was the younger from whom Fisk's parents borrowed the name. Pliny Fisk covered much of the ground in the Levant that had been ruled by this noble pagan and, like him, committed a good deal of his time there to fathoming the success of a rival faith and to writing, writing, writing.[9]

That itch to put pen to paper—and the sheer luck of his record surviving—makes Fisk the most constant witness to the story that unfolds in these pages. During his years in the Ottoman Empire, he would fill five stout, nearly ledger-sized volumes with entries in his private journal and notes on his reading, to say nothing of the hundreds of pages in official reports and letters that he dispatched back to the United States. And Fisk started writing well before his missionary career, spinning a lifeline that threads from the early American republic of the 1790s through the Levant of the 1820s. It might have snapped at several points: most of his papers lay somewhere in Beirut or Constantinople (Istanbul) for most of the nineteenth century, then were shipped across the Atlantic to sit in a cellar or attic on the East Coast, then got sold off to libraries in the mid-twentieth century, only to go missing in their stacks for many more years. If a good man is hard to find, Fisk must have been one of the best, so long were his literary remains scattered and lost. Only now recovered in full, the record of what he made of his worlds—both in the United States and in the Ottoman Empire—startles.[10]

Fisk speaks most directly in his private journal, an extraordinary chronicle spanning all his years abroad. The final version of the missionary reports published in religious periodicals and regularly devoured by so many American readers were the work of pious, circumspect editors back in the United States who culled the official journals sent from the field, red-penciling with a free hand. But well before that censoring, missionaries themselves composed their official journals with a close eye to the expectations of their sponsors, readers, and editors. They chose their news, even their words, carefully and padded their accounts with boilerplate pieties and prim rectitude. Among the many revelations of Fisk's private journal, then, is the distance between the Ottoman world he experienced and the version he and the other Palestine missionaries concocted for home consumption. Among its delights is the company of a diarist who bears no resemblance to the caricature of nineteenth-century Protestant missionaries as sanctimonious prigs and smug ignoramuses, clueless about non-Western cultures and proud of it.

But the real import of Fisk's private journal abides in its chronicling his encounters with Islam and with individual Muslims. Among the latter was a notorious American convert whom he finally tracked down in Alexandria; there was also a sheikh in Jaffa who drilled Fisk in Arabic and the teachings of the Qur'an. Fisk's efforts to understand this competing creed disclose the fundamental threat that Islam posed for evangelicals, their conviction that some secret accounted for its success, and their determination to find it out. Yet there also emerges from his private journal a deepening complexity in Fisk's response to Islam, a growing fascination with its similarities to all forms of Christianity, and even something approaching a cosmopolitan sensibility. To read closely in these pages is to glimpse the possibility that more missionaries of Fisk's bent might have produced different outcomes in the earliest relations of the United States with the Muslim world.[11]

If much of this story traces the arc of curiosity about Islam traversed by evangelicals such as Pliny Fisk, a militant crusader marches through its final chapters. As Fisk sought to discover the sources of Islam's power, his partner Jonas King strove to enlist this rival faith in enhancing the appeal of evangelicalism. In King's case, the name and the man made a perfect fit, as if fating him for this future role. His namesake, Jonah, a figure out of ancient legend, found his way into both the Old Testament and the Qur'an by claiming to have been swallowed by a great fish. Telling the first fish story is no small accomplishment, and it might have impressed upon King, a Bible reader from boyhood, the importance of making the most of his own powers of invention. That skill has long prospered among Westerners in the Middle East, and during the 1820s British and American evangelical missionaries joined their ranks. Stiff as the competition was and is, King had few peers, and he brought that talent to bear on one of the problems besetting evangelicals in the United States.

Many obstacles stood between nineteenth-century evangelicals and the fulfillment of their ambition to outstrip rival Christians, but two posed the most abiding difficulties. The first was their division over slavery, which splintered the major evangelical communions into northern and southern churches by the 1840s and embittered their relations for decades after the Civil War. Daunting as that challenge was, a second has proved even more formidable: persuading more American men to commit to evangelical Christianity. Then as now, men took less readily than did women to a faith that demanded a deeply emotional submission to a sovereign deity, and the result was—and remains—a preponderance of women in the pews. That gender gap troubled evangelical leaders far more then than it does now, and they spent most of the nineteenth century casting about for strategies to close it. One of the most ingenious came from King, who found inspiration in his embattled encounters with Muslims to endow his kind of Christianity with an indisputable purchase on masculinity.[12]

The work of both crusaders and cosmopolitans, inventing Islam reshaped evangelicalism itself. It was a consequence unforeseen by the founders of the foreign missions movement, but those in the present who take a long view of the past will be less surprised, seeing in that outcome yet another instance of a historic symbiosis. Over many centuries, portraying the East has figured as one of the most powerful influences on the West's self-definition. Through its reckonings with Islam, that process began to play out within the precincts of evangelical Protestantism at the opening of the nineteenth century, transforming its character with results that endure in the present. It was an ironic fate to befall those Christian believers who aimed—many of whom still aim—to convert all the world's peoples, especially its Muslims.[13]

*Part One*

# AMERICAN ORIENTS

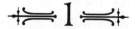

## THE AGE OF WONDERS

Let those of you who are willing to trade the life of this world for the life to come, fight in God's way. To anyone who fights in God's way, whether killed or victorious, We shall give a great reward.

—Qur'an, Women, 4:74

Pliny Fisk's practiced eye scanned the coded entries. Then he opened the small leather-bound book and transcribed the cipher. It was the fall of 1818, and he expected to be gone soon, not likely to return. If none who remained knew the code, the Brethren's earliest records would be lost. When they had first gathered a decade earlier, not a soul knew of the Brethren's existence—not friends, teachers, or even parents. They numbered among the many secret societies in the early republic, groups that concealed the names of their members and the rituals at their meetings. There were spoiled city boys who partied in clandestine social clubs, young swells who preferred to keep their revels from public view. More respectable and far more numerous were the Freemasons, whose ranks had included Revolutionary leaders such as Benjamin Franklin and George Washington. Now Masonic lodges drew otherwise sober lawyers and ministers, merchants and artisans, to conduct mysterious rituals in odd regalia. The Freemasons were also magnets for promising young men seeking useful connections, and Pliny Fisk would come to number among them. Here was someone who liked secrets.[1]

Neither he nor any of the Brethren seem like the sorts of people who would have secrets worth keeping. They were farmers' sons and preachers' kids, young New Englanders who had banded together not to get drunk and rowdy but to get serious and holy—to feed their dreams of becoming missionaries. The Brethren numbered barely a dozen when the eighteen-year-old Pliny first encountered them in 1810, two years after their founding, and how they had impressed him. There was first an exchange of letters with the prospective recruit—written in cipher like the minutes of their meetings—followed by long discussions with individual members, all several years his senior and who, as he drolly recalled, "spake of each other in such terms, as gave me a most exalted idea of them all."[2]

Exclusivity, like secrecy, appealed to the Brethren's founder, Samuel John Mills, Jr. He was a young man with a great deal to prove, blessed and burdened by his father's name. Remembered as a "giant in his physical frame," "Father Mills" was a patriarchal presence in every way, a preacher whose wit and eloquence made him the stuff of legend from his western Connecticut pastorate to Vermont's raw frontier settlements, where he often itinerated as a "domestic missionary." Alas, the junior Samuel, sawed-off and scrawny, favored his small, delicate mother; even friends described him as awkward, ungainly, and utterly humorless. He would make an unlikely leader of anything, this lackluster little fellow who spoke with a "croaking sort of voice." It was as if an eagle had sired a frog.[3]

Or so it seemed until young Mills "caught the missionary spirit," in the saying of the day, gathered the Brethren, and discovered within himself a genius for networking and organizing. Bolder than his father, he dreamed of expanding the scope of evangelical missions far beyond Vermont into every corner of the world. He aimed to forge the Brethren into a powerful order, as he believed a secret society with contrary aims, the Bavarian Illuminati, had once been, perhaps were still. A learned conclave of Western European intellectuals and statesmen, the order of the Illuminati had actually existed for less than a decade back in the late eighteenth century. It lingered much longer in the minds of conspiracy-mongers on both sides of the Atlantic who claimed that the Illuminati had provoked the French Revolution and schemed to destroy Christianity everywhere. After about 1800, most Americans repented their having credited this crackbrained fantasy, and even Mills might have come to doubt whether the Illuminati still lurked. But he remained convinced that wicked people of some description still plotted to undermine Christianity, and with the Brethren as his beginning he aimed to thwart those schemes. If the "devil" of the Illuminati had "put an en-

gine [organizing into secret societies] into our hands," Mills wrote to one
of the Brethren in 1810, "let us turn it against him and wield it like skill-
ful engineers." Far from dying out, their evangelical faith would spread
across the globe through the labors of missionaries.[4]

Being drawn into the Brethren made Pliny Fisk feel special, perhaps
for the first time in his life. As the sixth of eight children, the fourth of
five sons, he had no special claim on his parents' hopes or resources,
and in any case they had little of either to spare. The Fisks eked out a
competence from farming in Shelburne, a little upland village nestled
into heavily wooded, rolling hills that marks the first step on the ascent
from the Connecticut River valley into the Green Mountains. In this
part of western Massachusetts, the ground is rockier and the weather
colder than in Greenfield, Deerfield, and Amherst below, but its forests
are even more brilliantly afire in the fall, and in the winter its tall trees
glisten like the ramparts of an ice palace. Pliny's grandfather numbered among Shelburne's first settlers in the 1740s; after being routed
during the French and Indian War, he returned and put down roots.
His sons, including Pliny's father, Ebenezer, owned small farms and
relied on the labor of their children, whose formal education consisted
of a few months during the winter at a common school.

Not a few young people in early nineteenth-century New England
dreamed of escaping places like Shelburne. Among them was Ezra
Fisk, who, when he recruited his young cousin Pliny into the Brethren,
had gotten as far away as Williams College and hoped to get farther
still. Pliny had his eye on the same opportunities, so he, too, seized his
chance to enter the orbit of the Mills family, joining the Brethren and
making promises that might have given another young person pause.
He signed their constitution, pledging to undertake "a mission to the
heathen" and to keep free from any entangling "engagements" of a romantic nature. He professed "a firm belief in those distinguishing doctrines commonly denominated evangelical" and swore to keep secret
all of the Brethren's dealings. Less than a year later in March 1811, he
joined the sophomore class at Middlebury College and began his uphill battle for an education. He was obliged to break off his studies for
months at a time, doing manual labor or teaching school to scrimp
together the money to continue. He struggled to keep up academically as
well, having had only the scantiest training in the classics. Still, it must
have seemed a remarkable providence to Pliny, first his being admitted

to the Brethren, then his father's agreeing to forgo his help on the family farm. Perhaps Ebenezer Fisk harbored some hopes of the boy's bettering himself. Why name a son after two noble Romans if not to set him apart from all those Ichabod Cranes?[5]

As Pliny Fisk's dreams began to find their first fulfillment, so too did those of young Samuel Mills. Only two years after his first gathering of the Brethren in 1808, several like-minded ministers founded the American Board of Commissioners for Foreign Missions, and their first cohort of missionaries sailed for India in 1812. Over the next decades, missionaries from the American Board and other Protestant organizations overspread the globe; at the height of their influence a century later, there would be a hundred missionary societies in the United States sponsoring about five thousand men and women overseas. Mention missionaries today, and chances are that someone within earshot will claim a great-grandmother who taught in China or a distant cousin who preached in Africa. For more than a century after its founding, the foreign missions movement played a major role in defining the culture of evangelical Protestantism, inspiring devotion and activism among millions of believers. It all began with Samuel Mills's band of Brethren: it seems that they did have some secrets worth knowing.[6]

Here's one of them: Why did the campaign to build a global empire of the spirit draw its strongest original supporters from a narrow, exclusive elect of New England believers, nearly all immured in isolated farming villages and committed to an unbending Calvinism? How did such unlikely people—these self-righteous, tribal hicks—seize on so improbable a goal as the conversion of the world, including the Muslim world? It was as if a frog had sired an eagle.

The American foreign missions movement originated in an evangelical subculture known as the New Divinity. It claimed many, perhaps a majority, of small-town New Englanders during the decades around 1800, and its epicenter lay in northwestern Connecticut and western Massachusetts. The religious revivals that rippled throughout New England between the late 1790s and the 1820s also spread the New Divinity's influence east toward the seacoast and west wherever Yankees migrated—Vermont and New Hampshire, the Hudson River valley, and

Ohio's Western Reserve. Dense webs of kinship and friendship knit the sinews of this body of believers, and women typically outshone men as the most committed members of the laity. Not content with regular attendance at worship, women were far more likely to possess the spiritual fervor that led to their converting in revivals and then joining the churches as full members.

But it was the clergy—their ranks opened only to men—who provided the public face of the New Divinity. Charismatic ministers such as Father Mills seemed almost shamans to their parishioners. There was the woman who recalled repeating her pastor's name when, as a girl, she walked home alone in the dark, "with a vague impression that the repetition of this magical name would keep off all evil agencies," and the man who remembered in youth regarding his minister as "a sort of oracle." Some preachers had also spent time in the militia or the Continental army during the revolution, lending luster to their reputations even before they won renown for igniting revivals in their own churches and evangelizing frontier settlements in northern New England and New York. There they faced down challenges from rival Protestants, most formidably from the upstart Baptists and Methodists. Those fellow evangelicals set the same spiritual premium on a new birth, but the New Divinity scorned their poorly educated clergy and the unrestrained emotionalism of their worship. They also battled religious liberals: the few but pesky deists who rejected the Bible, the Universalists who offered salvation to all, and those within Congregationalist ranks who inclined toward Unitarian beliefs and questioned the divinity of Jesus.

New Divinity ministers and laypeople alike embraced a starkly conservative theology and a doctrinaire moral code. They smiled upon the chaste pastimes of sleighing and singing schools but grimaced at the vanity of balls and "frolics." Like many of their fellow Congregationalists and Presbyterians, they took their ideas about the relationship between God and humankind from the teachings of John Calvin. But no believers in New England took Calvin's ideas more seriously than did the adherents to the New Divinity. Even as they joined with more moderate Calvinists to promote revivals, the members of the New Divinity drubbed them for assuring sinners that good works and better intentions would win salvation. Only divine grace could transform the corrupt heart, the New Divinity taught, rooting out pride and

selfishness and instilling the capacity to act with "disinterested benevolence" for God's glory alone. They felt certain that even though the
sovereign God had made men and women bad to the bone, these fallen
human beings were nevertheless morally accountable for their sins.
Nothing in that conviction struck believers as contradictory, and it
aroused little debate, because they excluded from their churches anyone who did not share their religious views.

The New Divinity faithful may have peered at truth through a one-
inch pipe, but backward-looking they were not. Like their idolized
Jonathan Edwards some fifty years earlier, their ministers mounted an
intellectually rigorous defense of Calvinism for a post-Enlightenment
world, fending off charges of its being fatalistic, unreasonable, unfair,
and downright unrepublican. And as adroitly as evangelicals in the
present day, they flexed their power to shape the United States through
newfangled techniques. After 1800, that included founding an array of
what were then novel institutions—religious presses and publications,
libraries and moral reform associations, and domestic and foreign missionary societies. They established academies and colleges such as Middlebury, Amherst, Dartmouth, and Williams, as well as theological
seminaries, beginning with Andover. Their aim was to cultivate in the
laity, especially in young people, the piety and learning to promote
the New Divinity's vision of the future.[7]

If young Samuel Mills was their most fortunate son, Levi Parsons
was almost as much a golden boy. A shirttail relative of Pliny Fisk's and
the same age, Parsons boasted a background considerably more prosperous and genteel. As the young Fisk plowed his father's fields and mucked
out the barn in Shelburne, Parsons passed his boyhood in the nearby
village of Goshen, several slowly winding miles uphill from Northampton, Massachusetts. There his father—no hardscrabble farmer, but
the learned Reverend Justin Parsons—ministered for many years before presiding over two fledgling churches in Vermont and itinerating
tirelessly for domestic missionary societies.

That intensity his son more than matched. During his years at Middlebury, Levi matured into a magnetic religious virtuoso whose spiritual experiences met even the high standard set by the New Divinity.
These he freely shared in letters to his mother and sisters, who thrilled
to his pledges "to qualify myself to fight the battles of the Lord" and "to
climb up higher and higher, to be swallowed up by the Lord." A revival

in the fall of 1811 answered his striving: he experienced a classic New Divinity conversion, overcoming his repugnance to the dread doctrine "that *such* a God should reign" who "dispensed mercy to some and not others." After much anguish, he grasped at last the justice of himself, and all of fallen humankind, being sent to hell, whereupon "the world lost its charms—death was now only the gate to glory." New Divinity believers proved their spiritual mettle and gained assurance of their salvation by attaining such indifference to death's terrors, including the prospect of their own damnation. Such sentiments were proof of a regenerate heart, one so shorn of self-love that it had no other desire but to advance God's kingdom.[8]

Levi's future now spread before him. He had come to share the missionary dreams of the young man who had become his fast friend when they roomed together at Middlebury, Pliny Fisk. By 1816, the Brethren had gathered Parsons into their ranks, and a year later, shortly before graduating from Andover Theological Seminary, he delivered a fiery address to his fellows that signaled his plans. In the non-Christian world, he believed, Islam was an even more formidable foe than paganism, for in Muslim countries, "the kingdom of Satan is *firmly* established—favored by the *prejudices* of the *people*—strengthened and upheld by the power of *Magistrates*—by the arts, and subtilty of *Politicians*, the craft and influence of *superstitious Priests*." In Islamic dominions "where *every nerve* is braced against the truth," missionaries "who, at the command of Christ," carried "the standard of the cross" must "expect to fight, and fall by its side." But now, as in the days of the apostles, he concluded, "the blood of Martyrs will be the seed of the church."[9]

Pliny Fisk would have hung on every word, his dark, wide-set eyes fixed on his friend. What a brave, greathearted soul Parsons was, even more now than back at Middlebury. Classmates there had dubbed him "captain of the beggars" because he scrounged books for poor students, his roommate Fisk among them. Fisk had followed Parsons to Andover after scraping together enough from his teaching in country schools and the seminary's charity fund. Now Parsons's fervent denunciation of the Muslim world brought home to Fisk what their elders had been saying for years—that they lived in an "age of wonders." It was a time in which all things were possible, great evils and enormities as well as incomparable blessings and triumphs. A cosmic drama was playing out before their eyes, and in its final acts, pagans, Jews, and even the followers of Muhammad would abandon their former faiths and embrace Christianity. Should so superior a spirit as this "captain of the beggars" fall while bearing the standard of the cross against that of the crescent, what greater blessing than to die at his side? In his mind's eye, Pliny Fisk was already making his way to western Asia with Levi Parsons at his side.[10]

Martyrdom: that is how the first missionaries imagined their end. They numbered themselves among those apostles who would be called upon to give up their lives to convert the world. Only the era of the Reformation rivaled that of the early foreign missions movement when it came to the Protestant celebration of this self-immolating piety. John Foxe's *Actes and Monuments* (1563) riveted several successive generations of readers in England and New England with stories of the torture and death of Protestants at the hands of Roman Catholics. That cult of martyrdom renewed its claim on the imagination among many evangelicals after 1800, revived by their zeal for missions. But if most future foreign missionaries expected disease to claim their lives, those who set their sights on Islamic countries, like Fisk and Parsons, looked for a bloodier end: Muslims would step into the Catholics' role, wielding the assassin's knife or the executioner's sword.

A particular understanding of the past, present, and future forged the resolve of aspiring missionaries to become martyrs for their faith. Throughout youth, they were steeped in the history and prophecies handed down by New Divinity ministers who preached to local missionary societies and churches throughout New England in the years after 1800. Their sermons began by describing the first "apostolic age" during those centuries following the death and resurrection of Jesus, when, by their count, the largest number of Christians had walked the earth. But around the fourth century, the number of true Christians declined, a casualty, by the New Divinity's calculus, of corruption in the Roman Catholic Church, its idolatrous worship of the Virgin Mary and the saints, and the pretensions of popes to absolute authority. The rapid spread of Islam after the seventh century made matters even worse, a downward spiral finally broken by the Protestant Reformation and the providential invention of the printing press. And now at last—

during their own time—New Divinity believers felt certain that history had reached another crossroads: a new age of wonders had arrived, a second "apostolic age."

Some of those wonders were terrors that shook the world to its foundations. There was the bloodbath of the French Revolution, which unleashed a flood of "infidelity," an assault on Christianity. There were Napoleon's campaigns, which had set all Europe ablaze. Yet amid those horrors, there were wonders of another sort—wonders that assured true Christians that time was on their side. There were feats of exploration that had brought Western adventurers to nearly every part of the world and prodigies of new knowledge that they gained about other cultures. That expertise would soon see the Bible translated into every language, while innovations in print and transport would promote its dissemination around the globe. But of all the wonders that augured a new apostolic age, the greatest marvel of all was the foreign missions movement. Like a growing number of evangelicals on both sides of the Atlantic, the New Divinity believed that missions were God's appointed means for the final conversion of the world. Their confidence came from the conviction that they possessed an advantage over Jesus' disciples: print. It was an "engine of amazing power," as the Reverend Francis Brown assured a Maine missionary society, one that gave evangelicals "a hundred tongues," allowing them to "address at the same moment, persons on opposite sides of the globe."[11]

For all those reasons, glory awaited in the future envisioned by evangelicals. The new apostolic age, with its wonders both inspiring and terrifying, would culminate in the coming of the millennium, the thousand-year reign of Christ's saints on earth. But as Christianity's ultimate triumph over the Antichrist neared, a series of cataclysms would set history's crucible aboil—events of the last days that the devout found prefigured in the prophetic biblical books of Daniel and Revelation. They included the collapse of the Ottoman Empire, the return of the Jews to Palestine, and epic battles to topple what evangelicals identified as the twin horns of the Antichrist, the "imposture" of Islam and the "idolatry" of Roman Catholicism. That apocalyptic pairing of the two faiths and their gaudy rebranding—Islam became "the Mahometan delusion," Catholicism, the "Mystery Babylon" or "the mother of harlots"—evoke the visceral loathing those rival faiths aroused in evangelicals.[12]

End-of-the-world predictions draw ridicule today, but in the New England of Fisk and Parsons plenty of people took them seriously. "Learned treatises on the prophetic writings were favorite topics of discussion in social parties," one minister recalled of his boyhood in Stockbridge, Massachusetts. Parlors hummed with eager voices matching "signs of the times" spotted in the newspapers to biblical references plucked from the book of Revelation. Preachers made the most of this popular fascination. Many at the annual meeting of one missionary society in 1808 nodded in sober assent when the keynote speaker predicted that "within sixty years mahometanism and popery will be exterminated," because evangelicals saw hopeful signs everywhere. Why, Napoleon had occupied Rome itself, and as for Islam, both Russian challenges to the Ottoman Empire and religious schisms among Muslims foretold a grim future. Of particular interest were the Wahhabis of Arabia, known among evangelicals as "the Protestants of Mahomedanism," because of their opposition to the veneration of saints and shrines among some Sunnis. The Wahhabis, some New Divinity ministers predicted, would become their allies in any future struggle against other Muslims—an irony, given that this Islamic movement would later become the seedbed of militant jihadism.[13]

Yet more testimony that history had entered an age of wonders came from British evangelicals. As they lobbied Parliament to support the Christianization of India, they also barraged the public with stories and pictures showing the deplorable practices of the Hindus. Evangelical publications during the decades around 1800 overflowed with grisly descriptions of widows throwing themselves on the funeral pyres of dead husbands, pilgrims pitching themselves under the wheels of the car of "Juggernaut," parents drowning infant girls, and seers self-mutilating. The leading British religious monthly advanced the cause with a series of engravings depicting Hindu deities, a sinister pantheon that surely scared the bejeezus out of a generation of young evangelicals and kept them peeking under the bed for the rest of their lives. Here were wonders indeed, and so gruesome that their images migrated quickly across the Atlantic.[14]

The British evangelical who drew the largest American audience was a Scots chaplain in the East India Company, Claudius Buchanan. In 1811, he produced a Hindu-bashing classic with the deceptively tame title *Christian Researches in Asia*, which went into multiple editions on both sides of the Atlantic. The book's appeal is not hard to grasp: Buchanan was a move-over–Stephen King master of the Hindu horror genre, able to out-suttee and out-"Juggernaut" all comers in what was already a crowded field. But even before he set upon the Hindus, the resourceful Buchanan had found in Islamic ranks a wonder of another sort entirely: the Muslim almost instantaneously brought to Christianity through contact with the Bible. A number of those surprising converts turned up in missionary literature, but in 1809 Buchanan made two of them famous in what became the signature sermon of the early evangelical foreign missions movement, *The Star in the East*.[15]

Buchanan's star was Jawad Sabat, a Muslim from Arabia whose family could "trace their pedigree to Mahomet." His backstory—from Sabat's lips to Buchanan's ear—involved the conversion and "martyrdom" of another Arabian Muslim, Abdallah. Together he and Sabat had traveled as far as Kabul in Afghanistan; there they parted ways, and Abdallah embraced Christianity after a chance "perusal of a Bible." Fearing the consequences of his apostasy, Abdallah fled to Bukhara (in present-day Uzbekistan), where he had the misfortune to run into Sabat, who, outraged, betrayed his friend to Muslim authorities and witnessed his beheading. Stricken with remorse, Sabat wandered to India, where he, too, happened on the New Testament and, after comparing it with the Qur'an, "the truth of the word of God fell on his mind . . . like a flood of light." He took the name Nathaniel upon his baptism at the age of twenty-seven, and he was working as a translator for Protestant missionaries in India when he came to Buchanan's notice. No matter that Sabat's story (if his it was) seems a little sketchy: Buchanan dearly wanted to believe, because the convert made such a usable Muslim. Many other evangelicals wished to believe it, too. So famed was *The Star in the East* by the second decade of the nineteenth century that a Baptist pastor in then-remote Delaware County, Ohio, rendered it as an epic poem, and Andover students referred to its hero as "the celebrated Sabat."[16]

No small thanks to Buchanan, Britain's evangelicals carried their point with Parliament, which in 1813 loosened the East India Company's restrictions on allowing missionaries into India. Here was yet more evidence that anything was possible at the edge of history, where wonders begot more wonders. Or so it seemed to the younger Samuel Mills, who, upon hearing the news, exulted that the "present day is a truly interesting era."[17]


Believing that they lived in "interesting" times—poised on the cusp of the millennium—provided the New Divinity believers and all evangelicals with a powerful narrative. It ordered events and experiences into a meaningful pattern: nothing was random, and anything was possible. It made ordinary people into God's agents, doing their part for the imminent defeat of paganism or Roman Catholicism or Islam by supporting missions. It filled their lives with drama and significance, knowing that they were carrying out the divine will for human history and reshaping the world. Here was the same sense of purpose and order that Puritanism had offered believers in the sixteenth and seventeenth centuries, another period of intense millennial fervor. The foreign missions movement offered other satisfactions, too, that met the particular needs of young Americans in the Northeast.[18]

Centuries of practice had taught women to find fulfillment through selflessness, so it comes as no surprise that the elderly and matronly as well as the young and single flocked to the missionary cause. It found particular favor among those women coming of age in the early nineteenth century who had ready access to books, magazines, and newspapers and perhaps even an education at one of the growing number of female academies or seminaries. Many faced diminished or delayed prospects for marriage as the westward migration of men drained the Northeast's pool of potential spouses, while others preferred to remain single. Such women searched for other sources of fulfillment by teaching school, organizing reading circles and literary societies, and joining benevolent and missionary societies. They also wrote letters and kept journals that set forth their edifying, sometimes spiritually strenuous lives, some of which were edited into memoirs and shepherded to press by conservative evangelical clergymen.[19]

One of those memoirs became a blockbuster. It was the work of Leonard Woods, a New Divinity professor at Andover who saw a silver lining in the somber end of one Harriet Atwood Newell, an academy-educated young woman who became the wife of one of the first American missionaries to India. Because their arrival in Bengal coincided with the outbreak of the War of 1812, the British sent them packing, and the Americans scattered, hoping to find a new foothold for their mission. Harriet Newell had just turned nineteen when both she and her newborn infant died on an island off the southeast coast of Africa. That occasioned some murmuring against the foreign missions movement on the part of critics who detected within its ranks an insouciance about sacrificing the lives of women usually associated with the Hindus. But from the jaws of this near public relations disaster, Woods snatched commercial triumph: he devised a hybrid of pious memoir and adventure story from the letters and journals that Newell wrote during her short life. Although she had not shared the gospel with so much as a single "heathen" and died, like many women who remained in the United States, from complications of childbirth, Harriet Newell entered Woods's missionary pantheon of the "new race of APOSTLES AND MARTYRS." After all, she had forsaken friends and home for "burning India."[20]

This idealized heroine came to loom large in the inner world of many evangelicals, emerging as a model for future missionaries and supporters of missions, men as well as women. When Laura Chipman lay dying in 1818, the sixteen-year-old Vermonter looked forward to meeting Newell—known to her only from Woods's memoir—in heaven. Rufus Anderson, a Bowdoin student, fantasized about marrying Newell's sister, Emily: "If she be like her sister, God grant she may be mine;—that we may both cross the stormy ocean together, and administer the word of life to India's pagan inhabitants." Then there was Fanny Woodbury, who hoped to make a literary splash by publishing the spiritual reflections that she traded with her former schoolmates. Among them was the former Harriet Atwood, and Woodbury touted their connection ("It is unnecessary to say, she was one of my *first* and *best beloved* friends") shamelessly. And successfully: Woodbury's pastor published her journals and letters in 1814, shortly after her death. After reading them, Rufus Anderson marveled, "I never had, during my acquaintance with her, any idea that she was possessed of such talents. She was ever unassuming and opposed to ostentation of every kind." Ah, Rufus: little did you suspect that beneath the self-effacing exterior of such young women lurked an ambition to put their impress on the wider world, whether by breaking into print or taking up the cause of missions.[21]

The same drive animated young men, none more than the New Divinity's rising generation of ministers. They wished to imitate their fathers, biological and spiritual, to fight and win against their enemies. But they also aimed to outdo those redoubtable patriarchs by converting not merely Vermont but the whole world. Those outsized ambitions to win fame beyond the Berkshires, even the Green Mountains, did not set well with some among their elders: *Just who did these boys think they were?* In the rural milieus of the early republic, youthful strivings could arouse resentment among a less venturesome older generation. They surfaced in the accusations of "wanting a great name" that were leveled against Harriet Newell before she sailed for India. They echo in the suspicions of a cantankerous Vermonter that Levi Parsons was pocketing money from his missionary collections. They underlay the lavish assurances in the evangelical press that missionaries provided for the maintenance of aging parents before departing for the field. Warmly as most of the New Divinity tribe supported the missionary cause, not all of its older members were on board. Leave that field to the British, they warned: let the charity of American evangelicals begin at home with the poor, the frontier settlers, and the Indians.[22]

Even those young people encouraged by their families harbored complicated feelings about their missionary ambitions, particularly those who had imbibed the self-denying teachings of the New Divinity. During his years at Bowdoin, Rufus Anderson berated himself constantly for "this vile ambition! This enemy to vital godliness!" At one point, he feared that his zeal to become a missionary was giving way to "a stronger desire than formerly to improve myself in human science and literature," because the "love of applause seems deeply rooted in my heart." At the same time, Anderson fretted that he wanted to become a missionary only to win acclaim for his self-denial: "Is it that I may be known—that my name may be spoken of among men?" Most likely so, in his case. Once he made it to India with Harriet Newell's sister at his side, he wondered, "Will the hideous Jug[g]ernaut be compelled to witness the name of *Anderson* on the list of his opponents—classed with those who cross the mighty deep to contend with the kingdom of Satan? It is too much to expect; yet not too much." But most young evangelicals regarded missions as a sanctified outlet for their strivings. Committing to a missionary career was a pious expression of the passion for distinction, a way of purging the dross of worldliness from their ambition.[23]

Missions answered not only the personal aspirations of pious youths but also their sense of kinship with and obligation to faraway peoples. The same prodigies of travel, knowledge, and technology that announced the age of wonders to evangelicals also numbered them among a widening circle in the West who believed that succoring the world's less fortunate lay within their reach and hence their moral duty. Missionary sermons urged upon Christians the duty of a globe-spanning benevolence, showing compassion for every branch of "the great family of man" and ending the sufferings of "millions of our race"—which included, of course, their belief in the wrong kind of religion. Such rhetoric nurtured an emotional bond between evangelicals and what Leonard Woods called the world's *great family of immortals.*" "Imagine your children, parents, brothers, sisters this moment in the midst of India, worshippers of the horrid idol Juggernaut," he challenged his congregation. "But have not the Indians souls as precious as the souls of your kindred?—Nay rather, they are themselves your kindred; allied to you by the ties of a common nature . . . forget not the partners of your blood!"[24]

Promoters of missions thus affirmed Enlightenment universalism: the belief that human nature is the same everywhere. (The correlate was that everyone, the world over, would learn to embrace evangelical Protestantism along with the other practices of a clearly superior Anglo-American civilization.) With that enhanced fellow feeling came a heightened, sometimes even overwhelming sense of personal responsibility. Pliny Fisk admitted to experiencing years of "anxiety" about his "duty respecting missions," fearing that if he did not commit to that course, "the blood of souls may be found in my skirts." An indelible image and, coming from a man who did not often reach for a metaphor, it suggests that Fisk first heard the phrase in a missionary sermon and ever after it kept up a drumbeat in his brain. No wonder, so aptly did it express his fears that God would hold him responsible for the damnation of people half a world away from Shelburne. But there were within evangelical ranks some who scorned that kind of thinking, mainly members of an older generation who believed that charity should begin and end at home. Younger folks like Fisk who thought otherwise—who believed that their empathy and obligations as Christians extended beyond their homes and local communities—fell under suspicion among these elders for not keeping to their appointed place in the world.[25]

If newly intense and widespread stirrings of both ambition and humanitarianism drew many young evangelicals into the missionary orbit, their desire to vindicate Calvinism played a role as well. New Divinity ministers felled forests publishing their metaphysical contortions in Calvinism's defense, and they looked to missions for a practical validation of their theology. The inspiration for that hope came from their patron saint Jonathan Edwards's most popular work, a biography of his protégé, David Brainerd, who served as a missionary to several Indian tribes in the Northeast. Edwards emphasized the power of his and Brainerd's unflinching Calvinism to shape up Indian converts and challenged religious liberals to find "an instance of so great and signal an effect of their doctrines, in bringing infidels . . . to such a degree of humanity, civility, exercise of reason, self-denial, and Christian virtue." Not the weak tea of liberal theologies but only the potent elixir of Calvinism, he concluded, could win the hearts and minds of all the earth's peoples, transforming their cultures along the way. The conversion of the world would attest, once and for all, to its singular religious truth.[26]

Leaders of the early foreign missions movement adopted the same logic. Like Edwards before them, they believed that success in proselytizing among the besotted Hindus, the bigoted Muslims, and the benighted pagans would bear out the truth of their faith. And they would spare no rigor, demanding from those converts the same strict observance of God's law and the same evidence of an inward regeneration required of any candidate for membership in the New Divinity's churches. What they aimed for was no nominal pledge of faith but heartfelt experiences of conversion, rivaling in intensity and exaltation that of Levi Parsons. If those expectations struck others as loony—if they scoffed at the possibility of imparting religious sensibilities so foreign to non-Christians—well, that reflected only their critics' sorry underestimate of a sovereign God. As for the New Divinity believers and their allies, they were confident that the rest of the world would rise to their demanding spiritual regimen because theirs was an all-powerful deity, Calvinism prescribed the most acceptable form of his worship, and, as Leonard Woods avowed, the "laws of Christianity are suited to govern mankind of every nation and climate." In other words, the most exclusive and doctrinaire Christians in the early republic took up the cause of missions precisely *because* their prospects for success struck most Americans as so far-fetched. What was appealing to the New Divinity believers about converting the world was not that it would be easy but that it would be hard, seemingly impossible. It would be the crowning achievement of their faith, the ultimate display of divine glory in this new age of wonders.[27]

Many influences, then, drew evangelicals, most notably the young men and women among them, into the foreign missions movement. The ambivalence about ambition that bedeviled both sexes, the currents of enlightened universalism and humanitarianism, and the New Divinity's last-ditch defense of Calvinism—all combined to attract them to the work of missions. An uncompromising theology also lent a sense of urgency to their commitment. There could be no salvation without faith in Jesus, evangelicals believed, so the eternal outcome would be grim for those who died still deluded by Islam or Hinduism, paganism or unbelief. That meant hell was filling fast, and ministers never tired of doing the math to prove it. While their estimates of world population varied wildly, there was general agreement that pagans, Muslims, and Jews made up between two-thirds and three-quarters of the human race. By every count, pagans came in as the most numerous group and Jews as the smallest, and Muslims far outstripped Christians. There was also consensus that Roman Catholics and Eastern Christians outnumbered Protestants about three or four to one. One popular speaker on the missions circuit even computed the death rate among non-Christians who had reached "the age of discretion": he came up with twenty-eight thousand unsaved people dying per day, nearly twenty a minute. "While I am pleading they are launching forth," he warned his hearers. So many unsaved and so little time.[28]

Running those numbers disturbed evangelicals, not only because of the legions damned, but also because of the questions raised. If theirs was the superior religion, why were their ranks so small? Why were Protestants outnumbered by non-Christians, including Muslims—and even by Catholics within the Christian fold? It was inadvertent—to say nothing of inconvenient—but by bringing the religious loyalties of the world's people to the attention of a wide audience for the first time, the foreign missions movement got a great many Americans wondering about why their kind of Christianity was faring so badly.

Evangelicals were confident that they knew the answers, and none knew them better than the New Divinity. The predominance of pagans in the world made sense, they reasoned, given the long isolation of large parts of the globe, and the power of the papacy to keep the Bible out of circulation explained Catholic preeminence among Christians. As to Islam's superiority, evangelicals' answer differed little from the one that Christians had started giving in the Middle Ages: military conquest and forced conversions had spread Muhammad's faith, and its hold had endured through both the ruthlessness of rulers and the ignorance of their subjects. Since their earliest youth, Pliny Fisk and Levi Parsons had heard this explanation of why so many of the world's peoples were Muslims, and they were not supposed to learn any new answers from their ministerial training at Andover Theological Seminary.[29]

When it opened in 1807, Andover was a bastion of New Divinity Calvinism with an endowment double the size of Harvard's. The faculty understood its mission as training a Christian ministry with a three-year curriculum that consisted of teaching the Bible, Christian theology, and "sacred rhetoric"—meaning tips for preaching a decent sermon. Conspicuous by its absence was any instruction in the history of religion—not even the history of Christianity. The faculty believed that exposing students to the diversity of Christian belief might undermine their faith. But inevitably the interest in foreign missions among many of Andover's sponsors, professors, and students fostered curiosity about the world's religions, and with some unforeseen results.[30]

Shortly after arriving at the seminary in 1810, the younger Samuel Mills had organized the Society of Inquiry, a club for his fellow students considering missionary work. The Brethren, founded two years before, continued to thrive as a separate and still-secret group, and Mills seems to have used the society to recruit new members. Talking points for the society's meetings came from "dissertations" presented by its members, and during their time at Andover, Fisk and Parsons had the opportunity to hear or read two dissertations on Islam. The first came from Alvan Bond, who within a few years would become Fisk's brother-in-law; the second was the work of one Jacob Scales: both offered starkly negative images of Muslim cultures. Scales asserted that

Islam rotted all of its adherents in the same way: Muslims were mean, servile, ignorant, intolerant, and debauched. Bond opined that different Islamic societies rotted their peoples in differing ways, turning the Turks into oversexed dopes and the Arabians into plundering bandits, while conspiring to keep the Persians in "slavish subjection" to tyrants and the Egyptians in wretched poverty.

If those judgments show how well missionary sermons did their work, stray passages in both dissertations reveal a very different influence shaping their authors' views of Islam. With all the snippy assurance of the freshly informed, Scales dismissed "the opinion of some writers that Muslims believe women have no souls." "Whatever may be the opinion of the ignorant," he added, "enlightened Mohammedans believe them [women] to be immortal." Scales also credited Muhammad with reforming the "vile idolatries" of pagan Arabs and ending their practice of "burying their daughters alive at pleasure." Even more venturesome was Bond's assertion that Islam had not spread entirely by the sword. Muslims were active in "disseminating their own sentiments and successful in making proselytes," he contended, even in lands "where their arms have never penetrated."[31]

Bond and Scales had drawn all these judgments from the writings of George Sale. The Andover library contained only a small stock of books on Islam, nearly all of them polemical attacks, but like most libraries of any size in the early republic it also held a copy of his English translation of the Qur'an. First published in 1734, Sale's remained the best and most widely circulated translation in the West for nearly two hundred years thereafter. A solicitor by training and an Orientalist by passion, he was deeply read in the earliest enlightened Western scholarship on Islam, and he had picked up Arabic from two Syrian Christians of his acquaintance in London. His own spiritual loyalties are elusive. In the long "preliminary discourse" preceding his translation, he professed his belief that Protestants would play a providential role in the extinction of Islam and that an "impartial version" of the Qur'an was essential to expose Muhammad's "imposture." Sale then took the better part of two hundred pages—with a combination of lawyerly argument, learned historical references, puckish humor, and deadpan delivery—to counter the charges against Islam advanced by centuries of Christians. It was from the pages of the preliminary discourse that some Andover students learned new answers to the question of why there were so many Muslims in the world—answers that introduced them to the unsuspected ways in which Islam satisfied the spiritual strivings of its adherents.[32]

Key to Sale's case was proving that force alone did not account for the rapid spread of Islam. There was "something more than what is vulgarly imagined, in a religion which had made so surprising a progress," he insisted, and that something was Islam's eloquent testimony against idolatry and polytheism. Principled convictions—not ambition and lust—inspired Muhammad's prophetic career, and he took up the sword only in defense against his "persecutors," which put him in the good company of other armed prophets such as Moses. Sale also probed the contrast that Christians often drew between the supposedly peaceful progress of their faith in the Roman Empire and the military campaigns that accompanied Islam's expansion. If Christianity had "prevailed against all the force and powers of the world by the mere dint of its own truth" for its first three hundred years, thereafter an alliance with "public authority" had guaranteed its triumph and paganism's destruction. He judged, too, that Christians showed "a more violent spirit of intolerance" than either Muslims or Jews. Even more eye-popping to Andover students would have been the commonalities between Christianity and Islam that surface throughout the preliminary discourse, including discussions of how hard Muslims struggled to reconcile divine sovereignty and human free will and how doggedly they held that grace alone, not good works, saved believers. And because both faiths ascribed the same attributes to God, Muslims and Christians must worship the same deity. It was such a no-brainer, Sale shrugged, that he would not waste his time refuting "those who suppose the God of Mohammed to be different from the true God."[33]

No wonder the great eighteenth-century British historian Edward Gibbon joked that Sale was "half a Musulman." Less amused was mere Jacob Scales, particularly by Sale's suave assertion that Muhammad's God is the God of the Bible. Impossible, the seminarian sneered, because the Muslim deity presided over a paradise "far exceeding the vilest brothel the earth ever witnessed." Yet both Scales and Bond accepted some of Sale's other arguments, and they might have held back from owning even more in public. Like Fisk, many Andover students depended on the school's charity fund, and neither their professors nor their patrons would have looked kindly on students entranced with the opinions of "half a Musulman." Indeed, given the faculty's refusal to teach even non-Protestant Christian doctrines, these two dissertations on Islam seem almost daring. But now that Sale's Qur'an had breached Andover's walls, it was harder for all within that New Divinity fortress not to wonder why there were so many Muslims in the world.[34]

Whatever he made of this first brush with George Sale, Pliny Fisk spent his years at Andover worrying less about the Muslims abroad than about the Christians at home. He had known from the outset the long odds against his escaping Shelburne or someplace like it. He took heart that Vermonters seemed to like him—the children he had taught in winter schools and the congregations in which he had preached. Like those country people, he was a farmer's son of "simple habits" and talents of "the ready kind." Much as he enjoyed his studies, mostly the sciences, Fisk admitted that he liked even better "to be engaged in active employments." He spent many stray hours tramping about the countryside around Andover, long hikes to draw the sting of every slight inflicted within the seminary's austere precincts. There his confidence could be withered by "a single look from some man of intelligence, that tells me how I stand in his estimation." Among them were his professors, who set down Fisk as someone whose classical education was "defective" and "whose talents in general were more solid than splendid." Then—as even his friends admitted—there was his unkempt dress, his fondness for colloquialisms and other "hobby modes of expression," and, most damning of all, his manner, "remarkably affable and familiar," given to "levity." He was too rough around the edges, this rumpled hayseed, long on jokes and short on Latin. Andover's learned, genteel faculty was not impressed.

The blow came sometime in the summer of 1817, when his "respected Instructors" informed Fisk that they judged him unfit for foreign missions. Their vote of no confidence did not come as a surprise. "So others have thought before," he sighed. It would not do for them to encourage a fellow who had shown so little promise "in the study of languages and other things connected with a mission to the heathen." Especially because those "other things" would entail cultivating Western merchants, military officers, and diplomats stationed abroad, a community of gentlemen whose goodwill was proving essential to the success of missionary endeavors in India and elsewhere. Far better for Fisk to serve as a drone in the humming hive of evangelical organizations that begged money from the American faithful to provide every household with a Bible and to put religious tracts into every hand. Or he could become a domestic missionary in Vermont, where hardly anyone would notice his shortcomings.

Fisk was devastated. He had long felt called to foreign missions, and besides he had "two or three dear Brethren here [at Andover] who will probably go to Asia," Parsons no doubt among them, and "the prospect of being separated is exceedingly painful." That thought alone rallied Fisk, but what gave him the gumption to stand up to his professors was his unshakable conviction that the sovereign God disagreed with them. In response to his prayers, an authority higher than any at Andover endowed Fisk with "a comfortable assurance that I have *not* been deceived in thinking it my duty to devote my life to the service of the heathen." So he dashed off a letter to the faculty reaffirming his commitment, and shortly thereafter they relented and endorsed Fisk's future employment as a foreign missionary with the American Board.

What happened? Fisk's appeal alone would not have changed any minds. No, someone else had put a thumb on the scale, whispered the proper word into the right ear, and a good guess among mortals would be Levi's father, the Reverend Justin Parsons. Coinciding with the Andover faculty's change of heart was Levi's seminary graduation and ordination as a foreign missionary. Those events would have brought his father to Andover—and once there, to lobby for Fisk. After all, Justin's boy, gung ho but far from hardy, was set on going somewhere in Asia; who better to look after him than his robust friend of "ready" talents? And of Fisk's devotion, there could be no question. Sure enough, no sooner had the board accepted Fisk as a future missionary than he proposed to Parsons their partnering for a mission to Persia.[35]

That choice was not surprising. By the second decade of the nineteenth century, evangelicals were coming to regard Persia (present-day Iran) as an ideal entering wedge into the Muslim world. What promoted that opinion were the exploits of Henry Martyn, a British missionary who was drawing notice on both sides of the Atlantic for translating the New Testament into Persian and engaging in public debates with Muslim intellectuals in Shiraz. Evangelical magazines exulted over a letter reputedly from the "king" of Persia himself pronouncing Martyn's translation "highly acceptable" and commanding "Select Servants, who are admitted to our presence," to read it "from the beginning to the end." From his listening post in Russia, a Scots evangelical missionary concluded that Martyn's reception proved that Persians were tolerant and "fond of religious argument." From his mission at Ceylon, Samuel Newell agreed. An Andover graduate, a member of the Brethren, and the widower of the storied Harriet, he reported that Persia's "prince regent" had sent to England for a printing press—why, there was even talk of their translating the entire *Encyclopaedia Britannica*! Back at Andover, students like Alvan Bond felt confident that a missionary might "forfeit his life" in any Muslim country except Persia, where the Shia majority "aren't much prejudiced against other religions, seem positively infatuated with the English," and are "exceedingly fond of *hearing some new thing*." Soon there would be no telling Tehran from Boston.[36]

That was enough for Levi Parsons. When he read Newell's call to action, Parsons was itinerating on the Vermont frontier and waiting for Fisk to finish his final year at Andover. Now he began to press his friend about their future: "O what happiness to go to heaven from Persia after wearing out for Him who gave his life for us? What, and if we fall *martyrs* to the cause! It is the way in which multitudes have gone to glory." A few months later in the spring of 1818, he was still urging Fisk, "Can we go to Persia? How soon? In what way? I am not at home, nor shall I be, I hope till I am teaching the *Heathen* the words of eternal life."[37]

Word of Samuel Mills's death only fixed their resolve. A fever claimed him on the homeward voyage from West Africa, where he had been scouting land in Sierra Leone to establish a colony of free blacks. In the near future, he hoped, many would become missionaries, reclaiming a continent in thrall to pagan idolatries and Islam. Shortly before Mills discovered too many Muslims in West Africa, he had sounded the alarm upon discovering too many Roman Catholics between the Ohio and the Mississippi valleys. Like his fellow Protestants, he was repelled by Catholicism's set prayers, veneration of saints, and sumptuous worship settings. And now its adherents—whose first loyalties surely lay with the pope—were swarming into the heartland of the American continent, running their beads instead of reading the Bible, conspiring to snuff out republican liberty and true (Protestant) Christianity. Recall his batty beliefs about the Illuminati's conspiracies and hear the tumblers in Mills's brain clicking into a familiar place. Had he lived another decade, he would have stood foursquare with his fellow evangelicals whose charges of a sinister papal plot afoot to destroy American liberties ignited mob attacks on Catholic homes, convents, and churches.

As it was, no sooner had Samuel Mills's body come to rest at the bottom of the Atlantic than his name found a place beside that of Harriet Newell in the pantheon of missionary apostles and martyrs. Like Newell, he did not suffer death at the hands of those hostile to their faith, but as their fellow evangelicals judged the matter, the more martyrs, the better. Besieged by Enlightenment skeptics and rattled by Catholic incursions, they sought vindication in the willing sacrifices of their missionaries. From the past to the present, many believers in Christianity and Islam alike have looked to martyrdom to validate the truth of their revelations, and its cult presided, too, at the founding of the foreign missions movement.[38]

Even as he dreamed of following Mills into some part of the Muslim world, Pliny Fisk honored his memory in another way as well. When word of their founder's death reached the United States, the Brethren decided to decipher their records, and Fisk stepped forward. The society had kept their existence a secret, as he explained, only to avoid disapproval and ridicule by those people, including some of their own "good ministers," who regarded Americans' venturing into foreign missions as impractical, as "a boy's notion." A decade later in 1829, his cousin Ezra Fisk elaborated, recalling that the Brethren's charter members feared "the *possibility* of failure in the enterprise—*public opinion* then being opposed to us." To many people, schemes to convert the world smacked of "overheated zeal," he remembered, which meant that "*modesty* required us to conceal our association lest we should be that rashly imprudent and so we should injure the cause we wished to promote." It was risky for the young to get too far ahead of themselves, even in the new age of wonders.[39]

The Fisks' recollections poignantly evoke the rural culture of their youth. In that place and time, young men and women strove to shield themselves from the scorn that some of their elders would heap on anyone who betrayed the ambition to rise too high, to dare too much, or to stray too far from home. But it was not from New Divinity ranks alone that the Brethren dreaded criticism; they also expected to meet stiff opposition from a wider "public opinion." As well they might have, because a great many people in the early republic were developing views of Islam and opinions about their responsibilities to the rest of the world that diverged starkly from those of evangelicals. In fact, what Pliny Fisk and Levi Parsons idealized as a cause worth dying for somewhere in the Muslim world—as a romance of Christian martyrdom—other Americans saw as a suicide mission.

# 2

## "BY THE BEARD OF MAHOMET!"

People, We created you all from a single man and a single woman, and made you into races and tribes so that you should get to know one another.
                                        —Qur'an, The Private Rooms, 49:13

William Bentley loved the world. It was an unlikely affair for a man who rarely strayed far from home, but then, he was not built for travel, let alone for speed. Barely five feet tall and about two hundred pounds, Bentley was nearly as wide as he was long. Besides, many who lived in the vibrant seaport that was Salem, Massachusetts, in the early nineteenth century believed that the world came to them. That was the message sent by the annual procession of the town's East India Marine Society, a select club of sea captains who claimed the distinction of rounding the Horn of Africa. The event always drew a great crowd, and in 1804 it included Bentley. That would be him, the pastor of East Church, standing on tiptoes and craning his neck to see the parade. Or not: as one who had inspired the society's founding, Bentley might have claimed pride of place to view the procession. It was a show worth seeing. Each member carried "some Indian curiosity," followed by a "person dressed in Chinese habits and a mask" and palanquin borne by several of Salem's free black men.

The world came to Salem more often with the return of its merchants, sea captains, and sailors whose voyages spanned the globe—India and Ceylon, Java (Indonesia) and China, the ports of the Red Sea and the islands of the South Seas. Bentley estimated that by 1816 some ninety men from town had commanded voyages around the Cape of Good Hope, and two years later he counted fifty Salem vessels in the India trade alone. Sometimes the people plying those sea-lanes switched places for long spells: one was a Malay man who had settled in Salem; another, the son of a local couple, was editing a newspaper in Calcutta. Still another was a free black sailor who confided to Bentley that he was inclined to return to the Sandwich Islands, where for two years he owned land and "his rank in society was better secured to him" than in Salem.

Bentley cultivated all of these travelers. They provided him with some of the information that appeared in the summaries of world events that he regularly contributed to a local newspaper, the *Salem Register*. They also brought home the treasures that filled his cabinet of natural curiosities, that essential trophy for any enlightened gentleman. From Smyrna came a stuffed chameleon; from the South Seas the tooth of a whale and the eyes of a squid; from Siam (Thailand), a pelican's mandible and a rhino's horn. Even more important, Bentley's maritime circle connected him with far-flung correspondents. Among his most cherished was a German geographer, Christoph Ebeling. The two had never met but exchanged books and letters for twenty years. By 1805, he also harbored great hopes for his acquaintance with an Arab sheikh in present-day Yemen. With a sea captain serving as go-between, Bentley sent the sheikh his own telescope and received a gift of "sweetmeats" in return. Western Asia had aroused Bentley's boundless curiosity, prompting him to pester the British diplomatic resident at Mocha, a port city on the Red Sea, into sending the Qur'an and other books "explaining the principal tenets of the Mussulmen."[1]

How fortunate, it seemed, for such a man to live in what he called the "age of missionaries." Imagine what these world travelers could offer one of the early republic's most globe-spanning minds, to say nothing of its lesser mortals. Bentley did imagine—and he wanted nothing to do with them. He loathed the neighboring Andover Theological Seminary and its newly minted missionaries with their indifferent intellectual talents, their scanty knowledge of languages, and their zeal "in full consent with vulgar prejudices." Such ignorant young men, some even dragging their brides along—like poor Harriet Newell—on "Don Quixote adventures" abroad. Then there was the nonsense that their elders spouted when sermonizing on behalf of missions, "a compilation of all the extravagancies which would disgrace the dark ages." Model of civility that he was, Bentley made a point of keeping his opinions about other people's beliefs between the covers of his private diary. But he refused to take up collections for missions in his own church and gloated over poor returns in others.[2]

He also gleefully cataloged in his diary every disaster that beset the first American mission abroad. No sooner had the first cohort of American Board missionaries landed in Bengal—their arrival coinciding with the outbreak of the War of 1812—than the British East India Company sent them packing. Whatever did those "infatuated" men expect, Bentley wondered, barging into India without the consent of the British government? On top of everything else, some of the now wandering missionaries had deserted their New Divinity Congregationalist faith and turned Baptist. When a few of the others at last managed to establish a station at Bombay (Mumbai), Bentley delighted in reports from Salem sea captains that their mission was "neither conducted with ability, received with respect, or accompanied by any good effect whatever."[3]

Much as he despised everyone connected with Andover, Bentley probably could not have avoided crossing paths with Pliny Fisk. During the early summer of 1818, Fisk spent several weeks in Salem, organizing Sunday schools for African American families. For once, he felt that the wind was at his back: only a few months remained until his graduation, and thereafter, having wrung a recommendation from his professors, he hoped to head for Persia with Levi Parsons. Fisk might even have felt equal to approaching Bentley, who, after all, occasionally stooped to tutor Andover students in the several languages that he read with ease. He would have known, too, that Bentley was trying to add Arabic to that number and that his library included many treasures from western Asia. From his connections in Yemen, Bentley had acquired more than a score of Arabic and Persian manuscripts that included commentaries on the Qur'an, the hadith (sayings attributed to Muhammad by his followers), and treatises on Islam by Muslim authors. For his part, Bentley's long-standing interest in Salem's free black community might have encouraged him to suffer, if only briefly, young Fisk's acquaintance.[4]

Then, too, Bentley wished for everyone in the early republic to know about the world. That would be the world according to William Bentley—as opposed to that pack of numskull New Divinity ministers with their creepy cult of martyrdom and their wacky apocalypticism and their fathomless ignorance of Islam. What a disaster it would be if evangelicals came to dominate the channels that forged public opinion—the newspapers and bookstores, the schools and libraries, the churches and fraternal organizations. So it pleased him that the Salem Athenaeum, probably under his direction, had added to its own library a number of books offering the most scholarly and evenhanded treatments of Muhammad and his faith, starting with George Sale's translation of the Qur'an. Only the Athenaeum's proprietors—about a hundred of the wealthiest families in Salem—had access to those volumes, but Bentley reached the rest of his neighbors with that regular column for the *Salem Register.* "It may easily be granted that the benefits were more direct from his [Muhammad's] laws than his religion," he lectured the *Register*'s readers, but then "the design of this enterprising man was not directed to religion as his first object," but rather to gaining the consent of Arabia's tribes to "unite under the rule of law." This end Muhammad had achieved, Bentley continued, "with that wisdom which displays a comprehensive mind, and with that success which vindicates him from the character of a mere fanatic and wild impostor." A far cry, Bentley's George Washington of Arabia, from the bloody-minded, sex-crazed pretender of New Divinity sermons. Here was no God-struck prophet either, but a sober lawgiver—a founder of Islam for the enlightened.[5]

If Bentley was equivocal about Islam as a religion, other enlightened thinkers were outspoken in their criticisms. Many eighteenth-century French *philosophes* disparaged Islam for encouraging despotism, intolerance, and ignorance. Following their lead, Thomas Jefferson thought no better of Muslims than he did of evangelicals, on the grounds that both religious groups placed revelation above reason as the basis for their religious convictions. But the Enlightenment also inspired other Western scholars to work toward a fuller and more accurate understanding of Muhammad and his faith. Learned Orientalists like George Sale rejected the stock Christian narrative of an ambitious impostor who spread his religion by the sword. Intent on replacing fables with evidence, polemic with impartiality—the warlord Muhammad with the legislator—they influenced many Americans like Bentley.

That enlightened invention of Islam and its prophet was slowly trickling down to a wider reading public by the beginning of the nineteenth century. Bentley and others—historians, novelists, and contributors to newspapers and magazines—challenged old stereotypes about Islam by serving up the ideas of Sale and other early Orientalists in popular formats. Like Bentley, some regarded themselves as unblinkering the prejudiced and educating the uninformed. Also like Bentley, many were religious liberals who enjoyed telling evangelicals that the Middle Ages had called and wanted its view of Muhammad back. Combined, their efforts ensured that some of the Orientalists' careful research spilled beyond a handful of scholars in libraries, universities, and salons and into the awareness of a broader readership.[6]

These works popularizing the Orientalists' learning took their place among a rich array of other sources that purported to portray Muhammad, his faith, and the Muslim world, past and present. Remarkably diverse coverage of those subjects in newspapers and magazines, works of poetry and fiction, travel books and theatrical performances, informed and entertained an eager American audience. And by the second decade of the nineteenth century, learning more about the Muslim world became even easier because it figured as a frequent point of reference in the great debates of that decade over Christianity, women's rights, and slavery. It was becoming apparent, as William Bentley fervently hoped, that evangelicals enjoyed no monopoly on shaping the ways in which Americans understood Islam. The early republic resounded with a cacophony of differing opinions about Muhammad's faith and his followers, a veritable din in print.

The invention of Islam for an enlightened West began in the seventeenth century with a small number of scholars in England and on the continent of Europe. Students of Eastern languages, these Orientalists had come to regard Muslim scholars as more reliable than Christian authors when it came to information about Islam. The French scholars Barthélemy d'Herbelot and Antoine Galland leaned heavily on Ottoman sources to publish the first encyclopedia of Islam in 1697. A few years later, Jean Gagnier, a French convert to Anglicanism transplanted to England, translated the first biography of Muhammad written by a Muslim Arab, while Adriaan Reland, a Dutch Protestant, derided the legends that had surrounded the Prophet since the Middle Ages and translated a description of Islam from a Muslim text. Those efforts to make Eastern sources objects of serious study had introduced the term "Islam" into Western discourse by the middle of the seventeenth century, signaling an awareness, at least among some of the learned, that the older term "Mahometanism" mistakenly implied that Muslims worshipped the Prophet himself.

This pioneering research laid the groundwork for more positive assessments of both Muhammad and his faith. The most daring came from the eighteenth-century French historian Henri de Boulainvilliers, who pointed out that spreading his belief in the unity of God to the best and brightest from Arabia to Spain "corresponds but ill with the notion we have imbibed of this very Mahomet" as "a vile and odious impostor." Besides taking that can off the Prophet's tail, Boulainvilliers doubted that the promise of a sensual paradise could produce "an effect so grand and so permanent as the Mahometan worship." Most important, Boulainvilliers lent his voice to a growing Orientalist consensus that Islam was a religion based on reason. Even if Muhammad himself might have been "transported" by enthusiasm, he "undertook to prove his doctrine by dint of reason alone" and "without being warranted by any miracles, or juggling pretenses." Over the course of two centuries, Orientalist scholars from Reland to Boulainvilliers to Sale called for assessing Islam dispassionately and analyzing it historically. Challenging the views current among Christians since the Middle Ages, they concluded that Islam was no superstition, no heresy from Christianity, no heaven-sent scourge, and that Muhammad himself was no epileptic, no magician, no schismatic. Properly understood, Islam was one of the world's great monotheisms, remarkable for its simplicity and rationality, and its founder was a political and religious genius of extraordinary historical stature and significance.[7]

This invention of Islam by and for the enlightened fell hard on the ears of evangelicals, among them one of the founders of Methodism, John Wesley. In a review of Boulainvilliers's biography of Muhammad, Wesley dismissed it as "a dull, ill-digested romance, supported by no authorities at all." Orientalists enjoyed a delicious revenge with the appearance of William Hogarth's engraving of 1762, *Credulity, Superstition, and Fanaticism*: in this satirical depiction of a Methodist meeting, a minister, most likely George Whitefield, preaches to a crowd of worshippers (including John Wesley) who exhibit all of the unlovely qualities that the title advertises and more, with an emphasis on lust and hypocrisy. Looking on from a window is a small turbaned man calmly smoking a pipe, a Muslim appalled at the antics of Christian believers.[8]

Little as evangelicals might have liked it, Orientalist perspectives found their way into the United States through a variety of channels. The narrowest was by purchasing their great books, because the audience who could afford such works was small. Even Sale's translation of the Qur'an was available only in imported (and expensive) British editions. What enabled a wider circulation for some Orientalist works were the growing number of "social" or "membership" libraries in the early republic. Organized, funded, and patronized by private citizens, they provided books to their subscribers and sometimes, for a fee, to the general public. Perhaps five or six hundred such institutions existed in the United States, concentrated in the Northeast, between 1800 and 1820. The works of Boulainvilliers made an occasional appearance in their holdings, but the title best represented both in libraries and in bookstores was Sale's translation of the Qur'an. There were besides books by two steady-selling historians who distilled Orientalist learning about Islam for the less scholarly.[9]

The first was the eighteenth-century British scholar Edward Gibbon, who devoted one volume of his *Decline and Fall of the Roman Empire* to the life of Muhammad and his immediate successors. Every gentleman's library, every college library, and most social libraries included this Enlightenment classic. Its pages echoed the judgments of the Orientalists before him, praising Muhammad as a genius who preached "a simple and rational piety," celebrating the Qur'an as "glorious testimony to the unity of God," and venturing that a "philosophic theist [meaning a deist, as Gibbon was] might subscribe to the popular creed of the Mahometans." Sale's influence shows throughout: Gibbon adopted his view that by sometimes using the sword to spread his faith, Muhammad merely imitated Moses and "the judges and kings of Israel." Similarly, he followed Sale and Reland by presenting the Muslim paradise as offering more than sexual pleasure, because "the prophet has expressly declared, that all meaner happiness will be forgotten and despised by the saints and martyrs, who shall be admitted to the beatitude of the divine vision." If Gibbon stood on Orientalist shoulders, he speculated even more boldly on Muhammad's behalf. Was the Prophet an "enthusiast" who mistook his deep convictions for heavenly inspiration? Or had he at first believed in his divine mission and then over time, coarsened by bloodshed and corrupted by ambition, lost that conviction but kept up the pose only as a "necessary fiction" to replace idolatry with monotheism? If so, Gibbon concluded, his very imposture vindicated Muhammad, because in support of the truth "the arts of fraud and fiction may be deemed less criminal." Surely the Prophet "would have started at the foulness of the means, had he not been satisfied of the importance and justice of the end."[10]

Among the many readers intrigued by Gibbon's ruminations was John Bigland, a Yorkshire schoolmaster who earned modest fame by publishing *A Geographical and Historical View of the World* (1811). Its five hefty volumes sagged the shelves of most libraries and many schoolrooms in the early republic, and one tome included a long biography of Muhammad. An omnivorous reader, Bigland had grazed through many of the Orientalists and chewed Gibbon down to the nub, a diet that fed his call for understanding Muhammad not as "the enemy of our religion" but "as the legislator of a nation" who believed it "acceptable to God and conducive to the happiness of man" to "establish the rational worship of one Supreme Being." Bigland conceded that this "impartial" view of Muhammad would "appear too favourable" to most in the West—and "still more defective" to Muslims. In fact, his books' wide circulation shows how effectively the early Orientalists' reassessments were reaching a popular audience of both adults and children.[11]

Their influence also registered in a dictionary of world religions produced by Hannah Adams. A bluestocking cousin to President John Adams, she might have been the first American woman to make a living through literary pursuits, a career dictated by necessity, sustained by curiosity, and assisted by haunting her father's bookstore and some Boston gentlemen's libraries. Those opportunities gave Adams a grounding in Orientalist scholarship that left its mark on her dictionary. She offered an evenhanded description of Islam, allowing that Muhammad possessed "a subtle genius" and even suggesting that learned Muslims understood the Qur'an's sensuous paradise as an allegory.[12]

Orientalist influences did not penetrate everywhere. Patrons of libraries and bookstores in the early republic would have encountered plenty of less flattering portrayals of Islam and its prophet. Leading in that category was the bestselling *Life of Mahomet; or, The History of That Imposture Which Was Begun, Carried on, and Finally Established by Him in Arabia; and Which Has Subjugated a Larger Portion of the Globe Than the Religion of Jesus Has Yet Set at Liberty.* That left no doubt about the plot of this rambling potboiler, packed with sex and violence and punctuated by rabid outbursts against Jews and Catholics. Its anonymous author, apparently a British clergyman, spliced even more sensationalism into the standard evangelical depiction of Muhammad and at the end urged his country to invade the Ottoman Empire.[13]

How many people in the early republic read the serious works of Hannah Adams, Edward Gibbon, and John Bigland—or even the racy, almost hallucinatory *Life of Mahomet*? While literacy rates were on the rise, not many white Americans—preoccupied with the scramble for land and slaves, caught up in successive moves westward, distracted by wars with the Indians and the British, consumed by the passions of partisan politics, and addicted to drinking enormous quantities of alcohol—had the time, money, and often the sobriety to make their way through books on any subject. Even so, it was not only enlightened eminences with bulging bookcases like William Bentley or those with borrowing privileges at libraries who encountered the Orientalist learning that Adams, Gibbon, and Bigland popularized. Many ordinary people everywhere in the early republic were curious and thoughtful about Islam—as attested by the sheer volume and variety of information about Muslim history, beliefs, and practices in secular newspapers and magazines by the 1810s. Short articles published in these inexpensive forms of print, often passing from one hand to the next, introduced Islam—and even the ideas of the Orientalists—to Americans of slim means, little leisure, and rudimentary reading skills.

Some of the information being purveyed was even accurate—or almost. Washingtonians learned from their local newspaper that Friday was the Muslim holy day and that Islam's five fundamental religious duties were "the saying of prayers, giving of alms, fasting on Ramadan, making a pilgrimage," and professing the faith that "there is no God but one God and Mouhhamed is his messenger." Litchfield, Connecticut's town gazette instructed its readers that Muslims regarded the Qur'an as "a copy of the laws of God which are written on the table in heaven; and that God sent this copy by his angel Gabriel, who delivered it to Mahomet to teach men the way to eternal happiness." Other periodicals delved into more detail, and accounts appearing in one newspaper were often reprinted in many more. In a story picked up as far away as Natchez, Mississippi, Hartford's *Connecticut Courant* described the hajj rituals practiced by pilgrims to Mecca, such as the kissing of the Kaaba stone, drinking water from the well of Zamzam, and throwing pebbles against three stone pillars at nearby Mina. Many journalists took pride in showing off their stock of knowledge about Islamic ways, including a New York theater reviewer who sniffed at stage sets adorned with "pictures of ladies" for a play set in the Muslim world because portraits of "any living thing, did not belong in the house of a Mussulman."

Not a few periodical pieces dismissed some Islamic beliefs as "fanciful" or "superstitious," but others forbore any commentary. One Boston literary magazine left its readers to draw their own conclusions from "Mahometan History of the Creation and Fall of Man," with its obvious similarities to the account in the Old Testament. A New York publication went further, inviting its readers to admire an article it published under the heading "Morality," a "Mahometan Sermon" that celebrated God's unity, omnipotence, omniscience, mercy, and justice. Still other pieces noted with an air of slightly mystified approval Muslim prohibitions of drinking and gambling. Newspapers and magazines also offered widely varying impressions of Muslim societies. Reports on the severity of their justice appeared often, yet nearly every newspaper in the early republic latched onto an essay contrasting the harsh conditions in American debtors' prisons with the more humane treatment of bankrupts in Islamic countries. Many articles also countered the association of ignorance, indulgence, and intolerance with Muslim cultures. Scores of newspapers carried an account of their scholars' efforts to calculate infinity, while a Philadelphia literary magazine featured "Moderation in our Pleasures," verses purportedly composed by one of Muhammad's grandsons. The *Baltimore Patriot* doled out grudging respect to "the bigots of Mahomet" for being less bigoted than Roman Catholics, and a village newspaper in Maine agreed, asking, "What intolerant zeal of Mahometan enthusiasm could equal" that of the Crusades, the Reformation, or the Inquisition?[14]

The popular press offered as many different perspectives on the life of Muhammad. Secular newspapers sometimes followed the evangelical script, portraying him as an impostor who spread his faith by force and the promise of a licentious paradise. Some accounts also repeated medieval Christian legends: allusions abounded to the powerful magnet said to suspend the Prophet's coffin in midair. Still other articles screwed up the simplest facts, like the upstate New York paper that decided that Muhammad had claimed to be the Messiah promised to the Jews. But plenty of periodicals did better. They offered accurate accounts of Muhammad being orphaned in his youth, marrying a wealthy widow, traveling as a merchant, and making his flight, or hegira, from Mecca to Medina. Those authors who tried to get his story straight were also inclined to venture that Muhammad was "a great man," remarkable for his courage and wisdom, eloquence and grace. Following Sale and other early Orientalists, many cast Muhammad as a lawgiver who brought monotheism to Arabia. They repeated Sale's judgment that Islam triumphed less through armed force than through its compelling message and imitated his strategy of comparing Islam with other religions. In that spirit, a southern Ohio gazette noted that just as Muhammad had promised paradise to any warrior who died in his cause, so did Christian nations by "their prayers, hymns, illuminations, and solemn festivals" for fallen soldiers, which prevented anyone from doubting "their future felicity."

Whether damning or laudatory, informed or inaccurate, coverage of Muhammad and his faith made the pages of the popular press with surprising frequency. And by the spring of 1815, anyone who strolled along Broadway could enter—for only twenty-five cents—one Monsieur Naudin's "Grand Cosmorama" and gape at his top-billed attraction, "the interior view of the famous Mosque, and the Tomb of Mahomet, at Medina." (No doubt with coffin suspended in midair.) Those with a bit more to spend could attend a production of Voltaire's tragedy *Mahomet*, which played as far north as Albany and as far south as Philadelphia, or thrill to an opera of the same name. Popular culture made ordinary Americans so familiar with Islam that an army officer stationed on the Great Lakes described Tenskwatawa, the Shawnee spiritual leader of Ohio valley Indians, as "a great prophet (imposter, being somewhat similar in his conduct hitherto to Mahomet)." So familiar that Aaron Burr's enemies dubbed him "Mahomet Volpone, the Grand Impostor." So familiar that the phrase "the mountain came to Muhammad" tripped as easily off American tongues as did the oath "By the Beard of Mahomet!" So easily and so often that by 1807 the young Washington Irving—who would write a sympathetic biography of Muhammad decades later—riffed on this slang in his hip *Salmagundi* magazine by tossing off all sorts of jokey new oaths: "By the hump of Mahomet's camel!" and so forth. In any case, Muhammad's was a name worthy enough to be taken in vain, well known enough to be uttered with good effect, and more acceptable to swear by, even in a family newspaper, than that of the founder of Christianity.[15]

Muhammad's time had come again in the West—and for the first time in the United States—for many reasons. Napoleon Bonaparte's shooting star sparked interest in other great men who combined military glory with radical monotheism. Napoleon was a deist, and his lightning conquests transfixed the world during the decades around 1800, just as the triumphs of Muhammad and his successors had more than a millennium earlier. Some accounts of his life also cast Muhammad as a self-made man, that model for nineteenth-century strivers, who prospered in his first career as a merchant before founding a faith followed by millions of people. Finally, for those many Americans who still regarded the world as an enchanted realm shot through with magic and mystery, traditions concerning Muhammad offered yet more wonder lore. Besides the coffin hovering within his tomb, there were the miracles attributed to him by some later Islamic chroniclers. At the Prophet's command, they wrote, water flowed from his fingertips; he took his sword and cleaved the moon in two.[16]

Popular fascination went well beyond the person of Muhammad to Islamic cultures, past and present. If millennial expectations and missionary sermons stirred interest in Islam among evangelicals, pirates made many less pious Americans want to know more about Muslims. For centuries the Barbary States of North Africa—Tunis, Tripoli, and Algiers—had seized Western ships in the Mediterranean, enslaving their crews and demanding ransoms. The Barbary nations held an estimated seven hundred Americans in bondage between 1785 and 1815, and their plight aroused popular sympathy, particularly in northern seaports. Churches raised money for ransoms, wax museums exhibited "Barbary scenes," and circuses performed benefits for returned captives. That created a ready audience for narratives of captivity in North Africa, real and fictional. Most popular was the tale of Maria Martin, an imaginary heroine enslaved in Algiers and then imprisoned for rebuffing the advances of a Turkish official. A succulent mix of seduction, sadism, and piety (the earliest editions depicted Maria topless and in chains), it went into multiple American printings under a variety of titles between 1806 and 1818, even one in German.[17]

More widely read were *The Arabian Nights' Entertainments*—the

Harry Potter books of the early republic—a collection of folktales from the Middle East and India that found their way into the West at the beginning of the eighteenth century. The adventures of Aladdin, Sinbad, and Ali Baba captured youthful imaginations and inadvertently provided some accurate information about places from Cairo to Damascus and Mosul to Baghdad. Helpful footnotes in the editions that circulated in the early nineteenth-century United States explained why Eastern peoples ate with the right hand, how Muslims computed the year according to Muhammad's hegira, and what it was like to lodge in a khan. Some young readers were still addicted in college, including one Yale student so godless that he studied on the Sabbath and then read *Arabian Nights* to relax, much to the disgust of his evangelical roommate, Isaac Bird, who groused about "having an enemy in my room, who seemed to feel envious to all who were firmly resolved to be strictly religious."[18]

Those who outgrew *Arabian Nights* found plenty besides captivity narratives that purported to depict the Islamic world. Magazine romances and morality tales featured Muslim characters in "Oriental" settings, though both were so short on verisimilitude that their plots might as easily have unfolded anywhere. More authentically situated and much in vogue among American readers were Lord Byron's poems from the 1810s, which featured several noble Muslim heroes. Travelers' accounts also described Islamic places, people, and customs, and the popular press reprinted long excerpts and reviews of such books, bringing Muslim worlds to readers without enough money to meet the requirements of their imaginations. For the price of a newspaper, anyone could indulge vicariously in the pleasures of a Turkish bath, waggishly detailed by a young American naval officer in Tunis. Other readers saw Constantinople through the eyes of the physician to the British embassy there. Transported on the magic carpet of his prose, they surveyed "the marble domes of St. Sophia, the gilded pinnacles of the Seraglio glittering amidst groves of perpetual verdure, the long arcades of ancient aqueducts, and spiry minarets of a thousand mosques," where, at the call of the muezzins, "the followers of Mahomet are pouring in." Then there were the widely excerpted travels of "Ali Bey," a Spaniard and most likely a Christian, who posed as "a Mussulman and prince" and did things "which no other Christian has ever had the opportunity of doing." That included, according to a breathless blurb in a New York City newspaper, slipping into mosques at Mecca, Jerusalem, and Constantinople.[19]

It is likely, too, that black Americans raised awareness of Islam among some white Americans, especially in the South. Thousands of Muslims—perhaps even tens of thousands—numbered among the Atlantic slave trade's victims. It is impossible to know how many retained their Islamic faith or vestiges of it, but identifiably Muslim names turn up in slaveholders' records and runaway advertisements, particularly in Louisiana, coastal Georgia, and South Carolina. Slaves of all faiths tried to conduct their worship in secret, but occasionally whites witnessed Islamic devotional practices, and some masters judged that the Muslims among their bondspeople were superior in intelligence, dignity, and appearance.[20]

But it was chiefly through the world of print that most Americans received their knowledge about Islam and its founder. They came across that information, accurate and otherwise, not only when searching for entertainment but also, quite by accident, when keeping current with the most pressing concerns of their times. Anyone in the early republic who took an interest in the spirited controversies over the doctrines of Christianity, the rights of women, and the future of slavery—all contests gathering intensity during the 1810s—would also pick up odd bits of knowledge and even some Orientalist learning about the Muslim world. Ambiguous and multivalent as it was, the image of Islam proved irresistible to partisans on all sides of those great issues in search of rhetorical fireworks.

William Bentley loved the world in general, but some of his neighbors in New England, not so much. Evangelicals of every sort—"fanatics" in his diary eruptions—set him off. Merely disdainful of Baptists and Methodists, he found his bête noire in New Divinity believers. He despised their ministers, dismissing them as "farmer metaphysicians" ignorant of German higher criticism of the Bible. He despised their seminary at Andover, scorning "its known opposition to enlightened men in New England." And he most heartily despised their demonizing Christians whose beliefs differed from theirs and creating a hostile climate that poisoned public discourse. As Bentley's contempt attests, religious loyalties were polarizing in the early republic, and to understand the embittered relations between liberal and evangelical Christians is also to discover one of the unexpected—and ironic—ways that Americans came to learn more about Islam.[21]

If New Divinity evangelicals held the most conservative theological position on the spectrum of Christian belief, Bentley occupied the ultraliberal extreme. He was a Socinian: not a word on every lip today, but most of his contemporaries knew exactly what it meant, and evangelicals were second to none when it came to hissing its sibilant syllables. Socinians denied the divinity of Jesus. Theirs was the most radical strain of Unitarianism, the belief that Jesus was an extraordinary moral exemplar but altogether human. Only the deists—who rejected not only the divinity of Jesus but also the divine inspiration of the Bible—were in worse odor with Trinitarians, the overwhelming majority among Christians everywhere in the West. Subscribing to Socinianism put Bentley in a small but fast company. His revered friend the British chemist Joseph Priestley was a Socinian; so was Thomas Jefferson, at least during the latter part of his life.[22]

While Socinians lay sparse on the ground everywhere in the early republic, there was no shortage of other liberal Christians to provoke and return the hostility of evangelicals. Among them were the far more numerous Unitarians who held to Arianism, the belief that Jesus was half divine—the miracle-working Messiah prophesied by the Old Testament and a being higher than the angels but not equal to and one with God. President John Adams claimed that he "could fill a sheet" with the names of all the Unitarians he had known in New England even before the revolution. He could have filled many more sheets a few decades later, as Unitarianism of this moderate stripe gained strength, particularly in eastern Massachusetts. Until 1825, when its adherents hived off to form a separate Unitarian denomination, they worshipped alongside the many other religious liberals in Anglican, Presbyterian, and Congregationalist churches.

Relations between evangelicals and all liberal Christians, Trinitarian and Unitarian alike, grew increasingly strained between about 1800 and 1820. Their divergent understandings of Christianity detonated controversies that rocked the churches, with New England as ground zero. Even as evangelical Protestantism flourished in some quarters, many other Americans were coming to question the reliability of the Bible, the divinity of Jesus, and the reality of hell. And even those liberal Christians who continued to accept all three beliefs were spurning Calvinism for a creed that put less emphasis on the heart's sinfulness and more on the head's ability to help human beings believe and behave. Differences over and doubts about religion went down to the grass roots, plaguing ordinary people, dividing families, and tormenting souls.[23]

For a closer look at those struggles, meet the whole flock of Birds— the relatives of Isaac, last seen at Yale College. Recall his resisting the enchantments of Scheherazade, and imagine how hard the heterodox opinions of his western Connecticut family fell on his New Divinity ears. There was his aunt Betsey, who had no use for Calvinism and "placed her hope for salvation on her former good conduct saying that she had never done anything for which she should be sentenced to eternal misery." There was his uncle Haunchy, who not only doubted "the doctrine of the fall, of the trinity, and of the holiness of the Sabbath" but also judged "Moses incorrect in some of his history." One of Isaac's brothers, William, inclined toward the belief in universal salvation, because it seemed "unreasonable that God knowing that man would rebel would create him and punish him forever." More dismaying was his brother Henry, an outspoken atheist "determined to treat religion with almost every species of contempt of which his tongue is capable of expressing." As for Isaac's father, he rarely joined in family prayer and accepted no blame for not being "born again" because "God had given him the disposition which he now possessed."

An opinionated bunch, the Birds, with evangelical Isaac as the cuckoo in the nest. Their religious convictions ran from liberal Congregationalism (Aunt Betsey and perhaps Bird senior, both of whom trusted that their good works and God's good sense would get them into heaven), to universalism (brother William, who believed that everyone would go to heaven), to rank infidelity (brother Henry, who had no fear of hellfire). This range of opinions that the Birds so freely disgorged suggests how fundamentally enlightened rationalism was reshaping the religious outlook of ordinary people, even in evangelical strongholds such as western Connecticut. While the Birds might have bred more than their share of doubters, they turned up in all families: even Levi Parsons's rock-ribbed New Divinity clan included his lawyer uncle who doubled as an occasional Unitarian preacher.[24]

The contentious religious climate that divided families and neighbors inevitably fostered curiosity about non-Christian faiths. As inevitably, Muslim belief and practice aroused particular interest, in part because Islam claimed a basis in divine revelation superseding that of Judaism and Christianity. To follow the path by which religious perplexity could lead to inquiries about Islam, eavesdrop on an exchange between Isaac Bird and yet another brother, James, who was racked by all the doubts that could turn a person toward Unitarianism, deism, or even atheism. The lack of clarity and consistency of the Bible troubled James: Why hadn't God revealed his truths plainly so "that all men can understand it alike"? And didn't the existence of "different nations of men" argue against "the assertion of the Bible that all mankind descended from one pair"? He wondered, too, about the evidence for Jesus' divinity: Couldn't mere "sleight-of-hand" explain Jesus' so-called miracles? Most fundamentally, James could not decide whether religion actually benefited humankind: Why did competing religious sentiments often produce disputes and even war? When Isaac suggested that the martyrdom of early Christians attested to the truth of their creed, his brother was ready. "Mahomet and his followers [also] suffered exceedingly for their religion," he shot back. Unmistakably, at some point in his spiritual pilgrimage, what James learned about Islam had sharpened rather than assuaged—perhaps even aroused—his doubts about Christianity. And even this Yankee farmer with only the most rudimentary formal education had taught himself enough about Islam to drop references to Muhammad's prophetic career.[25]

Like many people in the early republic, James Bird could have acquired his knowledge of Islam from the same sources that fed his doubts about Christianity—the debates between evangelicals and religious liberals, especially the Unitarians. Islam came up often in those encounters—as it had ever since the seventeenth century. In the polemics of that earlier era, Trinitarian English Protestants described Socinians as "much more *Mahometans* than Christians" and as "scouts amongst us for *Mahomet*." Two centuries later, evangelicals on both sides of the Atlantic were still pillorying deists and Unitarians by pointing up their affinities with Islam: like Muslims, they denied the divinity of Jesus and emphasized upright conduct rather than divine grace as the way to heaven. Typical was the salvo fired in 1814 by Alexander McLeod, the Presbyterian pastor of a large New York City church, who asserted that "the creed of the Mussulman is essentially the same with that of the Socinians," and "did worldly policy answer, there can be no doubt that Unitarians would rather bear the name of Mahomet" and "would prefer the Koran to the best system of Christian theology." Salem's evangelical pastor Samuel Worcester agreed that even moderate Unitarians were so fuzzy in their beliefs about Jesus and his redemptive mission that they could enter into "blessed fellowship" with Muslims, who also "believe in Jesus Christ as a good man, and a great prophet." There lurked not far beneath the surface of such rhetoric the implication that liberals were spiritual one-worlders who deep down believed that all religions were alike.[26]

Evangelicals received even more encouragement to stay on the attack from an unexpected source. During his short-lived invasion of Egypt in 1798, Napoleon Bonaparte had issued a proclamation affirming that "there is no divinity save Allah; He has no son and shares His power with no one." He went on to assure the country's Muslim majority of his respect for Muhammad and "the admirable Koran" and to announce that the French were "*true Moslems*," friends of the Ottoman sultan, and enemies of the pope. Though he later admitted that the proclamation was a strategy to enlist Muslim support, evangelicals did not see it as much of a stretch for Napoleon or any other deist to seek common ground with Muslims, and the episode's notoriety reinforced for many the link between liberal religious sentiments and sympathy for Islam.[27]

A few liberals parried evangelical thrusts by turning the tables, arguing that Calvinists shared with Muslims a fatalistic belief in God's "absolute predestination." Hence Thomas Jefferson condemned Calvinists as "mere usurpers of the Christian name, teaching a counter-religion . . . as foreign from Christianity as is that of Mahomet." But being linked to Islam sent most liberals into a defensive crouch of denial. That was the strategy of William Ellery Channing, the spiritual leader of Boston Unitarianism. "We indeed believe Mahometanism false, notwithstanding its progress," he insisted in a sermon of 1813. Muhammad was a "deceiver" who pretended to prophesy, "brandishing in one hand the sword, and extending the Koran in the other," he continued, and what a contrast to the history of Christianity, in which "we see no warrior, no hosts, no conflicts." Those words would have flowed as easily from the quill of a New Divinity preacher.[28]

What prompted Channing's insistence that religious liberals had not gone squishy on Islam was the sensation created by one George

Bethune English. A man who knew how to call attention to himself, this scion of a Boston merchant family lingered in the memories of his Harvard classmates for flashing "a huge Turkish scymetar [scimitar]" before their bedazzled eyes. It was the perfect affectation for a wispy, whey-faced swat whose intellectual passions ominously combined biblical criticism and military science. He entered the ministry but did not preach for long, finding that eloquence deserted him in the pulpit. Then faith deserted him, too—belief in the divinity of Jesus and in the inspiration of the New Testament. At loose ends in 1813—a spoiled, rich twentysomething with the run of the Harvard library—English published at his own expense a long treatise arguing that Jesus was not the Messiah foretold by the Old Testament but rather "a mistaken enthusiast"—a mere man, albeit one of great moral purity, who suffered from delusions and hallucinations. Styling himself a missionary to Bostonians who found foolish solace in their specious Christian beliefs, English piled on: "The expiring Indian dies in peace—holding a cow's tail in his hand," he gibed. "Would you not endeavour to enlighten him, and make him ashamed of his superstition?"[29]

Like earlier polemicists among British deists, English leaned on Islam to attack the divinity of Jesus. He contended that Christian scriptures describing his miracles were no more reliable than those Islamic traditions that made the same claims for Muhammad. English also borrowed from the Orientalists in listing other arguments that "the Mahometan might urge in behalf of his Prophet"—and against Christianity. For starters, Islam had "made more progress in one hundred years than Christianity did in a thousand," and while the religion of Jesus was "skulking and creeping among the mob of the Roman Empire for some hundred years before it dared to raise its head in public view," the Qur'an was "embraced by the noble, the great, the wise, and the learned, almost as soon as it appeared." Nor did the sword account for that success, in English's judgment, because "vastly more nations embraced Islamism *voluntarily*, than there were who *freely* received Christianity."

All of those opinions, as William Bentley observed in a triumph of understatement, "made the work of Mr. English very interesting to the clergy"—none more so than those inclined toward Unitarianism. On the upside, English's attacks offered these moderate Arians the rare opportunity to flay someone even less orthodox than they. Not a few, like Channing, jumped at the chance to speak up for Jesus as a supra-human miracle worker, the Bible as divine revelation, and the suppos-edly peaceful spread of Christianity. But on the downside, English had handed evangelicals a prime opportunity to charge that anyone who argued for a less than divine Jesus might any day start bowing toward Mecca. Why didn't the man just put on a turban and be done with it? Channing and his fellow liberals yearned for this evil jinni to disappear back into his lamp, and they got their wish, at least for a while. When the liberal luminary and future Harvard president Edward Everett lobbed his mortar of a book—five hundred pages chock-full of exam-ples of English's academic dishonesties—its target disappeared from Boston in a puff of smoke.

With rival Christians (and the stray non-Christian) so often slash-ing each other to ribbons with the scimitar of Islam, American readers accidentally learned a lot more about that faith. Most Americans today no longer speak the language of theology, but in the early republic even ordinary people were fluent in that lingo—as the pointed questions of James Bird indicate. They could follow the sophisticated debates stirred up by the likes of George English, and they came away learning—to the satisfaction of some, the dismay of others, and the surprise of all concerned—that Christians, liberals and evangelicals alike, held not a few beliefs in common with Muslims. Some of the same men and women took as much interest in another contest gathering momentum in the 1810s in which the example of Islam kept coming up: the debate over the nature and rights of women.[30]

Though a lifelong bachelor, William Bentley liked the company of women, the brighter the better. So it tickled him, visiting Salem's "Female School" in the spring of 1819, where "for the first time ever in a public school I saw young Ladies answering questions in Geometry, Nat. [Natural] Philosophy and in Latin." Some private academies had begun to offer challenging subjects to female students, and even public schools, at least in some larger towns like Salem, were giving the same advantages to girls from less affluent families. A growing number of Americans endorsed educating young women; it was one of the few points on which religious liberals like Bentley saw eye to eye with New Divinity believers. Some in the early republic went even further, encouraging their participation in politics. But by the 1810s a backlash had begun: a swelling chorus of pundits and pastors were urging women to retreat from political rallies and parades and to curb their interest in partisan politics.[31]

Signs of a battle brewing surface in the popular press's fascination with the status of women in Islamic cultures. Editors from New York to Natchez knew that columns about polygamy would grab attention, so they pandered. One much reprinted item alleged that affianced Muslim brides were "generally kept close, and are fattened for the purpose, corpulence being considered a mark of beauty." Even more widely circulated under the heading "Turkish Gallantry" was the tale of a Western woman who reproached the Turkish ambassador on the subject of polygamy: without missing a beat, he responded, "We allow it, madam, that we may find in several, all the qualities which are found in you alone." Though such articles tickled and titillated, they also encouraged women readers to conclude that whatever civil disabilities they might face in the United States, they fared far better than Muslim women. Those poor Eastern dears, mere livestock being plumped for the harem—or like mushrooms, kept in the dark and manured in flattery. This wretched subjugation resulted, as many articles insisted, from the Muslim belief that women were flesh without spirit. Newspapers made frequent (and incorrect) references to Muhammad's teaching that women had no souls and could not enter paradise. A poem featured in the *New-York Weekly Museum* in 1816 summed up the standard indictment: "In the Mahometan countries, where men look on / Woman but as dust / A soulless toy for tyrant's lust." Deprived of education, Muslim women were "unable to benefit their country, even by instilling good principles in the breasts of their children." Here was the cue for female readers to count their blessings for being honored as "republican mothers" who reared patriotic offspring and elevated the nation's moral tone.[32]

The stereotype of Muslim culture as repressive and misogynist dominated coverage in the popular press, but even there it did not pass without contradiction. Washington Irving and his collaborators on *Salmagundi* magazine goofed on this notion in several letters from "Mustapha Rub-A-Dub Keli Khan," a fictional Muslim visitor to New York. Having left behind twenty-three wives in Tripoli, Mustapha asked his friend, the "principal slave-driver" to the "bashaw," to look in on his harem, to discourage them from sticking their noses out the seraglio, and to "feed them plentifully" so that his return would find them "sleek as the graceful elephants that range the green valley of Abimar." How favorably the lives of these Muslim ladies compared with those of Gotham's women, Mustapha continued, who were "suffered to run about in perfect freedom." That's what came from "treating women as rational beings and allowing them souls"—American females who "absolutely talk themselves thin," and some who "usurp the breeches of men." It was a wicked burlesque of those authors who invoked Muslim misogyny to reconcile American women to their subordinate status.[33]

If *Salmagundi*'s subtleties slipped over the heads of some readers, not so the get-up-in-your-grille opinions of Lady Mary Wortley Montagu, the wife of an early eighteenth-century British ambassador to the Ottoman Empire. So indelibly did she depict her short year in Constantinople that excerpts from her *Turkish Embassy Letters* still made for hot copy in American periodicals a century later. Many reprinted her judgment that, thanks to their veils, Turkish women of rank were freer than British ladies because that "perpetual Masquerade gives them entire Liberty of following their Inclinations without danger of Discovery." So much for the image of Muslim women confined to home and harem. As for Muhammad's slighting the spirituality of women, several newspapers picked up *The Connecticut Courant*'s testimony that "Her Ladyship flatly denies the so common report, that women, according to the Mahometan creed, have no souls, and are excluded . . . from any share in the sensual paradise promised by the pretended prophet." No doubt editors believed that Lady Mary's contrarianism had an upper-crust charm all her own, but some might also have endorsed the feminist sympathies that showed in her challenge to standard depictions of Turkish women by Western men. What better way to confound those who painted a damning picture of the lot of Muslim women abroad in order to discourage American women from seeking full citizenship at home?[34]

The emerging debate over women's rights opened yet another portal of print through which ordinary people might pass and, without even intending to do so, acquire greater familiarity with the Islamic world. And again, readers came away with mixed, often contradictory messages about Islam. Similar confusions arose even in the most direct sources of information about the Muslim world available to the average American in the early republic—newspaper coverage of diplomacy and warfare there and the captivity narratives of their countrymen who had been enslaved in North Africa.

At the end of October in 1816, William Bentley brought the world to Salem, as he did every week, with his newspaper column. As always, he strove for a measured tone in summarizing the great happenings around the globe, but that might have been harder on this occasion because his subject was Algiers. A frequent visitor to Salem's wharves, Bentley must have known some of the mariners held captive over the years in Barbary, so it grabbed his notice, the news that Britain, now freed from the threat of Napoleon, was determined to end North African piracy. A few months earlier, an Anglo-Dutch fleet had shelled Algiers's harbor defenses until its ruler freed more than three thousand Western slaves and promised to take no more. But Bentley was skeptical, advising his readers that the only effective deterrent would be "a general consent of nations to maintain a naval force to prevent the excesses of the Barbary States."[35]

Other newspaper reports did not strive for Bentley's restraint, and the Anglo-Dutch assault prompted yet another recital of a familiar litany. Many articles dwelled on the injustices against people and property inflicted by Barbary's governments; others denounced their rigid adherence to an Islam that sustained despotism. In 1819, the press was still abuzz, stirred up by Mordecai Noah, an American journalist and playwright who had written an account of his short stint as consul in Tunis. He pledged that "if men should range themselves under the banners of the cross" and march against all of Barbary, "I should feel and say, that such a crusade was a holy one, and would be prepared to join it myself." A considerable statement, coming from an observant Jew.[36]

A long history of enslaving Westerners accounts for this demonizing of North African Muslims. For decades, their dark presences had filtered into the imaginations of American readers through accounts of Barbary captivity. Most of those narratives emphasized the cruelty of Muslim masters to their Western slaves and their contempt for Christians. As the fictional Maria Martin assured her readers, "The very word [Christian] in their language signifies dog; and [Muslims] are continually seeking means to destroy them." These were the stories from which Americans first learned that the question to ask about their conflicts with Muslims was "Why do they hate us?" and that the answer was "Islam." It comes as a surprise, then, to find that this genre could also lend itself to more nuanced portrayals of Muslims and their faith.

Those more thoughtful renderings appear in a cluster of captivity narratives first published in 1817 and 1818, accounts written by American mariners shipwrecked off the Saharan coast of Africa and enslaved, along with hundreds of other Western sailors, in the sultanate of Morocco. Saharan chroniclers also stressed Muslims' "bigotry" against Christians, but some took an interest in Islam and remarked on the solemnity with which their masters performed religious devotions. And whereas earlier captives portrayed all Muslims as barbarians, Saharan slaves praised individuals and entire sects within Islam for their charitable and peaceful ways. Most important, a number of Saharan narrators acknowledged that Muslims had no monopoly on savagery and emphasized that Christians engaged in the slave trade, too, behaving with equal brutality. Among them was Judah Paddock, a New York shipmaster, who recounted his Muslim master remarking that if he, a dark-skinned man, had been shipwrecked on American shores, he would have been "doomed to perpetual slavery." "You are too lazy to work yourselves in your fields," his master concluded, at which Paddock "felt the sting of this reproach in a manner I can never forget."[37]

Saharan authors drew on their experiences of captivity to put forward the same critique of slavery that Royall Tyler had advanced in a novel. A lawyer and a successful playwright, the Boston-born Tyler first published *The Algerine Captive* in 1797, with a second edition appearing nearly twenty years later, shortly before the Saharan narratives. Like some of those authors, he took an interest in Islam; unlike them, he had read George Sale's essay on the Qur'an and so fully adopted its "liberality," he explained, that he composed his novel not only to end slavery but also "to do away with the vulgar prejudices against Islam." In a dialogue between the novel's hero, Dr. Updike Underhill, and an Algerine mullah, Tyler, following Sale, noted the many similarities between Islam and Christianity. He also pointed out a major difference: whereas Algerine masters freed slaves who converted to Islam, masters in the American South kept their fellow Christians in bondage.[38]

An even more radical perspective on slavery, Christianity, and

Islam found its way into the press's coverage of the bombardment of Algiers. A month after Bentley's piece appeared, a contributor to Washington, D.C.'s *Daily National Intelligencer*, a gadfly identifying himself as "Mustafa," deplored the hypocrisy of Western critics who reviled the Barbary States for enslaving Christians but looked the other way at the use of Muslim slaves in Spain and Italy. In a second letter published a few weeks later, "Mustafa" lamented that ever since "the victorious banner of Mahomet was first unfurled, the hatred of Christians has followed us." What made that enmity all the worse, he added, echoing Sale, was that the "God of Mussulmen differs not from the God of Christians." It was a sentiment shared by a tiny minority among "Mustafa's" contemporaries, but his letters signal how diverse the American conversation about Islam had become by the 1810s.[39]

Such were the many and often contradictory images of Islam that circulated in the early republic. For some readers, that variety was an intriguing curiosity; for others, a source of confusion, doubt, even outrage. Pick up the *Salem Register*, and there was William Bentley praising Muhammad, the legislator. But page through any evangelical publication, attend any missionary sermon, and up popped Muhammad the impostor. That negative image appeared in some secular newspapers and magazines as well, but it was evangelicals who were coming to own it. They condemned Muhammad and his faith all the more stridently as their investment in foreign missions deepened and the suspicion dawned that Americans of non-evangelical faiths or of no faith might be questioning the centuries-old Christian loathing of Islam. Those who felt most embattled were New Divinity believers, as their increasingly rancorous disputes with liberals splintered Congregationalist and Presbyterian ranks. Isaac Bird, a student at Andover by the spring of 1818, captured the mood in his diary, remarking that a classmate "compared us to a collection of rulers in time of war met to reproach themselves . . . for failure in duty when the enemy were in the very act of sacking the city and house in which they were holding their consultation."[40]

William Bentley believed that evangelicals had only themselves to blame; surprisingly, Pliny Fisk agreed. In September 1817, the latter completed an essay at Andover that lit into all partisans in religious debates who could see "but one side of a subject." He charged that their zeal arose from "disappointed ambition," which made them willing to play upon "the prejudices of the public"—sentiments that could have come straight from Bentley's diary. Still more remarkably, Fisk praised the "few favored geniuses" who had "thrown off the shackles of bigotry and tradition" and looked "with compassion on the pitiable multitudes who are still covered with the fugs and clouds of popery." Among those "geniuses," whether Fisk knew it or not, was Bentley himself, who for years had helped small groups of Catholics to establish their worship in Boston and Salem. He did so without a trace of Fisk's condescension, but then, Bentley had not spent his life among people who referred to the Roman Catholic Church as "Mystery Babylon" and "the mother of harlots."[41]

Their more irenic view of Catholics put Fisk and Bentley in a small and shrinking minority among evangelicals in the United States. Far more typical was Isaac Bird, who observed with no little apprehension the gathering presence of "popery" in Boston. Most likely, Bird had never met a Catholic until he spent two vacations from seminary visiting the city's jails, a seamen's hospital, and poor neighborhoods crowded with free African Americans as well as newcomers from Ireland, Germany, and Spain. Then he met entirely too many. Among them was an illiterate sailor's wife who asked Bird to bring her daughter a spelling book and then beamed (as he blanched) when the little girl "knelt before me at her mother's request and said her Roman Catholic prayers, creed, Hail Mary, etc." There was a black woman on the Boston Neck who told Bird that she "would stick to her religion," despite his pointing out "the unreasonableness of praying to the saints" and attending a worship conducted in Latin. Still more unnerving to Bird was his visit to the prison where a black Catholic man asked him some shrewd theological questions and "seemed to feel that Protestants were all making a trade of preaching and praying." Their devotion made so powerful an impression that Bird spent hours at a Catholic chapel, watching with rapt attention as two young women took the veil. Over the next decade, this anxious fear of Roman Catholicism would become one of the defining features of the evangelical movement on both sides of the Atlantic.[42]

Caught up as he was in this subculture so intolerant of Catholicism, Islam, and even liberal Protestantism, where had Pliny Fisk found encouragement to cultivate broader religious sympathies? Most likely in his secret life—not with the Brethren, but among the Freemasons. Fisk had joined the Masonic Order shortly before or after he entered Andover, probably during one of his stints of keeping school and preaching in Vermont. Besides his fondness for secrets, Fisk's hopes of becoming a missionary would have recommended membership. As one of his contemporaries recalled, joining a lodge was "a supposed passport to society in foreign countries," Masonic signals being "a sort of universal language." That made the fraternity a magnet for the movers and shakers in the British Empire, including those merchants, colonial officials, and military men who might prove useful connections to an American abroad. Then, too, some Masons in the early republic were urging their lodges to support the foreign missions movement by underwriting the expenses of those sent abroad and defraying the costs of translating the Bible.

Whatever drew Fisk into Freemasonry, frequenting its lodges exposed him to a climate of ideas far different from any known to him before. Mention the Masons today, and what comes to mind are middle-aged white guys trading business cards and Republican Party pieties. Not so in the early republic: Fisk's lodge brothers prided themselves on being enlightened cosmopolites, unmoored from provincial prejudices, and they included men who controlled the key nodes of communication with the wider world—printers and postmasters, librarians and newspaper editors, artists and ministers. A lifelong Freemason, William Bentley incarnated their ideal. So even if Fisk never mustered the courage to seek out that grand dragon of Socinianism during the summer of 1818, he might have met Bentley at Salem's Masonic lodge. Feature Fisk in that setting, marveling at how much his Masonic brothers differed from the Brethren—and perhaps taking on board greater charity, at least toward his fellow Christians.[43]

But most conservative evangelicals did not believe that wider sympathies and greater civility would answer the challenges that they confronted. On the contrary, they were convinced that consolidating their own ranks, beating down their liberal enemies, snuffing out the Catholic menace, and impressing on a wide public the proper opinions about Islam and all the world's religions demanded a take-no-prisoners leadership and a network of well-funded institutions. In the fledgling foreign missions movement, they would find a powerful means to serve all of those ends.

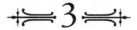

# 3

## "A PERFECT ROMANCE"

Those believers who stay at home, apart from those with an incapacity, are not equal to those who commit themselves and their possessions to striving in God's way. God has raised such people to a rank above those who stay at home—although He has promised all believers a good reward, those who strive are favoured with a tremendous reward above those who stay at home—high ranks conferred by him, as well as forgiveness and mercy.

—Qur'an, Women, 4:95–96

It would make a cat laugh—that's how preposterous it was. Preposterous, and downright dangerous, that some Americans took their opinions about Islam from a bunch of ink-stained wretches trying to boost their newspapers' circulation. Or from that near infidel William Bentley, that prating schoolmaster John Bigland, that scimitar-toting twit George English. Far too many wrongheaded, even outrageous views of Islam circulated everywhere in the early republic—its bookshops and libraries, newspapers and magazines, colleges and academies, parlors and Masonic lodges. To drown out those voices would take more than New Divinity men preaching missionary sermons. It would require a united front among evangelicals who knew their enemies and who were properly informed about the world and who were committed to bringing all its peoples the only true religion. And who better than himself—as if the Reverend Jedidiah Morse needed to ask—to lead the charge? Throughout the second decade of the nineteenth century, even as those whom he loathed gained a bigger audience, Morse put in place the scaffolding of the foreign missions movement, institutions through which he hoped to hand his liberal opponents their heads.

Like many people with a flair for making enemies, Morse imagined even more than he actually had. His list began with the Illuminati: in the years around 1800, no American had done more to trumpet their conspiracy for sowing anarchy and atheism everywhere in the West. No sooner had the alarm over the Illuminati subsided than Morse found another threat to take its place—the one posed by those radical Unitarians, the Socinians. Like the Illuminati, he warned, they worked by stealth; from their beachhead in the churches of eastern Massachusetts, they were beaming their subversive ideas that glorified humankind and debased Jesus Christ. No matter that every Socinian in the early republic would have fit comfortably into William Bentley's lodgings: Morse founded a magazine, the *Panoplist*, devoted to attacking their beliefs and those of other religious liberals. By then, the middle-aged Morse, a suave charmer in youth, had taken on an almost raptor-ish look, like some ancient Puritan bird of prey. It was as if years of spewing polemics had sharpened his chin, arched his eyebrows, and lengthened his beak. Perhaps fortunately, no surviving portraits show his teeth.

Some people in every age, often the young, find it impossible to resist those armed with adamantine certainties about what ails the world and how to right it. So it was with the New Divinity's rising generation: Morse's fixations set them afire. No sooner had young Samuel Mills gathered the Brethren than they joined in Morse's campaign to purge the republic of Socinians. And when they began to push for the entry of the United States into the foreign missions field, Morse numbered among the first ministers whom the Brethren approached. From its earliest years, he served on the American Board of Commissioners for Foreign Missions. He also led the campaign to found Andover Theological Seminary and kept up a correspondence with many of its graduates who became missionaries. His was a name that Levi Parsons and Pliny Fisk would always have heard or dropped with due reverence— or, at the very least, trepidation—throughout their years at Middlebury and Andover in the 1810s. He was always the man who, if not center stage, stood just behind the scenes as the Palestine mission took shape. Though not a birthright member of the New Divinity tribe, Morse was their constant ally, a reliably conservative Calvinist evangelical who broadened their constituency by enlisting others like himself to build the institutions of a new evangelical world—the schools and colleges, the print media and associations.[1]

For many Americans, he called into being the wider world as well. While conspiracies came and went for Morse, geography—and the money he made writing about it—proved lifelong lusts. In 1784, while still a tutor at Yale, he wrote a text for beginning students that would enjoy steady sales for more than three decades, and ten years later he brought out the first of many editions of *The American Universal Geography*. It was his most ambitious work, two doorstop-sized volumes that became a fixture in the curricula of colleges and academies and a staple in subscription libraries and gentlemen's studies. Here was an indispensable guide to almost every known fact about the countries of the world—not only their topography, climate, population, and major cities, but also their commodities traded, crops grown, manufactures produced, antiquities preserved, costumes worn, languages spoken, and customs observed. Exhaustive coverage made the *Universal Geography* the go-to introduction to the world for serious readers both within and without evangelical ranks in the two decades after 1800.

More than just the facts, Morse's big book offered factoids—most notably, thumbnail sketches of "national character." Only Britons and New Englanders escaped almost unscathed from Morse's appraising eye; the rest of the world's inhabitants he embalmed with only the faintest praise before burying them in rebuke. The Peruvians were lively but licentious; the Norwegians brave but litigious; the French ingenious but "given to empty ostentation and gasconade," while avarice, Morse's own pet vice, also proved "the ruling passion" of the frugal Dutch. Though the Chinese were mild and affable, their rich were lazy and their poor filthy; more remarkable for cleanliness were the Turks and Persians, but the former were too passive and the latter too passionate. And so on: master of the lethal adjective, Morse wielded his poison pen to put down peoples throughout the world. Better scholars—among them William Bentley and his friend the German geographer Christoph Ebeling—winced at Morse's snap judgments and dismissed them as so much . . . gasconade.[2]

Morse warmed to no subject more than religion, and in the tropics of his outrage, factoids flourished. He went so far as to praise the Buddhists of Ceylon for showing "a prodigious superiority of good sense to the visionary Brahmins" and did not so much as cock an eyebrow over the Yap peoples of the Caroline Islands who "worship a kind of crocodile." But Hinduism he reduced to an array of "fanatic penances, suicides, and other superstitious frenzies," and Islam, too, came in for a shellacking. Though he knew better, Morse sank to rehashing medieval legends about Muhammad—that the Prophet had relied on a Catholic monk to concoct the Qur'an and that he had passed off his epileptic fits as divinely inspired trances. It was a dose of Christian trash talk to counter the more impartial, even glowing depictions of Muhammad and his teachings that were gaining an audience in the United States.[3]

The final signature of the *Universal Geography* was its author's hand-in-glove relationship with the foreign missions movement. When he brought out its sixth edition in 1812, Morse acknowledged his debt to missionary publications for information about the world beyond the United States. In his 1819 edition, he drew directly on his private correspondence with American missionaries to lend currency to his coverage—which gave even greater weight to his judgments. From Adoniram Judson in Rangoon, he learned that the volatile political situation in Burma (present-day Myanmar) showed signs of settling down. From India, Gordon Hall provided an even choicer tidbit in yet another Hindu mode of ritual suicide, this one involving a saw, "so constructed and placed, that the person wishing to sacrifice himself, might fix his body under it, and then set it in motion with his feet, so as almost instantly to tear himself to pieces." Just as Morse used missionaries to sell his geographies, he used geographies to sell the American public on missions. His "particular object" in the *Universal Geography*'s 1819 edition was "to describe the various *missionary stations* in the different quarters of the world for the gratification of the Christian community." In other words, Morse made Protestant missions as much an essential article of geographic knowledge as the location of Hudson Bay and the Black Sea. By treating missions as simply a new feature on the landscape, he naturalized their expansion and enlisted readers in believing that the conversion of the world was inevitable.[4]

For decades, Jedidiah Morse reached a vast audience in the early republic. The *Universal Geography*'s sheer heft and ubiquity lent gravitas to its deliverances, affording evangelicals an immense advantage in shaping the way in which all Americans understood the world and its religions. No one appreciated more than Morse how much power that could confer on his kind of Protestantism. More Americans seeing the world's religions his way would lend even greater urgency and legitimacy to bringing all its peoples into the fold of evangelical Protestantism, and expanding missionary stations and publications would in turn afford evangelicals even greater ability to influence the ways in which Americans viewed the countries and cultures beyond their borders. Among the most prized of their hoped-for victories would be stilling the cacophony of opinion about Islam in a contentious public sphere and settling sentiment in evangelicals' favor.

As crucial in Morse's reckoning was the potential of the missionary cause to soft-pedal the doctrinal and ritual differences that divided leading evangelical churches—the Congregationalists, Presbyterians, Baptists, and Methodists. Like his geographies, missionaries' reports from abroad would invite readers to chuckle at the silly beliefs and to gasp at the grisly rites of evangelicals' great religious rivals the world over—Roman Catholics, Hindus, and Muslims—and then to recognize the common ground held by Protestants of their stripe and the pettiness of their squabbles. Building an empire of the spirit abroad would thus promote solidarity among evangelicals at home, a union ensuring their victory over religious liberals and enhancing their ability to contain the budding Catholic threat. In the fullness of their strength, evangelicals might realize their grandest ambitions within the United States: by dominating schools and churches, voluntary societies and the print media, they would gain leverage over the public opinion that, in the end, influenced government policies.[5]

Morse's undertakings would draw disparate groups of believers into a coherent, self-conscious, and powerful evangelical movement. Among the defining marks of its identity, perhaps none would prove so enduring as the commitment to converting the world, a crusading spirit forged by the distinctive popular missionary culture that first emerged in the second decade of the nineteenth century. No one did more than Jedidiah Morse to conjure this new realm for the play of imaginations and the patterns of association among his fellow religious conservatives. Once set in motion, that culture would shape the destinies of the first American missionaries to enter the Middle East and their inventions of Islam.[6]

The memories never left him. He was only nine or ten years old in 1815, when the second party of American missionaries left for India and the first sailed for Ceylon, but word of their going "greatly excited" his imagination. It captivated his grandmother, too, and she talked about missions throughout that winter he spent with her. When he returned home, he loved to listen as his father read from a magazine devoted to foreign missions. He could see himself still, a few years later at thirteen, kneeling on the rye scaffold in the family's barn "where I thought no one would see or hear me," repeating the prayer that he had composed consecrating himself to the missionary cause. He confided his hopes to a schoolmate, and they "took the names of prominent missions": he became "Ceylon" and his friend "Bombay." "The whole enterprise was a perfect *romance* to me," he recalled, "and I was for months nearly bewildered by it—and for years intensely interested in it." So he remained all his life, "tho' with feelings somewhat sobered by time." The author of these recollections chose to remain anonymous, perhaps because he had never realized his youthful dreams of becoming a missionary. Yet he could never forget "how my childish heart was stirred to its depths," which "I took to be a type of the feelings of hundreds of children as well as adults then living in Christian families."[7]

This romance of missions suffused the sensibility of Yankee evangelicalism, as "Ceylon's" recollection attests. It took hold during the first two decades of the nineteenth century, as missionary sermons became staples of pulpit oratory, and there sprang up in every village at least one society dedicated to praying for missionaries, collecting money and clothing for them, and discussing the latest news about them. Their members made up the devoted readership of missionary memoirs and the subscribers to religious periodicals publishing reports of missions. All those venues—the sermons and societies, the magazines and the books—elevated missionaries into iconic figures and spiritual virtuosos. Missionaries served as models especially for devout young men and women: here were the people whom they wished to become when they grew up, even though most, like the anonymous "Ceylon," did not. By about 1820, commitment to missionary institutions and ideals had become essential to the profession and practice of a growing number of northern Christians. Thereafter its influence would expand far beyond the circles of conservative Calvinist believers and across the United States, flourishing well into the twentieth century.

Jedidiah Morse handpicked the man who put in place the mechanisms for sparking and sustaining the intense emotions—that "perfect romance"—which came to surround foreign missions. Later in life,

Jeremiah Evarts would wage a heroic, doomed crusade against Indian removal, but in the 1810s he was a pious young lawyer, looking down his long nose at the dancers and drunkards, the Sabbath breakers and infidels, whom he denounced in occasional contributions to the *Panoplist*. Impressed by this capacity for pious contempt, Jedidiah Morse plucked Evarts from a failing New Haven legal practice in 1809 and put him in charge of editing the magazine. Under Evarts's editorship and with Morse's full support, the *Panoplist* (later rechristened the *Missionary Herald*) became the flagship publication for the American Board, devoting most of its coverage to foreign missions.

Much of what filled the *Panoplist*'s pages came from the journals and letters of missionaries. As the American Board's corresponding secretary, Salem's Reverend Samuel Worcester maintained an extensive correspondence with missionaries and with supporters of missions throughout the United States. He and his successors in that job also took a free hand to all missionary communications before they appeared in the *Panoplist*, censoring anything that might bark the shins of donors, real or potential. His workload piled up as more and more columns of a longer and longer magazine featured extracts from the reports of both British and American missionaries, describing creeds and customs, people and places, triumphs and trials, and throughout presenting the evangelical Protestant perspective on the world's other religions. Not only the most trusted source of news about the world for many Americans, the *Panoplist* and similar religious periodicals (which borrowed liberally from its pages) brought into being a national community of like-minded readers who had the same knowledge about the history of missions, the same familiarity with the doings of individual missionaries and their stations, and the same fund of hopeful signs and setbacks in their progress toward the conversion of the world.[8]

As Worcester oversaw much of the copy for the *Panoplist*'s pages, Evarts put his shoulder to expanding the missionary enterprise. He strove to increase the magazine's circulation, to publish weekly rather than monthly, and to enhance the quantity and quality of information from abroad by planting mission outposts in more parts of the world. Growing those operations would require raising money, and being appointed treasurer of the American Board shortly after becoming the *Panoplist*'s editor positioned Evarts to do exactly that. He proved nothing less than a corporate visionary and an organizational dynamo.

When he advised that evangelicals "must exhibit some of that enterprise which is observable in the conduct of worldly men," he meant business. While other Yankees tinkered to speed up spinning machines and to perfect eight-day clocks, Jeremiah Evarts was inventing the public relations campaign and state-of-the-art fund-raising techniques. Under his direction, the American Board morphed into the largest corporation in the early republic and an outfit with global reach.[9]

As a first step, Evarts encouraged the formation of auxiliary missionary societies in every New England village, each funneling its collections into the board's treasury. By 1818, there were five hundred such local societies, their membership often made up predominantly or exclusively of women. Their hearts set afire by Harriet Newell, women of every age—widowed, wed, and single—swelled the ranks of groups such as the Female Beneficent Society and the Female Bombay Society, the Female Cent Society and, inevitably, the Female Newell Society. When needed, Worcester played the fixer, composing gallant letters to those women who complained when their society's contribution went unacknowledged in the *Panoplist*'s back pages or when their subscriptions failed to arrive on time. Not a few had definite ideas about the conduct of missions. On a tour of Vermont to drum up donations, Levi Parsons ran into one woman who "undertook to show the impropriety of [mission schools'] educating male children to the neglect of Females." When he explained that such decisions were "left to the discretion of the Board and the Missionaries," she shot back, "No matter for that, if I subscribe, I wish to direct!"

When their female benefactors spoke, Evarts and Worcester had no choice but to listen. They counted on women to "keep up the missionary zeal" by forming new societies, locating potential donors, and even raising money themselves through the sale of handmade clothing. Most members of female auxiliaries took up collections locally, often going door-to-door, but they were not Louisa Battelle. A single woman of independent means and spirit, she traveled a circuit stretching from Saratoga Springs to Washington, D.C., drumming up donations and signing her reports to the board with a proud flourish, "Louisa Battelle, Agent." When Evarts intimated that she was shaking down her targets in Philadelphia too hard, prompting some to criticize her "misguided zeal," she fired back that "a *Gentleman* on the same business, would never have collected half as much in this City."[10]

Louisa Battelle was part of a network of agents whom Evarts dispatched throughout the United States, keeping close tabs on the performance of each. Those in New England had the easiest sell, for that region was the center ring of missionary hoopla. Ordination ceremonies drew enormous crowds, and the embarkation of missionaries for foreign fields attracted even more people. Two thousand onlookers lined Newburyport's wharves to bid farewell to the first American mission to Ceylon in 1815. Reborn pagans drew even better than departing missionaries, so Evarts hoped to rake in handsome collections for the first Sandwich Island mission by parading a few native Christians before rapt crowds at Salem and Boston.

To appreciate how deeply "the missionary spirit" stamped the piety of Yankee evangelicals, read over Samuel Worcester's shoulder as he sifted through letters from pious donors. One sent five dollars to "the fund for educating heathen children," as "a mother's thank-offering for the birth of a son," while a man in Newburyport gave twelve dollars to maintain an orphan boy in Ceylon, "which sum I shall continue, if life be spared for four years." A bereaved mother donated fifty cents left behind by her little girl who had once cried over the sufferings of children in Africa. "The death of Martha Ann has filled our souls with anguish," the woman wrote. "She was our only child." Then there were the hundreds of eager donors who sponsored a child at a mission school in India and Ceylon. That "heathen" boy or girl would thereafter bear whatever Yankee name was endowed by the American donor. Sponsors' choices ranged from foreign missionaries and popular ministers to prosperous merchants and pious matrons to Martin Luther and John Calvin. Some even rechristened those distant children with the names of their own dead sons and daughters: among them were the parents of Levi Parsons, who named a child in Bombay after a son who had died at the age of six. More than a whiff of superstition that evangelicals would have called "popish" hangs over these donations. Many laypeople endowed their support for missions with a kind of magical power, as if such gifts could prolong life, heal grief, cure sickness, promise fertility, or reincarnate a lost child. In that respect as well as in its creation of a new Protestant pantheon of apostles and martyrs, the missionary culture taking hold in the early nineteenth-century North eerily replicated some of the devotional practices of Roman Catholicism.[11]

While the cause of missions quickly caught on in the North, Jeremiah

Evarts saw that the South would be a harder nut to crack. On a tour of Georgia and South Carolina in the spring of 1818, he wrote to Worcester that "religious people" there knew far less about missions than did northerners. Nor did southerners have "that hardihood of character, which is requisite to enable them to resist and overcome opposition;—for opposition and objections will be augmented as the number of benevolent institutions is increased." Yet there was plenty of money, particularly among the planters with whom Evarts hobnobbed—far more, he believed, than in New England. "The question has dwelt a good deal on my mind," he reflected. "How are we to obtain a regular succession of donations to our Board from the people of the South?"

He was only a few miles north of Georgetown in South Carolina when it came to him: a direct-mail campaign. The board would send out fund-raising letters worded to make each recipient "feel that the appeal is made to him particularly, and aimed directly and boldly at his heart." They would take different forms, one "designed for a very rich man," another for people of more modest means, "calculated to impel them to make a regular, unsolicited, and punctual remittance to our objects." Yet another would address "persons of whom less could be hoped, in a systematic way, but who would do something handsome, if the subject were brought powerfully to their minds" through facts and arguments. A member of the American Board or an agent would sign the letters, adding a few handwritten lines, "so that the receiver should feel as though his character were known, and something expected of him." The direct-mail campaign would take fund-raising to a whole new level, allowing the American Board to "make a deep impression."[12]

If popular missionary culture had found its presiding genius in Jedidiah Morse, its master builder was Jeremiah Evarts. To invest American Protestants both emotionally and financially in the cause, to turn them into consumers of missionary literature and donors to the American Board, took careful planning. It took millions of words, spoken and printed, to instill the conviction that a Christian's duty was to convert the world. And it took knowing when, where, how, how often, and whom to ask for the money to do it. Without Evarts's publishing the *Panoplist*, dealing with auxiliary societies, dispatching agents, making spectacles from missionary ordinations and sailings, and balancing the books, there would have been no "perfect romance" of missions.

Then again, the new foreign missions movement might have drawn even fewer critics.

If evangelicals' ambition to convert the world raised eyebrows, even hackles, among others in the early republic, most of those critics kept quiet about their concerns, at least at first. Among the most restrained was William Bentley, who confined to diary entries his mounting alarm about the impact of missionary enterprise on Americans. Maddening as it was to him—the prospect that people would get their ideas about the world from Jedidiah Morse's geography books and the *Panoplist*'s missionary reports—even more galling were the ploys Evarts was devising to "milk my friends." Bentley's anger built to a crescendo over the board's practice of taking subscriptions, printed pledges that committed to missions a portion of what each donor produced. Farmers would "apply land to be cultivated for Missions," Bentley explained, while the "mechanic is challenged for his house and the manufacturer for his profits." Clerks and mariners would set aside a percentage of their salaries, fishermen a cut of their best catch, and women "of every age and name" would subscribe to spend one day of each month collecting or sewing for the missionary cause. The board thus made "a Business of Missions," one designed to garner enormous wealth and, with it, political influence for conservative evangelicals.[13]

A few Americans took that concern public. Among the first was "Avarus Homunculus," the anonymous author of an 1813 letter to a Boston newspaper who condemned foreign missionary societies for depriving "our own poor" in order to enrich "money-craving priests" and "here and there a sly-fingered lawyer"—a dig at Evarts. Assisting them in their "money-catching scheme" were "female mendicants" who were "thrusting themselves into all our families," pressuring reluctant donors to subscribe, and even going public with names and the amounts promised. As for the cockeyed scheme of converting the world, why, "you may just as well set the Andes afloat on the Rio Grande, and convey them through the Atlantic in order to sink the island of Great Britain, as attempt to lead the followers of the great prophet of Mecca to abjure Islamism." In the unlikely event that missionaries gained adherents, "the introduction of a new religion" would lead only "to wars and fighting." Besides, "Avarus" added with the antic glee of a writer who loves his work, Christianity would destroy "the intense conjugal affection that leads wives to die on the funeral pyres of their husbands."[14]

Ever since, foreign missions have been fodder for satirists. Few have reached the comic heights scaled by Charles Dickens with his send-up of *Bleak House*'s "telescopic" philanthropist Mrs. Jellyby, who fixes her charity on distant Africans instead of impoverished Britons at home. But he stood on the shoulders of many, and his American forerunners besides "Avarus" include Joseph Tinker Buckingham, a prominent politician and the editor of several Boston publications, including the *New-England Galaxy and Masonic Magazine*, which he founded in 1817. Not a few Masons in the early republic urged their fraternity to support Christian benevolence, but the *Galaxy* emerged as a forum for critics of Bible, tract, and missionary societies. Buckingham himself entered the fray, taking aim at the legions of "silly women" who "gadded" house to house in quest of donations, as well as attacking missions from a new angle. Missionaries "can effect but little," he advised, "while Christians, in the East Indies, are continually encroaching on the Natives with fire and sword; while the Jews, throughout Christendom are held in contempt and derision; while the Indians on this continent are hunted like wild beasts of the forest; and while the Africans are held in the most abject slavery." If Masonic lodges in the United States supported foreign missions, he added archly, "our [Masonic] brethren in the East" might well fund "disseminating the knowledge of Mohammedism."[15]

No doubt Buckingham received encouragement from the man who had helped him to launch the *Galaxy* right before taking his own swipe at foreign missions. Lawyer, literary gadfly, and a regular orator at Masonic festivals, Samuel Lorenzo Knapp not only contributed weekly columns to the *Galaxy* but also tried his hand at the literary trope of inventing a Muslim visitor who exposed the faults and foibles of the West. Surveying Boston from the statehouse roof, his "Ali Bey" declared Christianity in Boston on the verge of "a mighty schism" and announced his plans to "step in and take advantage" of the disputes between evangelicals and liberals by converting the city's inhabitants to Islam.[16]

These blasts aside, what is striking about public criticisms of missions before 1820 is how few and timid they were. Prominent liberal Christians like Bentley, Thomas Jefferson, and John Adams consigned their carping to the privacy of diaries and personal correspondence, and most of New England's Unitarians in the making even went on the record endorsing both foreign and domestic missions. Striking, too, is that their earliest critics argued against foreign missions strictly on practical grounds—the dim prospects for success, the diversion of funds from domestic charities, the enriching and empowering of evangelicals. As yet no American dared to wonder in print whether "the heathen" needed Christianity to improve their lot in this life and to enjoy heaven in the next. But in private exchanges some were asking those questions, and in their sermons a few liberal ministers were giving daring answers. The same enlightened universalism that inspired evangelicals to view foreign missions as their obligation to the great family of man suggested to other Christians that the rest of the world's people could find God in their own ways and should be left alone to do so. Would a just and loving God have spent centuries stuffing hell with heathen souls? By heightening popular awareness of the vast number of non-Christians, the foreign missions movement had raised that inconvenient question.[17]

If doubts about missions were deepening on both sides of the Atlantic, the British were bolder about venting them in print. Some opponents of Christianizing India ventured that the Hindus, if they led good lives, could enter heaven. Others went further, contending, as George Sale had earlier, that believers in different religions all worshipped the same God. Such sentiments drew the ire of the two speakers featured at Pliny Fisk's ordination at Salem in the fall of 1818. Samuel Worcester condemned the "delirious dream of infidelity" that "all nations acknowledge and worship the true God, only under different names, and with different rites," while the Andover professor Moses Stuart railed against the view that "the heathen do not need the gospel; that they are already as moral and happy as Christian nations; and have as good ground to expect future happiness." What a mercy, Stuart added, that Americans voiced such sentiments far less often than did the British.

Despite efforts to hold it at bay, the camel of religious relativism was wedging its nose under the big tent of Christianity in the United States. It was all the more unwelcome to some evangelicals in a newly founded nation still charged with apprehension about the separation of church and state. Would full religious liberty encourage more accepting attitudes toward peoples of many faiths and of no faith? Would more Americans conclude that all religions had some validity, perhaps even that believing in Christianity was not essential to salvation? Would religious freedom lead to religious relativism and relativism to outright skepticism? American evangelicals received encouragement for this kind of catastrophizing from the British evangelical Charles Grant, who had led the fight in Parliament to Christianize India. To him, the notion that all religions "are much the same as to their end and efficacy" led to the conclusion that "there is no such thing as divine revelation." It followed for Grant that critics of missions in India or anywhere else could not be real Christians.[18]

That was the logic which unnerved William Bentley: evangelicals were making support for missions the litmus test of faith. In fact, so successfully had Evarts and Worcester identified the sincerity of Christian profession with their enthusiasm for the missionary cause that they had all but stifled public opposition. Of course, Worcester and Evarts saw themselves as uniters, not dividers. They wished to rally all Protestants to affirm their faith's singularity and superiority, and they envisioned God's providence bringing about the conversion of all the world's peoples. In pursuit of both goals, they sought to create an evangelical Protestant consensus in the Christian nation of the United States. What could be more inclusive?[19]

Sadly, members of the Christian public were fickle. They grew discouraged by anything less than quick success, and they were easily drawn from one good cause to the next. Jeremiah Evarts would have reminded himself of as much when, at the end of 1818, he detected "a flagging of the missionary spirit" and a falling-off in donations. It alarmed him enough to consider recalling all of the missionaries abroad, a mere eight men in India and Ceylon, some with wives and children. But then he decided that a bold stroke might revive the board's fortunes. He and Worcester proceeded with plans to send the first American mission to the Sandwich Islands, where the British had already made some native converts. As for Pliny Fisk and Levi Parsons, they were to head somewhere in western Asia—which might mean anywhere from Persia to Turkey to Arabia—and, once they had learned Arabic, to headquarter in Jerusalem.[20]

Persia had once seemed the obvious choice for an American mission. But lately its stock tumbled among evangelicals because of the sudden notoriety of Jawad Sabat, the Muslim Arab convert and celebrated "Star in the East" who had helped Henry Martyn translate the scriptures into Persian. But Sabat's story took an unexpected turn when he spurned evangelical Protestantism and, still worse, wrote a defense of Islam, claiming that he had feigned conversion only "to comprehend and expose" Christian doctrines. By the middle of 1817, stunned reports of his apostasy were circulating as widely as had earlier stories of his piety. Sabat subsequently decamped to Malacca (in present-day Malaysia) and there, in what is rarely a wise move, turned from religion to politics. Sure enough, he quickly made enemies who stuffed him into a sack filled with rocks and tossed it into the sea—or so the evangelical press reported with grim satisfaction. With that embarrassment still so fresh, perhaps the less said of Persia the better.[21]

Wherever they went in western Asia, Fisk and Parsons would go as unmarried men. To such uncharted territory, in which no country came under the aegis of the British Empire, the board would send only bachelors. That brought Parsons back to Andover in November to join in "covenant" with Fisk, who had just finished deciphering the records of the Brethren. They held a private ceremony, pledging with "sincerity of heart, and with earnest prayer for divine assistance, [to] give ourselves to each *other*." They exchanged promises "to live in love; to maintain the most perfect harmony of feeling, of design and of operation; to unite our strength, our talents and our influence, for the conversion of the heathen"; and never to separate unless duty demanded, "having our hearts knit together as the heart of one man." Those vows bespoke an intense attachment between the two men, platonic yet romantic. A few weeks later in December, with Fisk now in the South raising money to support their mission, Parsons wrote from Vermont, "Time passes rather slowly since we parted. It gives me pain to count six months forward and to travel over 1200 miles to find the whole of *one*. Did you know that I was often with you by the way? Forget not this evidence of our recent union. It will be lasting; it will be immortal."

Their covenant ceremony formalized the commitment that had deepened between Fisk and Parsons since their days at Middlebury. A year earlier, in October 1817, Parsons, then a new Andover graduate itinerating in Vermont, wrote an extraordinary letter to his friend, who was finishing his last year at seminary. He began by listing what he believed had caused serious "dissensions" among the first American missionaries to India, including a lack of "frankness in relating faults." Because he already considered himself paired with Fisk for any missionary venture, Parsons proceeded to set forth his friend's shortcomings and urged him "in your letter deal out my faults plentifully. I will *love* you for it." After covenanting with Fisk, Parsons continued to press this "course of faithfulness"—meaning mutual criticism—on him. Fisk's side of the correspondence has not turned up, but it must have challenged his ingenuity to find any fault in such a paragon of New Divinity piety. Parsons's greatest spiritual struggle seems to have been taming the pride that he took in their future as missionaries, because it would surely tarnish the luster of any martyrdom awaiting. "It is but little to [be] bound in irons while the world are beholding with admiration our courage and zeal for the Lord," he confided to Fisk. "It will be a delusive test of piety to march to the stake, while we are sensible that it [is] the path to immortal fame." There was a power in Parsons's selflessness, a "purity," as his partner sometimes expressed it, that a more complicated man—the man that Fisk was becoming—might have coveted.[22]

The bond between Fisk and Parsons did not keep them from developing close friendships with women. As future missionaries, they often met and corresponded with young and old, single and married. Parsons even struck the occasional flirtatious note, hinting that his marrying at some future date might not be out of the question. Perhaps the prospect crossed Fisk's mind as well: his pleasure reading included Hannah More's popular novel, *Coelebs in Search of a Wife*. But Fisk stood by the original design of the Brethren, which included lifelong celibacy. Their founder, the never-married Samuel Mills, set the tone, reminding one of their fraternity that the man "is not fit for a missionary who sighs for the delights of a lady's lap." The same attitude echoed in the historical sketch of the Brethren that Fisk composed in 1818 while transcribing their minutes. "It was the first the united and *decided* opinion" of the charter members "that missionaries should not marry," he huffed. "In regard to this, some of them, at least, have changed their opinion."[23]

Having an intimacy founded on years of friendship made Fisk and Parsons an odd couple among missionary pairs. Their contemporaries typically received encouragement to marry, because the board's leaders believed that marriage would prevent missionaries from falling into sexual dalliances abroad. But in the 1810s there were not enough eligible women willing to accept the risks involved, or more likely, there were too many parents, relatives, and friends discouraging them from such unions. As a result, missionaries had trouble recruiting mates, and those who succeeded often wedded women with whom they had little acquaintance, meeting and marrying on the fly, a few months, even weeks before sailing to their destinations. "Providential" was the description favored by Evarts and Worcester for this hasty way of finding wives.[24]

Anyone walking past the American Board's "missionary rooms" on Boston's Market Street early in 1819 might have heard the wheels whirring. It was the sound of Jeremiah Evarts's well-oiled brain processing the implications of a national financial crisis—what would soon be called a panic. Contributions to all philanthropies would plummet in that economic downturn—he had seen the ominous signs at the end of the preceding year—and make the competition for donations even sharper. But scaling back foreign missions was no longer on the table: Evarts had decided to tough it out. After all, the evangelical public was responding enthusiastically to the board's planned mission to the Sandwich Islands, and he was reaching a decision about a destination for Fisk and Parsons that seemed nothing short of inspired: Ottoman Turkey.[25]

The deliberations of European diplomats had lately put the Ottomans on evangelicals' radar. At the Congress of Vienna in 1815, Austria, Prussia, and Russia had agreed to a treaty known as the Holy Alliance, pledging to promote Christian virtue in all their dealings. Some American and British evangelicals took the treaty to augur what they called a "second crusade" in which "the banners of the Holy League shall be established on the ruins of the temples of Mahomet." One pious contributor to a New York newspaper believed that this holy war against Islam had already begun, inaugurated by the Anglo-Dutch naval vessels' recent bombarding of Algiers. In the wake of an inevitable Christian victory over the Ottomans, the writer predicted that the "infidels will be forced to receive a treaty dictated at the discretion of the Holy League, and then our missionaries will pour into the Mahometan dominions." None other than Jedidiah Morse lent his imprimatur to the hope that big change was coming for the Ottomans, spelling it out in the 1819 edition of the *Universal Geography*. "The influence of

Russia is rising," he declared, which might in turn embolden Greek Christians to resist the Turks. As the means of "overthrowing the Mahometan power on the part of Russia" increased, the way would open for "the introduction of pure Christianity into this region of imposture and moral degradation." In this atmosphere newly charged with possibility, Morse surely urged sending Fisk and Parsons somewhere in the Ottoman Empire.[26]

That was a big place with many possibilities: Constantinople, Alexandria, Cairo. In the end, the board settled on Smyrna, a major seaport on the coast of Turkey. It hosted a large Western enclave, even a handful of American expatriates, to ease the missionaries' entry into this new world. Another consideration weighed in Smyrna's favor as well, especially for those as attuned as Evarts and Morse to the ways that spiritually colonizing the Islamic world might also pay dividends for evangelicals at home. That city had lately landed in the public eye with the appearance of a slim volume titled *Letters from Asia* by a "Gentleman from Boston." "Asia" meant mostly Smyrna, and the gentleman was George Barrell, whose family orbited alongside that of George Bethune English in the same Brahmin galaxy. His father's early death and a substantial fortune freed Barrell for many footloose years of roaming the sea-lanes from Scandinavia to the Levant on merchant vessels. Sometime in the late 1810s, he made port at Smyrna, beckoned because reading "Eastern Tales" had "beguiled many of my leisure hours" in youth. There he received a warm welcome from family friends and business associates; a few years earlier, one of them might have sent George English that scimitar.

It was paradise, and Barrell went public with his realizing that the "prejudices of the Christian world against the professors of Mahomet's creed . . . led me to fear a thousand dangers where none existed." How Ottoman commerce flourished, the fragrant bazaars loaded with "jewelry, furs, pelisses, Persian silks and Cashmere shawls," along with loads of goods from Europe. Provided they did not pursue Muslim women or show disrespect within a mosque, Westerners "may enjoy more liberty, and as much happiness in Asia, as in any part of the world," owning houses and other property without being taxed by the government. Then there was Islam itself, with its mosques so chastely elegant in which Muslims "worship the same God as we do." But much more fervently: "When a Turk once commences his prayer, nothing but the immediate preservation of his life would tempt him to cease before he has ended it." What Christians could equal Muslims' devotion? To say nothing of their honesty, according to Barrell, for theft was unknown in the Ottoman Empire. What's more, their firm belief in predestination not only inculcated a noble stoicism but also made Turks daring capitalists, keen to take risks and insouciant in the face of business failures. Thus the consummate cosmopolite from Boston gave voice to the tolerant ideal of the Freemason—which Barrell was already or would soon become.[27]

The prevailing image of Ottoman Muslims in the early republic was far darker. As every schoolchild who read Jedidiah Morse's textbooks learned, Turkish men immured their women behind veils and harem walls and debased them by polygamy; otherwise, these divan potatoes did little but lounge about, drinking coffee and smoking tobacco. Indolent and sensual, the Turks ranked among Morse's least favorite peoples, their morals, he tutted, being "loose in the extreme." Many other Western writers shared that low estimate. The Turks' epic consumption of coffee produced little in the way of activity or reflection, the Spanish traveler Ali Bey al-Abassi helpfully explained, because of their fondness for opium, to say nothing of "reiterated excesses of enjoyments appointed by or contrary to nature." The other distinguishing mark of the Turks was their "wonderful self-conceit," in the words of William Eton, whose *Survey of the Turkish Empire* found a place on the shelf of most American libraries. Islam was the source of that arrogance, because if many nations had believed themselves "favourites of the Almighty," among no people had "this folly appeared more disgustingly conspicuous than in the Turkish nation." Eton went on to catalog the wages of Muslim bigotry: the restrictions on Christians' dress, even on the color of their houses, the prohibitions against building and repairing churches, and the Sublime Porte's humiliation of Western diplomats.[28]

But contrary opinions were circulating about the Turks even before George Barrell weighed in. Not far behind Lady Mary Wortley Montagu's letters in public notice was her countryman Thomas Thornton's *Present State of Turkey*, first published in 1807. For many years a merchant in Constantinople, he lauded the Muslim Turks for their honesty in business dealings, charity to the poor, and hospitality toward strangers, and he endorsed Montagu's claim that Turkish women did not lead miserable lives. Like Eton, he found the Turks proud and indolent, but Thornton attributed those qualities not to their religion but to their despotic government. As for their insistence on Ottoman exceptionalism, "this haughty conceit of superiority appears as strong in the abject Jew, or the Christian puritan, as in the most bigoted Turk." By Thornton's lights, Islam possessed "an intrinsic worth" as a religious creed, and if some of its followers were intolerant, they violated the spirit of the Qur'an and the life of Muhammad himself. John Bigland agreed that the Turks harbored contempt for Westerners, but their religion was not to blame, because Islam "is not more intolerant in its nature, than most of the Christian sects have shewed themselves in practice; nor have the Mahomedans ever treated the Christians so ill, as the Christians have treated one another."[29]

None of these more dispassionate appraisals sat well with the leading men of the American Board, especially Jeremiah Evarts and Jedidiah Morse. And now here was George Barrell offering full-throated praise of both the Ottomans and Islam. Worse still, American readers could not get enough of his *Letters from Asia*: the book went through several printings in 1819, and many newspapers published excerpts. Could there be a more timely opportunity for missionaries to intervene in the rancorous debate over the Muslim world? Members of the board felt confident that Fisk and Parsons, once stationed in Smyrna, would send home reports that exposed every error in Barrell's fawning description of that place and its people. Their missionary efforts would also refute his parting shot that "the combined power of the whole Christian world would not be able to persuade a virtuous musselman to change his faith."[30]

Encouragement came from an unexpected quarter as Pliny Fisk prepared to depart for Ottoman domains in the fall of 1819. He paid a farewell visit to Shelburne, where "with my aged Father I enjoyed as much real solid happiness [as] in any visit before." Those words hint at tension between them in the past, as Pliny had struggled through college and seminary, the only one of his siblings to stray from the family home. But Ebenezer Fisk seems to have come to terms with his son's ambition, and "he rode about with me as I visited my friends and spent much time in giving me admonitions, exhort[at]ions, and advice." They also stopped at the graveyard, where Ebenezer pointed to the tomb of his wife, Pliny's mother, telling him, *"If you ever come home I shall lie there."* Another person might have sensed a reproach, but Pliny felt only gratitude at "so much calmness, such Paternal tenderness and still such Christian submission." A few weeks later, he made a triumphal departure from Boston.[31]

It capped more than a week of pious fanfare. The celebrations marked the sailing of twenty-three missionaries and their wives for the Sandwich Islands—the largest group dispatched by the American Board and the first ever to venture into the Pacific—as well as the departure of Fisk and Parsons for the Levant. Among the participants was one Julia Adams, a country schoolteacher from Medfield, Massachusetts, on a visit to Boston. Not particularly pious but bookish and curious about the wider world, she attended an evening "missionary party" of nearly a hundred people. The star attractions were four young men from the Sandwich Islands who attended the Cornwall School, an institution for native converts recently founded in Connecticut and sponsored by the American Board. Charming and at ease in company, they "made the white gentlemen, who went bowing round, appear quite clownish," she reported. One of them "spoke a declamation in the language of the Owyhee [Hawai'i] Isles" and then "repeated the Lord's Prayer in the same language." It took Adams a little aback: "To see a heathen instructing Christians in their own religion is a solemn and interesting scene." Here was exactly the sort of spectacle that Evarts delighted in staging.[32]

As he hoped, the departure of the Sandwich Islands mission only pumped up public interest in the "Palestine mission," as it was now called. A week after the contingent bound for the Pacific had sailed, Levi Parsons delivered an afternoon sermon on the conversion of the Jews, but his partner's evening performance generated even greater excitement. Word seems to have traveled through the evangelical grapevine that Fisk had acquitted himself admirably in the South, where he had proved a popular speaker and, if not exactly a good old boy, good enough to ingratiate himself with donors in Savannah and Charleston. Perhaps that cracker-barrel sense of humor so distasteful to the Andover faculty disarmed white southerners who were expecting a starchy Yankee. In Georgia, Fisk had even wrung enough money from the Freemasons to support the first year of his mission. Making his way back to

Boston, he glad-handed more lodge members in the mid-Atlantic and even met with Secretary of State John Quincy Adams in Washington, D.C. (Known among evangelicals as "a pillar of socinianism," Adams swallowed his disdain for missionaries long enough to provide Fisk with letters of introduction abroad.) Not bad for a bumpkin.[33]

That word of mouth filled the Old South Church to bursting on the night of Fisk's sermon. The church was more crowded, the *Panoplist* crowed, "than we almost ever recollect to have seen any place of concourse." People jammed into the pews, spilled out into the aisles, squeezed on the stairs, thronged both galleries; in the crush, "it was with great difficulty that the boxes could be circulated for the collection." Fisk's performance did not disappoint, and even though many were obliged to stand, "the profoundest attention was observable to the close." The crowd was expecting rhetorical red meat, and his farewell answered their hunger. Somewhere in the audience was Julia Adams, who hung on every word of what she called his "very extraordinary sermon." For many Americans, this mission was special, she explained, because of "its being to Jerusalem, which and around which, has been the seat of the most important events in our world" as recounted in the Bible.[34]

Playing to that fascination, Fisk emphasized the mission's ultimate destination in "Judea" or "the Holy Land," even though he and Parsons planned an indefinite stay in Smyrna. In "this land rendered sacred in the eyes of every Christian by a thousand religious associations," he declared, they expected to encounter peoples who were not "sunk in such stupidity and such brutal ignorance, as are the Hindoos of India, and the Hottentots of Africa," or, he might have added, as were the pagans of the Sandwich Islands. That made the Palestine mission more daring, because its objects did not "contemplate the character of Protestant nations with that respect, which is felt for civilized men among more untutored tribes," but rather with "contempt" and "a haughty sense of superiority." There were the "benighted" Eastern Christians, the self-righteous Jews, and, most formidable of all, the "Mahommedans, who are the masters of the country," "followers of that artful impostor," whose "religion was first propagated and is still defended, by the sword." Because "cruelty and blood" were among the "most prominent characteristics" of Islam, Fisk implied that missionaries to this part of the world might easily fall victims to martyrdom.

Those words echoed the sermon preached at his ordination in Salem only a year before. "Blood has followed the track of the crescent, ever since it was first displayed by Mohammed," Moses Stuart had told the congregation. That being the case, he continued, addressing Fisk, "if Jewish obstinacy, or Pagan superstition, or Mohammedan cruelty should light the fires of persecution; and seize you . . . as you ascend the scaffold there, planted on the spot where Jesus' blood was shed—proclaim once more, with your dying breath, a crucified, an all suffi-cient Saviour." After Fisk spoke at Old South, Samuel Worcester picked up on the same theme as he read aloud the board's instructions: "You will take all prudent care that you do nothing rashly . . . that you do not inadvertently or needlessly expose yourself to resentments, rapacities, stratagems, or acts of violence,—startle prejudices, excite suspicions, or offend against laws, or customs, or ceremonies, or opinions." Such cautions only heightened the sense that the pair walked on a knife's edge in Ottoman dominions. No wonder nearly all in the audience stayed to catch every chilling word.[35]

How artfully Fisk had learned to convey the romance of missions—and the romance of martyrdom. And how heartened were his elders at having enlisted someone with his powers to endorse the evangelical view of Islam from within the Ottoman Empire and to rout any con-tenders who dared disagree. Here too, they felt certain, was an ideal apostle for those Americans awaiting assurance that Islam had rotted the Ottoman Empire from within. Jedidiah Morse could not have been more pleased.

What went through Fisk's mind as he looked out on the cavernous space of the Old South meetinghouse? Perhaps he thought of the long road out of Shelburne—and how at last he had impressed those people to whom he had so much to prove. For the moment, even that fortu-nate son, Levi Parsons, stood in his shade. Fisk had become the latest hero of the missionary culture created during the last decade by Morse and Evarts in the hopes of vanquishing their spiritual competitors at home and abroad. He was poised to enter the Protestant pantheon of new apostles; soon his might be the name that pious sponsors endowed on "heathen" children in mission schools. Already he was a public pres-ence who had inspired a humble donor, identified only as "a friend of missions," to send the board three dollars, the proceeds of selling water-melons grown in the corner of a garden consecrated to that purpose.

By now, Fisk had to know that the way he had described Islam to the packed congregation at Old South was not beyond dispute. He knew that others in the West had a far different understanding of Muhammad and his faith, and he had doubtless met more than a few among the Freemasons. He might even have known that his fellow Mason Joseph Buckingham had lately denounced the Palestine mission in print as the most "useless" and "absurd" of all evangelical philanthropies. Had those dissenting voices with their enlightened inventions of Islam awakened any doubts in Fisk's mind? Perhaps: stowed away in the ship that would carry him and Parsons to Smyrna was a crate of books that they had lately purchased with the board's funds. Among them, inevitably, was the latest edition of Morse's *Universal Geography*—but so was Thornton's *Present State of Turkey* and Barrell's *Letters from Asia.*[36]

It would have made a cat laugh, pawing through that crate—if that cat were William Bentley. How preposterous, he would have thought, these two Andover graduates putting the likes of Morse on a par with Thornton and Barrell, who had actually spent time in Turkey. Here was yet another harbinger of the disaster certain to befall these hapless young men in Ottoman domains, and how eager Bentley would be to catch word of it, his ears itching for news from those Salem captains who sailed to Smyrna. But fate—or providence—cheated him of that satisfaction. At the end of 1819, when Pliny Fisk and Levi Parsons were basking in the balmy Mediterranean off the island of Malta, bitter cold gripped New England. As the darkness gathered one evening, Bentley scurried through the icy streets to his lodgings—too fast for a fat man of sixty who suffered from chest pains. He never made it home, dying with his curiosity, to the end, unsatisfied.

# Part Two

# JIHAD

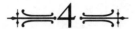

## BRITISH CONNECTIONS

So [Prophet] leave those who reject this revelation to Me: We shall lead
them on, step by step, in ways beyond their knowledge; I will allow them
more time, for My plan is powerful.

—Qur'an, The Pen, 68:44–45

His name conjures up an old gent with chin wattles and muttonchop
whiskers, so it's hard to feature William Jowett as he was in 1820. Sleek,
fair-haired, handsome, barely past thirty: watch him striding down
the sun-splashed streets of Malta's principal port, Valletta, heading
for the lazaretto in the harbor. At his side was a perfect English rose,
blue-eyed, blond Martha Whiting Jowett, carrying a basket filled with
oranges and a book. It was the young English missionary couple's farewell present to the two Americans awaiting what would be the last of
their visits before sailing on to their final destination at Smyrna. They
had met at the lazaretto—a quarantine for recently arrived ships'
passengers—almost every day over the last two weeks. There Jowett
had shared his experiences in the Levant over the last four years and
his hopes for the future. As Pliny Fisk wrote to the Brethren back at
Andover, they conversed "about his plans and our plans" and "cemented
our hearts together." Thus was forged another link in the chain of alli-
ances between British and American evangelical missionaries, partner-
ships that had begun a few years earlier in India and would soon spread
around the globe. The British, of course, expected to be the senior partners of this enterprise, and William Jowett was no exception. "Large and
well laid" was how Fisk described the plans of his new British colleague
in the private journal that he had begun to keep. And Jowett now included the newly arrived Americans in his project to bring all of the

peoples living along the Mediterranean into the evangelical fold, starting with his beachhead in Malta.

Glimpsed from a distance, Valletta seemed almost a celestial kingdom: the domes of white stone churches glittered in the brilliant sunshine, the wheels of two large windmills spun in the sea breeze, lush gardens bloomed on terrace roofs. The Jowetts knew better. Four years' residence there had taught them that for all its seeming beauty, this city fortress—like all of Malta—was a sinister spot, where, as William remarked, "no device seems omitted, which may entwine the cords of superstition fast round the imagination of man." It was a paradise for Catholics and a purgatory (had they credited so unbiblical a notion) for evangelicals like the Jowetts. Perhaps it had been for the best, then, that the Americans had not—and would not—set foot in the city. Quarantine restrictions confined Fisk and Parsons to their vessel, allowing only occasional trips to the lazaretto to meet with visitors. They consoled themselves by gobbling lettuce and fresh peas. Imagine having such treats in January, they gloated to friends and family in wintry New England. They liked the city's church bells, too. On Christmas Eve, a delighted Fisk heard them "ringing merrily most of the day—sometimes they chime quite musically."[1]

There you have it, as William Jowett might have put the matter. How easy it was to beguile the senses—and how long Roman Catholics had played upon that frailty. That was the litany running through all his journals and letters home. Start with the street corners in Valletta, which could not help but catch his eye, because each served as a niche for images—sumptuously painted, lamps glowing at their feet—of saints, angels, often the Virgin herself. Passersby stopped and crossed themselves before those idols, even mumbled a Paternoster or an Ave Maria, for some images bore inscriptions in the bishop's name, promising forty days of indulgence in the afterlife to any who performed this devotion. Call on any tradesman, and there was a saint or a sculpture of purgatory perched in the corner of his front door; even the wineshops and coffeehouses had little recesses in the walls for images bedecked with artificial flowers. Everywhere seen, popery could also be smelled: the faint scent of incense tinctured the air.

Worst of all, it could be heard—perpetually. Every church had two bells, some three, and for Jowett, unlike Americans, their chimes held no charm. Nor did the small bells tinkled by the white-robed altar boys who accompanied priests as they passed through the streets, bringing the consecrated host to the sick and dying. "Whole streets" fell to their knees, heads bowed, Jowett snorted. ("I always keep out of the way.") But festival days devoted to the Virgin (the "God-Mother") held the greatest torment, "the cannon firing and the bells going mad." Candles in their hands, worshippers paraded an immense gilt throne bearing her image through the streets; men pulled off their hats and caps as the procession passed. Only during the week before Easter did the bells fall silent—a dubious reprieve, because they were replaced by rattles, clattering like so many corn mills needing to be fed. "Grinding Judas's bones," the poor, deluded fools called it, whirling their toys.

Legion, the superstitions of these people, but what else could be expected from the centuries of Roman Catholic sway? Jowett glimpsed its most vivid emblem from the terrace of his airy, elegant villa: the looming twin towers of St. John of Jerusalem, a great, gaudy Baroque pile perched near Valletta's summit. Before the high altar and a huge statue of Saint John baptizing Jesus, the congregation bowed their heads and knelt. Now *there* was a testimony to the power of faith, given how freely the faithful spat on the floor—even the priests and sometimes the women. ("I have never mixed in the crowds at Church, without some apprehension for my clothes.") How could the people revere such a clergy—among them that buffoon of a Capuchin monk? (Disgusting, his mimicry of a false penitent in his sermon—ranting, laughing, and crying—as if he were standing on a stage instead of a pulpit.) Jowett's sole satisfaction came from the knowledge that St. John's exterior walls—built, like all of Valletta, from soft, crumbly limestone—were peeling in thin layers. The great church was flaking away like a giant's sand castle whenever a sirocco beat up, the wind that made people so melancholy that sadness seeped into their very dreams. But the sirocco did not blow often or hard enough to suit Jowett. Malta's lying sky nearly always shone clear and serene, as if this island fortress of crusader Catholicism were not every inch as much the dominion of Satan as the lands ruled by the sultan of the Ottoman Empire. Since 1800, it had also been a dominion of Britain.[2]

If Malta bore only traces of Islamic influence, it was not for lack of effort from the Muslim Arabs. Between 870 and 1090, they had held this archipelago of seven islands off the coast of Sicily; thereafter, European Christians had ruled, most constantly the soldier-monks of the

Knights Hospitaller who became its masters in 1530. For decades, the Knights used their prize as a staging ground for harassing Muslim ships and pilgrims and for fending off the Turks' retaliatory raids. By the opening of the nineteenth century, there was not a single mosque anywhere in the archipelago, though the country folk still spoke a dialect of Arabic. Yet in European eyes, Malta marked the midway point between East and West and remained a place of strategic significance. Capturing the islands from the French in 1800 came second in the trifecta of British triumphs during the Napoleonic Wars—after Admiral Horatio Nelson's naval victories in the Battle of the Nile (1798) and before the Battle of Trafalgar (1805). That made the British masters of the Mediterranean, and some had big ideas about how to translate their hard-won military superiority into profit for the empire by growing its commerce.[3]

William Jowett had big ideas, too, and a temperament well suited to a spot so long overrun by crusaders. Barely off the boat from England, he began to campaign against Valletta's theater, which played to packed audiences even on Sunday nights. As the town's few devout Protestants left their worship service, he groused, "the first object which presents itself to our eyes is a large painting, with figures of a ludicrous and profane description (such as Harlequin and the Devil) coarsely hung up on the walls opposite to the Palace, announcing the play for the evening." He would have complained to Malta's governor, but Sir Thomas Maitland stood entirely too ready to remind the young clergyman of "the necessity of keeping the people quiet here" and of his duty "to protect the Religion of the natives," who resented the presence of Protestant missionaries. Then, too, Sir Thomas was fond of the theater. So the show would go on, and this meddling missionary would keep his distance from the Catholic Maltese.[4]

No great loss by Jowett's lights. He regarded Roman Catholics as almost beyond redemption anyway, what with their rank superstitions and, worse, their devotion to "the Infallibility and Universal Headship of the Bishop of Rome." He had much higher hopes of winning over Jews and even Muslims, because like Protestants both were people of the book. Not the right book, of course, but it was a start. The grand plan of evangelicals like Jowett—a sort of domino theory of conversion— was to replay the Reformation in Levant's Eastern Christian churches.

Their missions would first target the Greek Orthodox and smaller groups such as the Copts of Egypt, the Maronites of Syria, and the Abyssinians of Ethiopia. Once reclaimed, those converts would banish their worst borrowings from Roman Catholicism—sweeping statues and pictures from their homes and churches, halting the sale of relics and indulgences—and start reading the Bible. Seeing Christianity in all its primitive purity for the first time, Muslims and Jews throughout the Ottoman Empire would abandon their faiths and follow Eastern Christians into the fold of evangelical Protestantism. Roman Catholicism would simply wither away.[5]

Immodest ambitions, but William Jowett came by them honestly. His father and uncles—affluent tradesmen and merchants, lawyers and professors—had long moved in the orbit of the Clapham Sect, an influential network of British evangelical reformers and moralists who had taken the leading role in founding the Church Missionary Society twenty years earlier. At the end of 1815, that organization named Jowett its "literary representative" to the Mediterranean, a missionary charged with gathering information about its religious groups, sussing out the best spots to plant new stations, promoting the circulation and translation of the Bible, and waiting for the dominoes to topple. Four years later, the American Board gave the same instructions to Fisk and Parsons on the eve of their departure—the imitation was deliberate—and urged them to seek out Jowett's assistance.[6]

The two Americans were a little in awe of so polished an English gentleman and altogether smitten with his wife, who was, in their estimate, the ideal missionary spouse. Martha and her William saw eye to eye on the dirty, ignorant, lazy Maltese, with their unscriptural devotion to the "God-Mother" and their grotesque religious festivals, but then, she had the opportunity to know her husband's mind on every matter. Late into the night, after long days of tending the flock of small Jowetts, overseeing her servants, and keeping school for thirty Maltese girls, she made fair copies of his journals and letters in her dainty cursive script. For his part, Jowett regretted that the Americans were not the fellow Oxbridge men he longed to lure to the Mediterranean as missionary colleagues. Still, he hoped to bring these Yankees up to scratch, which explains the book nestled in Martha Jowett's basket of oranges. Perhaps it was even she, clever girl, who hatched the idea to present the Americans with this newly published memoir of Henry Martyn.[7]

Its author was one of their own Clapham circle, an Anglican country parson named John Sargent. Less than a biographer but more than a compiler, he stitched together extracts from the writings of Martyn, an old college friend, with his own commentary. The resulting memoir, first published in 1819, would rocket Martyn into the pantheon of missionary apostles and martyrs venerated (had they engaged in so popish a practice) by nineteenth-century evangelicals. Even before his death at the end of 1812, Martyn had won notice in evangelical circles for his translation of the New Testament into Persian and its purportedly warm reception by the shah. That advance publicity ensured an awaiting audience for Sargent's *Memoir of the Rev. Henry Martyn*, and they were not disappointed. Among its most eager readers was William Jowett, whose largest and best-laid plan was to convert the Muslims of the Ottoman Empire.[8]

Besides sounding a clarion call for Christianizing the Islamic world, Sargent's pages offered much more. As powerfully as *Arabian Nights* stirred the fantasies of less pious readers in the West, his memoir of Martyn conjured a new Orient for evangelical Protestants. Muslims were its most compelling characters, cast in an image that diverged from earlier evangelical representations. The book put forward a new invention of Islam, one that influenced the ways in which many Christians envisioned the Muslim world for many decades thereafter. Martyn's missionary career as storied by Sargent became the basis upon which evangelicals founded their designs for bringing down history's curtain on Islam. And for their missionaries to Muslim cultures, Sargent's Martyn served as a model—as *the* model—for making sense of Muslims and for setting expectations of themselves. In every situation, in times of confusion and frustration, fear and despair, Pliny Fisk, Levi Parsons, William Jowett, and others who followed them always asked, What would Henry Martyn do?

For much of his life, Henry Martyn could not catch a break. His family tree did not spring from the rich soil, well mulched with money, that forced the leafing and flowering of the Jowetts' spreading branches. All that sustained Martyn's claims on gentility were his university degrees and his ordination in the Church of England, and all that saved him from genteel poverty was his Cambridge mentor, the Reverend Charles Simeon, landing him a chaplaincy in the East India Company. By 1806, Martyn was coming to a slow boil in sultry Dinapur, then a military station on the frontiers of British Bengal. His longtime crush back in England kept spurning his marriage proposals, which fated him to become the model for the fictional St. John Rivers, the aspiring missionary turned down by Jane Eyre. Male camaraderie did not fill the void. Most army officers took "no more notice of me than a dog," he wailed, and their contempt cratered after Martyn, swollen with righteousness and rigid with Calvinism, scolded a general for swearing. Most rank-and-file soldiers avoided their chaplain too, some because they could not understand his sermons, others, the Catholics, because they understood them entirely too well. For most Hindus and Muslims, he was a target of ridicule or anger.[9]

At last, Martyn took refuge in studying Sanskrit and translating the New Testament into Urdu, Persian, and Arabic. The Hindu pandits and Muslim munshis who assisted him in those labors provided more tribulations, impervious as they were to his efforts to convert them. More often than not, their challenges seem to have left him stumped. One of his munshis showed "remarkable contempt for the doctrine of the Trinity because 'It shews God to be weak (he says) if he is obliged to have a fellow,'" while his pandit pointed out that, unlike Jesus, "neither Brahma, Vishnu, nor Seib were so low as to be born of a woman."

The standout in this studious household was the erstwhile Muslim convert Jawad Sabat, only a year older than Martyn and more celebrated in evangelical circles. Years later, as payback for his apostasy, one of their British neighbors in Bengal sizzled up a Sabat who towered over the weedy Martyn like some maleficent jinni out of *Arabian Nights*. With his arched eyebrows, "fierce black mustachios," and "a voice like rolling thunder," this bronzed giant sported shiny earrings, embroidered shoes turned up at the toes, and a "jeweled dirk" dangling from the belt of his silk jacket. But whether his Christian conversion was fervent or feigned, it was Sabat who propelled Martyn from India to Persia. Besides collaborating with Martyn on Arabic and Persian translations of the New Testament, Sabat encouraged him to become a missionary to Muslims and even defied him to challenge Bengal's Islamic scholars to public disputations.[10]

Martyn shunned such open debates, explaining that he was reluctant to excite "the attention of the whole country and the government." What spooked him was the backlash against missions that followed the 1806 mutiny of Indian troops at Vellore, which many East India Company officials took for a protest against efforts to Christianize India. Sabat had no such scruples, and by the end of 1808 he was engaging in "daily disputes" with learned Muslims. According to another East India Company chaplain, Sabat arrived at one meeting to find "above one hundred Mollahs [mullahs] collected to banter with him." While Sabat "withstood them to the face," he advised the chaplain "not to argue with the Mahomedan doctors, lest they should by their logic shake my faith in Christianity."

Irked at being upstaged by this Arab Christian, Martyn started thinking about where in the Islamic world it might be safe to imitate him, and Persia came readily to mind. But Sabat's role in inspiring Martyn's new mission received no mention in Sargent's memoir. That was because just as Sargent's work neared completion, the news of Sabat's renouncing Christianity and returning to Islam reached the West. A most inconvenient turn of events, and Sargent dealt with it by giving Sabat as little ink as possible in the memoir, dismissing him as a tempestuous diva—an "unsubdued Arab spirit."[11]

So after nearly five years in Bengal, Martyn—with barely a nod at explanation by Sargent—set out for Persia, and just as unaccountably the memoir jumped literary genres. Following Martyn from England to India, Sargent served up the standard fare of evangelical devotional literature. He recounted his subject's spiritual anxieties, social humiliations, romantic disappointments, battles with temptation, strivings for resignation, bouts of spiritual dullness, and general mortification. He badgered his readers to imitate this exemplary Christian by subduing their passions and submitting to God's will. But once in Persia, Sargent's Martyn suddenly morphed from goat into stallion, and his edifying memoir turned into an adventure story.[12]

He began to grow out his beard as soon as Calcutta sank from sight at the beginning of 1811. He disembarked at Bushehr, a walled port town hugging the Persian Gulf whose ten thousand inhabitants lived in homes built of sandy stones encrusted with shells and in huts made from date trees. But he did not dress for the beach, attiring himself instead in a pair of "huge red boots" and "large blue trousers," a tunic and waistcoat of chintz, a heavy overcoat, and an "enormous cone" of a hat made of black sheepskin. To pass among the men of Persia, at least those farther inland, he must match their imposing appearance: here would be giants, at least in Henry Martyn's estimate. Besides, the giants' clothes concealed his wasted frame, and the whiskers disguised his sunken cheeks— the ravages of tuberculosis. "You will give me credit for being already an accomplished Oriental," he boasted to a friend in England. And to the woman who rejected his proposals, he wrote, "Imagine a pale person seated on a Persian carpet, in a room without table or chair, with a pair of formidable mustachios, and habited as a Persian, and you see me."[13]

After that makeover, Martyn traveled by caravan from Bushehr to Shiraz and took up residence in the household of an elite Muslim family. They introduced him to a circle of learned men with whom he conversed about religion while revising Sabat's translation of the New Testament with a Persian calligrapher and poet. Before leaving India, Martyn had promised General John Malcolm, who had led three British diplomatic missions to Persia, that he had "no thought of preaching" there or "of entering into any theological controversies." But he didn't mean it: Martyn promptly plunged into a round of private and public religious exchanges with Muslim clerics and professors of law, discussions probing the fine points of both Christian and Islamic theology.

Martyn might have regarded the city itself as signaling the imminent collapse of Islam. Shiraz's population of perhaps nineteen thousand had been declining for several decades, and despite its spacious, well-stocked bazaar and an array of mosques, colleges, and public baths, many public buildings were falling to ruin, bridges and gates stood in disrepair, and houses sat deserted. Such was the dismal legacy of an Afghan invasion nearly a century earlier that had triggered the fall of the Safavid dynasty and ushered in almost a century of chaos among rival tribes and the rule of plundering warlords. Now, with the Russians chiseling away at Persia's borders to the north and British India sprawling to the southeast, apprehension readily seized the city's inhabitants. As news of Martyn's doings spread, so did a swirl of rumors that he "was come to Shiraz to be a Mussulman, and should then bring five thousand men to Shiraz, under pretence of making them Mussulmen, but in reality to take the city."[14]

Those anxieties prompted other leading men in town to take a closer look at their uninvited guest. A respected mujtahid—a jurist expert in Islamic law—invited Martyn to a dinner party, one that in evangelical circles would become nearly as well known as the Last Supper. At eight sharp on the day appointed, servants ushered the missionary into "a fine court, where was a pond, and by the side of it a platform, eight feet high, covered with carpets," on which were ensconced "in opulence and ease," his mujtahid host and "a considerable number of his learned friends." The Muslims looking down from the platform had arranged this impressive show to awe their English guest, and they succeeded. Recalling the moment, Martyn disclosed his anxiety by joking that "the swarthy obesity of the little personage himself [his host] led me to suppose that he had paid more attention to cooking than to science." But when the man began to speak eloquently and in a manner so "confident and imposing," Martyn "saw reason enough for his being so much admired." There ensued what he regarded as his "first public controversy with the Mohammedans." In the wake of that exchange, the mujtahid Mirza Ibrahim Fasa'i—most likely Martyn's host—published a defense of Islam, to which Martyn fired back a scathing refutation, contending that Muhammad was no prophet or miracle worker but a mere upstart whose "Koran is full of gross absurdities and palpable contradictions."

Those Sabat-like forays into public debate made Martyn, at least in his own mind, a marked man. Boys pelted him with stones whenever he walked through the streets, shouting, "Ho, Russ [Russian]!" or "Feringee [Frank, or Westerner]!" Meanwhile, the city's Muslim leaders were reloading: the local prince invited Martyn to his palace to engage in another debate before a great body of learned mullahs. Sargent's staging etched what followed in the mind's eye of evangelicals throughout the English-speaking world. Entering the court of the palace, Martyn faced down a "room lined with Moolahs, on both sides and at the top," headed by Fasa'i. He was about to slip into a seat of inferior rank down at the door until "beckoned to an empty place near the top," opposite Fasa'i, "who, after the usual compliments, without further ceremony, asked me, 'what we meant by calling Christ—God?'" That was a shot straight across Martyn's bow: "War being thus unequivocally declared, I had nothing to do but to stand upon the defensive. Mirza Ibraheem [Fasa'i] argued temperately enough, but of the rest, some were very violent and clamorous."

Owing to Martyn's wit and courage, Sargent concluded with a flourish, "the imposture of the Prophet of Mecca was daringly exposed, and the truths of Christianity openly vindicated, in the very heart and centre of a Mahometan Empire." That was the man ever after embalmed in evangelical hagiography; his was the lone, courageous voice proclaiming the divinity of Jesus in the deepest recesses of the Islamic world. That was the Henry Martyn whom the first Palestine missionaries, as well as many future generations of evangelicals, strove to emulate. Here was a Christian with whom Muslims had to reckon.[15]

But here, too, were formidable Muslims. Some polite and decorous, all learned and accomplished, they were worthy adversaries by Martyn's measure, possessed of "uncommon subtlety" and impressive intellectual powers. He spent years striving to match them. Back in Bengal under Sabat's tutelage, he had worked to master Arabic and Persian. He also made a close study of the Qur'an and "considered with myself why I rejected it as an imposition, and the reasons appeared clear and convincing." He then set about reading "everything I can pick up about the Mahomedans." "A European who has not lived among them [Muslims]," he wrote to his mentor Charles Simeon after a year in Shiraz, "cannot imagine how differently they see, imagine, reason, object, from what we do."

But however different their ways might be from those of the West, reason they did. So it came as a shock to Martyn that Shiraz's learned Muslims, when presented with what he took to be his irrefutable arguments, stoutly defended their convictions. Here was a revelation: Islam commanded the wholehearted (and full-throated) loyalty of smart, cultivated, articulate people. Muhammad's teachings won their assent not, as Western Christians had long insisted, because of the blind allegiance bred by custom or beckoned by lust but because the Prophet's creed satisfied the demands of a well-honed critical intelligence. Momentarily, Martyn despaired that "my labour is lost . . . I have now lost all hope of ever convincing Mahomedans by argument. The most rational, learned, unprejudiced, charitable men confessedly in the whole town cannot escape the delusion." Then he recovered his resolve and returned to trading salvos with them.

Nor was it only the Muslims of Persia who won Martyn's respect. In Bengal, he had engaged in frequent exchanges with the Muslim munshis who assisted him in the work of translation, as well as in private discussions with Islamic teachers. On one occasion, he spent two hours with a Muslim nawab who offered "the proofs of the religion of Mahomet" and asked Martyn how to reconcile God's sovereignty with human free will. Martyn left "delighted with his sense, candor, and politeness"; indeed the man's "whole manner, look, authority, and copiousness constantly reminded me of the Dean of Carlisle," a clergyman admired by the Clapham Sect. Martyn came away from his conversations with Bengal's Muslims convinced that "these men are not fools, and that all ingenuity and clearness of reasoning are not confined to England and Europe." It was a regard he did not extend to Hindus in India, to Jews in Persia—or to Catholics and Methodists anywhere.[16]

How he wished that Muslims would return the compliment. Martyn admitted that "the contempt of the learned Mohammedans" in Shiraz for his Christian views was "even more difficult to bear than the brickbats which the boys sometimes throw at me." It stung, too, when, invited to an entertainment at the vizier's, he found himself "appointed to a seat . . . which I afterwards perceived was not the place of honor." No doubt Martyn's tenuous hold on gentility and his bitter memories of being snubbed by British officers made him all the more sensitive to such slights. But the Persians' disregard cut him to the quick because, in his mind, their judgment mattered. Muhammad's faith had won and held the loyalty of many learned men, and this Westerner had learned that their respect was worth having.

Henry Martyn wowed the evangelical world with his bold challenge to Islam. In fact, he was on safe ground in early Qajar Persia, because the British hoped to make that country the western outpost of their Indian empire. To that end, the British government was providing military aid to Persia in its war with Russia, training its soldiers, supplying its weapons, and paying a handsome subsidy to Fath Ali Shah. Of these advantages, Martyn was fully aware, though Sargent withheld them from his memoir. "I am sometimes asked whether I am not afraid to speak so boldly as I do against the Mahommedan religion," Martyn wrote to Charles Simeon. "I tell them . . . You know the power of the English too well to suppose that they would let any violence be offered to me with impunity." Indeed, as the aim of the stone-throwing boys improved, his Persian host (also the British agent in Shiraz) complained to the governor, who ordered a bastinado for anyone insulting Martyn. So when Martyn completed his Persian translation of the New Testament, it must have taken only a nudge from the British ambassador to induce the devoutly Muslim Fath Ali Shah to issue that letter of royal gratitude so widely reprinted in the evangelical press.

Besides the British aegis, Martyn benefited from—and enhanced—the reputation for intellectual curiosity and religious toleration that Persians had long and justly enjoyed in the West. Since the seventeenth century, travelers had praised the liberty of conscience and the freedom of speech accorded them in the shah's domain, as well as the refinement and sophistication of Persian elites and their fondness for religious and philosophical debate. The Afghan invasion and its grisly aftermath kept Westerners out of the country for most of the eighteenth century, but by the opening of the nineteenth there was Martyn, refurbishing that venerable image of Persia—and one with considerable basis in fact. Local mullahs in Isfahan had drawn one early nineteenth-century Roman Catholic missionary into raucous exchanges, and a Shiraz mujtahid told a later evangelical missionary that he enjoyed contesting with Western Christians because "it sharpens the understanding." Martyn claimed that Muslims came "in such numbers to visit me, that I am obliged, for the sake of my translation-work, to decline seeing them," and he engaged in frequent debates with Sufis and Jews in Shiraz as well. Arguably, Qajar Persians were more tolerant of Christians than many Christians in Britain or the United States were of each other. Protestant Gordon rioters in Britain during 1780 and mobs in Boston and Philadelphia during the 1830s and 1840s attacked Roman Catholics with abandon, snuffing out lives and destroying property.[17]

Put another way, Martyn's standing up to mullahs and mujtahids was not what made him daring. Far more venturesome was his using Persians (as well as East Indians) to make the case to an evangelical readership that Muslims prized learning and reasoned debate and that Muhammad's teachings drew accomplished people who cherished those values. By portraying Muslim cultures in this positive light, he became the first evangelical to join a select company of other Westerners who defied the prevailing opinion that Islam encouraged its adherents to revel in their ignorance, to read nothing but the Qur'an, and to cling to their faith out of habit, fear, or lust rather than rational conviction. The seeds of that prejudice had taken root centuries earlier but flowered vigorously in the full sun of the Enlightenment and the heat of Protestant revivalism; by the beginning of the nineteenth century, it had become a commonplace among many secular and religious thinkers alike. Both groups liked to repeat the statement attributed to a seventh-century Muslim general who had ordered the destruction of the library of forty thousand manuscripts collected by the Ptolemies: "Burn these books. If they contain only what is in the Koran, they are useless, and dangerous, if they contain anything else." In keeping with that spirit, the British consul at Tunis duly warned William Jowett in 1817 that the Muslim faithful were "strictly prohibited from studying, or even reading, any other works than the Koran, and the various comments written in explanation of it."

From the conviction that Muslims were people of only one book followed the widespread belief in the West that Islam itself discouraged education and opposed progress. The New Divinity's intellectual hero, Jonathan Edwards, denounced Muslims as "an ignorant and barbarous sort of people," because Islam itself operated "to debase, debauch, and corrupt the minds of such as received it." Half a century later, his fellow evangelical, the Scots minister Robert Adam, agreed that in Islamic cultures "knowledge is not only neglected but despised; not only the materials of it are banished, but the very desire of recovering and applying them is totally extinguished." Many enlightened secular thinkers were equally damning, arguing that Islam, like all revealed religions, could only be hostile to science and every other form of knowledge.[18]

But the decades around 1800 also saw the emergence of a differing view. In the English-speaking world, its most forceful advocate was one of the most eminent citizens of the republic of letters, Sir William Jones. A polymath like his friend Benjamin Franklin, he spent the last ten years of his life in British India (1783–94), codifying a digest of Hindu and Muslim law and mastering Sanskrit, which he discovered to be the common ancestor of the classical languages of India, the Middle East, and Europe. Before venturing to India, the younger Jones had learned both Arabic and Persian, and early in the 1770s he wrote a history of Turkey, a study that places him in the ranks of those Enlightenment Orientalists bent on rehabilitating the image of Islam. All that survives is its introduction, first published three decades later in 1804, in which Jones tackled head-on the "ridiculous notion" which "prevails among us, that *ignorance is a principle of the Mohammedan religion,* and that the *Koran* instructs *Turks* not to be instructed." In his view, "there is not a shadow of truth in this: *Mohammed* not only permitted, but advised, his people to apply themselves to learning." Jones described the Qur'an as a "strange book, where there are many fine ideas mixed with the heap of rubbish," yet he cited with approval the Prophet's sayings that "*the ink of the learned and the blood of martyrs are of equal value in heaven,* and that *learning is permitted to all believers, both male and female.*" Indeed, as Jones saw it, "there would be no end of quoting all the striking expressions of this singular man, and the ablest professors of his religion, in praise of knowledge and letters."

The man who made Sir William Jones's novel views on Islam known to a wide public was his friend John Shore, governor-general of Bengal, later Lord Teignmouth, and an ardent evangelical. Among the odder couples of British India, they became fast friends despite Jones, a deist, writing "hymns" addressed to Hindu gods and translating a racy Indian play and an erotic poem. What transcended their differences was devotion to the British Empire: despite his deep appreciation of Eastern cultures, Jones, like Shore, was an unabashed imperialist. Accordingly, when Shore retired to Clapham, then a rural village outside London, he not only worked tirelessly as the first president of the British and Foreign Bible Society but also shepherded to press all of Jones's unpublished essays, including his defense of Islam. Widely read on both sides of the Atlantic, the collection turned up in the holdings of many libraries in the early American republic as well as in the "missionary library" that Fisk and Parsons transported from Boston to Smyrna.[19]

Different aims prompted William Jones and Henry Martyn to challenge the image of an Islam indifferent to learning and opposed to rational exchange. Jones was intent on hauling Western prejudices before the bar of reason and banishing them with the empirical observations. A cultural relativist, he defended even as he derided the Turks' "ridiculously bombastic rhetoric" that fell so hard on his ears, because "such is the genius of the nation; and we can no more wonder that their rules of composition are different from ours, than that they build their palaces of wood, and sit on sofas instead of chairs." But more striking to

Jones than the differences in world languages and cultures were their underlying similarities. Scratch a word in Greek or Latin, and there was Sanskrit at the root. Translate into Sanskrit the Thirty-Nine Articles, which spelled out the essential doctrines of English Protestantism, and "they might pass well enough for the composition of a Brahman." And like many other Enlightenment intellectuals of his age, Jones found in Eastern religions a handy foil for criticizing what he disliked in Christianity.

Martyn came to his positive assessment of Islam's intellectualism from the opposite direction—out of his hopes to secure the triumph of Christianity. Nothing could have been further from Jones's admiration of non-Christian creeds than Martyn's snarl that Islam was "a filthy religion." Yet Martyn staked his life's work on the proposition that Muslims were not deluded fanatics but thoughtful people who would read his translations of the New Testament and discern the superior reasonableness of Christianity. In fact, he conjured his new model Muslims—people willing to debate points of theology, to entertain arguments against Islam, and to read books other than the Qur'an—in order to sustain the confidence that missionaries like himself stood a good chance of success. That image of Muslims also reflected what Martyn and other evangelicals took to be their own likeness as thinking Christians with as much claim to being bathed in the glow of the Enlightenment as deists or Unitarians.[20]

To be sure, Martyn had no illusions that his rarefied scholarly circle in Shiraz and earlier in Bengal represented the generality of Muslims in Persia or India. In one of his rare close encounters with an ordinary Persian—a merchant described by Martyn as "a plain Mohammedan, that is, a compound of bigotry and ignorance"—he let the man "talk away," thinking "it worthwhile to see the state of the middling rank of Mohammedans." The merchant told a bemused Martyn "that the Mohammedans had formerly taken all Europe, and that we still paid tribute for being permitted to live"—and then tried to convert him to Islam. But bigoted and ignorant as most Muslims might be, nothing in their creed would corrupt their reason or keep them from reading the books that would open their minds and change their hearts.

How unexpected that this more positive valuation of Muhammad's faith struck root within evangelical ranks. How curious that their first apostle to Muslims shared with Sir William Jones a deep regard for the intellectual powers of Islam's learned circles. And how ironic that what prompted Henry Martyn's surprising invention of Islam and promoted it among devout Christians on both sides of the Atlantic was the very intensity of evangelical missionary zeal.[21]

William Jowett was only the first in a long line of evangelical Protestant missionaries who would find their inspiration in Sargent's memoir of Martyn. Coming of age in the Clapham circle, Jowett would have been party to countless conversations about his hero's trials and triumphs in Persia until Martyn's death in 1812. And a few years later, as he established his mission at Malta, word would have reached him about the subsequent labors of John Sargent (with Charles Simeon looking over his shoulder) to complete Martyn's memoir. Everything that he heard about and then read in the memoir itself strengthened Jowett's confidence that evangelicals would ultimately prevail against Islam. They would do so by making the case for Christianity's superior merits to eminently reasonable people. He and his wife strove to nurture the same expectation in the newly arrived American missionaries by slipping Sargent's memoir into that basket of oranges. More grandly, Jowett hoped to impress the certainty of their inevitable victory upon evangelicals throughout the West by writing a book of his own.

Jowett had a literary bent. As he traveled throughout the Mediterranean between 1816 and 1819, he kept official journals filled with finely observed details and evocative vignettes. In the Armenian quarter of Smyrna, he noted that the little girls begging on the streets, "poor and ragged as they are . . . do not neglect the petty finery of dipping the tips of their finger nails red." It must be an ancient custom, he speculated, possibly even the inspiration of Homer's phrase "rosy fingered morn." The charm of such reflections was lost on the sepulchral Josiah Pratt, the chief administrator of Jowett's sponsoring missionary society, who chided his brother-in-law for "vivacity degenerating into levity" and balefully pleaded for briefer and duller reports. But Jowett kept storing up fodder for the book stabling in his brain. Only a few months after meeting with the American missionaries at Valletta's lazaretto, he would return to England to see his manuscript through the press. It was an exhaustive survey of every religious group in the Mediterranean with a strategy for turning them all—including Muslims—into evangelical Protestants.[22]

Jowett also filled his journals and correspondence with ploys to proselytize among Muslims and hopeful signs for their success. He toyed with a project to "collect and put together the errors of the Turks, with answers to them from the Gospel," and to pair those passages in the Qur'an that "speak respectfully of Jesus, of the Virgin Mary" with some from the New Testament. And he seized on every morsel of gossip from travelers that suggested Muslims were becoming more receptive to Western influences. Why, a British naval officer of his acquaintance who had visited North Africa "was always permitted to enter the Mosques only taking off his shoes at the door," and some of the "Moors drank [alcohol] with him." More puzzling is Jowett's conviction that being introduced to the enlightened ideas of the French had aroused "a spirit of inquiry" among Muslims throughout the Ottoman Empire. It seems not to have occurred to him that reading Voltaire could prove as corrosive to Christianity as to Islam. Reinforcement for his belief that spiritual seekers now abounded in the Muslim world came from a long-time British resident in the Levant, who told Jowett that the Wahhabis of Arabia were "pure Deists" and that their sentiments had spread to Persia as well. Surely, Jowett concluded, this new division opening within the ranks of Islam presented evangelicals with a prime opportunity.[23]

Seeing all these straws in the wind blowing his way, Jowett tried to marshal the British church and state for an all-out offensive against Islam. He wanted the British government to step up by stationing "intelligent English agents" at Constantinople, men charged with persuading Ottoman officials to abolish the death penalty for renouncing Islam. Lest that goal seem far-fetched, Jowett lectured the British naval commander in the Mediterranean that "Britain is girding herself with a spirit that fears not the greatest" and that its imperial agenda should include the Church of England applying itself to "the direct work of the conversion of the Mahometan world." Jowett was doing some girding of his own, for he added that "the ministers of our church will do perfectly right at the peril of their own safety to encourage the victims of Imposture [Muslims] to brave death, rather than remain as they are." But if blood were shed, most likely it would not be British. "No blame is attached to a Preacher, if a Turk voluntarily joins a Christian assembly," he assured Josiah Pratt, for "the danger impends only over the convert; his blood, should it be spilt, would be on his own head—a crown of glory."[24]

Jowett's expectations battened with every letter that he received from Dr. Robert Richardson. A physician of evangelical sympathies, he was touring the same places for pleasure that Jowett visited on missionary business, and he shared his friend's confidence that Muslims were relenting in their hostility to Christianity. Richardson deplored the ignorance he found throughout the Levant, and it surprised him that even at Cairo there were no books, "no journals, no newspapers, no printing-press, no universities, no houses of parliament, no lectures on law, physic or theology, no courses of mathematics, chemistry, or botany, no learned men, or learned professions." Yet he added, echoing the sentiments of Henry Martyn and Sir William Jones, that "a Mussulman is not necessarily ignorant as a consequence of his religion" and that there was "nothing in the religion of a Mussulman that ties him down from the exercise of his intellectual faculties." Unenlightened the sultan's domains might be, but that was not the doing of Islam, and once shown the superior reasonableness of Protestant Christianity, Muslims would recognize and embrace it.

In Richardson's view, evangelicals also had an aesthetic edge, and he predicted that relations between the two faiths would flourish once the shared simplicity of their worship settings came to light. "It is no bad medium of success to please the eye," he wrote to Jowett, so evangelicals should take encouragement from there being "nothing in the garniture of an English Church to offend a Mussulman." What a pity that the Christian churches in the Ottoman Empire belonged to Roman Catholics and Eastern Christians who "disgraced and profaned" them with paintings and statues. Richardson could well understand why Muslims, because "the unity of the deity is constantly in their mouths," regarded Eastern Christians as polytheists and idolaters, no better than a pack of pagans. Like other evangelicals, he blamed those practices for the continuing hold of Islam throughout the region. How different the future would be once evangelicals prevailed, for "we have no stumbling blocks of graven images and painted saints, and if we kept our dogs out of them and put off our slippers when we entered them, a Mussulman might walk through an English Church in those countries and know very little difference from his own Mosque."[25]

Richardson meant to spur Jowett on, but his observation that mosques and evangelical churches were nearly indistinguishable as worship settings also raised disturbing questions. Could it be that the Levant's Muslims rather than its Christians had a religious sensibility more closely akin to evangelical Protestantism? And how could missionaries persuade those Christians to change religions if something beyond reason secured their faith? Jowett was already looking for answers in the fall of 1816 when he spent several days on the island of Corfu, observing the devotional practices of the Greek Orthodox family of one Emmanuel Polymenos. His host immediately flustered Jowett by kissing his hand in greeting, as he would that of a Greek Orthodox priest, before whisking him to the upper floor of his home to show off a prized shrine. A hanging lamp kept constantly burning lit the large, rectangular wooden frame that Polymenos had filled with saints' pictures, crucifixes, wax candles, and other treasures that he had purchased at considerable cost during a pilgrimage to Palestine of nearly three years. Silly as this shrine seemed to Jowett, he admitted that "the desire of this man's heart has been abundantly satisfied" by seeing "all that the Monks show," including "the prints of our Saviour's foot, which he impressed when he ascended into Heaven."

It was undeniable, the appeal of this sensuous devotionalism. The "Papists treat Man as if he were all Sense; while some Protestants treat him as if he were all Spirit," Jowett wrote to Pratt, "but indeed you must visit these parts, would you *feel* the force of the former." Certainly Jowett felt it while studying a painting of scenes from the Apocrypha that covered one wall of his bedchamber in the Polymenos home: "red and yellow . . . plentifully spread upon the canvass; so that even a child . . . would see at once the beauty of the picture." It struck him again when Polymenos and his son Spiridion showed off their box of relics. While opening it, they "repeated a few words in a low voice" and then took out five small pieces of a saint's bone, "a vesture and a pillow used by S[aint] Spiridion," and "a silk slipper cut to the shape of the print of our saviour's foot on his ascension." After this display, Polymenos produced with equal pride a printed indulgence given to him by a Greek Orthodox bishop.

Jowett strove to get past what seemed to him the Polymenos family's want of "genuine spiritual piety." He tried to view the Christian world from their eyes, imagining that "to timid minds familiar in their devotions with a multitude of human ceremonies and respect, *we* [Protestants] perhaps present a mien too free and undisciplined." He assured Pratt that a "residence of some time in these parts seems to be necessary, before prejudices purely circumstantial can wear away" and "a general sympathy" be established. Jowett judged Greek Orthodox religious beliefs and practices to be every bit as idolatrous and superstitious as those of the Roman Catholics at Malta, even if his response to them ran to dismay rather than to the contempt that he showered on Catholicism. After all, the Greek Orthodox were crucial allies—the linchpins of the evangelical strategy to convert the Ottoman Empire, to say nothing of being enemies to Rome—so he backed away from confrontations. Yet he could not dispel the sense of something nearly heathen lurking in these so-called Christian practices, especially Emmanuel Polymenos's treasured indulgence, "which will serve his purpose not a whit better than an African Greagrea [charm]." He pressed the man about his pilgrimage—what had induced him to make this long journey, what spiritual benefit had he derived from it? Could there be "any secret in this—will God forgive your sins any more on this account?" But Polymenos "answered in a way that seemed to shew, that upon this subject we had not two ideas in common." Try as he might to make himself understood, Jowett concluded, "it was as if I had talked in a foreign language."[26]

That profound estrangement from the religious sensibilities of the Levant's Christians jostled against Jowett's conviction that the universal power of reason ensured gathering all the world's people into the evangelical fold. Confidence in the commonality of human nature and the plasticity of culture, the optimistic legacy of the Enlightenment reinforced by the logic of the early foreign missions movement, kept uneasy company with his nagging sense of the Levant as essentially alien. And what made for that difference was not only the distance between his kind of piety and that of a Greek Orthodox believer like Emmanuel Polymenos but also a racist contempt for some of the region's peoples. The same William Jowett who rhapsodized over the rosy fingertips of little Armenian girls also detected a "savagery" in Jews and Arabs from the shape of their mouths and the clenching of their teeth, attributing those features to "the guttural nature of their language." Such remarks announce the stirrings of the racial pseudoscience that would become far more prominent in Western views of the world in only a few years.[27]

Perhaps that explains why Jowett did not mingle much with the Levant's Jewish communities, save for stray encounters with a few rabbis. Nor, for all his skulling about Islam, did Jowett engage with Muslims often—or much to his satisfaction. At Alexandria, he encountered one "Sheik Ibrahim," an Islamic scholar and spellbinding orator, whom he peppered with questions about the justice of inflicting the death penalty on apostates from Islam. When the sheikh defended that practice, Jowett switched subjects, remarking that "Mahomet had spoken well of our Gospels." Again the sheikh proved no pushover, dilating at length about how divisions among the early Christians had corrupted their scriptures. Should Jowett have been surprised? Henry Martyn himself had served notice that Muslim ranks drew no shortage of quick-witted, well-read, silver-tongued believers.[28]

The side of Jowett that saw the Levant's people as fundamentally unlike himself comes into sharpest focus in his frequent references to secrecy and conspiracies. He pestered Emmanuel Polymenos for the "secret" that lurked in his making a long pilgrimage to Palestine. And despite spending little time in their company, he felt certain that the "Jews of Spain, Africa, Syria, and Asia Minor correspond very much in the Spanish language, under the disguise of the vulgar Hebrew Character," which revealed, at least to him, "the discovery of a new world under-ground." Somewhere the shade of Samuel Mills smiled—and the corners of Jedidiah Morse's mouth might even have twitched—as Robert Richardson saw and raised his friend's crackpot fantasies. The doctor professed to have come upon "a college" of dervishes at Cairo who "seem cemented in a sort of Freemasonry, and pervade in their correspondence the whole of the Turkish Empire." But the greatest enigma was the appeal of Islam itself. Westerners had been studying this rival faith for centuries, yet Richardson concluded, "with all our knowledge I think that the hidden man of Islamism is still secret to us."[29]

*The hidden man of Islamism.* If only evangelicals could learn the mystery of its strength, the Muslim faith would fall to ruin, and, as Richardson's telling phrase suggests, they identified that mystery as masculine. To find the "hidden man of Islamism" would be to fathom the deepest springs of men's devotion to their Muslim creed. The promise of a sensual paradise had to explain part of the attraction, Jowett and many others thought. Evangelicals also suspected what they saw as Islam's soft-pedaling human depravity, which, like liberal Christianity, flattered self-esteem and spiritual pride. But to discover the whole truth about Islam's attractions, especially to men—an enigma even more elusive than the Polymenos family's devotion to their glowing shrine—would require Christians of wit and courage. It would take men like the new evangelical hero who had, at John Sargent's summons, stepped from the side of Henry Martyn. It would take men who liked secrets.[30]

The book tucked into Martha Jowett's basket of oranges made an impression on the American missionaries that exceeded even the fondest hopes of her husband. Pliny Fisk was reading Sargent's memoir when their vessel docked at Smyrna harbor, and Levi Parsons might have done the same while still under sail. "How insipid does this work make the books seem that I have read on my passage," Fisk exclaimed. That list included both *The Iliad* and *Childe Harold's Pilgrimage*, but neither dimmed his certainty that "Martyn's reputation will shine with eternal lustre," while the renown of Homer and Byron "will fade and vanish."

It would be only the first of many readings of a book that, like the Bible, repaid regular resort for guidance and inspiration, comfort and affliction. "I love to read it," Fisk confided to his private journal, "and yet it always torments me by mortifying my pride and wounding my conscience." He and Parsons as well as the future members of the Palestine mission returned to Martyn's memoir so often that they even picked up his odd turns of phrase. A particular favorite appears to have been Martyn's description of growing out his whiskers en route to Persia: as he put it, "My beard and mustachios have been suffered to vegetate undisturbed." Sure enough, when American missionaries did the same, they traded jokes about their own vegetating "mustachios." What better way to dress for success when hunting "the hidden man of Islamism"?[31]

Their idolizing Henry Martyn should come as no surprise, for he was like no model these New Englanders had ever known. The missionary icon of their youth had been David Brainerd, embalmed in the widely read memoir composed by his mentor Jonathan Edwards as a meek and long-suffering Christian and a patient, tender pastor to the Indians of New England and New Jersey. By contrast, Sargent's Martyn was an adventurer who charged into the heart of Persia and challenged the mullahs and mujtahids. And he was so deliciously flawed: Martyn admitted to being peevish, proud, arrogant, and short-tempered, and at least once when his rage simmered over, he hurled a knife at a Cambridge classmate. Along with the anger, Martyn's ambition was on display for all to see. Imagine Fisk's feelings as he took in the memoir's account of its hero's dogged rise from a modest background. Nor could it have slipped past his American admirers that even as Martyn lacerated himself for every lapse, he also boasted of "the power I shall soon possess of making known the gospel in two such large countries as India and Persia." One of his contemporaries got Martyn exactly right. "I do not know another instance," he remarked, "of a man at once so self-asserting and so self-denying." Of course: Martyn's self-denial was itself a form of self-assertion, a paradox that spoke directly to the anxieties of young New Englanders at once consumed and shamed by their own ambition.[32]

What would prove as important as Martyn's incarnation as a new kind of missionary hero was his invention of an eminently usable view of Islam, one that held out the possibility of converting Muslims to evangelical Christianity through reasoned argument. That invention undercut the assumption that the West was an empire of enlightenment and the East, its opposite, a backwater of fanatics, ignoramuses, and enemies of learning. True, Martyn could talk out of both sides of his mouth—in one breath widening the gulf between East and West by trashing Islam as a "filthy religion," in the next narrowing the distance between Muslims and Christians with his insistence that both held an equal purchase on rationality. In that respect, his writings reflected the contradictory premises at the core of the foreign missions movement as a whole. On the one hand, the East had to be converted because it was so radically different from the West; on the other, it could be converted because the world's peoples were so similar.

Put another way, the paradoxical demands of evangelicalism depended on both "othering" non-Christians to demonstrate the urgent need for their conversion and "brothering" them to nurture optimism about that possibility. But with the possible exception of their fellow Christians the Roman Catholics, evangelicals put no group past the pale of reclamation. They had no choice but to "brother"—to search for common ground—if they planned to win over the Ottoman Empire through the force of persuasion and debate. And to believe that the fullness of their triumph would extend to Muslims obliged evangelicals to embrace an image of the Islamic world as much under reason's sway as was the West.[33]

## ﴾ 5 ﴿

## "OUR GREAT WEAPON"

> Read! In the name of your Lord who created: He created man from a clinging form. Read! Your Lord is the Most Bountiful One who taught by the pen, who taught man what he did not know.
> —Qur'an, The Clinging Form, 96:1–5

It would be a long drop into hell, but one look at Smyrna told Pliny Fisk that he was already there. "We see now before us a city containing more than 100,000 souls," he jotted at the end of Levi Parsons's first letter home, all "led captive by Satan at his will." No sooner had the two disembarked at this busy seaport on the Turkish coast than Fisk began to map it. Muslims predominated: about half of the population, he estimated, concentrated in the southern part of town. Nearly as many Greeks clustered at the eastern end of the city, along with a smaller neighborhood of Armenians; Jews lived in enclaves scattered throughout. Western expatriates numbered only about 5,000 souls, most of them European Catholics, and resided along the harbor.

Ottomans referred to the lot of Westerners as "Franks," who returned the misnomer by not using the city's Turkish name, Izmir. More egregious displays of Western arrogance could provoke deadly retaliation. The worst trouble in living memory, as Fisk got the story, started when an Ottoman janissary tried to stop an Italian sailor from muscling his way into a performance of "jugglers or rope-dancers," and the tar shot him dead. The Venetian consul's refusal to surrender the killer to Ottoman justice triggered a rampage of plunder, murder, and arson, reducing the Frank and Greek neighborhoods to smoldering rubble. That had taken place more than twenty years earlier, but, as Fisk explained more calmly than he felt, Westerners still lived near the harbor and thus were "very conveniently situated for escaping, in case of necessity, to the vessels." After so many smooth assurances from their fellow evangelicals about the imminent demise of Islam, the two Americans were more than a little daunted to discover how premature such predictions were and to find how vulnerable they felt in the midst of a Muslim majority. "What would you think," Parsons wrote to his family, "of a man approaching you, of gigantic stature, long beard, fierce eyes, a turban on his head, which if stretched out would make a blanket, long flowing robes, a large belt, in which were four or five pistols and a sword?" Here's what he thought: that it was "impossible to forget that this people [Muslims] have power to make war with the saints, and to overcome them." Like Henry Martyn, Parsons supersized his Muslims.

Everything about Smyrna drove home the message of Muslim preeminence to the newly arrived missionaries. Approaching the city by sea for the first time, they spied the broad harbor ringed like an amphitheater by cloud-robed mountains, their sloping hillsides planted with red-roofed dwellings and cypress, fig, and olive trees. Straightaway, Fisk started counting: towering above the houses, even the cypresses, were the domes and minarets of the city's largest mosques—twenty in all—which, as another Western traveler clearly heard, "speak the power of the false Prophet." Spoke loudly, too: some of Smyrna's Franks suspected that the black-and-white marble checkering the chief of these mosques had come from headstones and monuments in the English cemetery. Such rumors revealed the expatriates' lingering insecurity, despite the city's well-deserved reputation as the most Westernized spot anywhere in the Ottoman Empire.[1]

The real threats to all of Smyrna's dwellers were natural catastrophes. Earthquakes and the fires that inevitably followed killed thousands in any given year. Blazes spread rapidly, because neighborhoods were so crowded and streets so narrow that a single camel, bells jingling and burdens bulging, left little room for pedestrians to pass. The two English families who kept coaches were obliged, as Fisk reported, "to send a messenger before them that they may meet nothing" in the only street wide enough for a wheeled vehicle to squeeze through. So many packed so close made Smyrna a perfect petri dish in any season, but summers were the worst. As sherbet sellers hawked ices on every corner and mosquitoes feasted, plague devastated the sweltering city, in some years claiming tens of thousands of lives.

A few weeks after their arrival, Fisk was still measuring Smyrna against his only other experience of the exotic—Savannah. While some Ottoman houses were handsome stone structures, "2, 3, or 4 stories high," the homes of most Turks were "miserably bad, more like negro houses in Georgia than anything else." More invidious comparisons abounded, and Fisk aired them all in a letter to his Freemason sponsors back in Georgia. He deplored the "barbarous despotism and superstitious ignorance" that "has been felt here in all its degrading force" in "this land of darkness and disorder." There could be no security of property under such a tyrannical government, and as for "female education" it was "scarcely thought of." Nor was there "a newspaper or a periodical work of any sort published in all of Turkey." How lucky his brother Masons were, living in enlightened Christian Savannah. Fisk's letter was all that the American Board could have wished—their man in Smyrna puncturing that windbag George Barrell—and best of all, some newspapers picked it up and printed it. But in spite of himself, there were moments when this new setting charmed Fisk: long strolls through the streets bedazzled him, there being "every where people of different dresses and complexions."[2]

Less enchanting were Smyrna's Franks, starting with Francis Werry, a merchant for the Levant Company and the longtime British consul. Spry and sharp-tongued at seventy-five, he took real pleasure in strafing the pious. An American missionary who later passed through Smyrna recalled being hectored by Werry in his "squeaking tone": "I hear that there are a great many in the interior of America that have never been baptized,—why don't you go and take care of them?" His victim rendered speechless, the consul finished him off: "Well, well, every trade must live, and s'pose you have good salaries and come here to see the world and live on the fat of the land." His advice to Fisk and Parsons was just as deflating: they might labor among Eastern Christians as much as they liked, but, Werry warned, he could protect no one who meddled with the Muslims. So much for the missionaries' fantasies of engaging in Martyn-like debates with Smyrna's mullahs.[3]

There followed their sinking realization that this "open infidel" set the tone for the rest of the Frank community. Like Werry, most made their money in trade, and once they shut their ledgers, these expatriates were hard partiers, caught up in a swirl of dining, billiard playing, card playing, and dancing. Observing that the women kept up with the men in these revels, Fisk pointedly advised the board that spouses should accompany all future missionaries. To his shock, the Americans were the worst of this bad company: a small coterie chiefly from Boston and Salem, they dominated the opium trade. Cheaper and harsher than the drug sold in Western markets to make medicines such as laudanum, Turkish opium found a brisk market among Asia's poorest addicts. It was a sordid business, one that dealers justified on the grounds that the drug was less harmful than alcohol.[4]

His first year in Smyrna soured Fisk on Turks and Franks alike. "If there are any incarnate devils on earth, these Turks are the men," he wrote home to New England, condemning them as more "haughty, unmerciful, oppressive, pharisaical and anti-christian" than the worst of humankind. He would stick to this view, he added with George Barrell in mind, "notwithstanding all that some merchants who have been here may say in their favor." It was only because a profitable commerce had so clouded their judgment that "almost every body" among the city's expatriates "speaks highly of the Turks as honest and good men." Fisk was having none of it: he liked nothing about these Franks and their ways of partying, doing business, and defending Muslims. If Sargent's memoir of Martyn had planted in his mind any new notions about Islam's influence, they seem to have fled, at least temporarily.[5]

Misfits though they were in Smyrna, the two Americans perfectly suited William Jowett's designs for the Mediterranean. From his post at Malta, a mere week at sea away, the man whom they now called their "elder brother in the Missionary work" cultivated Fisk and Parsons with frequent letters and friendly counsel: *Learn languages. Don't ask other people for advice if you think they will be offended at its not being taken. Keep your own secrets, but try not to have any. Avoid intrigues with any party. Always wear a turban to soak up the sweat.* As their explorations yielded "discoveries," he added suavely, "let me beg the favour of your correspondence as far as you can grant it without impropriety." Flattered out of their wits, the two Americans proved more than willing to take their initial direction from him.

Jowett's plan was simple. He had begun to implement it during the four years before the Americans arrived, enlisting the help of a fellow evangelical Anglican, the Reverend Charles Williamson, who served as the chaplain of the Levant Company at Smyrna. Print, these two decided, held the key to transforming the religious culture of the region by reprising in Ottoman domains its historic role in the West during the Reformation. Receiving and reading the Bible and other devotional publications in their own languages would persuade first Eastern Christians and later Jews and Muslims to reject their false beliefs and modes of worship and to embrace evangelical Protestantism. That the overwhelming majority of Ottomans were illiterate did nothing to discourage the missionary pursuit of what struck others as a quixotic enterprise. Evangelicals believed that the power of print was protean, rivaling that of any picture, image, or relic. It was the superhighway between the Holy Spirit and the soul, and as such, it could not only command the reason but also awaken the emotions and stir the senses. The targets of this campaign were not slow to recognize its new crusading fraternity's fetish: Levanters dubbed the evangelicals filtering into their homelands "Bible-men."[6]

To follow the first Bible-men about the Mediterranean, flash back only a few years before Fisk and Parsons landed at Smyrna. Those pioneers numbered among the many British and Continental evangelicals determined to translate the scriptures into every language and to circulate them as widely as possible. As they read it, the Bible's message was plain and straightforward: God was a Protestant. No wonder, then, that the Vatican did not want the Word to get out and even prohibited the faithful from reading any translations not approved by Rome. That gave Henry Drummond his bright idea. Thirtysomething, the archconservative evangelical heir to a British banking fortune, he became the financial angel of a printing press in Naples, and by 1817 it was cranking out copies of an Italian translation of the Bible—the work of the Roman Catholic archbishop of Florence. How could the Vatican object to its distribution, even if by Protestants?

Giddy at the prospect of spiking the pope's guns, Jowett agreed to help Drummond spread his Catholic Bibles throughout the Mediterranean. Both were high-tech honchos with a thoroughly modern grasp of print's potential. Their shrewdness matched that of another British entrepreneur, this one plotting the expansion of the empire's trade, the Scots merchant John Galt. While carousing through Greece and Turkey with Lord Byron, Galt had also eyed Malta and concluded that there "we may be said to possess a fulcrum, on which we might construct engines sufficient to move the whole Mahomedan world." By "engines" he meant printing presses, which could pump out pro-British propaganda—books, newspapers, and pamphlets—translated into all the region's languages. Whereas Galt was looking to promote commerce, Jowett sensed the same possibilities for promoting Protestantism. "*With* a press, we are just in the state to move three continents," he promised Josiah Pratt. Amen to that, American evangelicals agreed.

Jowett did not see eye to eye with Drummond on everything. The latter represented a new strain emerging in British evangelicalism, one distinct from that of the humanitarian reformers and moralists of the Clapham Sect such as the Jowett clan. Believers of Drummond's stripe were doctrinaire in their Calvinism, literal in their interpretation of the Bible, and darkly apocalyptic in their millennial outlook. They stood at the beginning of a direct line of religious descent to the Fundamentalists who would emerge in Britain and the United States at the end of the nineteenth century. Still, Jowett could not help but admire Drummond's take-no-prisoners approach to Rome and his plans to found local organizations for circulating Catholic Bibles. Drummond even turned up at Valletta to help Jowett organize the first of these "bible societies," and they projected gathering more in some twenty other Mediterranean ports. Jowett believed that most Eastern Christians would receive the scriptures "with joy and gratitude," and thereby, he added, they would draw "a deeper and broader line of distinction between themselves and the Roman Church." In other words, evangelicals hoped to turn Bible reading into the wedge that divided Eastern Christians—Greek Orthodox and Armenians, Syrians, Copts, and Abyssinians—from Roman Catholics and that realigned them with evangelical Protestants. Theirs was a strategy for deepening religious differences in an Ottoman world already riven with fault lines.[7]

To begin this crusade called for a Bible-man with more zeal than prudence, and one came forward in Christopher Burckhardt, a young Swiss evangelical in Drummond's employ. He might also have been a man with something to prove because his cousin was the explorer John Lewis Burckhardt. Dressed in the rude clothes of a common laborer and taking the name of Ibrahim, John had spent several years traveling about Syria, Egypt, and Arabia, even passing as a Muslim pilgrim to witness the hajj ceremonies at Mecca. Those experiences left him skeptical about circulating the Bible even among Eastern Christians. It would prove too pricey for most people, he advised, who in any case preferred "their prayer-books, liturgies, and histories of the saints." Then, too, their clergy discouraged "reading of the whole of the scripture." Intent on proving his cousin wrong, Christopher Burckhardt disembarked at Alexandria at the beginning of 1817 with six large cases containing five hundred copies of the scriptures in twelve different languages. He traveled from Alexandria to Cairo and then made his way to Jerusalem and headed up the coast into Ottoman Syria. At the start of each day, he plopped down in front of his lodgings, pitched his Bibles to all comers, and thereafter went about introducing himself and his books to Greek Orthodox bishops, Copt patriarchs, Jewish rabbis—any religious leaders who would listen. He sent Jowett regular dispatches bubbling with upbeat assessments, but in fact his efforts were drawing opposition from both Roman Catholics and Eastern Christians. Before the storm could break, a fever killed Burckhardt at Aleppo, a mere eight months after his mission had begun.[8]

No sooner had news of his death reached Malta than Jowett took steps to follow up on his work—and perhaps to repair the damage done. He sailed up and down the Nile at the end of 1818, offering free samples of Bibles and testaments to the region's Copt, Greek Orthodox, and Roman Catholic clergy. From Syria came the news that in one town all of the books "which Mr. Burckhardt sold or distributed . . . were collected and burnt by some of the Priests, who threatened with excommunication those who secreted them." Undiscouraged, Jowett located depots throughout the Levant to stash boxes of Bibles and testaments translated into every language spoken in the region. From those stocks devout Western travelers might take books to distribute during their journeys, thus converting tourists and merchants into Bible society agents. He hoped that "in course of time, few persons will take a journey, either on business or for pleasure or curiosity, without lending a hand to this good work." He also planned to enlist the Mediterranean's mariners in spreading the Word, even the captains of small boats called caïques, projecting that such little craft would become "the bearers of hundreds and thousands of Bibles and Testaments, from island to island, and from shore to shore." By all those means, Bibles would spread across western Asia.[9]

But it was tracts—booklets no longer than a pocket-sized ten pages—that became the mainstay of the evangelical print campaign in the Mediterranean. Not just any would do, but only those, as Charles Williamson urged, written in a style "adapted to the customs, and habits, and reigning vices of the people." A text from scripture should head each, because the "best pioneers for Bibles are Religious Tracts." He and Jowett composed a few of their own, including one that explained the contents of various parts of the Bible and pointed up which ones were the best to read first. That would get readers off on the right foot, Jowett believed, for "if you put a Bible into the hands of an ignorant man, he is liable to begin with some part, either obscure, or perplexing, or less interesting." Powerful as they believed the Word to be and transparent as they held that its meaning was, evangelicals had to admit that not every chapter of scripture was a page-turner.[10]

It was even more essential for tracts to evoke images that elicited strong emotions. Jowett dismissed most of those sent from London as "too generally dull, because they deal more in abstract truth than in living pictures." That opinion shows how thoroughly he had gone to school on the strongly visual bent of Christian devotionalism in the region. It was not time wasted, the months that he had spent among the Greek Orthodox, filling pages of his journal with descriptions of how they crowded their churches and homes with pictures of biblical scenes and the saints, delighted in liturgical spectacles, and prized relics. He regarded them all as "living pictures" to the faithful, operating on their senses to awaken profound religious feelings, and he aimed to make tracts the literal and literary equivalent for Mediterranean readers. His was an effort to marry the Protestant means of print with the sensuous appeal of Roman Catholicism and Eastern Christianity to attain evangelical ends.

That ambition accounts for the missionaries' habit of observing and recording their tracts' emotional impact. They became adept at reader response, searching the faces of tract recipients for expressions registering sympathy or sadness and construing those reactions as reliable signs that the "living pictures" conjured by a text had touched hearts as well as minds. Evangelicals believed that vivid images in print were important in attracting audiences everywhere in the world but that they were essential for infiltrating the worship cultures around the Mediterranean. Endowed with extraordinary power by the Greek Orthodox and other Eastern Christians, the visual constituted the common ground between their religious sensibility and that of Roman

Catholics, who excelled at incarnating the spiritual through paintings, statues, and the sacrament of the Mass itself. By finding words that would serve the same purpose, Jowett hoped to deprive the pope of monopolizing that advantage.[11]

By the beginning of 1820, there were two new Bible-men in the Levant— his "pupils," according to William Jowett. Once settled in Smyrna, Levi Parsons and Pliny Fisk took a tour of several weeks in the surrounding hinterland villages and then spent a few months studying modern Greek on Scio (present-day Chios), an island off the Turkish coast. What made the deepest impression on them were the Christian worship services that they witnessed—Armenian, Greek Orthodox, and Roman Catholic. Like Jowett, they were stunned by these sensuous modes of worship: the Greeks waving their incense pots, the Catholics chanting their Latin prayers, the Armenians kissing their holy pictures. What drew Fisk's particular notice was that the churches of all three faiths burst with paintings, some small enough to be passed among the faithful, others set in casements plated with gold. At an Armenian church, Fisk could barely peel his eyes from a scene of heaven and hell, all "liquid flames—devils in the shape of serpents with extended mouths and horrid teeth," seizing sinners as they fell into the abyss. Then there was the chapel of a Greek monastery where tiny hands and feet wrought from metal dangled before the pictures of two saints to represent their healing miracles. The missionaries were at once fascinated and astonished to find that in all of these worship settings, the congregations appeared fervently engaged.[12]

It would be no easy contest, competing with "living pictures" that offered so immediate an appeal and inspired such intense devotion, but Fisk and Parsons plunged in, promoting their kind of religion. How they went about it seems odd to anyone unfamiliar with the strategizing of Jowett and other evangelicals. In the first place, the two Americans spent most of a year introducing the scriptures and evangelical principles to people who were already Christian. Aside from the occasional trip to a synagogue and a few conversations with individual Jews, they devoted their days to touring schools and distributing testaments and tracts among Eastern Christians, primarily among the Greek Orthodox. Preaching to any gathering was out of the question.

As Charles Williamson explained, because any Christian missionary would "expose his own life should he attempt to convert a Turk," it was "next to impossible that missionaries should gather any fruit from this flinty soil or surface, by preaching." Even among the Levant's Eastern Christians, he warned, Protestant missionaries would "meet with almost insuperable difficulties . . . by *preaching* of the Gospel," because of opposition from their clergy.[13]

Odder still, print thus became the preferred and only medium for proselytizing largely illiterate peoples by the new American Bible-men. Fisk and Parsons promoted tracts in particular with single-minded devotion, scattering them by the thousands in the monasteries and nunneries, schools and colleges, on Scio and around Smyrna. As soon as they acquired a smattering of modern Greek, they translated "The Dairyman's Daughter," a tract recounting the exemplary life and death of a young evangelical woman on the Isle of Wight, and Fisk himself tried his hand at writing one with the unbending title "Advice to Children." While directed mainly at Greeks, the tracts distributed by both American and British missionaries appeared in a range of languages— Hebrew, Arabic, Persian, Turkish, Armenian, Italian, French, German, Dutch, English, and Russian. They meant for their message to reach everyone in the Mediterranean, whether inhabitants or visitors.[14]

Like their British counterparts, Fisk and Parsons were keenly attuned to the ways in which their tracts were received. The head of the Greek college at Scio delighted them by admitting that he could not read "The Dairyman's Daughter" without weeping. But then, this learned scholar presided over the center of Greek literary culture on an island of 120,000 inhabitants, some of them retired merchants with commercial houses in Europe's major cities. So it gratified the Americans when their tracts met with a warm reception in smaller, more remote spots. Fisk crowed at the news that one of the tracts he had given out so gripped a Greek villager that the man rose in the middle of the night to read it again. Parsons claimed that no sooner had the people of Castello Rosso, an island between Rhodes and Cyprus, spied his tracts than "a multitude thronged in the streets, each crying aloud . . . Sir, will you give me a tract?" But the Americans also acknowledged that their activities, like those of Bible-men before them, aroused opposition among both the Roman Catholic clergy and some Eastern Christian prelates. The Greek Orthodox professor who sobbed over "The Dairyman's

Daughter" refused to print copies on his college press for fear of offending the "Superior of the [Greek] Press at Constantinople," who had not
examined the tract. Even with the clergy's imprimatur, the two Americans knew that there might be grassroots resistance to anything "be-
stowed by a Foreigner" and so recruited schoolteachers and other local
inhabitants to distribute their tracts in the countryside.[15]

They also suspected that less than pious motives might inspire
some of the clamoring for printed material. Smyrna had no press until
the spring of 1821, when an enterprising Genoese printer began to publish a weekly newspaper in French—the city's first periodical of any
sort. That addition made for three printing presses in all of Turkey,
none conspicuous for their output. As little issued from two others operated by monasteries in Syria and Lebanon and one just getting under
way outside Cairo, which brought to a total of six the number of presses
in the Ottoman Empire. With print still a curiosity, many flocked to
missionaries scattering tracts, and even schoolchildren, by Fisk's account, when they "learn that I have books for them . . . crowd around me
in the most irregular and noisy manner." And those for whom print itself held no fascination had a keen interest in acquiring paper, a scarce
commodity in the eastern Mediterranean. It was in demand among
druggists for packaging their pills and powders and among gun owners
for making cartridges. Finally, some who sought tracts and testaments brought them straight to their priests for burning. None of those
risks escaped the notice of Fisk and Parsons. To guard against their
books' being "abused," they insisted that anyone receiving them demonstrate the ability to read. Still, they measured their success by the number of tracts distributed and testaments dispensed, confident that the
circulation of print itself would work wonders.[16]

That's what baffles. How did evangelicals come by this cast-iron
confidence—this trust bordering on the magical—in the power of print?
As they saw the matter—as all Protestants had since the Reformation—
the influence of the Holy Spirit operated through the Word, drawing
readers toward divine truth and changing hearts and lives. But how
could tracts and testaments transform the religious landscape of the
Ottoman Empire when most of its inhabitants lived and died illiterate?
What headway would even an avalanche of print make against that

obstacle? Evangelical authors took pains to appeal to humble folks by populating their tract narratives with orphaned children, dissolute fishermen, and simple farm girls and ennobling them with the capacity for high thinking and pure feeling. But if the largely unlettered men and women living around the Mediterranean could not make out the words in a few short pages, what did it matter how enticing those "living pictures" were?

Then there was the problem of the literate minority, who, by Western lights, did not know the proper way to read. Christians and Muslims alike, as Dr. Robert Richardson complained, restricted their worship to repeating set prayers. That meant "private reading, meditation, or conversation with others, or with themselves, forms no part of their plans of felicity, or domestic enjoyment." His friend Jowett could accept that Levanters did not read in silence to themselves, because most could not comprehend a book "till they have made it vocal," reading it aloud "with a kind of singing voice; moving their heads and bodies in time, and making a monotonous cadence at regular intervals . . . although not such an emphasis, pliant to the sense, as would please an English ear." But when Jowett tried to demonstrate the "right" way of reading aloud—"inartificially and naturally," as the English did—they "laughed, and said, 'You are not reading: you are talking.'" A British traveler to Syria around the same time had the same response: listening to a group of Catholic schoolboys at their lessons, he described them as "bawling rather than reading Arabic."[17]

What were they thinking? What sustained the confidence of both British and American evangelicals—beyond the belief that their all-powerful God could work wonders—that print would transform Ottoman religious cultures? In part, it was their experience back in Britain and America, where membership in evangelical churches was surging as their Bible, tract, and Sunday school societies pioneered the latest print technology and marketing techniques. In many parts of the British Isles and the United States during the opening decades of the nineteenth century, readers were still scarce and opportunities for even basic schooling spotty. But the flood of printed material, much of it pouring from religious presses, put a cheap means of practicing to read into the hands of increasing numbers of people. By 1820, the founding chapter of the American Sunday School Union alone had published six million books sold at bargain prices and beamed at beginning readers, and by the Civil War basic literacy among white men and women was nearly universal in the United States. That was no coincidence.[18]

Evangelicals expected the same process to unfold the world over. They believed that the greater availability of printed material in vernacular languages would spur literacy, which would inevitably produce a great many more evangelical Protestants. As Levi Parsons saw the future playing out, "Distribution is our *great* weapon." Other evangelicals followed secular authors in comparing the press to a lever or an engine or an artillery—machines that would lift the world's peoples into the ranks of the literate and the saved. In short, the wide circulation and accessibility of print would both fuel the desire of ordinary people to read and improve instruction in the schools. Fisk summed up the consensus after visiting a predominantly Greek village outside Smyrna, "a community of say, 1,500 souls," where "only 55 children are found at school, and for the instruction of the female sex no provision is made. Yet I often perceive evidence that the Greeks are capable of learning with great ease, and when they have advantages they are very fond of books and study." The power of print to command a universal response had become an article of faith among the supporters of missions by the 1820s. And the younger these prospective converts were, the easier it would be to send the right spiritual sparks shooting across their synapses. For that reason, the Americans scattered copies of "The Dairyman's Daughter" among Greek children, expecting them to morph into Ottoman versions of pious young Americans.[19]

That evangelicals attributed to print such sweeping power reveals that at least on this score they saw no essential difference between East and West. People the world over would prove equally susceptible to the Word. Sentimental tracts would draw readers from everywhere, regardless of race, ethnicity, or creed, touching hearts and changing minds. In other words, evangelicals believed that all human beings were hardwired in the same way, gifted by God with equal potential for and powers of reason, feeling, and apprehension. Once provided with print and the ability to read it properly, these thinking, sentient beings would instantly recognize the superiority of evangelical Christianity to all other creeds. Not to have endorsed this Enlightenment view of an equally endowed human nature would have been tantamount to declaring that the conversion of the world was impossible—that their kind of

Protestantism was not for everybody. And as the desire to universalize their faith prompted evangelicals to embrace the Enlightenment's view of all human beings as possessing a common sense and sensibility, that perception in turn limited the extent to which evangelicals could regard those whom they targeted for conversion as "others."[20]

Bolstering the stock of universalist sentiment were the scores of sermons all devout New England evangelicals had heard from childhood. When addressing their congregations or local missionary societies, ministers spoke of unchurched farmers on the New England frontier in the same breath as the "pagan" Cherokees in Georgia and the "heathen" Hindus in Bengal. In a typical effort, one New Divinity pastor in Maine declared that "the situation of many in this District is not more favorable to salvation, than that of the superstitious Hindoos of Asia, or the wild Boschemen [Bushmen] of Africa." To another minister, "the new settlements" of New England were merely "the margin of the moral wilderness" that included "the western and southern sections of the American continent," as well as "the eastern world." Savages all, shrouded in the same spiritual darkness but capable of being saved by the same means and medium of print.[21]

Or more precisely, by the same means and medium adapted to the needs and preferences of different groups. Just as Eastern Christians would require Catholic versions of the Bible, Jews would accept only the Old Testament. Parsons discovered as much when he offered to give tracts to some Jewish schoolchildren, only to be turned down because they contained material from the Gospels. Christopher Burckhardt even hatched a stealth plan to attract Hebrew readers: a book "containing memorable actions and sufferings of the Jews since the time of Christ," which "should have the power to entertain" and take a compassionate tone, while carefully avoiding "whatever might startle too soon the prejudices of the reader, and make him throw the book away." Then at the end there would appear "a lively exhortation to examine the Christian Religion." Even the look of the type could make a big difference in a book's reception: according to Jowett, the poor eyesight of many Egyptians and the dark churches of Abyssinia (present-day Ethiopia) mandated the use of large fonts and wide spaces between lines.[22]

Important as pitching their message to Jews and Eastern Christians might be, evangelicals intent on proselytizing through print studied

Muslim preferences the most closely. If the influence of Sir William Jones and Henry Martyn encouraged their hope that Muslims would read books other than the Qur'an, there remained Islamic readers' aversion to typographic print itself. To eyes that had feasted on calligraphy, typographic print was a fast. As a British traveler to Turkey explained, Muslims considered "characters formed in writing . . . as more pleasing to the eye, and as capable of being connected and combined in a more beautiful manner, than in printing." How providential to evangelicals, then, that among new technologies in this age of wonders was lithography, which allowed printers to reproduce handwriting—even to approximate calligraphy—and thus to turn out books that looked nearly like manuscripts. Missionaries in the Mediterranean were all over this new invention, one that Jowett regarded as "a gift which Providence has given to our times" to evangelize the Islamic world. His enthusiasm for lithography also reflected the recognition that Muslim devotionalism shared with that of the Levant's Christian cultures a strong visual component. Despite Islam's prohibition of human images in artistic productions, exquisite calligraphy made the text itself an enchantment to the eye, a means of enlisting the senses in the service of spirituality. That approach offered another way of turning words— literally—into "living pictures," and Jowett meant to make the most of it through lithography.[23]

There were some Westerners in Ottoman domains who believed that the problem went beyond print. Chief among them was Christopher's cousin John Lewis Burckhardt, who judged that the Arabic translation of the Bible being circulated by Protestant missionaries would not make "the slightest impression" on Muslims, for they "could not read a page in it without being tired and disgusted with its style." "So uncouth, harsh, affected, and full of foreign idioms," this translation of the Bible simply could not compete with the Qur'an, "the purest and most elegant composition" in Arabic. "If Mussulmans are to be tempted to study the Scriptures, they must be clothed in more agreeable language," Burckhardt warned, "for they are the last people upon whom precepts conveyed in rude language will have any effect." Discouraging words, but they did nothing to diminish evangelicals' certainty that Muslims would bend before the power of print. It was Henry Martyn who had first instilled this conviction, declaring that the translation of the New Testament into Persian and Arabic, "whenever it is done properly, will be the downfall of Mahometanism."[24]

The deep satisfaction that evangelicals—and particularly their missionaries in the Middle East—drew from believing that the Bible would deal a deathblow to Islam points to another reason for their vesting print with such power. The dawning awareness that their kind of Protestantism might have much in common with Islam instilled in evangelicals a mixture of intense curiosity, heady optimism, and profound anxiety. If their shared fondness for reasoned debate and simplicity of worship raised hopes for Muslim conversions, more unsettling was the recognition that both were proselytizing faiths. Evangelicals and Muslims alike believed that spreading their creeds was a religious duty, that failing to do so invited divine displeasure, and that succeeding would bring matchless rewards in the afterlife, especially for martyrs. What Muslims knew as the lesser jihad, evangelicals called "catching the missionary spirit" for the "conversion of the world."

But that connection with Islam—one, ironically, enhanced by the gathering momentum of the foreign missions movement itself—came too close for comfort. In response, evangelicals drew a sharp distinction between their own proselytizing faith and that of Muhammad by emphasizing that Protestant means of conversion were noncoercive, unlike the violent methods that they attributed to Islam. "The sword propagates and maintains their creed," Jowett insisted, whereas Christians of his sort appealed to the mind and heart, using persuasion rather than force. Part of what wedded evangelicals to print, then, was the determination to distinguish their practice of jihad—their struggle to convert the world—from that of Islam. "The English have hearts white and pure as paper," one Christian Arab in Beirut remarked a few years later, a metaphor that caressed the ears of the American missionary who overheard it.[25]

In March 1820, the American missionaries at Smyrna opened a packet from the United States and fished out a diamond ring. It came from a woman in Charleston, South Carolina, probably someone whom Fisk had met on his travels there. Here was telling testimony to the personal stake in missions felt by many evangelicals, as well as to their high expectations of the Palestine mission. Religious periodicals back in the United States were celebrating Fisk and Parsons as advance scouts of a new crusade against Islam. Such hopes would only grow more outsized when Henry Martyn's memoir reached bookshops in the United States. But how many pious women would part with their diamonds for missionaries who could not be confused with Sargent's stalwart missionary hero? If the fondly anticipated influx of Muslim converts into the evangelical fold was not forthcoming, for how long would the Palestine mission hold the attention and command the donations of the American faithful? Burdened by those worries, Fisk and Parsons confided to the American Board their concerns about disappointing supporters. By the end of the year, Parsons wrote even more candidly to a woman friend, "Sometimes we fear since our exertions are so limited and our success so far below the expectations of our Friends that Christians will be weary, and discouraged . . . that we have not done *more* is a source of deep humiliation." Then, out of the blue, both of their British masters departed, and the Americans got the chance to make their mark as independent agents. Jowett decamped to London for a long visit in the fall of 1820, and shortly thereafter death claimed Charles Williamson.[26]

Levi Parsons took off for Jerusalem. There he made preparations to headquarter a permanent mission, in part because the Americans believed that pilgrims would attach greater sanctity and value to any tracts received in this holy city. Parsons also visited Eastern Christian prelates and handed out tracts and testaments, as Burckhardt had done there before him. But he was as intent on setting down long, detailed descriptions of the sacred sites in and around Jerusalem and noting their connection to the people and events in the Bible. No doubt in his mind's eye, he could see his journal extracts prominently featured in religious periodicals. He even drew a pencil sketch of the mosque built over Solomon's temple, the Dome of the Rock, perhaps in hopes that the *Missionary Herald*, as the *Panoplist* had been rechristened, would begin to put pictures in its pages.[27]

Fisk stayed on in Smyrna, hoping to join Parsons later in 1821. Bereft of his partner's company, he set himself the challenge of learning Arabic. It would have surprised his Andover professors to know that languages now came easily to Fisk. He could already get by in modern Greek and Italian, even preach in French, when he began Arabic lessons with Constantine Dracopolis, a schoolmaster who had earlier accompanied Jowett to Egypt. Possibly, too, Fisk took up Arabic with another goal in mind. Little more than a month after his lessons started, Dracopolis introduced Fisk to his first Muslim acquaintance, a Turkish teacher named Suleiman Effendi, and the two visited on four other occasions, conversing through an interpreter. To Fisk's delight, when first offered the New Testament in Turkish, Suleiman accepted, "putting his fingers to his chin and forehead in the manner which is often used in this country to denote gratitude." "This is the first opportunity I have had to put the gospel into the hands of a Mahometan," Fisk exulted. But the next visit dashed his hopes: Suleiman told him that the New Testament was "a book for Christians" and "said with some emphasis, 'one God.'" "I suppose he thought too much was said of Christ," Fisk glumly concluded—and stuck to the psalms in the Old Testament for their next visit.[28]

He also drew out Suleiman by speaking "of the prevalence of learning among Mahometans in the time of the Caliphs, etc. and enquired how it is now." For Suleiman, those were the glory days: "Ah, he said, they loved books and schools and learning then, but now they find it necessary to devote their whole time to the acquisition of money and the means of subsistence." Still more discouraging, when Fisk asked about the Turkish printing press at Constantinople, Suleiman replied that the press had issued a few books during the reign of the last sultan but now printed nothing. Fisk's intimacy with Suleiman made little progress because "we could converse only by an Interpreter; and I always find my Interpreter, whoever he may be, much more fond of talking himself than of interpreting for me." But even as their conversations lagged, Fisk was striking up a more promising connection with another Muslim.

He was a cosmopolite, a bibliophile, and a Moroccan diplomat, first identified by Fisk as "Seid Mahomet Effendi." He had tracked Fisk to his lodgings, looking to buy a Turkish testament for his library. Shielded by his high-ranking connections, he was unconcerned with giving offense to Muslim authorities by visiting a Christian missionary. With Italian in common, the two men began to talk about languages. By the end of May, they were reading the alphabet together in Arabic and English, and through that exercise Fisk learned, much to his satisfaction, the proper way of writing the Moroccan's name: "Mohamed Sayed Albakaly Effendi." Now their discussions were delving into Ottoman politics and the Turkish navy. The two also had agreed to exchange lessons in their languages when Mohamed returned from a trip to Constantinople, and he had invited an eager Fisk to inspect his "library of several hundred volumes." "I have not met with a mussulman before who seemed to care so much about learning," Fisk marveled, not a little flattered by the notice of a man who was also "said to have been intimate with *Hallit* Effendi, a celebrated Counsellor of the Porte [the Ottoman sultan] who had his education in France." At last, a Muslim who seemed to have stepped from the pages of Sir William Jones's defense of the Turks, someone who made Fisk feel almost like . . . Henry Martyn. He made no mention of their discussing religion.

What Fisk did record about his first Muslim acquaintances offers a revealing contrast, a self-censoring that suggests the limits of what his American sponsors wished to hear. Whereas the official journal that he dispatched for publication to the board in Boston detailed his every encounter with Suleiman, which ranged from dismaying to unsatisfying, it mentioned nothing more than his first meeting with Mohamed. Only to his private journal did Fisk confide his growing intimacy with the Moroccan. Evidently, he believed that news of his proselytizing a Muslim, whatever the results, would be more acceptable to his evangelical audience than reports of his having hit it off with another aficionado of books and languages who also happened to be a servant of Allah. Fisk's pleasure in Mohamed's company was too palpable, their relationship a little too chummy, for him to risk disclosing more.[29]

What might have been? What if Mohamed had returned from Constantinople and continued his conversations with Fisk? What if Fisk's Turkish had improved, and his talks with Suleiman had continued? What if Fisk had widened his circle of Muslim acquaintance in Smyrna? But all those possibilities gestating in the womb of time during the spring of 1821 never came to be born. What history delivered instead arrived in blood and terror.

In the middle of April, Fisk returned to Smyrna from a trip to the ruins at Ephesus with two visiting Boston gentlemen. As they entered the city's Turkish quarter, armed men swarmed. Some shouted that the Greeks had rebelled, others said that the Franks had taken up arms against the

Turks, and still others that the Turks were poised to attack a French warship in the harbor. With that entry in his private journal, Fisk announced the beginning of the Greek bid for independence from Ottoman rule. A few days later, he was reporting "great consternation" among Smyrna's Greeks, who were hiding in their homes or fleeing to vessels in the harbor. Within a month, word spread through the city that the islands of the Peloponnese had followed the Danubian provinces of Moldavia and Wallachia (in present-day Romania) into rebellion.

By then, carnage had begun in Smyrna, and every day the slaughter claimed tens, sometimes scores, of Greeks in the city. Gangs broke into the homes of families who had not escaped town, plundering their property and seizing women and children to sell as slaves. On one occasion, Fisk, who had taken refuge at Francis Werry's home, watched from the rooftop as a Greek man attempted to escape his Turkish pursuers by jumping into the sea and swimming for a boat. "The bullets often hit the water within a few inches of his head . . . This was the first time that I ever saw one of my fellow creatures fire upon another." Only an outbreak of the plague at the beginning of July brought about a lull in the violence for the next two months. Meanwhile, the Greek archipelago erupted, trapping Parsons in the cross fire on his return voyage from Jerusalem. On more than one occasion, Greek soldiers boarded the vessels carrying Parsons and other pilgrims, searching for Turks and warning the other passengers that if "you are arrested by a Turkish Vessel you must expect immediate execution."[30]

Many of Smyrna's Franks blamed the fighting on the Greeks. They "began the war of extermination and carry it on regularly by putting to death all the Turks they make prisoners," Werry wrote to Parsons. While neither of the Americans ventured an opinion about the origins of the conflict in their official journals, both believed that the Greeks behaved as savagely as the Turks. Parsons reported that Greeks had set afire Muslim villages in the vicinity of Salonica, causing the Turks to retaliate in kind. Fisk, too, though he had witnessed atrocities only against the Greeks, reported to the American Board that both sides roasted their captives alive and killed pilgrims returning from Mecca or Jerusalem. As for the Jews, "some follow the Turkish Army and buy the plunder" seized from the Greeks "at very low prices." "Human blood flows freely," Fisk concluded. "All of the selfish, revengeful, cruel and licentious passions of which human nature is capable are indulged without restraint."[31]

Here was a hell beyond any that Fisk could have imagined when he disembarked at Smyrna a year and a half earlier. For a person steeped in the Bible's prophetic books, it must have seemed that the fourth horseman of the Apocalypse astride his pale mount had charged into the Levant, bringing death by the sword, plague, and wild animals—the last, in human form. Beyond their sheer brutality, what stunned Fisk was the power of these events to defeat his expectations and to contradict his certainties. From a window in Werry's house, he had watched as one of the consul's Muslim janissaries stepped between a boatload of Greeks and the muskets being leveled at them by "a company of Turks." For this "humane and courageous act" that saved many lives, Fisk "could have embraced him as a brother." But why had the same man "since boasted of having killed 6 Greeks in the streets himself"? A world far more complicated than the one he had seen a year and a half earlier now met his eye.[32]

But perhaps Fisk's first impression of Smyrna's inhabitants—that they were "led captive by Satan at his will"—had been more discerning than he knew at the time. They were all "incarnate devils," as he realized now—not only the Muslims but also the Christians and Jews. Fisk did not set down the slaughter that he was witnessing and the savagery that he had heard about to some uniquely Turkish or Muslim ferocity, some Eastern bloodlust or Islamic fatalism. No, by his lights, the depravity common to all humankind, the worst passions of which fallen nature was capable, had wrought this hell. Here was yet another kind of universalism, a darker one, and experience was teaching him to fathom its depths. How worthy a subject to have pursued with that learned Moroccan, Mohamed; their conversations might already have inflected Fisk's thinking. But once chaos swallowed Smyrna in the summer of 1821, his new Muslim acquaintances disappeared from the pages of all his journals. Pliny Fisk was about to find his way further into Islam through a most unexpected route.

# Part Three

# HEGIRA

# 6

## TURNING TURK

Say [Prophet] [to the Jews and Christians], "How can you argue with us about God when He is our Lord and your Lord?"

—Qur'an, The Cow, 2:139

Captain Arthur Philip Hamilton held the dinner guests spellbound. To capture the magic, Pliny Fisk wrote down his stories that very night in his private journal. An officer in His Majesty's navy, Hamilton had covered the globe—"went with Napoleon to St. Helena—has been in China—on Lake Ontario and in the river St. Mary's in America." His greatest adventure had come at the ill-fated siege of Constantinople in 1807, Britain's naval campaign in support of its ally Russia against the Ottomans. There was Hamilton, standing on the deck of the frigate *Ajax* when it burst into flames and "casting himself into the sea before she blew up." The last year he had spent knocking about Egypt and Syria and found "not the least danger in traveling" either place. Not that so bold a man as the captain, a stranger to fear surely, would have noticed any threat. Passing through Jerusalem, he had met Levi Parsons, and together the two had visited the Jordan and the Dead Sea. What Fisk would have given to have joined them!

And how he envied the captain. No one in Smyrna hung on Fisk's every word. Most Franks found him a killjoy, struggling to stifle a reproof whenever the Casino—the city's hot spot for gambling and dancing—came up in conversation. Still worse, he felt useless. Ever since the violence had flared in the city, he had been unable to distribute tracts or visit schools, and at the end of May he had confessed to Parsons, "I do not see that I am doing any good or that I am likely to do any." By now, the late summer of 1821, outbursts of renewed fighting and the onset of the plague kept him cooped up in the Frank quarter, where he passed the time polishing his French, Greek, and Italian and tutoring the children of a wealthy Dutch merchant. All the more reason for that flicker of jealousy in his account of Captain Hamilton's active life and the adventures that won him so many admirers. Fisk consoled himself by striking up an acquaintance with the captains of American merchant vessels, men who, like Hamilton, had seen much of the world. They became his boon companions, and their dinners together often ended with earnest talks about religion. Betraying his boyhood far from the Atlantic, Fisk made note of every visit aboard their vessels, and one or the other usually invited him to preach to the crew on the Sabbath. Such pious gentlemen—at least in the missionary's presence— and so unlike Smyrna's Franks.[1]

Early in September, another sojourner turned up—a raconteur to rival even Captain Hamilton. A chubby New York City lawyer in his late thirties, Luther Bradish had junketed through the Greek islands, Syria, and Egypt—running into Captain Hamilton at the pyramids— before winding up in Smyrna, many stories richer. Both Bradish and Hamilton confirmed what Fisk had already observed: the Greek Revolution had set off fierce fighting among ancient religious rivals, and the Greeks were as guilty of atrocities as were the Turks. Hamilton had seen the corpses of two Jews "who had been roasted to death by the Greeks" and heard that a Greek Orthodox bishop of Naxos had urged his people "to murder the few Catholics on the island and take possession of their lands." Bradish gave it as his opinion that what set off the war was the Greeks entrapping in a mosque and then slaughtering nearly three thousand Muslim Turks.

Bradish was in a position to know a great deal, because he had first come to Turkey a year earlier at the behest of John Quincy Adams, the secretary of state. It was a choice tale, but sadly, it could not be told, for he was Adams's secret agent, negotiating with the Sublime Porte to open the Black Sea to American shipping. Though his mission failed, Bradish was at no loss for other stories to tell Fisk and his posse of sea captains. Had they heard that the niece of William Pitt, Lady Hester Stanhope, presides over a household of thirty servants on Mount Lebanon? That the Arabs esteem her a prophetess and kneel to pray before one of her horses—a beast with a peculiar back, which one of their holy books predicts "that the Almighty himself should saddle"?

Did they know that Mehmet Ali, the pasha of Egypt, the son of a Turkish Muslim "risen from nothing," sent the sultan "a jewel which cost 30,000 pounds in England"? That he has received a large supply of books in different languages from Europe and aims to establish a school for his military officers? That he supports an army of 150,000 men? Quite a comer, the pasha, and for all his projects, he "employs many Europeans."[2]

It was then that Fisk thought to ask about a fellow New Englander, a former clergyman, whom he believed to be in Egypt. Surely Bradish would have heard of him, and Fisk could not help but be curious: George Bethune English was a hard man to forget. He was also a hard man to forgive, at least in Boston, where his no-holds-barred attacks on Christianity several years earlier had blighted his prospects. His comparing the religion of Jesus unfavorably with that of Muhammad had put him at the end of even the Unitarians' patience. Luckily, English counted John Quincy Adams among his few remaining friends, and that secured him a commission as a first lieutenant in the Marine Corps in the spring of 1817. English also stuck in Fisk's memory because only a year later the lieutenant jumped ship in Smyrna. He was "an imprudent young man," his mother's old friend William Bentley sighed at hearing of English's desertion, "who studied divinity before he knew his own mind" and who went to Turkey "because [he was] discontented with Christians." But not for long. English's next commission—a promotion—came from Mehmet Ali, who made him a general of artillery in Egypt's growing army. Even before assuming that command, English had proclaimed himself a Muslim, taking the name of Mohammed Vehbi Effendi. By the summer of 1820, while waiting to join the pasha's expedition to the Sudan, he was with one hand composing a treatise on the superiority of Islam to Christianity and with the other tinkering to make vehicles with "wheels of scythes," like ancient war chariots.

Word of English's apostasy made its way back to the United States early in 1819, where it was reported in newspapers from Vermont to South Carolina to Ohio. The secular press took a snarky tone, noting that English had accepted the pasha's commission "in the hope of one day attaining promotion in the military service of that country, more advanced than he could ever have expected in ours." The religious press smugly described the now Mohammed Vehbi Effendi as the "author of a deistical publication." (See what came of denying the doctrine of the Trinity and the divinity of Jesus?) Those few still willing to identify themselves as English's friends managed only a few forlorn lines in a Charlestown, Massachusetts, newspaper, insisting that "the rumour" of his apostasy was unfounded. More likely, they were friends of his mortified father.[3]

But by the fall of 1821, the best-informed source on George English happened to be Luther Bradish. While in Egypt, he had not only spoken with Mehmet Ali about his new American general of artillery but also read English's manuscript "in proof of Mahomentanism." It was "superficial and unsound," Bradish remarked, "though somewhat plausible."

That was higher praise than it might seem, coming from a devout evangelical and future president of the American Bible Society who described Islam as "a deformity." Bradish might also have learned more about English's doings from two British travelers, George Waddington and the Reverend Barnard Hanbury, who had cold-shouldered the pasha's American general when their paths crossed in the Sudan at the end of 1820. What other reception could English expect "from those whose religion he had deserted?" Waddington sneered. Despite, or perhaps because of, the contempt he aroused, English delighted in reinventing himself—adopting a new religion, a new political allegiance, a new name. According to Waddington, he had acquired even "the grave and calm look of the Turks," including "the slow motion of the head and roll of the eyes." Yes, George English had outdone himself, surpassing the notoriety of his Boston days.[4]

Pliny Fisk knew of other Westerners who had professed Islam. Only months after the news of English's apostasy rocked the early republic, readers in William Bentley's Salem were pondering the strange fate of one John Porl. He was just nine years old in 1806, a cabin boy on the ship *Essex* out of Salem, when its captain quarreled with a Muslim official at a port in the Red Sea. It ended badly: all the crew murdered, throats cut ear to ear, except for little John, who was spared and subsequently adopted by a local sheikh. Or so all of Essex County at last learned thirteen years later when a Newburyport ship captain, Charles Cook, chanced upon Porl, now Abdallah Mohammed, in Yemen. Conversing proved difficult, Porl/Mohammed having forgotten much of his English, and by Cook's account, the sheikh "has been careful to educate him in the religion of Mohammed, and had done everything in his power to prevent any recollections of his native country." Cook urged him to return to Salem, but Porl/Mohammed explained that he had a wife and children and that he could not think of leaving Arabia so long as his adoptive father was alive.

Other apostates came to Fisk's notice once in the Levant. Francis Werry told the cautionary tale of an Englishman who embraced Islam and found himself ostracized once back in Britain. The man returned to Constantinople, taught engineering and translated two books of Euclid into Turkish, "but was so much neglected and so badly treated that he died of grief." Quizzing an American opium trader in Smyrna, Fisk learned that five or six of their countrymen had embraced Islam, one of them "a black who was employed afterwards to seduce other sailors," another "a carpenter who is gone to Algiers." Finally, there was Thomas Pewett, the subject of one of the longest entries in Fisk's earliest private journal. When the two met on Scio in the spring of 1820, this former sailor in the British navy claimed to have been drunk when he accepted Islam. Fisk believed Pewett "to possess a good degree of intelligence and to have been instructed in Christianity," so he urged the sailor to renounce his Muslim faith and to reaffirm his belief in Christ, exhortations that "seemed to make him sometimes solemn, sometimes uneasy." As well they might, because the Ottoman penalty for apostasy from Islam was death.[5]

Conversions to Islam struck a nerve among evangelicals, as Fisk's dwelling on Thomas Pewett suggests. Another sign of their sensitivity is a letter, its author identified only as "Calvin," that appeared in a periodical published in the New Divinity bastion of New Haven in the fall of 1819. "Calvin" began by noting that "a few Englishmen in Asia, a short time since, renounced the Christian faith, and declared themselves Mohammedans." Those apostasies raised the pressing question—at least in the circles that "Calvin" traveled—"*Why are you not a Mohammedan?*" He plunged in, rehearsing the stock evangelical objections to Islam with stalwart conviction, as if imams were about to descend on Connecticut like a Muslim version of American Board missionaries. The prospect of the crescent unfurling over Yale College was not, of course, why "Calvin" asked his question: it was the defection of George English. He was no terrified child, no disgruntled, barely literate sailor; he was a well-educated, well-connected gentleman, one trained as a Christian minister, who had chosen Islam freely and with full knowledge.[6]

His apostasy fretted Fisk, too, like sand under his shell. English was only five years his senior, a fellow New Englander, and a former Congregationalist clergyman. Yet could two people have chosen more opposite courses? There was Fisk, striving to turn the Ottoman Empire's peoples into evangelical Christians, and there was English remaking himself into a Muslim. How could anyone betray the cross for the crescent, especially now, at the very moment when evangelical forces were mustering for a crusade against Islam everywhere in the world and when the signs—at least as Fisk read them—had never been clearer that Muslims were on the losing side of history? Searching for an answer to that question, Pliny Fisk followed George English through the looking glass to begin a spiritual odyssey stranger than any he could have imagined and one that would reveal the deepest sources of evangelical anxiety about Islam.

*Renegadoes*: ever since the late sixteenth century, that was what Western Christians called those who deserted their faith for Islam. They had "turned Turk," it was said, or "taken the turban." Some of the million or more Christian men, women, and children held captive in the Barbary States of North Africa between 1500 and 1800 converted to Islam, many hoping thereby to gain a reprieve from the most arduous labor or to escape slavery altogether. Westerners who were not slaves also embraced Islam. Religious conviction drew some, and for others it was a matter of expedience, the condition of their enlisting in the Ottoman military or joining the Barbary corsairs. Whatever their reasons for turning Turk, *renegadoes* aroused an anxious fascination among early modern Europeans. Here were apostates casting their lot with the Muslim enemy just as the West seemed to be faltering. The Ottoman Empire was steadily expanding its control over eastern Europe during the sixteenth and seventeenth centuries, pressing west as far as Vienna, swallowing up Egypt and North Africa, and snatching captives from ports as far distant as England and Ireland, Iceland, and Newfoundland. As the crescent carried all before it, Christendom imploded; the Protestant Reformation plunged western Europe into a century of carnage. With Christianity in such dire straits, feeling ran high against those who denied the cross, and dramatists tapped into that outrage: *renegadoes* often strode the Elizabethan stage, cheered when recanting or hissed when getting their just deserts.[7]

The number of captives had dropped off sharply by the end of the seventeenth century as bribery and reprisals by Western governments prodded the Barbary States to curtail their depredations, and by 1800 the ranks of *renegadoes* had thinned even more. Yet even as their numbers were shrinking, renegades, as they were coming to be called, began to occupy a larger place in the imagination of many in the United States. Accounts of captivity in North Africa stirred interest because some of the several hundred American sailors enslaved in Algiers, Tripoli, and the Sahara turned Turk. Those renegades and other Westerners who had taken the turban figured prominently in the memoirs that returned American captives published during the first decades of the nineteenth century.[8]

Typically, their accounts depicted renegades prospering, at least temporarily, implying that they had embraced Islam out of either self-interest or weakness. As typically, the renegades lived to regret turning Turk and longed to return to Christianity and the West. Scenes of their comeuppance cued readers to hoot and hiss, just as Londoners in the Globe's pit would have done three hundred years before. But if the arc of renegades' rise and fall recalled the plot of Elizabethan plays, American captivity narratives also expressed anxieties characteristic of a new republic where national allegiance was still a work in progress. The Barbary States represented no direct military threat to the United States, but attacks on American shipping and demands for tribute humiliated the fledgling nation. All the more egregious, then, were turncoats who colluded with North African pirates and pashas.[9]

What received even more emphasis was the renegades' betrayal of Christianity. Captivity narratives dwelled on those renunciations, while their authors (like Elizabethan dramatic heroes) gained stature because they resisted turning Turk. Among them was the Connecticut sailor Archibald Robbins, whose bestselling account of his Saharan captivity made his doughty struggle against converting to Islam a key element of the narrative. At first, Robbins humored his Muslim captors by joining them at prayer, but he later stopped, "thinking it sacrilege to offer up worship to a prophet whose followers shew so little of humanity in their practice." So resolved was he to demonstrate "not the least conformity to the faith of Mussulmen," Robbins even made a point of "feasting" during Ramadan. Whether he would persist in his determination to "resist this apostacy [sic] to the last" lends as much suspense to Robbins's story as when and how he would finally make his escape from slavery.[10]

Even more riveting than those captives who held fast to Christianity were those who did not. That, at least, was the calculation behind the climax of Judah Paddock's story of redemption from his Saharan Muslim masters. One of his fellow captives, an English teenager named Jack—a "treacherous, lying rascal"—had developed a good command of Arabic and always joined "with the Arabs in their prayers." Once ransomed and brought to Mogador (present-day Essaouira) on the Moroccan coast, Jack ran off to live with the Muslims in town and finally "declared that he had embraced the Mahometan faith, had been circumcised . . . and he claimed protection from the man whom he called his adopted father." Despite efforts to reclaim him, Jack held fast to his newfound faith, and the Muslim community celebrated by parading the boy about town, mounted on a horse, "the followers singing and shouting in a merry mood, gratified by the grand acquisition they had made."[11]

Other popular diversions attest that apostasy lost none of its power to grip the imagination of Americans, despite dwindling numbers of renegades. The saying that "a renegade is worse than a Turk" became a staple of political mudslinging, lobbed at men who switched party loyalties. One of the most widely reprinted stories in American newspapers during the 1810s recounted the fate of Athanasius, a Greek Orthodox youth who bent to pressure from his Muslim master and converted to Islam, only to repent—whereupon he was beheaded by Ottoman authorities. Renegades also took to the American stage. In 1818, crowds packed theaters up and down the Eastern Seaboard to catch *Bellamira; or, The Fall of Tunis*, in which the leading character had turned Turk. Although flayed by critics ("new food for reflection, upon the incapacity of our present race of writers"), its author, the Irish playwright and politician Richard Sheil, knew what audiences on both sides of the Atlantic liked: his earlier productions include *The Apostate*. He was simply capitalizing on the success of Frederick Reynolds, whose "musical drama," *The Renegade*—which featured the spectacular destruction of a "Moorish vessel" by a waterspout—crossed the Atlantic to open in American theaters in 1813.[12]

In part, the fascination with renegades reflects the novelty of North African captivity for Americans. The three decades after 1785 marked the first time that a substantial number of them languished in Barbary prisons. It did not matter that few actually became Muslims. Any betrayal attracted outsized notice because of another novelty of those decades—the religious free market emerging in the United States. Renegades became culturally resonant figures for many Americans of every faith and none, as they worried or marveled over how far popular spiritual loyalties might stray from Trinitarian Christianity now that the United States was embarked on the radical experiment of separating church and state. In the late 1780s, critics of the "godless" federal Constitution's prohibition of religious tests for federal office holding warned that "pagans, deists, and Mahometans" would vie for such positions, even dominate the new national government. The youth of many of the renegades suggests that their religious allegiances aroused especially acute concern. Finally, there were those positive portrayals of Islam in novels like Royall Tyler's *Algerine Captive* and in occasional pieces in the popular press, coverage which encouraged the conclusion that such apostasies were not inconceivable.[13]

If renegades commanded general notice, those who turned Turk were particularly disturbing to evangelicals, none more than those who promoted foreign missions. What could be more confounding to their expectation that Christianity would conquer the world than these turncoats to Islam? And while their numbers were hardly legion, why were there so many more of them than there were Muslim converts to evangelical Protestantism—or to any form of Christianity? Still more troubling, why had the most famous among them, Jawad Sabat, returned to Islam? Small wonder, then, that the premier student of renegades—a man whose books would soon attract huge audiences in the United States and Britain—was the evangelical missionary with well-laid plans for the conversion of the Ottoman Empire.[14]

William Jowett began to fill his private diary with accounts of those who turned Turk during his tour of Ottoman domains in 1818. By now, the majority of renegades were not captives but common seamen who professed Islam at their own initiative. What might have been Jowett's first encounter with one of them took place at Smyrna in that year, when he witnessed the ceremony of converting to Islam. It left an indelible impression not only on him but also on many pious readers, for Jowett included a chronicle of the event calculated to send shivers up their spines in his 1822 bestseller, *Christian Researches in the Mediterranean*. Curious to observe the proceedings, Jowett and John Werry, the son of the British consul, waited at the apartment of Smyrna's mayor, unnerved by the sound of "a man in the yard suffering the bastinado" who "at every stroke . . . sent forth a terrible howl." At length, another fellow, a pale, sullen American ship's carpenter surrounded by Turks, entered and remained standing among them at the end of the room farthest from Jowett and Werry. Asked by Werry "why he wished to turn Turk," the man muttered that "he could not live by his own religion!—He had been on board many years, and suffered ill treatment." To Jowett's inquiry of what he would do on Judgment Day, having denied Christ, he made no answer. "You see," said Mr. Werry, "that he is lost." With coaching from an Islamic cleric, the carpenter stumbled through a brief declaration in Arabic that ended with the words "There is but one God, and Mahomet is the prophet of God." Then Muslim officials led him away to be bathed and circumcised.[15]

The ritual left Jowett so shaken that he returned to it in conversations for days thereafter. A longtime British resident of Smyrna, Dr. John Lee, counseled him to forget the matter, because "the character of some of the lower Europeans" in the Levant was "so bad" that it seemed "almost necessary to let them suffer their deserts." But Jowett could not let it go. He was convinced that desperation, drink, and lust brought most Westerners into the Muslim fold and that bravado, shame, and force kept them there. Seamen he regarded as being especially at risk, "for they are very whimsical and obstinate; whimsical because they have so limited a knowledge of society on land; obstinate because their understanding is fully grown without having been properly exercised." Grudges against ship captains pushed common tars to take drastic action: once ashore, they "get into drinking-houses, and when drunk promise to turn Turk." A boast blurted out in a crowded tavern or a promise whispered to a Muslim lover could end in apostasy, sometimes with three or four shipmates egging each other on and turning

Turk together. Too often, there was no going back, because reneging on the vow to convert would open sailors to ridicule, even a flogging, aboard ship where "they would never be able to hold their heads up again."[16]

Why did they do it? In *Christian Researches*, Jowett served up his list of the reasons for "Europeans choosing to become Mahomedans." While some, typically common seamen, were desperate to escape debt, punishment, or prosecution for a crime, others, usually of greater means or prestige, were "so connected with Mahomedans by marriage, trade, or some profession, as to feel no desire to withdraw from them." Then there were those, high and low, who believed "all religions are alike" or harbored "that grossly delusive fancy, that a man may be a Christian at heart, and a Turk in profession."

Most revealing in this list is the reason that's missing: some Westerners were drawn to Islam by its spiritual power. Among them were veterans of Napoleon's campaigns in Egypt, officers who remained in the country and converted, finding Islam both essential to promotion and congenial to their rationalist outlook. Poorer men, too, experienced Islam's appeal. Some renegade sailors might have known little of Christianity and cared less, but others displayed an unexpectedly sophisticated knowledge of Christian doctrine. Among them was Thomas Pewett, who asked Parsons and Fisk whether "denying Christ is the unpardonable sin." Other seamen felt confident enough in their knowledge of Christianity to tell Jowett—as he admitted only privately—that "they considered Mohamedanism as a better religion than their own." After that acknowledgment, Jowett scribbled, "Therefore it follows they knew nothing of their own—tell this to the Sailor's Bible Society." That brusqueness betrays his apprehension that some Westerners, white and black, learned and unlearned, might judge Islam superior to Christianity.[17]

As for Pliny Fisk, he had to wonder about George English. Did this American Muslim number among those whom "the hidden man of Islamism" had claimed, heart and mind? Or was his profession of Islam driven by desperation or expedience rather than real conviction? His glee in defying authority made English even less likely to succeed as a marine lieutenant than as a clergyman, so it could be that he entered the pasha's service and accepted Islam because he had run out of options. Maybe he had written that manuscript "in proof of Mahomentanism"

only to impress Mehmet Ali. And perhaps now—as Westerners suspected of all renegades—he repented turning Turk. Whatever the truth
about English, the power of renegades to compel their attention was
the unwitting tribute that early nineteenth-century evangelicals paid
to Islam. Their missionaries in the Mediterranean never mentioned
Westerners embracing Catholicism or Judaism, never so much as hinted
that those faiths could hold any allure for Protestants. Islam was another matter entirely, and its appeal a point of sometimes furtive but
always keen interest. For that reason alone, Pliny Fisk would find
George English a hard man to forget.


His conversations with Luther Bradish piqued Fisk's interest in renegades. So much that he wrote to the American Board, asking for a copy
of Robert Adams's Saharan captivity narrative. As his request slowly
floated back to Boston, Fisk was also trying to gain a fuller knowledge
of Islamic theology and ritual practice from sources unmediated by
Western commentators. More than a year earlier, he had read George
Sale's translation of the Qur'an and along with it, as a kind of spiritual
prophylactic, the most celebrated Christian polemic against Islam, a
set of lectures by the eighteenth-century British Anglican cleric the
Reverend Joseph White. But by the end of 1821, when he accompanied
a Dutch merchant's family to their country house in the mountain village of Sediqui, he took along a classic work of a very different kind.
Borrowed from the library of Jowett's friend Dr. John Lee, it made for
heavy lifting and even heavier reading: four volumes in French detail-
ing Islamic history back to the first caliphs and describing in every
particular the Ottoman Empire's civil and religious institutions. Un-
daunted, Fisk dug in and kept going even after its author announced in
the introduction his intention to offer a defense of Islam. By the time
Fisk had tunneled through all four volumes, his own stout "Book of Extracts" bulged with more than thirty pages of notes on *Tableau général
de l'empire Ottoman*. Here was his first glimpse of the Islamic world as
seen from within.[18]

Well, almost. The book's author was Ignatius Mouradgea, a man
whose life straddled East and West. Born in 1740 at Pera, then a suburb
of Constantinople, the son of an Armenian Catholic father and a French
Roman Catholic mother, he served first as a dragoman and later as the

minister plenipotentiary and head of the Swedish legation to the Ottomans. Disgusted by the distortions of Western authors, he spent decades doing research on every aspect of Ottoman life, past and present, studying Islam with the help of a lawyer and a theologian, both Muslims, and even interviewing female slaves to acquire reliable information about the sultana and the harem. In 1784, he began a stay of ten years in Paris, where he took the surname d'Ohsson and, in 1787, at last completed the remarkable book—a quarter century in the making—in which he sought to explain the Ottoman Empire to the West. Nothing could be more necessary, in his view, because "religious prejudices" posed a formidable barrier to understanding between the two cultures, filling European minds with false notions about Ottoman laws, customs, manners, and religion.[19]

D'Ohsson's grand theme is that Islam should bear no blame for the difficulties confronting the Ottoman Empire. A proponent of modernizing reforms, he denounced the corruption afflicting its politics, the apathy inhibiting public improvements, and the suspicions barring the adoption of Western technologies. Those evils, according to d'Ohsson, resulted not from Muslim teachings and laws but rather from "fatal prejudices" and "false opinions," such as belief in the power of astrology, divination, and magic, as well as fascination with omens, portents, and prodigies. All were contrary to the Qur'an and repugnant to the true spirit of Islam, a religion of "rational precept," he claimed. "Enlightened spirits" among the Ottomans and those schooled in Islamic doctrine and canon law "openly scorn these chimeras."

There were plenty of such right-thinking and no shortage of well-educated Muslims, d'Ohsson insisted, because their creed neither disdained resorting to reason nor discouraged acquiring knowledge, Western or otherwise. Muhammad himself was a "celebrated Legislator," a genius as well as a "subtle politician," and the Ottoman religious and legal code had "a peculiar grandeur in many of its tenets, a striking sublimity in the generality of its moral precepts, an affecting dignity in its religious ceremonies, a profound wisdom in its laws, and a natural and pleasing simplicity in its customs and manners." From that foundation, he confidently asserted, "an intelligent, enlightened, enterprising Sultan," backed by civil and religious officials, would be able to effect sweeping reforms. Here was a perspective on Islam utterly at odds with that of the Reverend Joseph White but sustained by other authors with whom Fisk had become familiar, most notably Sir William Jones and Henry Martyn.[20]

What gave Fisk still more to think about was d'Ohsson's reconstruction of Islamic religious belief and practice, a survey that, like those of George Sale and some other early Orientalists, drew attention to its affinities with the various forms of Christianity. There were parts of d'Ohsson's Islam that Fisk would have called popish: Muslims venerated Muhammad's relics—including his robe, part of his beard, even a few of the Prophet's teeth. They believed in the miraculous powers of their saints and in the immaculate conception of Jesus; they prayed and gave alms to shorten the sufferings of their dead in a purgatory-like place in the afterlife. Some of the devout fingered chaplets, a string of ninety-five beads much like a rosary. Yet Islam shared with Protestantism in general and its evangelical strain in particular so much more. Such was the Muslims' reverence for scripture, d'Ohsson claimed, that they would touch the Old Testament only when "in a state of legal purity," "kissing and carrying it before them with profound sentiments of respect and devotion." Such was the Muslims' regard for the gulf separating the human from the divine that they permitted no statues or pictures in their mosques. And what Westerners scorned as Muslim "fatalism," d'Ohsson explained as a belief in predestination indistinguishable from the Calvinist tenet that God had foreordained the eternal fates of men and women, sorting out the elect from the reprobate before the beginning of time. Like the heirs of the Reformation, Muslims believed that "one could obtain heaven" not through good works but "with faith alone."[21]

D'Ohsson gave particular emphasis to the devotion that Islam inspired in its faithful. The muezzins' call from the minarets—"awful and majestic"—brought life to a standstill as Muslims, whatever their rank or condition, abandoned everything to worship God. Five times daily—in mosques, houses, shops, markets, even the public streets—men, women, and children prayed. They did so with "constant and scrupulous attention," no turning heads or wandering eyes. Throughout cities and the countryside, there were oratories set close by wells or fountains, so that even travelers had places to purify themselves before prayer. Their common regimen thus drew together rich and poor, clerics and laypeople, the pious as well as the skeptics, because Ottomans dreaded above all else being reputed irreligious: one's good name could not survive that taint. Through their spiritual observances, then, d'Ohsson approvingly concluded, "this immense people" seemed "to form only one religious society."

Fisk had to wonder: Why had this godly society become a reality among Muslims at Constantinople but not among Christians in Boston? Gone were the days of the Puritans, who designed their governments, as Muslims did their sharia law, to endow civil institutions with divine sanction and to bring every aspect of life under divine authority. But even—indeed, especially—as the separation of church and state proceeded apace in the United States, the great goal of evangelicals and the main aim of their revivals and voluntary associations was to make their kind of religion pervade civic life and define national identity. They worked tirelessly to steep the new republic in Protestant piety so that men and women would not feel ashamed to display their religious commitment in the public square and even infidels, duelers, and drinkers would cease their scoffing, lay down their pistols, smash their gin bottles, and join everyone else at church.

But it was the followers of the Prophet who stopped in their tracks to pray; it was in a land of minarets, not church spires, where doubters shrank from showing their true colors. Even men—especially men—openly displayed their faith. How it had struck Fisk, when still new to Smyrna and out strolling one evening, to spy three or four Turks kneeling on a patch of grass, their faces toward Mecca and bowed to the ground, their hands clasped. And it was in the Ottoman Empire, not the United States, where magistrates listened and punished the wicked when clerics, twice a day in some mosques, inveighed against vice, luxury, and the corruption of manners. There was more, enough to make Fisk wince, thinking about New England's Protestant churches charging pew rents to exclude the poor, while in mosques men sat without distinction on carpets or mats. Or noticing the contrast between Muslim religious festivals, celebrated in "tranquility and silence," with none of the drunken rowdiness that accompanied some Christian solemnities in the great cities of Europe.[22]

Reading d'Ohsson confirmed for Fisk, if he hadn't taken it on board before, that Muhammad's teachings had left a more profound impress on Ottomans than those of Jesus, at least so far, had on Americans. To an evangelical, that was an alarming accomplishment, one proving that Islam was a real contender for the religious loyalties of the rest of the world's peoples. Truly, there must be a "hidden man of Islamism."

Those reflections appear to have prompted a fundamental shift in Fisk's perspective on religion, a change that surfaces in a fascinating scrap from his private journal. He made three lists, most likely during the last months of 1821, setting forth Protestants' similarities with and differences from Muslims, Jews, and Roman Catholics. Fisk's shorthand rendition of the comparison with Islam reads as follows:

### Points of Agreement with Mahometans:
One God—no images
Law of Moses—Christ and his Gospel
Resurrection and Eternal Punishment

### Difference:
Divinity and Atonement of Christ
Bible preserved uncorrupted?
Mahomet—Koran—
Trinity?—Fight for religion?
Polygamy?

Pay particular attention to the sprinkle of question marks. With the first two, Fisk was indicating that, like Muslims, many liberal Protestants rejected both the Trinity and the authenticity of the Bible. The last two question marks seem to signal George Sale's influence on Fisk's thinking: the acknowledgment that both Protestants and Muslims had fought to spread their faiths at some point in the past, and the recognition that practicing polygamy was not essential to Islam. Take away the differences marked as questions, and Protestants as a group had much in common with Muslims—considerably more, by Fisk's count, than with Catholics. Prompted by d'Ohsson, Fisk was thinking about religion in a completely new way—in comparative terms—and he was also dwelling on the affinities between Protestantism and Islam.[23]

Another influence was working on Fisk as well, and that was George English's turning Turk. Besides reading d'Ohsson during his sojourn at Sediqui, he leafed through a British diplomat's account of his time in Persia and zeroed in on a curious story buried in a footnote. It describes one Talamash, a Frenchman born in Constantinople, who had traveled through India, Afghanistan, and Persia posing as a Muslim holy man. In Persia, he passed himself off as a dervish and tested his powers of disguise by making visits to the diplomat, who finally discerned his true identity. After more wandering, including a stint as a privateer in the Red Sea, Talamash simply vanished. "It is a very rare instance of the successful assumption by an European of an eastern character," the diplomat concluded. "I have known, in Turkey, several *renegado* Englishmen, who could never sufficiently disguise themselves to be taken for original mussulmans." Surely this story drew Fisk's notice—it even ended up in his "Book of Extracts"—because he was searching for insight into an American Muslim's character. Was English merely another Talamash, taking on the colors of another culture and flaunting his chameleon feat? If so, then he might not be beyond reclamation after all.[24]

Everything except the Greek war flew from Fisk's mind when he returned to Smyrna at the end of November. Warned away when he reached the edge of the city, he learned that a street brawl had escalated into the slaughter of "great numbers of Greeks" and that the Turks, still enraged, now "threatened to burn Frank street and to massacre all the Franks they could find." Days later, the Turks received the pasha's permission "to kill Greeks wherever they could find them." Fisk still believed that Turks and Greeks bore equal blame for the bloodshed. But he had also begun to weigh the possibility that Ottoman Muslims saw the conflict as a holy war—a jihad against Christian infidels. Shortly after arriving in Smyrna, he and Parsons had assured the American Board that Muslims in general no longer sought to spread their religion "by the sword" and that the Ottomans in particular made "almost no efforts" to induce Christians or Jews within their empire to convert. Even by May 1821 as Smyrna spiraled into violence and Fisk projected possible outcomes of a failed revolt, he had speculated that only "the privileges of the Greeks" such as their access to printing presses and schools would be "very much abridged."

Now his imaginings had turned darker. He recorded in his journal a conversation with his tutor in Greek and Turkish, George Demetrius, who claimed that more than three thousand Greeks had been killed in and around Smyrna, but "frequently when any have been taken up," the Turks offered the prisoners their lives in return for converting to Islam. Was that a true report, or only one of many rumors flying about the city? If true, what would happen if the Greek bid for independence failed? Would the victorious Turks force a mass apostasy of Greek Christians to Islam? Only a few months later, in April 1822, the leaders of the newly formed Greek government would justify the rebellion in their "Declaration to the Christian Powers" in the West by playing on precisely those fears: "Already a conversion to Mahometanism appeared the solo safeguard to the wretched population [of Greek Christians] . . . Would Europe have wished to see the consummation of this gigantic act of apostacy [sic]?" That prospect was still troubling Fisk a few weeks later as he reread the preliminary discourse to the Qur'an and copied into his "Book of Extracts" Sale's view that the "Religion of Mohammed [was] not propagated by the sword only, but Embraced by nations who never felt the force of the Mohammedans arms." That meant sometimes the sword *did* spread Islam, and when victorious in war Muslims "make slaves of women and children, and put the men to death, unless they become Mussulmans or are otherwise disposed of by the Prince." Grim reflections, and for a time they drew Fisk's mind from those Western renegades who willingly turned Turk.[25]

He was distracted, too, by Levi Parsons, who returned to Smyrna early in December after a year's absence. Never as sturdy as Fisk, Parsons had suffered from various ailments ever since arriving in Turkey, and now his lungs troubled him. A physician recommended wintering somewhere warmer, so as the year 1822 began, the two boarded a ship sailing to Alexandria. Their plan was to establish an American mission at Jerusalem in the spring or, at the very least, to pass out their testaments and tracts to the pilgrims who flocked there for Easter. As for the prospect of converting Muslims, Fisk seemed in need of some encouragement. In one of the last entries in his private journal at Smyrna, he recorded the words that Dr. John Lee had inscribed on the last page of Henry Martyn's memoir, which the missionaries had given him as a farewell present. Lee predicted that "at no very distant period in Persia, will the abominable no-religion of that odious and satanical impostor,

Mahommed, be first rooted forth, never more to pollute the earth with the abominations of its desolations. So be it. Amen Amen Amen." Heartening as it was to recall his hero's triumphs, Fisk harbored far more modest hopes as he and Parsons set off for Egypt, the last place that anyone had sighted the American Muslim George English.[26]

# ┿═ 7 ═┿

## AN AMERICAN MUSLIM

People of the Book, do not go to excess in your religion, and do not say anything about God except the truth: the Messiah Jesus, son of Mary, was nothing more than a messenger of God, His Word directed to Mary, and a spirit from Him. So believe in God and His messengers and do not speak of a "Trinity"—stop [this], that is better for you—God is only one God, He is far above having a son.

—Qur'an, Women, 4:171

No sooner had Pliny Fisk landed at Alexandria than he struck the trail. The British vice-consul there, Dr. John Lee's brother Peter, readily shared his good news: George English had been persuaded of "his error in embracing Islam" and now stood ready to "return to his country and the religion of his Fathers." Eager for the details, Fisk turned up at Lee's residence the next day, where he received only the assurance that the vice-consul expected "Mr. English here daily in order to make his escape to America." Lee spoke more freely of other renegades, American and British, and of how, like English, they came to repent turning Turk and how he had "sent two such out of the country privately." On the third day, Fisk, still searching for the full story, took Lee's suggestion and wrote to the man himself. English was at Cairo, still recovering from a harrowing trek through the desert on his way back from Sudan during the previous fall. The letter sent, Fisk borrowed the vice-consul's copy of the Qur'an and braced himself to meet the former—or so he prayed—American Muslim. Those preparations proved premature. Three weeks later, English replied through Lee that he "dare not venture to answer" Fisk's letter, and "if he does not altogether follow the advice it contains, he shall always respect the purity of the motives which dictated it." The brush-off, definitely.[1]

Fisk had little time to care, because what he had dreaded for weeks was now a certainty: life was slipping away from Levi Parsons. Their voyage to Alexandria had left his partner so weak that Arab porters took him by chair from the harbor to the lodging Fisk had engaged. When Parsons asked to glimpse the city, it jolted them both, how easily Fisk lifted his wasted body and carried him upstairs to the terrace. Like many in Alexandria, they enjoyed a clear view from atop their flat-roofed dwelling, because no buildings rose higher than three stories, save for the city's two largest mosques. Look south and gaze upon a great stretch of desert pocked by palm trees. Look north and see the sparkling Mediterranean and twin harbors cinching the city. Look down and watch an ever-changing scene in the streets. Buffalo-drawn carts and droves of camels clattered through the narrow passages; shopkeepers sat cross-legged on their counters in the bazaar, plumes of smoke rising from their pipes. White veils whisking through a crowd signaled Muslim matrons; a flash of scarlet, the skullcap worn by single women. Far smaller than Smyrna, Alexandria claimed some thirteen thousand Arabs, Turks, Greeks, Syrians, and Jews; the tiny Frank community, perhaps two hundred people, kept to its own quarter. That neighborhood boasted wider streets than elsewhere in town, as well as a fashionable promenade, the Parade, where European travelers and adventurers strolled and flew kites. No wonder Parsons, sick and bored, longed for time on the terrace.[2]

He was scared, too. Now that death stalked him, Parsons no longer dismissed it, as he had in youth, as "only the gate to glory." "I have been led to view *death* as a near event," he wrote to a woman friend, and "when this hour approaches . . . then you will *feel* that it is a dreadful thing to die." Out of this urgency—and perhaps to master his fear—Parsons summoned the strength to draw up a list of advice for Fisk. Composed during the last week of January 1822, it revealed an even more remarkable transformation in Parsons, once the crusading zealot. Now he strove to impress upon Fisk the importance of taking an irenic approach toward those of other religious beliefs, counseling that one of the "most valuable methods of doing good in our mission is by easy, meek, and spiritual conversation with those who visit us." He also stressed the importance of "a critical, judicious and impartial examination of the religious creeds, ceremonies, and *hopes*" of different faiths. Their two years in the Ottoman Empire had inclined both men toward more accepting attitudes, but perhaps neither could admit to the other how far that process had proceeded until Parsons, staring into the abyss of his own dissolution, summoned the courage to give this parting advice to his friend.[3]

Parsons had been moving toward that more tolerant outlook over many months. Some evidence of a turn in his thinking appears in a letter to a male friend in western Massachusetts written a year earlier. He was sailing for Jerusalem, and among his shipmates were three Muslim Turks, "interesting men," in his estimate, "who give me the accustomed salutations of friendship." How "affecting" he found it to "see them prostrating themselves on the floor, in the service of prayer, and looking toward Mecca, the city of their beloved Prophet." A false prophet "to all those who know the truth as it is in Jesus," but the depth of their devotion moved Parsons. On the same voyage, some of the reasons for Ottoman reticence with Westerners also began to register with him. As he wrote to a friend at Middlebury for whom he had promised to collect mineral specimens, "Turks watch with a suspicious eye every motion of foreigners which has the appearance of searching for treasures." It was dawning on Parsons that Levanters would not welcome those who came as crusaders of any sort.[4]

Parsons's changing views owed even more to his close association with men of other Christian faiths. Like Jowett before them, the two Americans found some Greek Orthodox leaders receptive to their plans for blanketing the Levant with tracts and testaments, and Parsons developed close ties to at least two. There was the head of the college at Scio, whom he described as greeting him with "the affection of a Father"—a phrase tellingly redacted by an evangelical editor of his journals to read, "with great affection." There was also Procopius, a monk who served as the principal agent of the Greek Orthodox patriarch in Jerusalem: Parsons lodged at his convent, and the two became so close during his sojourn there that his new friend referred to him fondly as "Levi."[5]

More surprising was the shift in Parsons's stance toward Roman Catholicism. On his return voyage from Jerusalem, hostilities stranded him for nearly six months on Syra, an island in the Cyclades with a substantial number of Roman Catholics. At first, he filled his journals with hand-wringing over the venality of local priests, the credulity of lay Catholics, the fatuity of Latin worship, and the sacrilege of doing business on the Sabbath. But he also spent hours attending masses and even observing confessions. Like Jowett before him, Parsons was trying to plumb the appeal of a liturgical faith, but he went further, striving to establish what can only be called an interfaith dialogue. Out of his discussions with Syra's priests came Parsons's plan to print and distribute tracts with selections from the medieval Catholic mystic Thomas à Kempis. He grew even more accommodating toward Catholicism after falling ill. Delirious for nearly a month, he "was often in Jerusalem preaching with great success" and once, Henry Martyn–like, "reasoned before the Governor of Smyrna." If he had lost none of his zeal for converting the world, Syra's Catholics nonetheless endeared themselves to Parsons by nursing him back to health and—even more touching to a flinty Yankee—by haggling with doctors over his medical bills. Curiously, too, the tokens from Palestine that Parsons sent to friends and family members a few weeks later were not the usual Protestant mementos—vials of water from the Jordan or dried flowers from Gethsemane—but instead Catholic crosses and rosaries.[6]

Parsons shared his new outlook only with Fisk, who in turn told no one. Both men were already practiced in self-monitoring, and they knew, too, that the American Board would take particular pains to censor any dispatches from the Palestine mission. That was because as Parsons lay dying in Alexandria, he was becoming a celebrity back in the United States. Christian periodicals and even some secular newspapers were publishing parts of his Jerusalem journal, the first descriptions of biblical sites and Eastern religious rites from the pen of an American. By revealing the large and eager audience for such chronicles, Parsons jump-started what would become the cottage industry of Holy Land publishing in the United States: a later member of the Palestine mission cashed in with *The Land and the Book*, a lavishly illustrated bestseller that anchored many a parlor table in the 1850s.[7]

Parsons did not live long enough to know of his fame. Death came for him in mid-February 1822, leaving Fisk to suffer the raw grief of losing the love of his life: both men were a mere twenty-nine years old. Only a few months earlier, upon learning that Parsons's vessel had made a safe passage from Syra to a port near Smyrna, Fisk had confided to his private journal that "the prospect of meeting him so soon gives me a satisfaction and a pleasure wh[ich] I have seldom felt." Now he could wring no consolation from the death of "my dearest earthly friend," "though I was permitted to stand by his bed-side, and kiss his gasping lips." With his partner's death, "my chief source of happiness, as it concerns creatures, is taken from me," and Fisk felt "more than ever that I am a pilgrim and a stranger on the earth." He consoled himself by pledging to fulfill Parsons's last wish, establishing a mission at Jerusalem that very spring.

As the tide of time bore Levi Parsons ever further away, it carried Pliny Fisk deeper into Egypt. There he would become more intimately acquainted with all of that region's revealed religions and especially Islam. Since his first landing in Ottoman domains, he had tried to comprehend its meaning and import, and now Fisk let curiosity draw him on. He had learned enough in Smyrna to suspect that he was seeking a dangerous knowledge, one that could challenge the confidence that his evangelical Protestant faith was singularly true, its appeal universal, and its ultimate triumph assured. He was right: a reckoning there would be, and one from which there was no retreat once he closed in on the American Muslim George English.[8]

Some must have regarded an infidel German Jew as an unlikely, if not inappropriate, companion for a Christian missionary, but Pliny Fisk thought otherwise. Dr. Marpurgo—no first name turns up in the documentary record—had taken medical training in Vienna before settling in Alexandria. He made his share of enemies during seventeen years there. One of them, a British traveler, lambasted him as a scoundrel who cheated his patrons, poisoned his professional rivals, and squabbled over the price of treatment as his patients lay dying. But Marpurgo's care of Parsons won over Fisk, who sought out the physician often during his long first weeks of mourning. Fluent in English, French, German, Italian, and Arabic, Marpurgo "conversed very fast" in them all, leaving the slack-jawed Fisk "scarce time to say a word." He was also "quite a free thinker," which made him the American missionary's latest tutor in the ideas of the Enlightenment. A radical deist, Marpurgo rejected all revelation, whether Jewish, Christian, or Muslim, stripping down religion to "the worship of God and the practice of morality." And the guide to morality, he insisted, "was not to be found in the Bible in that perfection in which it was to be found in the writings of the Greeks." It got even more of a rise out of Fisk when the doctor regaled him with eye-popping gossip about Muslims' fondness for "sodomy" and the size of the pasha's seraglio.[9]

An antidote to gloom, his conversations with Marpurgo also inspired Fisk to read the work of another disciple of the Enlightenment, the French philosopher and historian who wrote under the name of Volney. Born Constantin-François Chasseboeuf, he spent two years traveling throughout Egypt and present-day Syria, Lebanon, and Israel and in 1787 finished his encyclopedic *Voyage en Égypte et en Syrie*—the same year that d'Ohsson began to publish his *Tableau*. Volney's book became the go-to guide in the West for many decades thereafter, and Fisk himself took twenty pages of notes in his "Book of Extracts." A starker contrast with d'Ohsson's views is hard to imagine: Volney blamed Islam for making the Levant poor, backward, and corrupt, sliding into decay along with the rest of the Ottoman Empire. In his view, the religion of Muhammad fostered hostility to learning, and "almost the whole Koran is a chaos of unmeaning phrases, puerile tales, and fables," instilling in the faithful "a fierce and obstinate fanaticism." Fisk, who omitted from his notes any mention of d'Ohsson's favorable estimate of Islam, readily set down Volney's hostile commentary.[10]

But no sooner had Fisk put down Volney than he returned to a book with a very different message. The Danish explorer Carsten Niebuhr's account of his travels in Egypt and the Arabian Peninsula during the 1760s was, as much as Volney's work, an Enlightenment compendium, cataloging every known fact about these regions, from agriculture to religion. The two authors had little else in common. What impressed Niebuhr was the diversity of Islam as practiced, both its myriad sects and the gulf between ordinary Muslim believers, whom he regarded as credulous and xenophobic, and their more liberal-minded brethren, who were curious about Western learning and welcoming of exchanges with learned Christians. As for Islam itself, Niebuhr held that in the form imparted by Muhammad, it fostered neither superstition nor despotism, nor oppression of women, nor intolerance of other faiths. In short, Niebuhr's estimate that Islam corrupted neither the mind nor the social order was closer to the opinions of d'Ohsson and Sale than to that of Volney.[11]

Fisk had first read Niebuhr while crossing the Atlantic two years earlier, and his picking up the book again suggests that the widely differing appraisals of Islam were weighing on his mind. Could it be that the evangelical critics of Islam and the enlightened ones like Volney were altogether wrong? Certainly Fisk's list of authors who disputed their view that Islam disdained reason and learning was getting longer: d'Ohsson, Niebuhr, Jones, and, perhaps most persuasively for an American missionary, Martyn. What's more, education seemed to be prospering under Mehmet Ali's rule. The pasha was establishing an "institute" to train his army and naval officers, as Luther Bradish had reported, and he had sent young Egyptian men to be educated in Europe in order to staff that school. One fresh from his Western education in France and Italy, Osman Efendi Nureddin, "now gives lectures at Cairo," Marpurgo had told Fisk, and another returning student "has brought with him a printing press." Then again, perhaps the pasha's efforts to educate his people signified nothing, for he was no observant Muslim—as the vice-consul Peter Lee informed Fisk—but rather "a perfect Deist." And what were the religious principles of this Nureddin and the other young Egyptians coming home from Europe? At the beginning of March, Fisk set off for Cairo, hoping to find out. True, the season neared when pilgrims would come flocking to Jerusalem, and Parsons's fervent hope had been to establish a mission there. But curiosity pulled Fisk in the opposite direction, bringing him closer—perhaps not coincidentally—to George English.[12]


Upwards of 350,000 Arabs, Copts, Greeks, Syrians, Armenians, and Jews jammed Cairo. Overhung by roofs and upper windows that nearly touched from opposite sides, its narrow streets wove the city into a dark labyrinth that crackled with the cacophony of baying dogs, grunting camels, and—the preferred way of wending through town—braying donkeys. Five times during every twenty-four hours, a sublime sound drowned out the din as a chorus of voices from minarets called Muslims to prayer. With no fewer than three hundred mosques, Cairo was an ideal place for immersion in Islamic culture, but Fisk seems to have spent most of his time in the Frank quarter, a warren of fewer than two hundred souls, mainly French and Italian. It was there, at the home of the British consul general for Egypt, Henry Salt, that Fisk met his host's chief dragoman, who now called himself Osman Effendi.[13]

Born William Thompson in Scotland thirty-four years earlier, Osman had come to Egypt as a sandy-haired, freckled fifteen-year-old surgeon's mate in the British army. By his account, the Turks had taken him prisoner and forced his conversion to Islam, but Osman assured Fisk that he continued to believe "in Christianity though he keeps up the appearance of a Mussulman." Bad sorts, the Muslims, the dragoman said: husbands practiced polygamy, so their wives "often go from home privately for bad purposes and even hire men to visit them." A sorry business, too, "the lewdness and sodomy which are practiced at Mecca." His stories went on: a veritable Zelig, Osman seemed to have known every Western adventurer who had passed through Egypt, including George English. Fisk had wasted no time asking after him. Ah, yes: Osman had helped English "to get off [from Cairo] secretly in the evening," just a few days before Fisk had left Alexandria. "We must have passed each other," Fisk mused in his private journal. And how the dragoman had "laughed at the idea that Mr. English embraced Islamism from a conviction of its truth." No, said Osman, it was impossible that English had made a sincere conversion to Islam—no more than the Scot had himself.[14]

Did Fisk question the value of assurances that one renegade might offer for another? He might have been less inclined to do so after Osman spent a week showing him the sights. He waited patiently at Saladin's citadel, a massive fortress overlooking the city, as Fisk counted ninety-five minarets before giving up. ("Doubtless there are many more.") They visited Greek and Coptic monasteries at Old Cairo and the pyramids at Giza. All the while, Osman kept up a practiced patter: Muhammad's followers were "totally destitute of morality" and "extremely lax in the observance of their own religion." As for the pasha's harem—why, believe none of the wild exaggerations—it includes "not above 100 or 150 women." Here was a man who knew how to show the Franks around town.

But the highlight of Fisk's visit was inspecting the new institute in the suburb of Bulaq founded by Mehmet Ali and run by Osman Efendi Nureddin—a Muslim Turk, as it turned out. Fisk could not stay away, visiting three times in the space of two weeks. It included a school for about fifteen boys, a library, and three printing presses. Fluent in both French and Italian, Nureddin spent most of his time translating books from those languages into Arabic and Turkish, drawing on a library of about three thousand volumes that covered every subject from history and geography to mathematics and the sciences, to philosophy, poetry, and "the Military Art." Fisk admired everything about the institute except perhaps that the schoolmaster was a Roman Catholic priest from Syria and the printer, originally from Beirut, was a Maronite. Even that did not dampen his enthusiasm. "To hear a learned Turk [Nureddin] speak deliberately of attempting to civilize his countrymen produced a peculiar effect on my mind," Fisk wrote. "Peculiarly affected," too, were his "feelings" when he spied an Arab boy setting type for the institute's press to print in Arabic a tract on the Lancastrian system of education that Fisk himself had been circulating in Cairo; plans were also afoot to produce a newspaper in Arabic.

No wonder the pasha's institute worked so powerfully on Fisk, drawing him back again and again. Here were grounds to wonder whether it would be Muslims or Roman Catholics rather than Anglo-American Protestants who made the printing press their engine to transform the Ottoman Empire. But if that thought crossed Fisk's mind, he did not express it. Instead, he found at the pasha's institute firm grounds for hope that evangelical missionaries would find among Egypt's Muslims avid readers of the printed page—perhaps even of Christian books and tracts. Here, too, he saw evidence—the school, the library, the printing press, the Muslim Nureddin himself—that once and for all laid to rest the notion that Islam itself opposed reason, education, and progress. Henry Martyn was right, and the implications were enormous. If Persia was no anomaly, an evangelical missionary to Egypt or anywhere in the Islamic world might follow in his heroic footsteps. But was the future of the Islamic world augured by the promise of the pasha's institute—or by the prospect of forced conversions among the defeated Greeks?[15]

By now, Fisk had picked up the traveler's trick of taming the new by relating it to the known. On his way up the Nile at the beginning of March 1822, he compared its width with that of the Connecticut River at Greenfield, Massachusetts, a few miles downhill from his boyhood home. Making his way downriver to Cairo nearly a month later, he observed that the people living along the banks "in their dress, food, and houses are almost perfectly in the same condition as the Negroes in the Southern states." But there was much more on his mind than the scene floating by the boat, and he hinted at it in a private journal entry: after "considerable reflection," he had decided to return to Alexandria and from there to sail back to Malta. *Malta?* Fisk had again postponed his trip to Jerusalem and for too many reasons, each a little lame. There was the arrival at Malta of Daniel and Rachel Temple, a missionary couple from New England; there was the chance for a cheap passage to that island; there was the report of disturbances in Syria; there was the desire to improve his Arabic.[16]

More likely, it was Osman who changed Fisk's plans. Taking his farewell, Fisk presented the dragoman with a copy of Martyn's memoir, and the two "conversed sometime." What they talked about emerges in Fisk's private journal once he reached Alexandria on March 27 and boarded the brig *Sicily*, the vessel promising bargain passage to Malta. That very day, he received a letter from George English: the renegade wished to meet. How did English know where to find Fisk—or even that he had returned to Alexandria? And why, after shunning Fisk's overture back in January, was English suddenly so eager for "an interview"? The two men did meet on the following day, and on April 1 Fisk abruptly jumped ship. He left the *Sicily* and—as his private journal announced in large letters—"embarked with Mr. English on board the Brig *Despatch*, Captain John Finley, for Malta."[17]

This trail of evidence leaves little doubt that George English was sneaking out of Egypt, and Pliny Fisk was helping him. Here is the scenario that best fits the facts: When Fisk turned up in Cairo, Osman saw in the American missionary a chance to arrange English's safe passage from Egypt. Their week touring Cairo together gave the dragoman plenty of time to size him up—and to persuade Fisk that English, like Osman himself—had not made a true conversion to Islam. Of course, a zealous minister of the gospel such as Fisk might even bring about English's heartfelt restoration to the Christian fold. At their last meeting, Osman sprang his scheme, asking Fisk to meet English at Alexandria and assist his escape to Malta. Fisk might have agreed immediately to the plan or only to consider it; in either event, Osman sent word to English in Alexandria that the American missionary was headed his way, and their first meeting on March 28 clinched the deal. Most likely it was Peter Lee—recall his boasting earlier about "privately" helping other renegades to escape—who settled on the *Despatch* as a safer vessel for English's escape. Likely, too, when the two men went aboard on April 1, English was posing as a servant—a subterfuge favored by renegades on the lam—which explains why Fisk paid for his passage.[18]

It is not hard to imagine why Fisk, always a sucker for secrets, went along. What better opportunity to explore Islam than with one who knew its beliefs and rituals from the inside? And what glee at the board back in Boston should Fisk reclaim this notorious renegade! Then there was the intoxicating whiff of danger: spiriting English out of Egypt was not in the same league with Captain Hamilton's jumping from the burning deck of the *Ajax*, yet it was a small, stealthy jab at the Ottomans. Fisk might never persuade a Muslim to take up the cross, but he might snatch a New Englander from the clutches of the crescent. More puzzling is why George English, a high-ranking officer in Mehmet Ali's army and one who had written a treatise in defense of Islam, was looking for a way out of Egypt. Had he become the classic repentant renegade, that figure so familiar in the imaginations of Westerners? Had he embraced Islam out of expedience and then come to regret his reckless, wicked choice?[19]

To search out an answer, follow English through his years in Egypt until his escape with Fisk. Everyone who knew him there—except for Osman—felt certain that English had accepted Islam out of "principle" rather than "convenience." George Waddington and Barnard Hanbury, the two British travelers who snubbed English as a despised renegade in the Sudan, described him as having accepted Islam "from conviction" and added that he even hoped to publish his manuscript arguing for Islam's superiority to Christianity. Both British consuls in Egypt, Peter Lee and Henry Salt, agreed that English's profession of Islam was heartfelt. And then there was English's long association with a sailor from New York whom he had met in Cairo and persuaded to take the turban and with it the new name of Khalil Aga. He followed English up the Nile, acting as his all-purpose factotum—shaving him and scaring up food—and then back to Alexandria on a harrowing trek through the desert. All the while Khalil kept a small journal littered with mentions of "Mohammed Effendi"; not once did he use English's Christian name. Some ten years later, an American in Turkey reported that Khalil Aga was still living in Egypt, still in the pasha's service, and still, evidently, a Muslim.[20]

But the strongest testimony to English's embrace of Islam comes from a man who knew more about apostasy than any renegade. Enter the Reverend Joseph Wolff, easily the gaudiest Western eccentric in the lush field of the early nineteenth-century Levant and the one who had taken the longest, strangest trip to get there. Born in Bavaria in 1795, the son of a rabbi, Wolff, for reasons never explained in his many memoirs, converted to Roman Catholicism at the age of seventeen. That first apostasy put the quick-witted young man with a flair for languages on a fast track to the College of Propaganda in Rome, the Vatican's boot camp for future missionaries. Denying papal infallibility got him excommunicated—or so Wolff claimed—and shortly thereafter he landed in the company of some well-heeled Anglican evangelicals who had big plans for this lapsed Catholic Jew. Wolff's particular patron was Henry Drummond, that archconservative, rabidly anti-Catholic, proto-Fundamentalist printer of Bibles and financial angel to the London Society for Promoting Christianity Among the Jews. Drummond's money sent Wolff to Cambridge and then financed his first missionary tour of the Mediterranean. Newly ordained in the Church of England, Wolff had just begun his journey when he came across English in September 1821. The two latched onto each other aboard a canal boat at Alexandria and sparred all the way to Cairo.[21]

It was kismet: a Jew turned Christian angled for the soul of a Christian (and an unwavering critic of efforts to convert the Jews) turned Muslim. "Mahomed Effendi (once Mr. English,) soon gave me his confidence," Wolff reported in his journal, "telling me the history of his turning to Mahomedanism from principle." According to English, his conversion had turned on his judgment concerning the authenticity of scriptures. He professed to accept the first five books of the Old Testament and the Qur'an as divine revelation but not the New Testament. From that exchange and many which followed, Wolff concluded that "the sincerity of his [English's] turning to Mahomed is not to be doubted." To show that he meant business, English swore, "If I ever can persuade myself that Mahomed was a mere enthusiast, I will renounce his religion at the risk of my life." To show that he, too, meant business, Wolff began his campaign by lending English his copy of Henry Martyn's memoir.[22]

As those two had floated from Alexandria to Cairo in the fall of 1821, English—besides smoking and disputing with Wolff—was mulling over how he might gain dismissal from Mehmet Ali's service with his head still attached to his shoulders. English had not had a good war in the Sudan. Plagued by eye trouble, he had joined the army late and left it early. His fellow renegade Khalil Aga described the expedition as "twelve months of misery and starvation," and he and English barely survived the return trip through the desert. Nothing could have prepared them for the sheer brutality of the campaign. What they had believed to be an incursion against "brigands" pillaging Upper Egypt was, in fact, a raid to provide conscripts for Mehmet Ali's army. In the single year that English served, the pasha's troops seized and sent north nearly two thousand men, women, and children; they forced some into the army and sold others as slaves. Once back in Cairo, he groused to his friend Osman that "he had been disappointed in respect to his pay and other things by the Turks and was wretched enough."[23]

But leaving Egypt was no simple matter for any renegade—especially for an army officer already at the end of the pasha's patience for deserting his command in the Sudan. Trying to escape the country now would be tantamount to renouncing Islam, for which, as English well knew, the penalty was death. Yes, taking the turban off would be trickier than putting it on. But do it he must.

English had realized as much the instant that Waddington and Hanbury looked down their long British noses at him back in the Sudan. True, Muhammad and his faith had received more sympathetic treatment in the popular press during the second decade of the nineteenth century, but most Americans and Britons would not look kindly on one of their own who had judged Islam superior to Christianity, especially now, in the wake of the Ottomans' repression of the Greek rebellion. No, a man with his big plans could not return to the West as a professing Muslim. Once in London, he hoped to publish a book about his travels in the Sudan, to garner acclaim for traveling farther up the Nile than most Westerners, and to rub shoulders with the bon ton of British scientists, explorers, and antiquarians in the Royal Society and the African Association. Then he would set sail for the United States, where his old friend John Quincy Adams was still the secretary of state and still in need of a treaty securing American merchant ships access to the Black Sea. Who better than English to become his man in Constantinople? So many fair prospects, and all English needed was what many other Americans in the Middle East have needed ever since: an exit strategy.

Here is where Wolff, and later Fisk, entered English's plans. His scheme for safely shedding his renegade status and returning to the good graces of those in the West inspired the passage of events that, had it been an Elizabethan play, would have been titled *The Renegade's Repentance*. Once he was back in Cairo and the good company of Osman, a plan took shape in English's mind. It began with his cultivating Joseph Wolff, his new acquaintance and unwitting partner in this bit of stagecraft, who suddenly noticed that his new renegade friend was softening toward Christianity, perhaps even sinking into the melancholy that preceded an evangelical conviction of sinfulness. By October 1821, English was telling Wolff that "a good Christian is better than a good Mussulman" and that "Christianity speaks to the heart," while the "Mahomedan trembles and fears."

Heady stuff for a novice missionary, especially when English confided that he had "written against Christianity for many, many years, and have perverted many," but if ever brought to recant, he would "write the motives of my final reconciliation with Christianity." Miraculously, a month later, English told him that he had "given up the idea of remaining a mahomedan." Wolff modestly disclaimed any credit, and in fact he had a great deal to be modest about. He hadn't even made it to the end of the Qur'an, and he found nothing fishy about English's explanation that his renewed Christian piety prompted him to pray five times a day. Nor did it strike Wolff as odd that the other American renegade, Khalil Aga, also fell into "a very distressed state," as if on cue, at exactly the same time as did English. This show of taking off the turban and putting on Jesus succeeded brilliantly. Completely gulled, Wolff spent the last months of 1821 trumpeting his triumphs among the renegades to Peter Lee in Alexandria and his benefactors back in England.[24]

English made sure that those letters singled out Henry Salt for lavish praise. Wolff described the British consul's Cairo home as a veritable nursery of Christian piety for recovering renegades—English, Khalil Aga, and even Osman. In fact, all three were in Salt's debt for food, lodging, and, in Osman's case, steady employment. In return, they provided him with antiquities to pass along to private collectors and the British Museum and with geographic knowledge to impart to the African Association. While in the Sudan, English had gathered fragments of ancient pottery for Salt, as well as passing along reports about pyramids and other monuments. Khalil had trooped about Upper Egypt scribbling Salt's name on choice statues for future pickup and presented him with his journal of the Sudan expedition. Even Wolff snooped around Greek convents on Mount Lebanon, searching for manuscripts about the Crusades. It all went into winning what Salt lusted after, a roar of recognition from London's Orientalist lions. But to succeed at social climbing, he also needed to burnish his reputation as a Christian gentleman, and here English was pleased to oblige. Reading off a script that English supplied, Wolff's letters to England emphasized that the renegades' changes of heart owed everything to pious encouragement from Salt himself. Laying it on with a trowel, English added that the good consul had also vanquished "his prejudice as an American against the English nation."[25]

English thus secured the assistance of both Wolff and Salt in escaping the reach of the pasha's power. Their connections would prove useful, too, as English made his way in London society. Most important, he would reenter the West not as a renegade but as a prodigal, always so winning to evangelicals. Being English, he also left himself some room to maneuver, just in case the pasha caught wind of his escape plans. While declaring that he had renounced Islam and making a show of pious repentance, English described himself as still "wavering" in his religious convictions even at his last meetings with Wolff. What a relief it must have been to give over his charade and disgorge the truth to Fisk once aboard their vessel and bound for Malta—probably no sooner than Alexandria sank beneath the horizon. Now English risked nothing by candor. No way would Fisk ever confess to the board that he had taken the risk of rescuing the most notorious American Muslim.

The two spent more than a month together during the spring of 1822. They shared a cabin aboard the *Despatch* throughout the trip to Malta and then a room at Valletta's lazaretto. All the while they engaged in "repeated and long conversations," during which Pliny Fisk learned why George English was a hard man to forget and an even harder one to know. Alas, Fisk disclosed little of what he found out; his official and even his private journals fall silent on those "long conversations." Nothing could be more out of character, given his anticipation of their encounter, as well as his habit of writing down important exchanges about religion. Had English confessed that he turned Turk only to get a commission in the pasha's army and yearned to return to the Christian fold, Fisk would have broadcast the news to Boston in a heartbeat. But he did not so much as mention English's name in any of his dispatches to the board or even to friends and family back in the United States. After their embarking for Malta, Fisk's only reference to English in his American correspondence appears in a letter he wrote in Valletta's lazaretto to a woman friend in Massachusetts. He described his "unspeakable satisfaction" at "passing most of the day alone" in the lazaretto, as "the gentleman who had occupied the room with me had gone aboard a vessel in the harbor." What a trial it was, he continued, "to be constantly in a small cabin with men of the world, where if you speak of religion at all, conversation will often take such a turn, that you will wish you had not mentioned it." That unnamed "gentleman" was George English.[26]

What had English revealed during their time together that Fisk could not bring himself to recount at any length? The only direct evidence comes from a letter that he wrote to English in May 1822, shortly before the two left quarantine at Valletta. For the last several weeks—as their vessel pitched toward Malta and then as they lodged together in the lazaretto—he had listened—just as Levi Parsons had counseled, with candor, impartiality, and patience—while English held forth. Then the two engaged in a protracted debate about religion during which the renegade vented the depth of his contempt for orthodox Christianity. Fisk's parting letter blasted English for having a "temper of heart" so perverse that "obstinate hostility to the truth is the prevailing temper of your soul." But the worst of it was that English had "known something about the gospel, and the way of life by Jesus Christ, and you have rejected it and I greatly fear you hate it." It was unlike Fisk, this impassioned outpouring, but then, he had lost his dearest friend and risked his own life for the conviction that receiving the gospel would turn all the world's people into evangelical Protestants. English's life defied—even mocked—that faith. By the end of their weeks together,

English's own religious beliefs had become so familiar to Fisk that he did not bother to set them down in detail, but his parting letter disclosed that the renegade had railed against Trinitarian Christianity and "in favor of Judaism, Mohammedanism, and Socinianism." There it was: English still embraced some Muslim beliefs in some form.[27]

There were other Westerners like him who found much in Islam that answered. Such men went beyond the shape-shifting Talamash—the Frenchman who, among his many incarnations, played Persian dervish. They were not taking hold of other cultures to test their powers of disguise or their capacity for spur-of-the-moment self-invention. On the contrary, Islam had taken hold of them, spiritually colonizing their hearts, minds, and souls. Listening to English, Fisk might have recalled Henry Martyn's description of a gentleman back in Bengal, a fellow member of the East India Company and one "advanced in years, and occupying a situation of great respectability," who lived "in a state of daring apostasy from the Christian faith, and openly professing his preference for Mohammedanism. He had even built a mosque of his own." An even closer parallel had come to Fisk's notice from Osman, who had once served as a retainer to the Swiss explorer John Lewis Burckhardt. Henry Salt sketched him at Cairo in 1817, portraying his friend dressed in a burnoose and turban. By then, Burckhardt's affinity with Islam was more than costume-deep: as he lay dying only a few months later, the explorer requested Muslim funeral rites—even though he never declared himself a convert. Unlike Burckhardt, English survived Egypt, and right before or after he sailed from Alexandria for the last time, he put off his robe, doffed his turban, and reclaimed his Christian name. Yet Islam still shaped his religious outlook. Like Burckhardt, he was not a cultural chameleon, not a mere spiritual voyeur spying on the Muslim world from within. He was yet another Westerner who had felt the force of "the hidden man of Islamism."[28]

Fisk's shadowing English from Alexandria to Cairo and back seems almost a pursuit. Irresistibly drawn on, he was as fascinated as he was repelled by English's embrace of Islam but unable to keep himself from trying to close in on the secret, to solve the mystery. The man's career so starkly defied his expectations—and the entire premise of the missions movement—that greater knowledge of the world's religions would turn pagans, Jews, and Muslims into evangelical Protestants. English's spiritual pilgrimage, to say nothing of those made by other once-Christian renegades, attested instead to Islam's appeal. How many more would follow? Would evangelical expectations be turned upside down? Would it be the Muslims who converted the world?

It is only in retrospect that those fears seem outsized. Consider how dramatically the globe was shrinking and how fully evangelicals grasped the implications of that fact. Improvements in transportation were making it faster and safer for travelers to reach far-flung destinations. At the same time, print's engines brought to more readers descriptions, accurate and otherwise, of Islam and the world's other religions. Probably no single agency contributed to that information revolution more than the foreign missions movement, with its publishing industry turning out magazines and books. Finally, knowledge about other faiths was reaching more Western Christians as disestablishment proceeded apace on both sides of the Atlantic, making religious belief a matter of individual choice. With all those influences opening up new realms of spiritual possibility, what Fisk glimpsed in English was a harbinger of the way that history was headed. In a smaller world blanketed in a blizzard of print, it was inevitable that seekers would multiply, especially in the West. And if English was any weather vane, the winds of change would carry some of them into Islam.

Fisk's fellow missionaries betrayed the same anxiety about Islam's appeal. Henry Martyn nervously joked more than once about the possibility of his embracing Islam, and even wrote to a colleague that because he read the Qur'an aloud and drank no wine, "the slander has gone forth" among his Christian neighbors in Bengal that he had "turned Mussulman." But privately, Martyn was not amused: he admitted to the fear that studying the Qur'an might draw him into Unitarianism or deism, even into the thrall of Islam itself. Troubled "with infidel thoughts, which originated perhaps from the cavillings of the Mohammedans about the person of Christ," he insisted that such doubts, although momentary, sometimes "penetrated more deeply," teaching him "that the grace of a covenant God can alone keep me from apostasy and ruin." In a similar vein, William Jowett confided to his diary a Greek Orthodox bishop's warning that Franks who went to Muslim teachers to learn Arabic, Turkish, or Greek found that "after the first lesson or two, they will begin to persuade their pupils to turn

Turk." With an almost audible gulp, Jowett "asked whether they would in this way trouble an Englishman, like myself, coming with good patronage and protection." "Not exactly in this way," the bishop replied, "but by degrees they would flatter, and say, what a pity, that a man of so much learning and genius should be in the way of error!"

What made them feel so vulnerable? Why did Jowett and Martyn fear that even well-educated Western Protestants such as they were (and as George English had once been) might succumb to Islam? The answer lies in the evangelical invention of that rival faith as a creed similar to the radical monotheisms of the West, the liberal, rationalist religions of Unitarianism and deism. Attacks on their enemies provided one venue for that process. Trinitarian Christians had dissed Unitarians and deists for centuries by charging their creeds were halfway houses on the road to Islam. Hence his enemies labeled the Socinian Joseph Priestley "half a Mahometan." Hence the English Baptist preacher John Macgowan gibed that the really interesting question was "whether the Mohammedans shall receive the prophet Jesus . . . or Rational Christians shall receive the prophet Mohammed." Hence William Jowett alluded to the "Unitarianism of the Mahomedan," and the Maine Baptist preacher Daniel Merrill "exposed" Unitarians as "Mahomedan Christians." Hence the satirist Samuel Knapp's fictional Ali Bey calculated that Boston's Unitarians would support his schemes for converting the United States to Islam. And then there was the Methodist leader Charles Wesley, who versified about Muhammad, "Stretch out thine arm, Thou Triune God! / The Unitarian fiend expel / And chase his doctrine back to hell."

Missionary narratives—most notably, Sargent's memoir of Martyn—also contributed to the evangelical invention of Islam as a form of religious rationalism. Far from posing obstacles to learning and intellectual exchange, the Islam professed by Martyn's learned Muslim circles in Shiraz won and held adherents by appealing to their reason. In a sense, that power to command the mind's assent was for Martyn "the hidden man of Islamism."[29]

Through such evangelical devising, Islam morphed into a kind of Unitarianism East. That's not surprising: this invention marked only the latest, but not the last, chapter in a long history of Western Christians remodeling Islam to mirror their own immediate religious anxieties and casting Muslims in the image of heretics and unorthodox

Pliny Fisk
(Alvan Bond, *Memoir of Fisk*
[Boston, 1828], frontispiece)

Levi Parsons
(Daniel O. Morton, *Memoir of Parsons*
[Poultney, Vt., 1824], frontispiece)

William Bentley
(Peabody Essex Museum, Salem, Massachusetts)

Jedidiah Morse
(Painting by Samuel F. B. Morse, Yale University Art Gallery)

Henry Martyn
(Cambridge University)

Jeremiah Evarts
(Philip Schaff Library, Lancaster Theological Seminary)

Sir William Jones
(Engraving by William Evans after A. W. Devis [London, 1798])

What Fisk and Parsons would have seen as their ship entered the harbor at Smyrna
(Lithograph from Eugène Napoléon Flandin, *L'Orient* 1 [Paris, 1853])

The wooden houses and narrow streets of early nineteenth-century Smyrna
(Edmund Spencer, *Turkey, Russia, the Black Sea, and Circassia* [London, 1854])

Mehmet Ali, pasha of Egypt
(J. Madox, *Excursions in the Holy Land* [London, 1834])

Jonas King
(Isaac Bird, *Bible Work in Bible Lands* [Philadelphia, 1872])

Joseph Wolff
(Joseph Wolff, *Narrative of a Mission to Bokhara in the
Years 1843–1845* [London, 1846], frontispiece)

The rooftops of Jerusalem
(Louis Lortet, *La Syrie d'adjourd'hui: voyages dans la Phénicie,
le Liban, et la Judée, 1875–1880* [Paris, 1884])

Acre with the al-Jazzar Mosque in the foreground as depicted by a British artist in the 1830s
*(Syria, the Holy Land, and Asia Minor in a Series of Views Drawn from Nature by W. H. Bartlett and William Purser with Descriptions of the Plates by John Carne* [London, 1836], p. 29)

The Plain of Esdraelon inspired not only Jonas King but also the Scottish artist David Roberts, who visited the Levant in the late 1830s. His paintings and lithographs of Biblical sites found a wide audience in the West. Christian pilgrims appear in the foreground of this piece.
*(The Holy Land: From Drawings Made on the Spot by David Roberts, R.A., with Historical Descriptions by the Rev. George Croly, L.L.D.* [New York: Rizzoli, 2000], 110–11)

Christians closer to home. What's ironic is that evangelicals found Islam so threatening not because they understood it as an alien and exotic Other but because they identified it as something altogether familiar— as yet another form of religious rationalism. In doing so, they became persuaded that this rival faith possessed the potential to draw many admirers, even converts in the West, perhaps especially from the ranks of deists and those Protestants who had abandoned or doubted Trinitarianism. Here was a prospect that raised even more pointedly the possibility that evangelicals might not own the future. Would these faiths of elegant theological simplicity—Islam and deism and Unitarianism— prove more appealing in a post-Enlightenment world than Trinitarian Christianity? Could it be that Joseph Priestley was right when he advised that Christians bent on converting Jews and Muslims would improve their chances by embracing Unitarianism? Were evangelicals and their missions on the wrong side of history?[30]

Being written here, too, was another chapter in the depiction of Islam as a religion for the West to fear and hate. While that antipathy has long figured as a strain in Western thought, its sources have shifted over the centuries. What inspired its first chapter was the dread of conquest by Muslim forces, from Muhammad's followers storming out of the Arabian Peninsula in the seventh century to the Ottoman Turks knocking at the gates of Vienna in the sixteenth century. What authors its most recent chapter is the terrorism of Islamic extremists, etched in the world's memory by the sight of planes slicing into the World Trade Center and plowing into the Pentagon in September 2001. But in the eighteenth and nineteenth centuries, even as many condemned the Muslim Turks' brutal treatment of Balkans and Christians, Westerners no longer feared their own peoples falling victim to violence from the forces of Islam. Far more directly troubling to the evangelicals among them were that faith's affinities with liberal Christianity and other forms of religious rationalism, with their shared emphasis on radical monotheism and moral duty. It was that conjunction which aroused profound anxieties among evangelicals for their own future success, lending the fear and loathing of Islam another lease on life.

Paradoxically, evangelicals also drew confidence from the kinship they detected between Islam and all forms of Christian belief—including their own. True, their rhetoric routinely juxtaposed the "darkness" of Muslim beliefs to the "light" of Christianity, but when beating the drum for missions, evangelicals often pointed up some of the common elements of the two faiths. In 1784, the Oxford don Joseph White promoted planting Protestant missions in India on the grounds that the Muslims there were not "in a state of barbarism" but "already a race of men and citizens, who by an easy transition might pass to a full belief of the doctrines of Christ." After all, Islam had prepared its adherents to "embrace the argument from prophecy," which also formed the basis of Christianity. A more frequent evangelical refrain was that Islam itself had spun off from Christianity. The American Board missionary Samuel Newell urged the translation of the Bible into Arabic and Persian, because, in his view, their speakers "rank as high on the scale of intellect as any people in the world." What augured the imminent success of spreading the gospel was that "Mussulmans are a kind of heretical Christians," a judgment echoing Henry Martyn, who, several years earlier, had characterized Islam as "a species of heretical Christianity." To early nineteenth-century evangelicals, then, Islam was at once a distinct, "dark" world religion and a kind of off-brand Christianity.[31]

The notion of Islam as a Christian heresy was by then a very old invention. It hatched in the brain of an eighth-century Byzantine bureaucrat turned monk known as John of Damascus, who included Muslims among the many heretics whom he denounced for departing from Eastern Christian teachings. His charge caught on in the West: for centuries thereafter, Christian polemicists dismissed Islam as a hodgepodge of Arab superstitions and borrowings from Judeo-Christian doctrines dreamed up by an ambitious impostor who, even with the devil's help, could not manage to concoct a better religion. But another, far smaller group of medieval Christian thinkers put a more positive spin on the idea that Islam was a Christian heresy, transforming what had been a slur against the Muslims into the grounds for optimism about prospects for converting them. It was this tradition that nineteenth-century evangelical missionaries carried forward.[32]

Preaching that message came at a price. If talking up Islam as a Christian heresy made the conversion of the Muslim world appear a more attainable goal, it also blurred the boundaries between the two faiths that missions were meant to reinforce. In turn, that obscuring of spiritual borders only heightened evangelical anxieties about the likelihood of Christian apostasies to Islam. After all, if Samuel Newell was right—that it wouldn't take much doing to bring Muslims back to the

Christian fold because the two faiths were so closely related—then by the same reasoning Christians would just as easily fall into the embrace of Islam. More easily, it seemed: as William Jowett's writings on renegades publicized so widely in evangelical circles, Christians in Ottoman domains turned Turk far more often than Muslims turned Christian.

It would not be surprising, then, if Pliny Fisk had felt apprehensive about finally coming face-to-face with an American Muslim. Certainly by the time they reached the lazaretto at Malta, he heartily wished English gone. It was unsettling, living so long and in such close quarters with a man rendered nearly unrecognizable by the distance he had traveled from the faith in which he had been bred. His was a spiritual journey that spoke powerfully to how porous and unstable the frontier was between Christianity and Islam, how easily a person might slip across that border. The worst of it was that Fisk had to wonder whether he himself was starting down the same path. Hadn't his experiences over the last two years in the Levant drawn him to recognize the many affinities between Christianity and Islam—even to suspect that the distance between East and West might be narrower than portrayed by that swelling chorus in Europe and America who were proclaiming it a chasm? Some of those revelations he owed to his own experience with Muslims like the Moroccan bibliophile Mohamed in Smyrna and Nureddin, the head of the pasha's institute, men cast in the mold of Henry Martyn's mujtahid scholars. Others had come in the course of his reading authors like d'Ohsson. And still others flowed from the pens and fell from the lips of his fellow evangelical missionaries.

"A man of the world": that was Pliny Fisk's final verdict on George English. But it would be more accurate to describe English as a man of many worlds, and Fisk knew it. True, by all reliable accounts, English had converted to Islam out of principle, and if his explanation to Joseph Wolff can be credited, he took the Qur'an to be a revelation superior to the Gospels. Yet in his farewell letter to English, Fisk described him as embracing a religious outlook that combined Islam with elements of Christian rationalism (in this case, Socinianism) and Judaism. English seems to have understood the three faiths as kindred monotheistic traditions, each offering some measure of truth and guidance, each worshipping the same God. From that insight, he had fashioned a belief system without spiritual borders, blurring East and West by drawing from different traditions to construct a syncretic personal theology. That made George English as unorthodox a Muslim as he had once been a Christian, a renegade from every form of fixed religious belief and loyalty.

It also made English even more threatening to Fisk than if he had professed himself committed to Islam alone. True believers, even true disbelievers like Dr. Marpurgo, made sense to Fisk—or more sense than the limber, eclectic English with his signature creed. It disgusted Fisk, what he regarded as the man's dog's breakfast of religious borrowings from Islam, Christianity, and Judaism and one that denied what evangelicals sought to affirm above all else—the special status of Protestant Christianity among revealed religions. It was also a tough set of convictions for Fisk to dispute. If English had been a radical deist like Marpurgo, dismissing all sacred scriptures as so many bogus fictions, Fisk would have known how to argue against him. But English had reached a conclusion still novel in the early nineteenth century. Unlike those religious liberals who believed that Islam, Judaism, and Christianity were all tolerable enough so long as they upheld decency and morality, he had come to the conclusion that each in its own way was *right*. That made English the avatar of a spirituality lived by so many people in the United States today that it is easy to overlook its relatively recent appearance in the West. English's position was an alloy of universalism (all religions have value) and individualism (so pick and choose the best elements from among them). An evangelical like Fisk found that smorgasbord spirituality much trickier to answer than outright unbelief, because it ruled out dismissing English as a miserable infidel who worshipped only his own reason. In fact, English was a man of faith—entirely too many faiths, in Fisk's view.[33]

The whole truth about their encounter would remain one of Pliny Fisk's secrets. By the middle of April 1822, he was making his excuses to Jeremiah Evarts for not being in Jerusalem. Though at the time he and English still shared the same small room in Malta's lazaretto, Fisk resorted to the vaguest explanations for his retreat from the mission field. What had knocked the stuffing out of him, he told Evarts, were "the journeys and voyages, the studies and anxieties, the scenes of Plague and Massacre, and the various disappointments of the last two years . . . and especially after the sickness and death of my Colleague and Brother." He had returned to Malta that "I might collect my scattered thoughts, review the way by which the Lord has led me, and as I hope, set out again with renewed strength of body and mind." That had been Fisk's hegira: a long flight from the horrors of the Greek Revolution and from the loss of Levi Parsons. He was fleeing still, striving to hold at bay all of the anxious doubts aroused by his "studies" of Islam and then deepened by the "disappointments" of his weeks with an American renegade.

Nothing had done more to batter Fisk's confidence in himself, in his faith, and in his mission than their time together. It had all the more impact coming at the end of the long period of his discovering that Islam had undergone many inventions by Western Christians and that credible alternatives existed to the evangelical version in which he had first been schooled. Evidence of that recognition appears in the advice that Fisk, around the time he parted with English, offered to an aspiring Andover missionary. He urged that the best preparation for proselytizing among Muslims was reading both George Sale's translation of the Qur'an and his preliminary discourse, with its spirited defense of Muhammad.[34]

As for English, he had come to the end of one hegira and the beginning of another: the flight from his reputation as a renegade. By now he was an accomplished escape artist who knew, if nothing else, how to cut his losses. From Malta, he made straight for London and another reinvention. He swaggered in that city's learned circles on the strength of his book about the Sudan expedition, but before its publication one small matter had demanded his attention. His old nemesis from their Sudan days who had never forgotten or forgiven that English turned Turk, George Waddington, had published his own book of Ethiopian travels, and in it he fingered the American as a renegade. Why, it was "an account of me not a little fabulous," English countered and demanded a retraction. Waddington duly apologized—or so English assured the readers of his Sudan book, which he dedicated to Henry Salt and published in London late in 1822.[35]

Meanwhile, in the United States, English's father and friends prepared the way for his rehabilitation at home. A few newspapers printed what purported to be a letter from English to his father in which he represented the Sudan campaign as a "romantic and fortunate expedition," a "most complete success" that had made him "the first civilized man" to have reached the main branch of the Nile. A less delusional but equally exculpatory spin of English's entire career came from a fellow Harvard graduate who identified himself only as a college friend; the piece achieved wide circulation in newspapers from Maine to Virginia. It acknowledged English's long history of "unsettled" religious views but described him as "a gentleman of amiable disposition, of frank and simple manners and of pure morals" whose career "well illustrates the enterprise of the American character" epitomized by Harvard men. As for English's conversion to Islam, "nothing certain is known." Surely he would clear up the matter upon returning to the United States.[36]

English did come back, but not for long. By 1823, he was living in Constantinople, dispatched there as the new secret agent of John Quincy Adams, who was still seeking navigation rights to the Black Sea for U.S. vessels. "I pass for an American mussulman who has come from a far distant country to visit the capital of Islam," he reported to his longtime patron. He failed in that mission, as Luther Bradish had before him; shortly thereafter, Adams secured English another job as an interpreter for a diplomatic mission to the Ottomans. But by the summer of 1828, even Adams had lost patience with his old friend. He had "repeatedly procured employment" for English, Adams complained to his diary, "notwithstanding his eccentricities, approaching to insanity," but now he could "no longer sustain him." English died of causes unknown at the age of forty-one during the fall of that year in Washington, D.C., still denying that he had ever turned Turk.[37]

*Part Four*

# THE HIDDEN MAN

# 8

## EPIPHANIES

God is the Light of the heavens and earth. His Light is like this: there is a niche, and in it a lamp, the lamp inside a glass, a glass like a glittering star, fuelled from a blessed olive tree from neither east nor west, whose oil almost gives light even when no fire touches it—light upon light—God guides whoever He will to his Light; God draws such comparisons for people; God has full knowledge of everything—shining out in houses of worship.

—Qur'an, Light, 24:35–36

Victory! No sooner had he settled into the diligence than the merchant from Lyon asked why he'd pointed toward heaven when parting from his friend. The two hoped to meet there one day, he replied, loud enough for all in the big carriage to hear. The merchant took him up, raising questions about the Bible's authenticity, which he answered so easily that even before they reached the outskirts of Paris, this same intelligent, respectable gentleman was helping him hand out tracts at every stop. Yet more triumphs followed as the diligence lumbered southward. He defended the Bible to three infidel army officers, who at first thought him a fool. Set beside the wisdom of revelation, he assured them, Rousseau and Voltaire were "mere pygmies," and only half an hour of his preaching persuaded them to purchase Bibles and the other passengers to join in scattering tracts whenever the carriage halted.

So unbounded, the enthusiasms of the French: maybe it did happen that way. But most likely it did not, because Jonas King had as boundless a talent for embroidering a tapestry of exaggerations, half-truths, and outright lies when recounting his life and times. He was working it hard with this account of journeying from Paris to Marseilles and thence to Malta, intent on impressing his new patron. King had been cultivating Sampson Vryling Stoddard Wilder for several months, passing every Sabbath in his richly appointed Paris parlor and finally moving in with the family. But who could have guessed that his connection with Wilder would prove so useful so quickly? When Pliny Fisk's letter arrived, asking King to replace Parsons in the Palestine mission, it was Wilder who stepped up with the money—his own matched by donations from other pious men of business in Europe. They became the charter members of the evangelical Paris Missionary Society and the patrons who sponsored King's new partnership with Fisk.

A protégé of Jedidiah Morse's in his youth, Wilder had risen from clerking at a Boston dry goods store to agenting in Europe for the city's merchant princes. Making big money gave Wilder the taste for—and the willingness to believe—stories of succeeding against all odds. As a man who spent most days ensconced in a round chair of red morocco leather while bargaining for ladies' finery—silks and satins, gloves and hosiery, ribbons and fans—he also craved the frisson of secondhand adventure, preferably with a dash of danger. As the financial angel of the Paris Missionary Society, he felt entitled to that return on his investment. King was happy in his reports to scratch where his patron itched.

As the diligence jolted farther south, the installments to Wilder continued. Two of its passengers warned that Roman Catholic priests might try to have King arrested, and one of those "dark ministers" took a tract and then "retired hastily as if going to give information to some one respecting me." Despite those threats, King insisted, fear never found him. At the Roman ruins in Lyon, he declared to a crowd of visitors that he did not have "the sword of Hannibal or Caesar," but held the Bible before which "all the nations of the earth are destined to fall." He liked dropping his name into the same sentence with Napoleon's, too.[1]

King's doings did beckon danger—just not to himself. At real risk were those Protestants in and around Nîmes among whom he sojourned several days, promoting foreign missions. For more than a century, religious conflicts had seared the southwest of France, and only seven years before King's visit Catholics had massacred as many as a hundred of their Protestant neighbors. His proselytizing might well have reignited the violence, but that possibility seems not to have troubled King, who sailed from Marseilles for Malta by the end of October.

A few weeks later, he was surveying his new missionary associates at Valletta.[2]

It made a certain sense that Fisk had turned to him. Both had weathered straitened boyhoods among New Divinity believers in western Massachusetts and struggled to pay for college and seminary. Like Fisk, too, King had an ambition to rise above his origins that set him afire. "My heart would beat for hours at the thought of shining as a general or as a man of science," King recalled of his youth, "or of having my name uttered with respect by every child." And like Fisk—or anyone in flight from dread obscurity—he grasped every opportunity. Fresh out of Andover, King went to Charleston as a missionary to sailors and the poor, but he quickly sought choicer connections by wangling preaching gigs at the city's richest churches, where "I was thrown much into society with those who were considered the most polished people in the United States and had opportunity for improvement in many ways." From those Carolina ranks he might have plucked the private benefactor who supported his studying Arabic in Paris with the famed Orientalist Sylvestre de Sacy.

For all that, Fisk and King were not a pair. No intimacy had grown up at Andover between the jovial, robust Fisk and the humorless, hypochondriacal King. The Brethren did not tap him to enter their fraternity, most likely because he set his sights on a scholarly career, and when Fisk's letter found him at Paris in the spring of 1822, King had already agreed to become the first professor of Oriental languages at Amherst College. Then he reconnoitered: What better opportunity to perfect his Arabic than a few years in the Ottoman Empire? Returning to western Massachusetts—the eternal winters, the runny-nosed students, the chilblained faculty—could wait. Now that he had the ear—and the purse—of Sampson Wilder, bigger opportunities beckoned to make his mark in the world. For starters, he arranged for his missionary journals to reach not only his sponsors in Paris but also the American Board's audience in the United States.[3]

Well before swanning into Sampson Wilder's parlor, King had learned that the company one kept was important. So it must have pleased him to discover that Pliny Fisk was no longer the bumpkin that he—that they—had once been. Fisk was still recognizable from his Andover days. A British evangelical leader visiting the Levant described him as a man of "solid sense, amiable temper, and strong constitution." Yet two years of travel and study had rubbed down his rough edges; he spouted modern Greek, French, and Italian and enjoyed a hail-fellow-well-met familiarity with the British naval officers and the sea captains who frequented Valletta. Such enterprise could only have impressed his new partner.[4]

Less satisfactory to King was that his new circle also included Joseph Wolff. Another year's seasoning had made Wolff less green but, to King's discomfort, no less a Jew. At first, he could not mention the man's name without adding, "this Christian Jew," or "this Israelite indeed, in whom is no guile." Off-putting, too, was the "want of manly dignity" that King detected in Wolff's demeanor, "a child-like simplicity of manners." Not that there was anything wrong with that: such traits appealed to "thousands and tens of thousands" of his fellow Jews. Or so King assured the man who was still footing the bill for Wolff's travels, the proto-Fundamentalist Henry Drummond. Besides blanketing the Levant with Bibles, Drummond had founded the Continental Society, which dispatched evangelical missionaries to the cities of Catholic Europe. Its vice president happened to be Sampson Wilder, so it was probably at his and Drummond's urging that Wolff had agreed to shepherd the two American missionaries on their travels. After all, Wolff had spent the last year in and around Jerusalem, their ultimate destination, and besides having German and Hebrew, he was already fluent in English and Italian and quickly picking up Arabic and Persian.[5]

More to King's liking was the senior missionary in the Mediterranean, William Jowett. The consummate Christian gentleman, so well connected to such wealthy people and so many of them. What's more, believers on both sides of the Atlantic were buzzing over Jowett's recently published *Christian Researches in the Mediterranean*, which offered descriptions of all the Levant's religious groups along with suggestions for establishing missions there. By now he had become an even stauncher advocate of proselytizing among Muslims. Christianity would never "regain its empire in Mahomedan Countries," he declared, without the "zeal to propagate the Gospel, with the willingness to suffer for it." During his early years in the Mediterranean, Jowett had subscribed to the indirect, "domino" strategy of converting Muslims by first reforming Eastern Christians. He had urged, too, that only apostates from Islam would face danger from the authorities, not the Christians who converted them. Now he acknowledged that any missionary seeking Muslim converts ran the risk of martyrdom, for once within Ottoman domains he "has passed a boundary beyond which no earthly power is present to afford him competent protection." Only daring would carry the day: if a missionary were "to *dwell . . . two whole years* in one of their principal cities, as a preacher to the Native Mahomed-ans," he ventured, it would be "just possible, though scarcely to be expected, that the person might be safe." Whatever the cost, Jowett urged, missionaries must go beyond handing out tracts and testaments and begin preaching to Muslims. Once they had spent a few years learning the region's languages and customs, missionaries must "openly combat Mohammedanism."[6]

It was a call to spiritual warfare for the missionary circle gathered at Malta, but this time Pliny Fisk would not rally to that standard. If they tried preaching to Muslims, he shot back at Jowett, "we should in all probability lose our lives, or at least be expelled from the country." Not so long ago, Fisk had thought otherwise. Shortly after arriving in Turkey, he wrote to an Andover classmate that Christ's apostles "never thought of ceasing to *preach* because men threatened their lives." But two years in the field had changed his mind. The sultan might tolerate Christian missionaries within his domains to keep Western nations from formally allying with the Greeks, Fisk believed, but British and American sympathy for the rebels rankled Ottoman Muslims, which made it the worst time to start preaching against Islam. With scenes of the carnage in Smyrna and of Parsons's death still fresh in his mind, martyrdom had lost its glory for Fisk.

For King, it never held any allure. Even so, he assured Wilder that witnessing the two senior missionaries joined in this "impressive and solemn" debate about preaching to Muslims left him feeling "as though my own life was involved in it." Decades before the camera's invention, King could step straight into its eye. In fact, he was about to become a key player in this earliest evangelical encounter with the Muslim world, and his representation of its peoples would have a lasting effect on that movement's relationship to Islam. Over the next two years, King and Fisk became the first Americans—and among the few Westerners— to spend months at Jerusalem, Mount Lebanon, Beirut, and the coast in between, to sojourn at Damascus and Aleppo, to seek out the company of Muslims in all those places, to read the Qur'an in Arabic, and to study Muhammad's teachings. That time marked for Pliny Fisk a final, fateful engagement with Islam and its "hidden man." But for his new partner, revelations of another order awaited: insights into the potential of this rival creed for strengthening the evangelical movement itself back in the United States.[7]

Joseph Wolff needed no encouragement to offend Muslims' religious sensibilities. During his first tour of the Levant, he had shoved tracts into their hands, read aloud from the New Testament in their midst, and once left a stack of New Testaments for sale in a Turk's shop. Now, spurred on by Jowett, he gave even freer rein to what Pliny Fisk, in a long reach for euphemism, referred to as Wolff's "eccentricities." The trouble started as soon as he and the two American missionaries reached Egypt at the beginning of 1823 and made for Rosetta, a city nestled near the Mediterranean on the Nile's west bank among palm and citrus groves, marshes and rice paddies. Because he had the best command of Arabic, Wolff took the lead, paying the missionaries' respects to the city's governor and then responding to questions from the mullahs in his retinue about the meaning of verses in the Qur'an. Prudence would have dictated his backing down; instead, Wolff presented those assembled Muslim dignitaries with an Arabic translation of the New Testament, prompting the governor to object that "these books are not for us" because they "made mention of 'Son of God.'" Undeterred, Wolff then roamed Rosetta's dusty, narrow streets, preaching and hawking testaments. If swearing hadn't fallen so hard on Fisk's ears, Jowett's name—right after Wolff's—would have risen often to his lips.[8]

Rumbles of the protest roiling Rosetta reached Cairo along with the three missionaries, and the authorities instantly descended on Wolff. Osman Nureddin, the head of the pasha's institute and soon to become his army's chief of staff, patiently explained that Christian proselytizing "disturbs the *rest* and *peace* of mind of many." Ismael Gibraltar, the admiral of the navy, added less patiently that "if in England," he would "mount the pulpit and preach" on the hatreds dividing Christians and the many mistakes in the missionaries' translations of the Bible. A few days later, the vice-consul Peter Lee scolded all three missionaries for stirring up "fanaticism" and "tumult" among Rosetta's Muslims, and as they began their cruise along the Nile, the consul Henry Salt himself dispatched a letter warning them to confine their efforts entirely to

Christians, because otherwise "you may get into difficulties from which it may not be easy to extricate you." Those dressing-downs did not so much as dent Wolff, who preached and passed out scriptures to Muslims as far up the Nile as the three sailed.[9]

What finally stopped him were the rumors drifting upriver from Cairo. Word had it that war between the Ottoman Empire and western Europe was imminent, that Muslims had massacred all of the Franks in Constantinople, and that they meant to do the same in other cities. Dire reports, and Fisk credited them. Faced with the prospect of actual danger, King snapped at Wolff that "it really seems not to be the time yet to speak much about Christ with Mussulmen, for their hand . . . is too much coloured with the blood of men." Back to Cairo the three scurried, stopping at the outskirts of the city and sending word to Salt asking whether they might safely enter. It "filled our minds with anxiety," as Fisk acknowledged, both "complaints that have been presented to the Pasha concerning us and the reports of a general massacre at Constantinople." To settle their nerves, they prayed and reread the part of Martyn's memoir recounting his time in Persia.

The scare sputtered out in anticlimax. No massacre had taken place in Constantinople, Salt assured them, and even the anger of Rosetta's Muslims was smoldering out. Fisk took grim satisfaction from being confirmed "in the opinion I have for some time entertained that it is our duty . . . to labor principally and almost exclusively for the present among Christians and Jews." Irksome as that course might be to Jowett, Fisk assured the American Board that the Palestine missionaries might still safely approach the minority of educated and widely traveled Muslims. Even that was risky, and Fisk knew it from the way that Nureddin and Gibraltar had lit into Wolff. But to cease any missionary efforts among Muslims would disappoint those many American donors who expected Islam's imminent collapse—and might take their money elsewhere.

Thanks to King, those hopes of a Christian triumph ran higher than ever. That was because he had done exactly what the board looked for all its missionaries to do, and what Fisk himself had done upon landing at Smyrna two years earlier: he sent home a devastating portrait of his host culture. King summoned a Cairo for Boston's readers where the "Turks walk about in pride, while the people groan under the deepest oppression," all so "ignorant and degraded and vicious" that every known sin "is literally committed here without a blush." He urged "raising up men" at Andover who will "gird up their loins, and come out to the combat, which must be fought with the bloody followers of the false Prophet." All the more reason, then, for the missionaries to keep proselytizing—carefully, if Fisk had his way—among certain Muslims.[10]

An ideal opportunity seemed to offer itself in the spring of 1823 when the three joined a caravan of some seventy men heading across the Sinai desert to Syria. As Fisk made his first, bemused acquaintance with a camel and King whined about the scorching heat, the blowing sand, his throbbing head, and his heaving gut, Wolff, as usual, went charging across spiritual frontiers. One member of the company owned a manuscript containing an interpretation of the Qur'an that Wolff, at their request, read aloud to the other Muslims—until he broke off to praise the "perfect toleration" prevailing in England. Some Turks countered that Muslim men in parts of their country not only married Christian women but also joined the Freemasons.

At that Fisk's ears pricked up. Could it be his membership was about to pay off in the middle of the Sinai desert? He joined the conversation, striking up an acquaintance with one Hadji Mohammed, a Russian dervish who, though not a Freemason, was well traveled and literate, able to read both the Persian New Testament and the Arabic book of Genesis that the missionaries showed him. In return, he displayed a Persian manuscript containing a poem describing Mecca and Medina, which they purchased, and much discussion ensued about the divinity of Jesus and the inspiration of the Qur'an. Fisk had not forgotten Rosetta, and he noted in his private journal that not all Muslims in the caravan were so welcoming of their books as was this Russian. While Hadji Mohammed "read in Genesis and said it was *very good*," another Muslim denounced it as "infidelity to say God *rested* on the seventh day of Creation," and yet another vented his contempt for Wolff by flogging his donkey and calling the poor beast "a *Jew*."

Still, their encounter with Hadji Mohammed seemed likely to appease Jowett and to play well in the evangelical press. But then, a few weeks later, the Russian turned up at Fisk and King's lodgings in Jerusalem, asking to borrow the Persian manuscript. Suspecting that he meant to make off with it, the missionaries refused, whereupon he went to one of the city's Muslim judges, known as a *qadi*, and charged them with theft. Rattled, they turned to Jerusalem's governor, a Muslim Turk, who ordered Hadji Mohammed bastinadoed and informed the *qadi* that "Englishmen could not be brought to trial before him." Fortunately for Fisk and King, they passed as English in Ottoman domains, although at first their national pride suffered from discovering that most of its peoples knew "no difference between us and Englishmen, having never before heard of America or Americans." It was a close call nonetheless. Another governor, one who did know the difference between the Americans and the English, might have ordered the missionaries bastinadoed instead.[11]

Another governor there could well have been, because rulers changed quickly on the ground that the missionaries now traversed—present-day Israel, Lebanon, and Syria. In the early nineteenth century, that territory comprised the Ottoman provinces of Damascus and Acre, each ruled by pashas appointed by the sultan, and ten different pashas ruled Damascus alone in the 1820s. To compound the political instability, rivalries between pashas for control of territory often erupted into armed warfare, each vying for the fickle favor of the Sublime Porte and support from village notables and sheikhs. Those local grandees held the real power in the countryside, but even they faced challenges from ordinary people whose outrage at high taxes, inflated prices, and military conscription flared into uprisings whenever village clans could put aside their own squabbles long enough to unite. The Bedouins presented yet another obstacle to order. Driven north from the Arabian Peninsula by warfare and drought, they pillaged villages and attacked caravans. Finally, there was the Greek Revolution, which taxed an already fragile and fragmented political authority by intensifying religious and ethnic tensions.[12]

Those political realities—and the sour memory of Hadji Mohammed—only deepened Fisk's reluctance to approach Muslims. Even Wolff seemed chastened, at least temporarily, and during his stay in Jerusalem he confined his mission to the city's Jewish quarter. It was King alone who saw in their brushes with disaster something other than a cautionary tale and glimpsed in those episodes other possibilities. If the facts were judiciously culled and the story properly told, here were adventures that would keep Sampson Wilder on the edge of his red morocco leather chair. That inspiration marked the beginning of Jonas King's efforts to make his own inventions—his missionaries and his Muslims—dominate the imagination of American evangelicalism.

His patron had given him the perfect opportunity to practice. Shortly before King left Paris, Wilder presented him with a small volume, its spine bound in red leather, its blank pages to be filled by the newly minted missionary during his time in the Ottoman Empire. Once inscribed by King with stories of memorable events, descriptions of religious sites, and pious reflections, he would return the little book to Wilder as a sort of devotional aid and a keepsake of his connection to the Palestine mission. King even hired a copyist to transcribe his scrawled draft into the elegant script that flows across its pages. With equal care, King chose the episodes that merited inclusion in this special journal. No mention, of course, of that embarrassing fracas at Rosetta, nor the mortifying retreat to Cairo, but plenty about crossing the Sinai. Slogging through "vallies of moving sand, which was carried along by the wind, like snow in New England," King was still able to forget his own "wants and privations, and pains and sickness" at the sight of "several of our company bowing, and worshipping towards Mecca." At that, he "bowed toward Jerusalem, and lifted up my voice to him who died there, that he would have mercy upon these deluded people." There could be no missing the implied comparison with Jesus' forty days in the desert, but King was also using Wilder's special journal to experiment with another message that would become essential to his missionary aims.

It surfaces first in his version of the missionaries' dealings with Hadji Mohammed. They wished to avoid being "conducted by a Janizary through the streets of the city, like criminals," to answer to the *qadi*, King explained, because "if we let this insult pass, we might be exposed to similar insults every day." And in the end, they received satisfaction from Jerusalem's governor, who assured them that even if "the people here did not know the character and rights of Englishmen," he did. "So we came out from the Governor with 'our horn exalted,'" King concluded. His reference to the missionaries' dread of being paraded through Jerusalem "like criminals" would have registered instantly with Bible readers. It echoes the passage in the Gospel of Mark in which

Jesus objected to being arrested "like a robber." But King's references to the missionaries' warding off this "insult" and gaining satisfaction from the governor's respect would have resonated with an even wider American audience.[13]

He was invoking the language of primal honor, the code of behavior prescribing that real men show no fear, avenge all insults, and thus gain public regard. This lingo sounds strange coming from a Yankee evangelical—a clergyman, at that. But if he belonged to a body of believers whose watchwords were restraint and respectability, King had often seen the code of honor in action when he was knocking around the harbors of Cape Cod as a day laborer and coastal South Carolina as a preacher. In both places, the currency of honor passed as the coin of masculinity's realm for seafarers and other working-class men, as well as among the genteel company King aspired to keep in Charleston. In the South, too, King had seen how evangelicals, mainly Methodists and Baptists, were accommodating that region's honor culture to win acceptance among white men. With ministers stepping forward as models of holy machismo, upholding patriarchal prerogatives and defending slavery, a new ideal of evangelical manhood was taking shape in the South, one which promised that the right kind of Christianity would do nothing to diminish the will and the power of real men to prevail over others. What King intuited is that a similar strategy—inventing missionaries as exemplars of Christian masculinity—might broaden the appeal of evangelicals everywhere in the early republic.[14]

Did they need it. Even before the revolution and even in New England, women had outnumbered men in the membership rolls of all Protestant churches, and the evangelical surge of the early nineteenth century had done nothing to reverse this "feminization" of American Christianity. To the contrary, the gender gap yawned ever wider, particularly when it came to involvement with foreign missions. Everywhere outside New England, men hung back as women flocked to local missionary societies. Much as ministers might rely on their female members to fill the pews of their churches and to take on the scut work of begging money to spread the gospel, it was men who held the purse strings in most families.[15]

That did not bode well for the financial future of the American Board, and no one knew it better than Jeremiah Evarts. The indifference of most men to missions irked him to the point of obsession: he could not stop noticing it, especially when touring the South in the 1820s. Spying "a respectable looking country physician" as he picked up his subscription to the *Missionary Herald* at a store in South Carolina lifted Evarts's spirits until later in the day, when he noticed a religious magazine at the home of a Baptist preacher. He saw that its leaves had been cut "where is some account of the missionaries in Burmah," only to discover that the reader was the minister's landlady. His heart sank again at learning that the wife of Petersburg's Presbyterian minister could reel off the names of every missionary in the Sandwich Islands but that the Presbyterian pastor himself at Norfolk was so "altogether ignorant on missionary subjects" that he took those islands to be somewhere "in the Atlantic ocean, near St. Helena." With their preachers so dim, what hope was there for the South's laymen? As Evarts sized up the crisis, everywhere outside New England "it is rare to find a man, even among the intelligent part of the community, who knows any thing about missions."[16]

Bad enough, but what threw the gender gap into even sharper relief was the foreign missions movement itself, which reminded Christians in the West that Islam enjoyed the wholehearted devotion of men in the East. Muslim males of every country and class appeared prominently in missionary accounts, conducting their daily regimen of prayers and ablutions and stoutly asserting their belief in the prophetic status of Muhammad and the oneness of God. The fervent dedication that Muslim teachings inspired in men raised the question all the more pointedly: If Christianity was the superior religion—and evangelical Protestantism its purest expression—why did Islam fare so much better when it came to commanding male loyalties? Why, unlike Islam, did evangelical Protestantism possess no "hidden man," no ineffable, masculine appeal? Here was a fundamental problem, and nothing except disputes over slavery did as much to corrode evangelicals' confidence about the future of their movement.

Like many evangelical leaders, then, Jonas King would have brooded over the dearth of men in evangelical churches and missionary societies—until he caught lightning in a bottle. What better way to command the attention of male readers, perhaps even draw them into the evangelical orbit, than by treating them to the exploits of dauntless adventurers in a dangerous place, missionary heroes who came away from every challenge to honor with their "horn exalted"? And what situation offered a better opportunity than the Ottoman Empire, where missionaries spent nearly all their time in the company of men? That lent no little fascination to their occasional sightings of Ottoman women. Fisk and Parsons watched from the window of their lodgings as a group of Scio's Greek women kindled a small fire to celebrate a saint's day, and "they amused themselves by running to jump over it," a sport that drew girls "who were gaily dressed and had no cause to be ashamed on the score of beauty." Fisk also confided to his private journal stealing a first, furtive peek at "a Turkish Lady's face" and hearing titillating gossip from one Westerner in Cairo that Muslim women there paraded naked about their rooftops. But the Americans' most regular and sustained encounters were with Ottoman men, among them Muslim sheikhs, clerics, and officials who held the advantage of arms, authority, or both.[17]

It was from their ranks that King drew his arch-villains, trying out his first inventions in Wilder's special journal. Throughout the Sinai desert crossing, he described their caravan being harassed by "formidable" Bedouins who "seemed to spring up like Hydras in every corner." When the missionaries tried to enter the desert tomb of a celebrated Muslim sheikh, "two Bedouins who looked like fiends from the world below followed us," demanding tribute, and, when refused, "they would come close to me and put their hand on the hilt of their swords." Two months later in a Muslim village near Jerusalem, "companies of Boys ran after us, threw stones at us and cried 'kill all the Franks.' One of them took a knife and drew it across his throat, intimating by this, what he wished to do to us." At the Garden of Gethsemane, "some dark, fierce-looking Bedouins, armed with spears and swords advanced on horseback," and "I was not without some fear that they would think me alone, and attack me." Two days later at the pool of Siloam, a reservoir outside the city walls, "a mussulman Arab . . . looked at me with all the wildness of a man possessed of the Devil," a figure as "frightful" to King as a lunatic he had seen in a Paris asylum. A stark contrast to Henry Martyn's Persians, King's earliest portrayals of Syria's Muslims foregrounded their anger and violence, their fanaticism and irrational hatred of the West. Here were monsters and madmen, the spitting image of Muslims conjured by some American opinion makers both before and after the events of September 2001.

Those caricatures would prove too crude for Jonas King. Crafting his Islamic adversaries became a work in progress, their depiction, like his own self-presentation, something that he developed during the years that followed. Muslims persisted in his reports as threatening figures, but over time he complicated their characterizations, as he gained a clearer sense of the ideal foils to challenge his new missionary heroes and the most compelling message about evangelicalism to beam at American men.[18]

Those who could left Jerusalem for the summer. The tiny, walled city was no spa in any season, but once temperatures rose, its sweltering inhabitants—some twenty thousand people squeezed into a spot not even three miles in circumference—spent as much time as possible atop their homes, catching the stray breeze. Small, gently sloping domes pocked the skyline, but those housetops still afforded space enough for families to lounge and walkers to navigate nearly all the city by roof hopping and crossing the arches that spanned its narrow, crooked byways. (Second-story travel was a popular choice year-round, because the streets were open sewers.) Joseph Wolff coped with the stench and sizzle throughout the summer of 1823, waiting until fall to strike out for Damascus. Jonas King only talked like a man who meant to endure. "I should rejoice to see a troop of such men as you are, here, so that the moment we should hear 'a moving in the tops of the mulberry trees' we might rush on to battle," he wrote to Charles Cook, a British Methodist missionary. A few weeks later, he decamped farther north and spent the rest of the year studying Arabic in the village of Dayr el-Qamar on Mount Lebanon, where all that moved the mulberries was a cooling breeze.

Pliny Fisk also left Jerusalem, touring Mount Lebanon and then exploring the coast between Beirut and Acre. His official journal chronicles his visits to Catholic monasteries (known as convents) and his meetings with William Jowett and other British evangelicals who visited Syria. But his private journal reveals that the last half of 1823 marked a transformative passage in Fisk's life, one which would set him on a course that diverged sharply from the expectations of the American Board and the trail being blazed by Jonas King.[19]

Those months began with Fisk's immersing himself in local cultures and training an almost ethnographic eye on Ottoman Syria's peoples.

He met a few grandees, but most did not leave much of an impression, including one of the grandest, the pasha of Acre. Fisk covered their brief meeting in a few sentences, describing how he diverted himself by watching the man's attendants "demurely smoking and drinking coffee" while the pasha kept him cooling his heels for two hours. When finally ushered into a small, neat room, he spied the pasha incongruously "squatting on a divan at the corner." So much for the high and mighty; the doings of ordinary people interested Fisk far more.

That included the household of a Jewish rabbi, where he slept in his study amid "500 Rabbinical books" and a heap of onions and delighted in listing each member of the family (Deborah, Solomon, Baruch) because "I love these Old Testament names." It also included an array of Eastern Christians who revered the Virgin Mary—the "God-Mother" so disdained by William and Martha Jowett. As Fisk learned, "all classes of people" in Syria accepted the tradition that Mary had died on Mount Zion before ascending into heaven and thus challenged a tract that he was distributing, which put her death on the island of Patmos. He took it seriously when "they demand of me proof" and asked the missionary printer at Malta, Daniel Temple, to remove the offending assertion from future tracts and to provide him with "any information you may possess respecting the tradition in favor of Patmos," especially because, Fisk added drolly, "we, in Syria, pretend to be strict Bible Men." No doubt he shared the Jowetts' disdain for veneration of the Virgin, but Fisk responded with respect to Eastern Christians when they upheld their traditions.

He also experienced a deepening compassion for the hard lives endured by many Syrian families. His private journal records at length an evening spent with his sometime guide Antoun, a Catholic Arab of Nazareth, who invited him to dine with his wife and seven children. Fisk inventoried the family's single-room dwelling: in one corner the kitchen, consisting of a jug of water, an earthen vessel serving as a fireplace, and two pots; in another a bedroom piled high with blankets; in the third, a nursery; and a sitting room—divan, mat, and carpeted window seat with two cushions—in the fourth. Their dress was plain, even ragged, but Antoun's spouse and daughters wore strings of small pieces of silver over the forehead and hanging down both cheeks. Fisk asked the couple if they wished to send their eldest son, eleven-year-old Yakoob, to Boston for schooling, then seemed abashed when his mother replied, "If he goes away from me there is nothing I sleep." (Meaning, as Fisk explained, that she would not sleep.) For dinner, there was bread and boiled cucumbers stuffed with rice, yet, Fisk wrote, "I take this to be a very respectable family in Nazareth. They probably live better by far than the greater part of the inhabitants."[20]

This widespread poverty weighed on Fisk, fueling his outrage at its cause, which he took to be Ottoman taxes, fees, and other levies. Such exactions had been rising in recent decades, the result of official corruption as well as the costs of rebuilding after earthquakes and arming for wars. Christians and Jews paid an added premium in the *jizyah*, a poll tax to ensure their protected status as religious minorities, and the Greek insurrection had hiked those levies. Jerusalem's governor and its head of police routinely imprisoned Greek Orthodox, Catholics, and Jews—Fisk estimated as many as twenty a day by late 1823—until their families paid the ransom demanded for their release. Christian convents also surrendered hefty sums each year to ensure their security.

Nor did it escape his notice that Ottoman demands also made life miserable for many Muslim Arabs. During his second stay at Jerusalem in the winter of 1823–24, Fisk watched as a coalition of Christians and Muslims who lived in and about neighboring Bethlehem drove out soldiers who had been quartered in their midst. Despised because they collected taxes, these poorly paid and provisioned troops aroused even more hostility by shaking down civilians for food, shelter, and money. In this instance, the soldiers retaliated by murdering an elderly Greek Christian peasant and impaling his head on one of Jerusalem's gates. Shortly thereafter, Ottoman troops marched to a Muslim community near Bethlehem, and Fisk saw "the red flag flying, and the smoke of their cannons" as they fired on the little village. He vented in his private journal, skewering Turkish officials and soldiers as rapacious bullies who bilked Jews, Christians, and Muslims alike.[21]

As Muslim Arabs came within the compass of Fisk's sympathies, his mounting anger at the Ottoman Turks did not translate into contempt for Islam. To the contrary, it was during these months that Fisk experienced his most profound sense of connection with that faith. It overtook him during a November visit to the graceful mosque built by Acre's late ruler Ahmad Pasha al-Jazzar. As he stepped inside, what instantly drew Fisk's eye was the reading desk standing in one corner of the main floor and the pulpit rising from the opposite. How remarkably this worship setting resembled a Christian church, he reflected. His gaze traveled to the stairs on both sides leading to two tiers of narrow galleries. How splendid this sanctuary must appear after dark, when many lamps blazed and the great chandelier suspended from the center of a lofty dome shimmered. The entire mosque would glow, alit from within.

It was a moment of epiphany for Fisk, an insight that went beyond acknowledging the affinities between evangelical Protestantism and Islam to grasping their import. The reading desk and pulpit attested to how profoundly Muhammad's followers, like those of Jesus, were a people of the book, its sacred stories and strict laws loud in their ears and sweet on their tongues, filling their minds, touching their hearts, and fortifying their souls. Then there was the brilliant light pouring from the mosque's windows and piercing the night's darkness: here was a powerful symbol of the zeal to transform the world shared by evangelical Christianity and Islam. If his encounter with George English had spiked Fisk's anxiety about the many likenesses among the world's monotheisms, that fear fell away as he stood within the Jazzar Mosque, lost in admiration. Spread before him were stirring emblems of what was shared between his faith and that of Muslims, and at least for the moment he embraced that unity.

His pleasure in the place followed Fisk into its courtyard. Beneath two domes, palm trees spread and fountains played; rows of cloisters lined three sides, one of them housing a library, the others, rooms for travelers and students. Here was an oasis in a "hot country," "a delightful spot" to Fisk, where "my imagination was filled with the idea of the learned Mussulmans in the times of the caliphs of Baghdad and Cairo passing their time in such places." Then his reverie drifted from the glory of the medieval Saracens to the present: "I was dressed in my Turban Khumbaz and Jeubbee [robe] with a beard already of tolerable length, and I almost fancied that I could soon become master of Arabic in such a place, surrounded by Mussulman doctors." Here were learned Muslims gleaned from the recollections of Henry Martyn, not those who haunted the pages of Jonas King's earliest journals.

Or the mind of William Jowett, who had come along on this excursion to Acre. His health shot, he was taking his last look at the Levant before assuming less taxing duties for his missionary society in London. During their final visit, he again impressed upon Fisk the importance of mounting an aggressive campaign against Islam and, as they toured the Jazzar Mosque, perhaps Jowett sensed his companion's thoughts or even reproved his remarks. Whatever he might have intuited or Fisk confided, it seems to have prompted the remark that appeared in the book that Jowett was then preparing about missionary prospects in the Ottoman Empire. No matter that the Jazzar Mosque's serene court-yard seemed to invite spiritual reflection, Jowett warned, for this scene was "well calculated to make the mind forget that there is, throughout all Turkey, more offensive filthiness than can be expressed." The spec-tacle of "Turks and Arabs, with most venerable silvery beards," per-forming their devotional ablutions at the courtyard's fountain "would carry the imagination far toward a good opinion of the morals inspired by these Mahomedan Ceremonies"—but only for those unfamiliar with "the abominations of the East."[22]

Fisk had found plenty to abominate about the Ottoman Empire, but much to admire as well. His surrender to the Jazzar Mosque's en-chantment showed the effects of his eclectic reading, his connections with other well-traveled Westerners, and his growing number of Mus-lim acquaintances—many of whom he did not mention in his reports to the board. But to his private journal, he confided his delight in these new circles, including an evening he had spent at the Cairo home of Ismael Gibraltar, the pasha's admiral. The gathering included Nured-din as well as "two or three men of learning, one famous for his knowl-edge of Persian," and a French physician "whose beard was I think 3 ft long. I never saw anything like it." The conversation flowed easily in French and Italian "about languages, printing, travels, poets, etc., etc.," a stream that bore Fisk further than he could ever have imagined from his narrow New Divinity world back in New England.[23]

Fisk had decided to travel farther still by the end of 1823. He wished to meet Muslims on their own ground and in their own dress; he hoped to converse with them in Arabic and even to enter the scenes that spooled in his mind's eye at the Jazzar Mosque. Like Martyn, he yearned for rec-ognition within an idealized masculine fellowship of accomplished scholars. And just as Martyn had drifted from India to Persia, Fisk hoped to explore Muslim societies beyond the Levant, seeking out their learned men. He confided as much to the printer Daniel Temple, his classmate at Andover and a fellow member of the Brethren. Though no attachment would ever rival his bond with Levi Parsons, Fisk had come to trust Temple and, only weeks before visiting Acre, wrote to him that his next destination would be "Armenia or Mesopotamia or Nineveh or Babylon or Persia," for "I am such a vagabond myself that I don't know that I shall ever find a home, I mean in the present life."

In the same letter, Fisk also alluded to a conversation with Temple on the night before he left Malta for Alexandria at the beginning of 1823. On that occasion, Fisk wrote, he feared that "he said too much" and that "he should make some retraction." What did he regret telling Temple—regret so much that remorse had dogged him for nearly a year? One possibility is that Fisk, fresh from sparring with English and demoralized by his two years in the Levant, had expressed doubts about missionary work, perhaps even speculated boldly about Islam, Christianity, or both. But the man who liked secrets was good at keeping them, too, and he never tipped his hand. What's certain is that the company he kept in Egypt and Syria was prompting Fisk to project future travels to present-day Iraq and Iran.

Seeing himself through the eyes of those others was also changing how Fisk saw himself. Particularly revealing is what may be the only instance of his complaining to Jeremiah Evarts. It came in a letter composed late in 1823 in which Fisk described himself as "mortified and vexed" by how the editors of the *Missionary Herald* mangled those parts of his journals that appeared in print. Passages omitted, place-names misspelled, and cities mixed up "may not materially affect the interest of the journal with most readers in America, but I cannot avoid looking at them as they must appear to Consuls, Merchants, Travellers, and Missionaries." It mattered to Fisk, his standing among those who knew the world. So if the *Herald*'s editors could not do better with his journals, "I beg you will not attempt to print them. You perceive that I write with Yankee frankness." To say nothing of impatience with yokels who confused Alexandria with Rosetta. He chafed at parochialism in another letter, this one to a close friend in New England, in which he urged that Americans show their patriotism "not by vain boasting, but by praying that God will save our nation from corruption . . . not by attempting to prove that Americans are better than other men, but by attempting to make them better."[24]

Was Fisk traveling toward true cosmopolitanism, a frame of mind that sought out, even celebrated differences among the world's peoples— including their religions? Was such a journey even possible for a missionary committed to the universal truth of Christianity? Surely not by the lights of anyone back at the American Board, so in his official journal Fisk balanced an admiring account of the Jazzar Mosque with assurances that he had not lost confidence in the conversion of Muslims. "Had I the faith, the wisdom, and the learning of Martyn," he dutifully declared, "I might perhaps . . . tell the [Muslim] doctors [jurists and scholars] that Jesus is the son of God." And no sooner had William Jowett gone back to England, never to return, than Pliny Fisk, now the senior evangelical missionary in all the Mediterranean, regained the full measure of his former zeal to convert the Islamic world.[25]


It had been Isaac Bird's dream, becoming a member of the Palestine mission and laboring with Fisk in Jerusalem. The two had bonded at Andover—a refuge for Bird from the liberal Christians and outright skeptics among his relatives—and when Fisk sailed for Smyrna, his friend idolized him from afar. "For some months I have been watching you and watching you, and often in imagination have seen you fleeing from persecution in one city, to another," he wrote from New England at the end of 1822. "I have now the full expectation that this letter will find you . . . testifying to both Turks and Greeks." In fact, Bird's letter had found Fisk holed up at Malta, still reeling from his encounter with George English. And at the beginning of 1824, when Bird at last joined him in Jerusalem, the younger missionary's dream lost a little of its luster.

He found Fisk immersed in the study of Arabic with his teacher, Jar Allah, pondering what it meant that Muslims, like evangelicals, believed that Jesus would return to earth to usher in the millennium. With one difference: Jesus would "descend from heaven, wage war with the Dajal [Antichrist], overcome and kill him," Jar Allah explained, and then establish Islam throughout the world. Christians featured Jesus arranging a different outcome, but what struck Fisk was that some of both faiths "pretend to calculate the precise time when the millennium shall commence." He agreed with Jar Allah, who "more prudently says, it will be when God sees fit." More than ever, Fisk was a man torn between seeking the common ground with Christianity that might promote Muslim conversions and dreading that he would find too much of it—enough to undermine, even to destroy, his belief in the singular truth of his own creed.[26]

It must have surprised Bird to find his old friend more intent on studying Islam in search of its "hidden man" than contesting it. To Bird's eyes, "the little cluster of houses, the common Arab huts," scattered about the countryside "with the Minaret of the Mosque rising from the midst of them" looked like "some country village in New England with the meeting house and steeple in the center." How hard could it be, converting the occupants of what looked like so many Connecticut towns? But Fisk parried his enthusiasm with caution, warning, "We know not yet how far we may venture in proclaiming the gospel to Mussulmans." For their first two months in Jerusalem, Fisk would sell scriptures only to those who came to their lodgings for that purpose. Then, early in February, he took the next small step, dispatching his dragoman to the convents and the market to offer Bibles there. For all his prudence, Fisk had gone too far again.[27]

A few days later, he and Bird opened their door to a company of Turkish soldiers. They brought the two before a Muslim judge, most likely the chief *qadi* for all Jerusalem, who sent them on to the governor with orders for their imprisonment until the pasha of Damascus could weigh in. This governor—like his predecessor who had sided with the missionaries against Hadji Mohammed—refused that order on the grounds that Fisk and Bird were "Englishmen," but he did not send them back to their lodgings. After spending a few hours in a ground-floor room crowded with soldiers smoking and playing chess, the two received an invitation to join the governor in his private quarters, where they were treated with pipes and coffee, a customary show of hospitality. Thereafter, they took a late supper with the governor's nephew, who, as Fisk noted, "said as many as 20 or 30 times 'Excuse us.' 'Be not offended with us.'" Despite these courtesies, the two Americans passed an uneasy night. As Fisk emphasized in all his reports of the incident, the "Turks are accustomed to inflict corporal punishment in order to obtain money or extort some confession which they wish." But in the end, nothing worse happened than an official proclamation ordering anyone who had received books from the missionaries to return them to the *qadi* and forbidding all Muslims, on pain of imprisonment, to acquire such books in the future. The soldiers also made a halfhearted bid for baksheesh from the missionaries, but without success.[28]

Fisk blamed the arrest on Jerusalem's Roman Catholics, and his suspicions were not misplaced. For months, he had been cultivating their bitter rivals, the Greek Orthodox, the city's largest Christian group, who proved so welcoming of his tracts and books that Fisk planned to launch a magazine for their benefit, a Levantine version of the missionary periodical. By making those friends, he inevitably inherited their enemies. So the Catholics might have sought to curry favor with the Ottomans, as Fisk believed, by telling the *qadi* that the testaments sold by the Bible-men—those partisans of the rebel Greeks— were ending up in Muslim hands. Strange bedfellows, the Catholics and the Muslims, but as Fisk was learning, the struggle over a spot that to most Westerners looked like God's last bag of sand could spawn intrigues to rival those of Machiavelli's Italy. By arresting Protestant missionaries to please Jerusalem's Catholics, the *qadi* not only succeeded in deepening divisions among Christians but also set a trap for the city's governor, who stepped right into it. By refusing to imprison the missionaries, the governor was truckling to these Christian troublemakers, or so the *qadi* wasted no time in telling his patron, the pasha of Acre. Meanwhile, the governor tattled to his patron, the pasha of Damascus, blaming the *qadi* for stirring up trouble with "the English"—those who must not be offended, lest they throw off their neutrality and back the Greek rebels.

Despite their labyrinthine rivalries, as Fisk found to his dismay, Muslim officials could agree about the missionaries' books. Bird reported that upon reading from their Arabic translation of Genesis that "the Spirit of God moved upon the face of the waters," the *qadi* "threw the book on the floor, saying, 'that is infidelity. Is not God everywhere? Has he need? Moving from place?'" As for the governor, an offending phrase in an Arabic Psalter made him exclaim, "'God forbid,' and spit contemptuously at the book." It was not the first time their books had met with rejection. Two years earlier, Fisk had struck up an acquaintance at a Valletta hotel with a party of Turks returning from Europe— familiarity enough, he thought, to present them with an Arabic Psalter and a Turkish testament. Both came back, the Turks telling him that "a great part of these books were drawn from the Koran" and ignoring his insistence that "the Koran must be drawn from them because they were written long first." The Methodist missionary Charles Cook likewise reported that while in company with several Muslim Arabs, he gave one a book of psalms who read it to the others until a servant "told them it was a Christian book . . . they soon after left off reading." Muslims' interest in books other than the Qur'an did not extend to Christian translations of the Bible.[29]

Fisk did not share his latest discouraging news on that score with the board. His official account of the arrest played up the role of Jerusalem's Roman Catholics in instigating the *qadi* and their intention to "continue to excite the Turks against us by all the means in their power." He stressed the missionaries' readiness to suffer for their faith in the very spot where, as they had been told by the governor's nephew, Jesus had been condemned to death. And he ended with their vindication: shortly after the missionaries' release, the pasha of Damascus himself told both the *qadi* and the governor that "we should be protected and treated with respect." "All parties regretted that they had meddled with us," Fisk concluded, because "a general impression was made, that men under English protection are not to be trifled with." Vilifying Catholics, invoking parallels with Jesus, vaunting "English" influence for bringing the Turks to heel, and "exalting" the missionaries' "horn"— all were tropes that Fisk had poached from King. And how well they played. Fisk's report of the arrest led the *Missionary Herald*, as well as other publications along the Eastern Seaboard. Thrilled by the notice it drew, Jeremiah Evarts started planning to bring Fisk back to the United States for a fund-raising tour.[30]

But Fisk kept from the board most of what happened in the aftermath of the arrest. "It was no small matter," he tersely informed Evarts, "that we were able to refuse money to the Turks, who had us in their hands." Because so many Eastern Christians, Jews, and Muslims had endured Ottoman extortion, they marveled that the two Americans had managed to stay out of jail without paying for the privilege. Only in his private journal did Fisk disclose how much goodwill he had actually won by standing fast. Shortly after the arrest, he and Bird visited Bethlehem, whose residents were still at swords' points with Ottoman officials. The two missionaries entered the village in the "Turkish dress" that they always wore to travel, and "we saw multitudes of men, women, and children looking earnestly at us from the windows and terraces as well as in the streets, as if anxious to know whether we were friends or foes." Then they recognized Fisk and Bird and broke into "friendly salutations"; Christians rallied around them as the two headed toward a convent guarded by Bedouins. It had been an ecumenical effort, repulsing Ottoman soldiers from Bethlehem, the Bedouins working in concert with the town's Arabs, a Muslim minority and a Christian majority. "Not yet knowing who we were," Fisk continued, at least a dozen Muslim defenders now stationed themselves at the convent's door, checking to make sure that their muskets were well primed. They stepped aside only when the village's Christians "cried aloud 'Inglis, Inglis.'"

Fisk recognized that broadcasting this episode would entail too many risks. If the beleaguered Bethlehemites hoped to bring the influence of the "Inglis" to bear against the Ottomans, that redress lay close to his heart but beyond his power. The board had strict rules against missionaries' meddling in local politics, and the Roman Catholics would waste no time informing Ottoman authorities if the Bible-men enlisted in Bethlehem's cause. In any case, plans to join the players on Ottoman Syria's chessboard were not what consumed Fisk's thoughts. He had been preoccupied by another matter entirely, one occasioning an intense inner debate.

"Perhaps there is something in our present mode of proceeding that is not exactly according to the mind of the Spirit," he mused in his private journal. Perhaps the arrest had been providence's way "to bring us to a more evangelical mode of attempting to spread the Gospel." That "more evangelical mode" meant public preaching, the course that Jowett had been urging—and Fisk resisting. Now he reconsidered. Could the missionaries' newfound popularity, so evident from their entry to Bethlehem, win a wider hearing for their religious message? Perhaps it was only right and just, their taking on the risk of preaching, because what any missionary might suffer was nothing "compared with what the Christian and Jewish subjects of the Sultan suffer daily."[31]

Martyrdom: that's what was on Fisk's mind—and had been for months, even before he and Jowett had sparred back at Malta. "How is the gospel to be preached to the Mussulmans," he had asked in his journal to the board shortly after leaving the Jazzar Mosque, if "the penalty was death for any who renounced their religion?" That led Fisk to rehearse the power of martyrdom to inspire mass conversions, reflecting that the early Christians had gained moral authority through their sufferings. In the Roman Empire, "it usually was only some of the principal persons or at least only a part of the Christians," who were put to death. That might happen again in the Ottoman Empire, and "if a few conversions should take place and be followed by immediate martyrdom and the blood of the martyrs again prove the seed of the Church, the persecutors would cease from their opposition." Or perhaps "some great political revolution is to open the door for the free preaching of the gospel to the followers of the False Prophet." Either way, latter-day apostles would have to mount a forceful defense of Christianity aimed at Muslims. That challenge would set off a wave of repression, snuffing out the lives of missionaries and converts alike, but there were times when upholding the truth demanded the ultimate sacrifice. In other words, Fisk had begun to believe that his own death might prompt mass conversions to the evangelical faith, and as that conviction took hold, the self-immolating piety of his years with Levi Parsons found him again.

When Fisk's reflections on martyrdom appeared in the pages of the *Missionary Herald*, they drew no shocked protests from readers. Why would they, when he was only echoing the sentiments that he himself had voiced in his farewell sermon at Old South Church years earlier and that other evangelicals still expressed both privately and in print? Among them was William Jowett, who, writing to Jeremiah Evarts in May 1824—a letter that quickly went public—ventured to hope that the members of the Palestine mission "may have the grace and courage boldly to follow the Captain of our Salvation . . . who shed his blood in Jerusalem for the redemption of the world." By the 1820s, this romancing of martyrdom—with its assumption that the success of their cause would cost many lives—had become commonplace in the rhetoric of the foreign missions movement. Indeed, Rufus Anderson—the man now serving as Evarts's assistant who once had fantasized his future in India with Harriet Newell's sister—was nearly cavalier about contemplating other people's sacrificial deaths. If you are called on to "pursue the flaming path" that took martyrs to heaven, he lectured Isaac Bird, it "will excite a wonderful interest in the churches here, if it does not throughout Palestine." "God uses his people as he pleases," Anderson shrugged, and "some can do more by dying than by living."

The ideal of martyrdom had struck a deep and spreading root in early nineteenth-century evangelicalism. Its pervasive power made Fisk's renewed embrace of this cult of self-sacrifice far less remarkable than his short-lived resistance to it. For all of the ways that he had distanced his origins, Fisk could not for long abandon the narrative that endowed his life—and that of his beloved Parsons—with meaning. If they were not martyrs—or martyrs in the making—then they were fools for traipsing about Ottoman domains, selling Bibles, and scattering tracts. As an expression of committed belief, to die willingly for one's faith holds a comparable power today in some quarters of Islam—and perhaps driven by the same impulse that propelled Fisk toward it again. Caught up in a world where boundaries between religions increasingly blurred, at once intimidated by its perils and captivated by its possibilities, Fisk at last reconciled his warring thoughts and emotions by reasserting his conviction that there was a religious truth and that he was willing to die for it. It was a retreat from the sense of connectedness that had overwhelmed him at the Jazzar Mosque, an uncompromising affirmation that his faith was distinct from Islam. Martyrdom would be no senseless sacrifice: it would be the answer to all of his questions.[32]

Whatever course Fisk took next would be one that he set. At the time of the arrest, no member of the board had written to him for more than a year. "It is so long since I received a letter from you, that I had almost forgotten that you were one of my correspondents," he chided Evarts in the spring of 1824. But by now being left to his own devices felt more like freedom than neglect. He was laying plans to tour Damascus and Aleppo and to improve his Arabic. And he was still enjoying his new-found celebrity as the "Inglis" who stood up to the Ottomans, playing that part to the hilt on the April day that he and Bird left Jerusalem.

Before a cloud of witnesses clustered at one of the city's gates, an Ottoman soldier took Fisk's horse by the bridle and demanded "a present." This exchange followed: "'Do you know,' said Mr. Fisk (looking him sternly in the face), 'do you know what *kilmi wahadi* means.' This is a common Arabic expression signifying *one word for all*. 'Yes,' said the soldier. 'Well,' replied Mr. F., *'one word for all*, there is not a para [a small coin] for you. Have you understood me?' 'Yes,' answered the soldier quitting his hold and smiling. 'Go on, God bless you.'" The witness to this scene was Isaac Bird, now restored to his old admiration of Fisk. Bird recorded it in his private journal, perhaps at Fisk's insistence that the board had no need to know. Fisk himself made no record of the episode. Then the two headed to Jaffa to meet the man who would never have squandered the chance to spread so choice a story from New York to New Orleans.[33]

Pliny Fisk's sojourn in the Levant had made him, more than ever, a man in search of meaning. If losing Parsons had cut him adrift from all hopes of fulfillment in fond intimacy, it had invested Fisk all the more intensely in other quests. A person of ordinary intelligence but driving curiosity, he was determined to understand Islam, its appeal, and its affinities with his own faith, and he did not allow unsettling discoveries to stop him. Fisk's experiences were also heightening his sympathy for ordinary people of all faiths in the Ottoman Empire. Finally, events were leading him deeper inside himself, as he wrestled with the question of whether to attempt the conversion of Muslims, believers whose faith seemed ever more kindred to his own. Other matters entirely seem to have preoccupied Jonas King. The shadow of a doubt lingers, because King's private journals—and he seems to have kept them throughout his time in the Levant—have not come to light. But the reckonings with religious truth, spiritual virtuosity, and social justice that appear repeatedly in all that Fisk wrote figure neither in King's official journals nor in his special journal for Wilder, nor in his private correspondence. The mask of the Christian crusader never drops in those pages, which raises the suspicion that King might not have been wearing one.[34]

Whether or not that role claimed King completely, he entered it even more fully during his stay at Jaffa. At the beginning of 1823—only days before the arrest of his friends at Jerusalem—King had settled there and spent the next two months entertaining epiphanies of a different order from those being visited on Fisk. It was a spot well matched to the man's temperament, this small seaport fortified by two watchtowers, two citadels, a moat, and an encircling wall mounted with cannons. King enlisted a local Muslim sheikh, Khaleel, to tutor him in Arabic, and the two set about reading and chanting the Qur'an. Not the stuff of suspense, but from a man with King's powers of puffery no circumstance was safe, especially now that he had acquired two new correspondents back in the United States. They were the sons of Jedidiah Morse, Richard and Sidney, who had recently begun to publish the *New-York Observer*, a weekly newspaper that showcased evangelical revivals, reform societies, and, of course, missions. But the Morse brothers mixed in coverage of secular matters as well, aiming to deliver all the news with an evangelical spin, just as their father had done for geography. Like him, too, they hoped to make the most of their missionary connections, soliciting not only King but also Fisk and Bird for reports on their missionary activities as well as "the fine arts and geographical and statistical subjects" as they pertained to Ottoman Syria.[35]

King knew just what the Morse brothers wanted—and would want even more once he gave it to them. Writing to Sidney, he described Sheikh Khaleel as "a large dark looking son of Ishmael" and "a genuine follower of the false prophet" who wished "to make me give up the Divinity of Christ" and "preaches to me hellfire and damnation in such a terrific manner, that my blood sometimes almost runs cold." Through the Morse brothers' good offices, this sketch found its way into the *Observer* as well as a number of secular newspapers. Encouraged, King pumped even more juice into the journal that he sent to the board in Boston, turning several weeks of learning Arabic in a sleepy seacoast town into a spiritual drama fraught with peril. There was the danger to Khaleel, who "expressed much fear . . . said it had been reported among the Moolahs and great men of the Mosque, that one of their number was teaching an Englishman their religion." Greater still was the eternal danger to King, as the sheikh made constant "endeavors to convert me to the Mussulman faith." Finally, there were "common people" in this largely Muslim place, "so noisy and impudent" that in conversations "they come at you like a mad bull, pawing and bellowing and throwing dust around them, and one is almost tempted sometimes to knock them down with weapons that are only carnal."

King had hunkered down into what would become a pet literary pose: the stalwart missionary standing up to hostile Muslims. Hostile, but with the appearance of Sheikh Khaleel, not unhinged. If Jaffa had its share of mad bulls, the learned, canny Khaleel, determined to prevail in debate, comes off like one of Henry Martyn's formidable mujtahids. As for King, he now portrayed himself not as a cowed Christian but as a man who had willingly put himself in harm's way, dared his adversaries to do their worst, and held his ground. And if martyrdom was to be his fate, he would not go quietly; to the contrary, King bragged about his impulse, barely restrained, to come out swinging when attacked.

His dispatches from Jaffa also taught King what the evangelical press did not want. Though he postured as a man besieged in a stronghold of Islam, in fact King had befriended a Muslim warlord with the stepped-out-of-*Star Wars* name of Ibrahim Aboo Ghoosh. Mewed up within Jaffa's walls after running afoul of the pasha of Damascus, Aboo Ghoosh and his entourage were looking to kill time and to finagle a way out of town, and they hoped that the American missionary might answer both purposes. So they dined with King and discussed the Bible, and on one memorable occasion Aboo Ghoosh "wrote a little love song in Arabic describing a beautiful Damsel, whose charms had power to open prison doors, unloose captives, etc." On cue, a member of the warlord's retinue asked King "if I knew the name of Moses' Mother, by the help of which, he said, a man might open a door, which was locked against him." King expressed doubts that any name could break locks but obliged anyway; a delighted Aboo Ghoosh declared that now "he should soon find a means to escape." So he did, with or without help from Moses's mother. That story numbers among the few of King's journal entries that never saw the light of print. He should have guessed that the *Missionary Herald*'s editors would never let slip in their pages that one of the board's missionaries was trading love ditties and magical incantations over a cozy supper with a Muslim warlord and his posse. That he didn't guess is telling, and what it tells is that King's pride in this camaraderie with Muslim men blunted his usually infallible instincts for what would fly with his evangelical sponsors and readers.

But he recovered and turned out a surefire crowd-pleaser with another of his tales from Jaffa. This one recounted his being poked by that other horn of the Antichrist, the superior of a nearby Roman Catholic convent. Looking King up and down, he needled, "Aha—a white turban—all Mussulman, you have turned Mussulman then—I must write to England, and let them know, that you have turned Mussulman." A good story and remarkably like one recounted in a memoir a few years earlier. The teller then was Henry Martyn, who nervously joked that his reading the Qur'an started gossip that he had embraced Islam. At least King was stealing from the best—well, the best so far. And the truth is that he was not only beginning to enjoy being mistaken for a Muslim but also borrowing more than a white turban to further his purposes. With his sojourn at Jaffa, King reintroduced himself to American evangelicals as a man who actively sought out danger to extend the sway of his faith and who found the greater glory and holiness in battling rather than dying. Here is not the model of a Christian martyr, for whom sacrificial death itself carries the ultimate spiritual significance, but ironically Islam's ideal of the fighting martyr.[36]

# 9

## AT THE GATES OF DAMASCUS

Shall I tell you who the jinn come down to? They come down to every lying sinner who readily lends an ear to them, and most of them are liars: only those who are lost in error follow the poets.

—Qur'an, The Poets, 26:222–27

Spires of minarets spiked the Damascus skyline, shimmering in the summer heat. White stone buildings spread for miles, studding forests of cypress and chestnut, olive and poplar, and once the riders drew closer, gardens and orchards hove into view. Nearly all of the city's 150,000 inhabitants were Muslims, well versed in the story that his first sight of Damascus so beguiled Muhammad that he refused to enter, saying that he would not have his heaven on earth. Jonas King was less impressed: "the scenery is indeed beautiful" yet "did not appear to me so enchanting, as it did to the Mussulman Prophet."

Nothing would stop him from riding his horse into town. As they approached one of the city's gates, Pliny Fisk reined in his mount, but King cantered through. He was asking for trouble, and he knew it: Christians and Jews were not permitted to ride horses within the gates of Damascus. Not long ago when the French consul had tried, Ottoman soldiers had pulled him from his horse, "cut his sword from his side, and struck him several times." King did not get far either. "Dismount, dismount," a soldier shouted, at which he did, all the while insisting that being under English protection, he could "pass where I please." What was he thinking? Of Joseph Wolff: several months earlier, some Jew-baiting soldiers at the same gate had ordered him off a mere donkey and made him run behind the beast while his Muslim guide rode into the city. It was a sin for missionaries "in whatever place we proclaim the Lord's name, if we trust in our own strength," he warned, but when in Damascus, "this fanatic town," it was "both sin and madness" not to rely on God alone. Wolff's humiliation must have irked King, and he meant his own act of bravado either as payback or as one-upmanship of the "Christian Jew."

King himself made light of his defiance, saying that he only wished to ascertain "whether he might not enter without being noticed." Like John Lewis Burckhardt and George English, he prided himself on passing for a Muslim. "I have put on the turban and the Arab dress, and my beard is so long that I am generally taken by strangers to be one of the sons of Ishmael," he bragged to friends in the United States. His disguise fooled even his old Andover classmate and fellow missionary William Goodell, who had come to Ottoman Syria with Isaac Bird. On one of his first walks through Beirut, Goodell "supposed the figure which he saw seated on a stone by the wayside was a genuine son of the desert, until suddenly addressed by it in unmistakable American vernacular." "Mr. King is a perfect Turk," his new colleague marveled. In fact, he came close—but not close enough to make it through the gates of Damascus.[1]

King and Fisk were constant companions from the summer of 1824 through the spring of 1825. After spending a few weeks in Damascus, they moved on to Aleppo for three months before returning to the coast and sojourning between Jerusalem and Beirut. Yet in all this time together, the two were headed separate ways, each pursuing plans laid months earlier. As King went charging through the Damascus gate, imagining how well it would play with an American audience, his partner who dismounted there began to implement a design for evangelizing the Islamic world—one that he hoped and feared would bring about his death.

The first, faint traces of this blueprint surface in Fisk's correspondence and the notes on his readings while in Aleppo. Being a commercial and cultural crossroads for millennia made it a good town for bookworms, and most likely Fisk was burrowing through a stall in the grand bazaar when he came across the French manual on lithography. Back in Smyrna, he had come to share William Jowett's appreciation for that technology's potential to reach calligraphy-craving Muslim readers, and now Fisk took six pages of notes on exactly what was needed. Then he wrote to Daniel Temple, the missionary printer at

Malta, for help in procuring the necessary "apparatus" and finding someone skilled in its operation. A recent *firman* prohibited the distribution of the missionaries' testaments, so Fisk aimed to elude the sultan's edict by publishing tracts instead and, by using lithography, to make them "more acceptable to the people of the country."[2]

It might also have crossed his mind that he would have an easier time transporting bales of these small booklets, rather than crates of testaments, to the Islamic countries that he hoped to visit in the near future. And that distributing tracts far and wide in western Asia would open the way for the even riskier work of his public preaching to Muslims. What lends substance to those speculations is that shortly after leaving Aleppo, Fisk spent two months in Jaffa studying the Qur'an with King's Muslim tutor there, Sheikh Khaleel. They kept at it for six hours nearly every day. Neither Fisk nor any of his fellow missionaries took up a sustained study of the Talmud, the central text of rabbinic Judaism, or of the writings of those church fathers prized by Eastern Christians. But his studies of Islam so consumed Fisk that for several weeks he committed little else to his private journal except the sheikh's commentary on the Qur'an and their exchanges. From Aleppo to Jaffa, all of Fisk's activities—the efforts to launch lithographic printing, the close study of Islam, the determination to perfect his Arabic—point to his intention to take his message directly to the Levant's Muslims.[3]

As Fisk pursued those projects, King controlled the narrative of their travels that reached American readers, mainly through his official journal for the board and his correspondence with the Morse brothers and Sampson Wilder. Those connections kept him current with news from the United States, and his awareness of the climate of opinion there came to shape his reports from Syria. Like others who excel at self-promotion, King could gauge how attitudes were trending among his target audience, and he positioned himself to keep pace, even to stay a little ahead of the pack. It was an invaluable instinct for an aspiring religious entrepreneur and one that lent even greater elasticity to his version of events. Some of the stories—his charging through the Damascus gate among them—stayed faithful to the facts, confirmed by Fisk or other eyewitnesses. Many others did not, and some Levanters were catching on to how little of what came from King could be loosely called the truth. Shortly after their arrival, Bird and Goodell rhapsodized that "Mr. King has received in this region, the appellation of 'the man that speaks the truth.' 'There,' say they, as he walks the streets of Bairout, 'comes the truth teller.'" Still novices in an irony-free zone, neither got the send-up of King's self-righteousness, dogmatism, and fact gilding.[4]

Back in the United States, King's dispatches commanded not mere credence but wild enthusiasm. Their prominent, often front-page showcasing in the American Board's *Missionary Herald*, the Morse brothers' *New-York Observer*, other religious periodicals, and even secular newspapers signals that they were a favorite among readers. "Everything from the pen of Mr. King is interesting," the *Observer* purred in preface to an excerpt from his journal. And how: he transformed his travels through Ottoman Syria into gripping tales, equal parts peril and glory, even as he made his Muslims into worthier adversaries than the fiends and fanatics who skulked and ranted through his earlier reports. He even rendered some of his missionary exploits in epic verse, a poetic self-apotheosis that began by announcing his intention to visit Jerusalem ("What awaits me there I know not") and ended by declaring that the "God of armies" under "whose banner we have enlisted, is sure to conquer."[5]

It's always tempting to underestimate people who defy caricature, and in King's case the temptation is almost irresistible. His name is unknown today, and because so few of his private papers have survived, the man himself disappears behind the bombast of his official accounts. Whether or not a more complicated character lurked within, King was not just one more in the ever longer line of Westerners who make up a Muslim world to suit their purposes and to satisfy their sponsors at home. His years in Ottoman Syria launched him into a lifelong celebrity that extended even beyond evangelical circles. Adept though he was at posing as a man who risked everything to challenge Islam, martyrdom had nothing to do with his winning that renown. On the contrary, Fisk's anguished struggles on that score must have struck him as mystifying, almost quaint. King's achievement instead was finding in his encounter with Islam the means to fortify evangelical Protestantism with its own "hidden man." Its influence endures to the present in some quarters of religious and political conservatism in the United States.

King's defiance at the Damascus gate was not an isolated episode. It was only the first in a series of confrontations with Muslim men that received rapt coverage in the American press. Once settled in that city, he instantly bridled at the effrontery of his Muslim tutor who "gave me a lesson in true Oriental style. I was obliged to sit at his feet like a child, and he taught, as if he were Lord of the World." A few weeks later when their caravan to Aleppo stopped at a famous sheikh's tomb and he and Fisk tried to enter that shaded enclosure, King heard some Turks exclaim, "God forbid, that a Christian should enter," and one vowed, "I will give my blood before that shall take place." At that, King rejoined, "Are you Mussulmans? Do you think you are so much better than all other men?" On the same trip, he ended up in a shouting match with "the greatest Shekh in the caravan" who had urged him to embrace Islam. And he lectured another member of the caravan, a man "who was very boisterous and talked, as if he thought the Mussulmans the only people on earth" to learn from "the fable of the Mouse, that was born and brought up in a chest." Like the mouse, which "marveled that the world was so large" once it left the chest, King huffed, this Muslim braggart thought "that the sultan's Dominions are the whole World;—whereas they form a very small part of it." Here was a whole new cast of Muslims, not one crazed fiend from his former repertoire among them. Their most remarkable trait was the arrogant assumption and assertion of Muslim superiority, and King's great virtue, having the chutzpah to set them straight. The trouble with Islam, as these stories told his readers, was that its adherents rejected the fundamental tenet of republican equality—that no one was better than anyone else.[6]

If King tailored this portrayal of Muslim men to appeal to his American audience, he also built on an earlier chorus of Western complaint about Muslim contempt for Christians. Its most commanding voice, even in the 1820s, remained that of Carsten Niebuhr, the Danish explorer who lamented at length that Christians and Jews in eighteenth-century Cairo could ride only donkeys and were obliged to dismount even those lowly beasts when passing the homes of Muslim magistrates and important mosques. A greater humiliation for Niebuhr was their being forced to "alight, upon meeting even the most inconsiderable Egyptian lord" who would "appear always on horseback," with a servant in the lead, "a great staff in his hand," warning them by "crying out *enfil*, get down." Niebuhr bridled, too, at some of the Egyptians' popular entertainments, including a "magic lanthorn" that turned "the dress and manners of Europeans to ridicule and dressing monkeys in Western style." The mortified Niebuhr, like King and other Westerners after him, took the behavior of these "extremely haughty and insolent" Muslims as an affront to the Christian faith.[7]

They took it, too, as an affront to their masculinity. More than a whiff of testosterone rises from these accounts once Western males sensed that their honor was at stake, and King's reports were no exception. His determination to ride mounted on horseback, a classic emblem of mastery, and his tirade at the shaded tomb recall the concern with reputation and respect that first surfaced in his response to Hadji Mohammed back in Jerusalem. As an evangelical, of course, King could not have resorted to physical violence except in self-defense, but he made a point of telling his devout readers that like any man of spirit he felt "tempted" to throw off that religious restraint. Standing up to Muslim men—even if it stopped short of going mano a mano with weapons other than words—was essential to his asserting evangelical manliness.

True, King provoked men of every faith and none, but he and his fellow missionaries never doubted that Muslims were the real men of the Middle East. How those Persian giants towered in Martyn's fantasies as he dressed for Shiraz. How Fisk yearned to be accepted into the learned fraternity of Muslim scholars that he conjured at the Jazzar Mosque. How Jowett fumed when several Turks on horseback sped by him at Scio, knowing they "despise a man who goes on foot." And how the missionary wife Abigail Davis Goodell thrilled when she and Ann Parker Bird perched on the shoulders of "half naked Arabs" to disembark at Beirut. ("Altho' I was not much pleased myself at the idea of riding in this new way," she added primly.) Even steamy gossip about the prevalence of "sodomy" did not impugn Muslim masculinity. Touring the pasha's palace in Cairo, King estimated that it held three hundred concubines and "also observed some small rooms, which I was told were occupied by boys, and for purposes, which I should blush to name." He concluded that Muslim men were sexually insatiable and degenerate—but not unmanly. If Islam made them supercilious, it had not turned them into sissies. Just the opposite.[8]

The missionaries found their esteem for Muslim men echoed in the writings of many other Western travelers and scholars that circulated in the decades around 1800. The tribesmen of the Arabian Peninsula

won universal acclaim for their courage, hardihood, and love of freedom, wringing even from Jedidiah Morse the admission that they "are
a people of great spirit and valor, and resolute in defence of liberty."
John Lewis Burckhardt agreed that the desert Arabs had not only "an
air of independence" but also an "altogether brave and manly appearance." Turks often came in for sneers that they were effeminate sensu-
alists and no match for any Westerner, above all the French. Or so
François René de Chateaubriand insisted in an account of his travels
through Turkey: got up like a dominatrix—booted, spurred, and whip
in hand—he claimed to have reduced janissaries and even an aga to
sniveling terror. William Jowett agreed that "Turks" were afraid of
Englishmen, and "intimidation was the only way in which you could
obtain good treatment from them." But others rose to the Turks' defense,
including the Irish traveler James Emerson, who gushed that they were
"the finest looking race of men in the world," with their "arching brows,
jetty eyes, and aquiline noses, their lofty figures and stately mien," to
say nothing of the Ottoman's "glossy beard," which "flings contempt
on the effeminate chin of the clipped and docked European." Weapon
envy also cast its spell: Emerson's idealized Turk came equipped with
"a pair of superbly chased pistols," "a yataghan [sword], with a jeweled
handle," and a scimitar.[9]

Western men of every sort loved the whole look—the robes and the
turbans, the beards and the arms, the works. As they told it, getting
decked out *à la turque* or *à l'arabe* was all about convenience and safety,
but—admitted or not—it was also about looking manly. No drag queens
could have been keener to trade their trousers for flowing robes, and
some Westerners saw the humor. When his missionary partner, Isaac
Bird, first "put on his Oriental dress," William Goodell joked that he
looked "like an Archbishop." But most Western men took such make-
overs seriously, recording the exact date of their assuming "Eastern"
dress along with full descriptions of their clothes. A few—including
Jonas King—posed for drawings in their new duds. Pliny Fisk did not
go that far, but he, too, took some pride in his outward transformation.
In a letter to his niece Clarissa back in Massachusetts, he confided, "If
we were to meet now, and I should be surprised to see how much you
have improved, you would be not less surprised to see me with a long
black beard, with large white turban on my head, and loose robes that
come down to the ancles [ankles]." No matter how strange he might

appear now to Clarissa, Fisk implied that he had "improved" over the intervening years, as had "the little girl who used to sit on my knee and play with me." On the flip side, failing the test of proper appearance stung. To shade himself while traveling about Mount Lebanon, one British army captain opened his umbrella, prompting a Druze peasant to jeer, "The shade is for women, not for men." Mortified, the captain still "could not help admiring the apparent sincerity of the fellow" and "acknowledged its force by shutting up my umbrella till he had got out of sight."[10]

Through King's chronicles, American evangelicals began to play their part in shaping the West's long-standing fascination with Islamic masculinity. Devils and lunatics receded from the ranks of his inventions as he joined the other Westerners who evoked Muslim men as inspiring a mixture of fear and envy, awe and emulation. Like Henry Martyn before him, King aligned with the many secular writers who, far from identifying western Asia as a feminized "Orient," conjured a preserve of manly (albeit undemocratic) Muslims against whom the best Christian men would prove their mettle and dispel their adversaries' contempt. And to dominate this imagined setting, King crafted a missionary persona who unfurled republican equality's standard on distant shores. Even more important, that ideal embodied a new model of evangelical masculinity, one whose attributes went beyond restraint and respectability, piety and probity, to include physical prowess, fearlessness, and daring. Here was a hero who might lend the sort of appeal to evangelicalism—a "hidden man"—that it sorely needed.[11]

Jonas King's inventions addressed the biggest challenge that faced evangelicals particularly and Protestants generally in the early republic. Just as John Sargent populated his memoir of Martyn with learned, reasonable Muslims to answer anxieties about converting the Islamic world, what prompted King's creations was the Protestant clergy's concern at the feminization of American Christianity. It was a clever, if counterintuitive, strategy: King hoped that by putting its image on steroids, the foreign missions movement—until then a weak draw among men—would become evangelicalism's star attraction. To that end, he devised a new kind of saint, the missionary as a man of action and honor, a

Christian more than capable of holding his own with men who set the gold standard for masculinity.

Sargent's memoir had heralded the appearance of this heroic persona, but his Martyn was strictly a verbal pugilist, and Persia's learned jurists and clerics were no more likely to come out swinging. By contrast, King represented himself as spoiling for a go at armed-to-the-teeth Turks and desert-hardened sheikhs, whose worth, like his own, showed in the capacity for action as well as the power to debate. His stories sent the message that missionary manliness would show Muslims that Christianity—real Christianity, of the evangelical kind—was a religion worthy of their respect. But that message also aimed to convince men back in the United States who had heretofore shunned religion—the workingmen of the North, all classes in the South—that evangelical Christianity was worthy of *their* respect.

The older image of the self-denying martyr—an ideal embraced, rejected, and then embraced again by Pliny Fisk—did not disappear from popular missionary culture. But the iconic figure for the coming age would be King's world-straddling hero, whose exploits announced the manly bona fides of evangelicals and whose fighting—far more than his dying—assured his moral authority with a wider male audience. Fisk himself endorsed enlisting Christians of conspicuous valor to recruit more men in the evangelical cause. Writing to a friend in New England, he drew an unfavorable contrast between American military officers and those among his friends in the British navy, who sold Bibles and formed Bible societies among the Greeks in the Mediterranean and even strove to convert their "deistical" fellows. "Is there any class of men in our army or navy of whom we can say this?" he asked, knowing the answer. "If there are any who *profess* to be religious, do they let their light shine, and openly and boldly serve their Lord?" (No such problem among Muslims, he might have added.)

But relating his arrest in Jerusalem marked the last time that Fisk would turn his own experiences into grist for the publicity mill that King was creating. Nowhere in his journals or correspondence did Fisk mention what he made of his partner's inventions of Muslims or missionaries, nor did he hint at any tension in their personal relations. But some of the stories about himself that Fisk withheld from public knowledge seem to imply a judgment of King. There was his confrontation with the soldier at the Jerusalem gate who demanded baksheesh. And there was another, more dangerous encounter, one detailed at some length in his private journal but that appeared nowhere in his official reports or even in his surviving letters to family and friends. An armed Druze robber accosted him while riding through Mount Lebanon, and a struggle ensued as the two wrestled for the thief's pistol until both wore out and agreed on a bribe—a bitter pill for Fisk. It's hard to imagine the frail King in such a fight, let alone walking away in one piece, but he had it all over Fisk when it came to pretending otherwise. Possibly, then, Fisk's public silences about his own displays of physical courage sound a quiet reproach to his partner.

Whatever Fisk's opinion of King might have been, both recognized that the foreign missions movement needed a prominent figure who would appeal to men as powerfully as the Harriet Newell of missionary-wife hagiography spoke to women. Just as her elevation into an "apostle and martyr" stood as proof for a female audience of evangelicals' commitment to upholding the spiritual equality of women, the right sort of missionary would send the message that evangelicalism only made men more macho. Little as he looked the part, King was more than ready to debut in that role.[12]

That set him on the cusp of a major change in the culture of American Protestantism. It was his generation of evangelicals who initiated the drive to bring more men into their churches by endowing their faith with a more masculine ethos. For the rest of the nineteenth century and to the present day, those efforts have continued, finding their fullest expression in the decades around 1900 with the vogue of "muscular Christianity," a strain of religiosity urging the need for "manly men" to spread the gospel both abroad and at home. King thus stood at the head of a long line of men who embodied evangelical masculinity, spreading the word about the manliness of godliness within and beyond religious circles. His most direct descendant today is the motorcycle-riding, pistol-packing Franklin Graham, founder of the global evangelical philanthropy Samaritan's Purse. The organization's message—that the God of Islam ("a very wicked and evil religion") is not the same as the God of Christianity—King would have found as congenial as Graham's carefully cultivated public image.

This combination of macho swagger with the fervent expression of Christian piety and an aggressive stance toward the Muslim world exerts a broad influence and appeal in the present-day United States. A legacy of popular missionary culture from two centuries ago, it constitutes a common strand of cultural DNA among some of the leading figures in today's right-wing religious, political, and military circles. It infuses certain strains in neoconservative foreign policy, and it helps to explain why a twice-born president with no experience of combat, days after declaring a preemptive war against Iraq, donned a flight suit, landed on an aircraft carrier, and proclaimed victory. Here was a bit of political theater beamed directly at those evangelical voters irked by the president's repeated claim in the wake of the attacks on the Twin Towers and the Pentagon that Islam is "a religion of peace." The strutting demeanor, the "Make my day" rhetoric, and the militant ethos evoked a masculine style and implied a stance toward Islam as reassuring to those believers as that of Franklin Graham and as old as the inventions of Jonas King.[13]

As Jonas King strove to shape the future of evangelicalism in the United States, events unfolding at home contributed to his success. Of particular importance was the emergence of a nearly universal sympathy for Greeks in their struggle against the Ottoman Empire—and a corresponding antipathy to the Turks in particular and to Muslims in general. King's timing—far from accidental, thanks to his well-placed correspondents—could not have been more perfect. His portrayals of missionaries and Muslims reached readers in the United States just as those sentiments were peaking in the mid-1820s. It was an auspicious climate for the new missionary persona that King had called into being: the man of action, dishing out the comeuppance that Muslims deserved. Standing up for Jesus' divinity and republican values in Ottoman Syria made him the right man for his time as this first wave of Islamophobia swept the United States. His invented Muslim Arabs, contemptuous of American liberty and democracy, served as perfect counterparts to the Muslim Turks represented in the secular press, almost uniformly vilified as tyrants bent on snuffing out the Greeks' bid for freedom.

It was a group of devout women in Brooklyn Heights who wrought the most vivid emblem of pro-Greek sentiment. In the fall of 1823, they emblazoned a mammoth cross with the inscription "Sacred to the cause of the Greeks" and erected it in their neighborhood to overlook Manhattan. Americans of all religious persuasions and none joined in, soliciting publicity, money, arms, and fighters for the Greek cause. Merchants pledged a percentage of their profits to the relief effort; ministers delivered sermons and took up collections; socialites sponsored auctions, fairs, and balls; actors gave benefit performances; college students held candlelight vigils; state legislatures passed resolutions. The well educated and wealthy, steeped as they were in classical learning, lionized Greece as the cradle of philosophy, literature, and democracy. People of humbler means identified the Greek insurgency with the American war for independence only half a century earlier. As for evangelicals, they believed that a Turkish defeat would deliver the deathblow to Islam. Typical were the sentiments expressed from one Boston pulpit that "the downfall of Turkey will remove that impassable barrier, which has hitherto shut out Christianity from Western Asia . . . Missionaries loaded with Bibles will feel their way into the farthest retreats of Mohammedan darkness."

Critics had always outnumbered Ottoman admirers in the West, and the latter's ranks thinned even more as the Greek struggle raged. Insisting that "we are no crusaders," the Boston *Evening Gazette*'s editors nonetheless acknowledged that "we would rejoice to see Palestine in the possession of Christians" and that an independent Greece would be "a wholesome check on the vagaries of his Sublime Negress the Grand Seignor"—an allusion to the Ottoman sultan. If racial epithets were rare, a more common tactic for reading the Turks into the ranks of the despised were graphic portrayals of what Boston's Greek relief committee called an "impious rage" against Christianity—Ottoman Muslims murdering Greek Orthodox priests and monks, turning churches into mosques, and desecrating Bibles. Among the outrages widely chronicled in newspapers was the fate of a Greek priest named Jesus, whom, it was said, the Turks crucified, covered with pitch, and burned.

With both the Greeks and many of their supporters in the West casting the struggle as a holy war, it proved a short step from denouncing the Turks to demonizing all Muslims. Secular and religious publications on both sides of the Atlantic kept up the drumbeat, characterizing the contest as "a war of the crescent against the cross" and referring to the Turks as "the ferocious disciples of Mahomet." By the same slippery elision that made the Turks stand for all Muslims, the Greeks came to represent all non-Muslims. In a statement circulated throughout the North, New Haven's Greek relief committee claimed that Islam inspired its believers with "a supreme contempt of all men not professing the same system of faith" and a determination to "establish the Mohammedan religion over the earth by fire and sword." Geographies drilled the same lesson into schoolchildren, who learned from a popular textbook that "Mahomet propagated his religion by the sword" and that his followers still harbored "a spirit of malevolence" toward all but Muslims. Even magazines patronized by an elite readership purveyed the opinion that Islam instilled antagonism to other faiths.[14]

A few dissenters took exception to depicting the Greeks' struggle as a holy war. Noting the "powerful effect" of Christianity on many Americans' view of the conflict, one contributor to a Hartford newspaper charged that aiding the Greeks had become "a mere crusade, and a most inconsistent procedure in us Americans, who assert as a natural right, the entire freedom of religious opinion." The same newspaper also printed the remarks of a sympathetic British traveler in the hopes of removing "those illiberal and unfounded prejudices which almost universally prevail against the Ottomans." Neither did balanced portrayals of Islam disappear entirely from the press. One contributor to a Philadelphia literary magazine praised George Sale's "soundness of judgment" in refuting the charges of "invention and imposture" against Muhammad and called on the West "to admit that science and the arts, the sacred cause of liberty itself, owes much to these eastern devotees [Muslim scholars]." Finally, a few fearless souls ventured the opinion that people of all faiths worshipped the same God and would meet in the afterlife. Among them was a liberal Christian minister whose sermon offered kind words about Muslim believers, inspiring one member of his Baltimore congregation to compose a poem that found its way into a few newspapers:

> TO ALL—each creature of his hand,
> Or Jew or Turk, simple or grand,—
> He doth extend one hand in love,
> And with the other points above:—
> The Christian and the Turk, and even
> The pagan, are in the same heaven.[15]

But far different sentiments had come to dominate most public discourse by the mid-1820s, muting those voices that had offered more positive appraisals of Islam earlier in the nineteenth century. Caricatures of Muhammad and his faith abounded. Among the most widely reprinted newspaper items was a comparison of Jesus and Muhammad, the latter "arrayed in armour and blood" and engorged with lust for his wives and concubines. In one of many purported historical illustrations of the violence inspired by "the power of that superstition of which Mahomet was the founder," the *Alexandria Herald* recounted a grisly procession mourning a Turkish military defeat centuries earlier in which 300 Muslims "with habits *dyed in blood*" murdered a Jew at every quarter mile, while "100 penitents mutilated themselves with knives." Hoary fables revived, too: newspapers throughout New England reprinted the tale of an American who traveled to Medina and claimed to have entered a vault—the first Christian ever to do so!—where he saw Muhammad's coffin was suspended by magnets. He "actually passed his sword at each side of the coffin, which very sensibly vibrated as the steel approached it." So much for the efforts of earlier decades to provide Americans with a more accurate understanding of Islam. By the mid-1820s, the reports dominating the press had come to echo, even to reinforce, the message that evangelicals had been beaming for decades: what defined America's enemies in the Middle East was not their ethnic or national loyalties but rather their adherence to Islam.[16]

Accompanying this surge of Islamophobia were efforts to demote Islam from one of the world's great monotheisms to a tissue of superstitions, even a sort of paganism. Earlier treatments of Islam, both religious and secular, had sometimes tagged certain Islamic beliefs as "superstitious," but during the 1820s that characterization became more sweeping and widespread, popping up in periodicals and schoolbooks, speeches and sermons. "The light of the gloomy crescent is waning fast," one New Hampshire newspaper promised, and "the falling fabric of savage superstition totters to its very centre." More striking was the judgment that Muslims were mere heathens, an opinion that had last commanded wide acceptance among Christians during the Middle Ages. One geography textbook explained to its youthful readers that "the Koran teaches the worship of one God, and forbids idolatry; but it requires an idolatrous reverence for Mahomet." The Boston *Evening Gazette* agreed that "almost any paganism is preferable" to the "doctrines of the Koran." It followed that the heathen adherents of so "savage" a "superstition" must be uncommonly credulous, and proof for many American readers came in the aftermath of a devastating fire that consumed Pera, a suburb of Constantinople, in 1823. Nearly every newspaper in the early republic carried accounts of the destruction, most followed by some version of this tale from the crypt: as one "Cheid Ahmet, reputed a sage and saint among the pious Turks, was making his prayer alone before the sacred coffin [of Muhammad in Medina]," he heard the voice of the Prophet himself complaining about "the vices and sins of the Mussulmen." Word spread back to Constantinople that Muhammad had spoken from the grave, convincing all of the Turks that the blaze was "an effect of celestial anger."[17]

Jonas King swelled this first wave of Islamophobia still higher with reports that reinforced the link between Muslim beliefs and superstition. At once shaping and shaped by public opinion, King's dispatches demonstrate the synergy that could develop between missionaries and their audience back in the United States. Evidence of occult doings had intrigued King from the outset of his travels in the Levant. Writing from Cairo to one of his Andover professors, he noted that some Egyptians "still practice magic, and have much to do with Serpents, which they keep and feed with milk," even held in their hands. For his readers, he described evidences of the similar occult notions among Syria's Muslims: a sheikh who urged him to embrace Islam proposed "to write certain words, on a piece of paper," for King "to put under my head at night, and in case I should dream of some one's coming to me and telling me that Islamism is the true faith, that I should turn Mussulman." But most fascinating to King were the jinn, or genies, spirits inhabiting both the visible and the invisible worlds who appear in the Qur'an and the hadith. Although the Bible features similar second-string supernaturals like angels and demons, King concluded that Muslim belief in the jinn crossed the line that separated faith from superstition.

That made him eager to know more. So eager that King offered a large sum of money to a Muslim Turk who visited his lodgings in Beirut if he could produce a jinni for inspection. The Turk admitted that the jinn had never actually appeared to him but insisted that "the thousands in Egypt who declare they have seen and known them" could hardly be wrong. Then he related "with an air of entire confidence in its truth" that a jinni who had a human wife and family in Egypt had been called to answer to a magistrate for allowing them "to wander about in poverty and rags." The jinni replied that he was married "in the other world and was forced to divide his attention between the two families. 'If,' he said 'you compel me to do better by my children down here, I must go and obtain a separation from those in the other world.'" The governor insisted, and the jinni complied. Once in Damascus, King pursued the subject with his Arabic teacher there, Mohammad el Attar, who replied that the jinn had visited him every night for the last nine months. By his account, they were male and female, of Muslim, Catholic, and Greek Orthodox faith, good and bad character; typically, they lived underground, often among the ancient ruins, and had the power to assume any shape they wished. In fact, he knew two "who appear to be men, and who go to the market and buy and sell, like men"; some married human beings, unions that produced exceptionally fine children. No surprise that the jinn quickly found their way from King's journal to the pages of religious periodicals. Could there be juicier evidence that superstition riddled Islam?

Intellectual consistency became zeal's first casualty in pressing that line of attack. Evangelicals had a long history of depicting Islam as superstition's opposite—as an ultra-rationalist religion, a Unitarianism East. Like religious liberals in the West, evangelicals charged, Muslims reduced religion to the performance of moral and ritual duties, investing too much regard in their powers of reason and will, and failing to grasp the depths of human sinfulness. King had no plans to give up that argument. On the contrary, he stored away in his journal—no doubt for some future assault on his liberal adversaries—an exchange in which Sheikh Khaleel asked if any Americans believed that Jesus was not God. Once King described the Unitarians, the Muslim replied "with much warmth," "Those men I should take by the hand, as Brothers. Those are good men." Yet when King was not slamming Muslims for being too rationalist, he did not scruple about scolding them for being too irrational—sunk in the grossest superstitions. A whopping contradiction, but one too useful for him and other evangelicals to abandon.[18]

By their lights, identifying Islam with superstition advanced the cause of Protestant missions. It enhanced the prospects of turning Muslims—a people who, though credulous, were as innately reasonable as other human beings—into Christians. By way of implied contrast, it also reinforced the congruence of Christianity to the canons of reason. The great goal of nearly all post-Enlightenment Protestants was to build a case for the reasonableness of their faith by showing that it rested on a foundation of common sense supported by the biblical "evidences" of miracle and prophecy. And the Protestants in the early republic with the greatest incentive to pursue that goal were evangelicals. Upstart groups like the Methodists and the Baptists faced a barrage of criticism that their revivals promoted emotional excess and social disorder, while more established denominations like the Congregationalists and the Presbyterians fended off charges that their Calvinist doctrines flew in the face of both reason and republicanism. With these challenges before them, tarring Islam with the brush of superstition—by definition an unreasoning belief or practice or awe or fear—helped to reinforce evangelical Protestantism's desired identity as a religion—the only religion—that could pass muster with thinking people.[19]

For a man who claimed to know Islam, Jonas King was remarkably cavalier when it came to the Qur'an. "Having always avoided reading it in English or French," he finally got around to it at Jaffa early in 1824. He read the Qur'an through—for the first and evidently the only time— in Arabic ("that *wonderful* language") under the tutelage of Sheikh Khaleel. "Its beauties consist in a fine jingle of words and harmony of sounds," King concluded, but its message showed that even men with "high thoughts of certain parts of the Divine character, may arrive at a very high degree of wickedness in this world." Pliny Fisk, too, would remain fixed in his judgment that the Bible far outshone the Qur'an, even though the latter had "many fine sentences, the style is often flowing and harmonious, and the sentiments expressed, particularly concerning the Deity, are often grand and sublime." But when Fisk took instruction from Sheikh Khaleel early in 1825, he had already read George Sale's translation and many books about Islam. And he had spent the previous months, as his travels took him from Jerusalem to Damascus to Aleppo and then to Jaffa, focused on gaining a full command of Arabic and a better grasp of the Muslim faith.[20]

What stands out is Fisk's resolve to get Islam right—to gain an accurate understanding of its core doctrines and practices. To that end, he quizzed his tutors in Arabic as well as any other Muslims whom he met. What he discovered was that, as among Christians, their beliefs and practices varied. Even to basic questions, such as whether Muslims prayed to Muhammad, his informants offered differing answers. During his night under arrest in Jerusalem, he found the presence of mind to ask the governor's nephew about this matter, and the young man "confirmed what we [he and Bird] had already heard that Muslems pray to Mohommed that they have a book of prayers to assist this part of their devotion." Still not satisfied, Fisk took that same question to his Arabic teacher in Jerusalem, Jar Allah, who convinced him that "this practice is not authorized by the Koran and if it exists, it is a corruption of Mohammedism." Fisk wasted no time informing Jeremiah Evarts but also kept checking; he raised the matter with Khaleel a year later, who agreed with Jar Allah.[21]

That was only one of many subjects on which Fisk quizzed the sheikh over the next two months. The two spent six hours together each day and made their way through the first half of the Qur'an. They chanted its verses together, breaking often for Khaleel's commentary and their discussions, which Fisk committed to more than thirty pages of notes in his private journal. Some of those conversations he set down in the form of a dialogue, as he had done before to capture the flow of his discussions with Jews and Christians, perhaps working from notes scribbled as Khaleel spoke. Fisk's questions ranged from the elementary to the obscure, along with any stray curiosity that crossed his mind. Did Muslims believe that human beings could sin by harboring bad intentions or only by acting on them? Did they include the Virgin Mary among their prophets? Must those Jews who wished to become Muslims first convert to Christianity? A good listener, Fisk asked questions designed to draw out his tutor, and he rarely challenged Khaleel's statements or held forth about his own religious views.

What better way to discover the source of Islam's appeal—its "hidden man"? Fisk ranked the sheikh among Syria's best and brightest, the sort of man whose loyalty to Muhammad's teachings continued to arouse the greatest curiosity among evangelicals. During the same month that Fisk began his studies in Jaffa, Britain's leading missionary journal declared that "the System of Mahomedanism is, as yet, but imperfectly understood among us," because whereas promises of a sensual paradise accounted for its hold "on the mass of the people," far less obvious were "the sophisms and subtleties by which it palliates its grossness and follies to acute minds, and retains such men in bondage." That was what puzzled Fisk, and before him William Jowett and Henry Martyn. How did Islam draw and hold the loyalty of "acute minds"?[22]

And why did some swallow so much of what seemed like superstition to Western Christians? Sharing King's fascination with the jinn, Fisk squirreled away in his private journal all that his partner's tutor in Damascus, Mohammad el Attar, had to impart about those beings. It was also one of the first subjects that he raised with Khaleel, who, to Fisk's frustration, if not his surprise, did not entirely agree with el Attar's descriptions of the jinn. No, Khaleel took great exception to the view that they were visible to human beings: "He [el Attar] is a fool. He is a madman and a liar. He is a genii himself and not a man. He deserves to be put in fetters until his senses return to him." With equal conviction, Khaleel related stories about the dark art of "enchantment." He had watched as a sorcerer "raised his long robe a little from his feet" and immediately thousands of mice "scampered forth and filled the room"; a second robe raising released "a multitude of weasels" that devoured all the mice, and a third rounded up the weasels. He also claimed to possess a book that enabled him to divine what someone else was thinking—as many as "a hundred times in succession."

Wonders all, rivaling those that King had broadcast back to the United States. But if Fisk was intrigued, he was even more mystified. There was the learned Khaleel, talking soberly of sorcerer sightings and mind readings. And before him, there was Mohammad el Attar, "said by the Christians to be the most learned man in Damascus" and "certainly a man of strong mind and well acquainted with Mussulman learning," who nonetheless, to Fisk's utter astonishment, appeared to believe "all this nonsense" about the jinn. What to make of this Muslim teacher who boasted in one breath about the handsomely endowed "Madressas" of Damascus with their "learned Shekhs" and in the next described "a book which contains a wonderful science by which a Shekh who understands it well can do anything he pleases" simply by writing "a paper"? Why, he himself had lately provided that service to the pasha of Acre, Mohammad confided, by writing a "paper" that restored him to favor with the Ottoman sultan. Fisk struggled to reconcile his high estimate of his Muslim tutors' intelligence with his low opinion of some of their professed beliefs. But unlike King, he hoped to understand rather than exploit what both men took to be superstitious elements in Islam.

Fisk suspected that what might account, at least in part, for learned Muslims' embracing what he found outlandish was their concern to uphold Islam's superior truth. During their two months together, Khaleel disclosed his devout belief in much more that Fisk believed to be as fanciful as weasels rushing from under a sorcerer's robes—but set down fully in his notes. There was the "Island of the Girls," inhabited entirely by women, their bodies "wholly of flesh without bones," who "marry each other and propagate their species." There was the "bridge of the Mohammedans" that all humankind must cross on the Day of Judgment, a span described by the sheikh as fifteen hundred miles long, "thinner than a hair and sharper than a sword." There was the great tree in paradise bearing on its every leaf "the name of some person and the length of his life"—only one of the wonders in this vast heavenly garden, with its buildings made of pearls and jewels and its fruits so magnificent that back in the time of the caliphs, when an apple fell to earth, even "a Camel could not carry it." Fisk knew that some other Muslims understood these wonders recounted in Islamic tradition as "metaphorical," and he offered Khaleel openings in their conversations to agree. But his tutor insisted on their literal truth. He did so stoutly, perhaps out of conviction, but possibly, as Fisk intimated, from the concern that any concession to allegory would diminish all of the truth claims of Islam in the eyes of a Christian missionary.[23]

The possibility must also have occurred to Fisk that men like Khaleel and el Attar claimed magical powers to fathom the depths of the missionaries' credulity—or to intimidate them. As he knew, ordinary people and elites alike in Ottoman Syria suspected that any Westerner in their midst was up to no good. They were either gathering military intelligence for a future conquest or searching for buried treasure in ancient ruins or scheming to steal money. By the mid-1820s, that apprehension had come to focus on the American missionaries. Rumors susurrated through Jaffa that they practiced witchcraft of such power that their spells had brought on the earthquake that leveled Aleppo a few years earlier. All of Beirut gossiped that the missionaries were "necromancers" who bribed people to become Protestants. Their

magic even ensured that the original sum of those bribes "always remained" with those who took the money, no matter how much they
might spend. These Protestant sorcerers also wreaked vengeance on
backsliders by drawing pictures of their converts and keeping them in
a book; if any deserted their new faith, the missionaries would "shoot
the picture," and the apostate would die. (No mean achievement, because the Americans had made not a single convert.) What better defense, then, against missionaries reputed for their skill in the dark arts
than for Muslim men to claim potent magic of their own? Or better
still, to possess the confidence that their faith actually endowed them
with such occult powers? Could that explain, at least in part, the elusive "hidden man" of Islam?[24]

Whether or not Fisk's speculations strayed in that direction, he felt
certain that Islam's appeal had something to do with its empowering
men. By the promise of magic, perhaps—at the expense of women
most certainly. Here was the other recurring subject of Fisk's notes: he
devoted many pages to the Qur'an's teachings and Khaleel's offhand
remarks about marriage, divorce, remarriage, and penalties for adultery, and most emphasize Islam's subordination of women and husbands' debasement of their wives. "There are few now in Jaffa who have
never divorced their wives," the sheikh declared. "Some 2–3 5–10 and
even 20 times." It need not come to that, he continued, because "if you
fear that they [i.e., your wives] will displease you admonish them—
separate from them in bed . . . and beat them." When Khaleel acknowledged that "there are many [men] who do beat their wives till their
heads are covered with blood and sometimes even till they die," Fisk
pursued the matter:

F. If a man beats his wife to death is no notice taken of it?
S. None at all. Nobody makes any inquiry about it.
F. He kills her as he would a dog.
S. Just like a dog. Such is the government of our country now.

Fisk did not regard the Muslim paradise as promising much
improvement. According to Khaleel, there "every man has at least
70 women," and for "Martyrs, Apostles, and Prophets" many more.
"Not such a heaven as I wish for," Fisk rejoined. Yet on this subject, too,
he sounded out the sheikh by mentioning that "a Christian who had

turned Mussulman"—none other than George English—had told him that "the best Commentators understood it [70 women for each man in paradise] figuratively." "Then he is not yet a Mussulman," Khaleel shot back. "Why Paradise if there are no women there?"[25]

Fisk never explained his aim in keeping so complete a record of his time with Khaleel, but it clearly served as more than a useful reference of the Qur'an's teachings. One purpose was for Fisk to establish to his own satisfaction, like Henry Martyn before him, that the Qur'an failed to pass muster at the bar of reason. To that end, Fisk offered a kind of higher criticism of the text itself, arguing that even though Muslims pointed to the very existence of the Qur'an as miraculous evidence "and impregnable proof of the truth of their religion," yet "by their own confession the Coran did not make its appearance at once in a complete form, nor even chapter by chapter, but a verse or a few verses at a time." It was the Prophet's successors who then arranged the verses in chapters, so that "in fact the book as it now exists is the production of the learned men of two or three generations." Little did Fisk suspect that similar approaches to the Bible would challenge the faith of many Christians in the near future.

By writing down his exchanges with the sheikh, Fisk also confronted his own inner struggles. Experience kept breaching the boundaries between his faith and Islam—rudely, in his encounter with George English; almost mystically, in his epiphany at the Jazzar Mosque in Acre. To restore a sense of boundedness, he had committed himself again to seeking his own martyrdom, and in some of his exchanges with the sheikh Fisk seemed to be searching for firm, bright lines of demarcation between his own faith and Islam that would justify that decision. His disgust over the treatment of Muslim women exudes an almost palpable relief at what Fisk took to be the superiority of evangelical ways. And then there was a brief, bitter exchange, the closest that he ever came to confrontation with Khaleel:

F. Yes, your religion is altogether by the sword.
S. Yes wholly by the sword. Excellent.—Is it not excellent by the sword?
F. To stand by the truth is better than by the sword.
S. The sword is truth. The sword is descended from heaven.
F. The sword is from hell.

Curious, the assertion that Islam "is altogether by the sword," coming from a man who had so long sought that religion's "hidden man" and acknowledged that Muslim beliefs often spread through peaceful means. He had at least heard as much at Andover and in later years appeared completely persuaded by George Sale and other Orientalists. Perhaps Fisk's sympathy for the embattled Greeks had at last taken its toll on his estimate of Islam.

Perhaps, too, Fisk was compiling his trove of notes with one eye trained on a prospective American audience. For months, Jeremiah Evarts had been urging him to write about his years in the Levant—to produce an American version of Jowett's books about the religions of the region and missionary prospects there. Some of the American Board's donors were getting restless—among them a Boston women's missionary society that had contributed freely to the Palestine mission but now threatened to withdraw funding. "Their alleged reason is, that they do not see any effects produced by the labors of the Palestine Missionaries," Evarts wrote. After three years of partnering with King, Fisk knew exactly how to write for such readers, and what the sheikh had spilled would make a real splash. The jinn and the sorcery and the divination. The giant apples, the boneless Amazons, the bridge like a razor's edge. Here was welcome copy for the American presses that were pounding Islam down to a superstition. And what would pry open purses in Boston quicker than a sheikh's testimony that Muslim women were treated no better than dogs in this world and then consigned to an afterlife abounding with men never "weary of coition"? To say nothing of the satisfaction those many Americans outraged over the Greek Revolution would take in Fisk's insistence that Islam "is altogether by the sword."[26]

Yet he never published a word of his conversation with Sheikh Khaleel. Whatever Fisk might have intended when he began taking down his notes, he never dispatched them to the American Board, never sent so much as a scrap to the Morse brothers. What held him back? Perhaps once immersed in his studies, Fisk had slowly realized that he would need to converse with a great many more Muslims before coming to any accurate conclusions about Islam, let alone the sources of its appeal. There were simply too many differences and discrepancies in the testimonies of those believers—all of them men—whom he had interviewed. That explanation suits this stickler for getting the facts straight, the man who took pride in his learning about the Ottoman Empire and who hoped to impress others familiar with that world. He would have respected the difficulty of the challenge before him, intent as he was on understanding—and not inventing—Islam. In any case, Pliny Fisk shared nothing about his months in Jaffa with his sponsors or his readers in the United States. That left telling the story of the Palestine mission's encounters with Muslims in Ottoman Syria to a man with an altogether different agenda.

According to Jonas King, it was the rumors about their practicing witchcraft that finally forced him and Fisk out of Jaffa at the end of March. More likely, the two had long planned to head for Jerusalem in time to proselytize among the Christian pilgrims flocking there for Easter. With temperatures rising and visitors packing the city, tensions ratcheted even higher when the pasha of Damascus showed up with some three thousand soldiers and set about collecting his annual tribute through intimidation, torture, and imprisonment. He also scattered the rebellious inhabitants of Bethlehem and neighboring villages, whose frightened inhabitants took up temporary refuge in the desert. Finally, the pasha tried to settle his long-running score with Ibrahim Aboo Ghoosh, King's dining companion in Jaffa, whose family had long treated the roads between Jaffa and Jerusalem as their private turnpike, demanding tolls from all travelers. That turned a tidy profit, and the pasha wanted his cut, so he nabbed Aboo Ghoosh's brother and held him for ransom. No sooner had the pasha and his prisoner headed back to Damascus than this terrier to the ruling mastiff sent two hundred of his men to prowl the roads around Jerusalem, seizing his own hostages and shaking down Jerusalem's Christian convents to raise the money.[27]

As spring seethed into summer in 1825, more people than ever wanted to get out of Jerusalem. With the city and surrounding countryside racked by a rampage of theft and violence, Fisk described its desperate inhabitants as "enraged and rendered mad by the oppression," which meant that "murders were frequent and there was no safety to him that went out or to him that came in [to Jerusalem]." When at last the convents caved and coughed up their bribes to Aboo Ghoosh, it seemed an opportune moment for the missionaries to risk the roads and make for Beirut.

What happened next, as recounted in King's journal, received full play in the American evangelical press. On the morning of their departure, who should turn up at the missionaries' lodgings but Aboo Ghoosh himself, demanding to know why King had been "afraid" to enlist his protection. Then their visitor wrote out a pass, and, as King boasted, he and Fisk set out for Beirut "without any guard whatever, except our muleteers . . . without the least molestation, and without paying a single para." The published portions of King's journal offered no explanation of why this dread Muslim warlord went out of his way to give safe passage to a pair of Christian missionaries, leaving the impression that his intervention was providential—or that so manly a fellow as King just naturally commanded special regard from Muslim leaders. In fact, Aboo Ghoosh, grateful for his escape from Jaffa, was repaying King with a safe passage out of Jerusalem.[28]

A good story—even if the whole truth would have made it better still—and King's best tale of all quickly followed. Fisk recounted a version of the event, too, which took place shortly after the two left Jerusalem with Aboo Ghoosh's pass in hand. Near Nazareth, a band of Arabs armed with muskets, swords, and clubs—Bedouins most likely—swept down on the missionaries' caravan. He was frightened at first, Fisk admitted in a letter to Daniel Temple. The marauders were trying to free two of their comrades who had been apprehended a day earlier while stealing a trunk, and their attack was "furious and wild as the whirlwind in the desert." Yet no member of the caravan sustained any serious injury, and as Fisk noted in his private journal, once "the Muleteers [of the caravan] told the Arabs that the man whose trunk was taken, was a Consul from the Pasha of Acre," they seemed scared and "cried out (*Aman*) safety or confidence and immediately began to collect the blankets, saddle bags and other articles of baggage which had been dropped . . . and bring them to us." What began in terror ended almost comically with their assailants trying to make amends by picking up the missionaries' luggage. Not a word about his partner in any of Fisk's accounts.

King told quite a different tale, one so gripping that the evangelical press published it under the title "Adventures on the Plain of Esdraelon." That was a stretch of land, as he reminded his audience, "famous for many a battle" in the Bible, and even before the marauders appeared, he "felt very sensibly, that our situation was now dangerous," because "I had seen the Arabs spring up like grasshoppers" in "the land of the Philistines." Then the "infuriated mob" rushed the caravan, "setting up a terrible yell, like the war-whoop of the savages of North America"; there was "no time for parley" because death "seemed to stare us in the face." When a dragoman leveled his gun at one of the Arabs, King shouted not to fire, at which another member of the caravan, a Muslim, "caught hold of the gun, and prevented him from shedding blood." Then King led the pack as they galloped in flight from pursuers who "knew every turn." He was unarmed, but even if "I had had arms, I should not have used them. I came here not to fight, but to bring the Gospel of peace." So "when an Arab Sheik came flying up to me on his steed, with a large club in his hand," King "addressed him, calling him brother." At that, the Arab—miraculously—stopped, then turned away, and even began to drive back some of his comrades. King granted that "the attack was a gallant one, and made by the Arabs as if they were determined to carry their point through life or death." Indeed, he had no doubt "that had one of their party fallen by our hands, it would have been the signal for the slaughter of us all." Now, how likely is it that Pliny Fisk, ever an admirer of men of action, would have passed over without remark such a display of coolheaded courage?[29]

What a career King might have had, scribbling those blood-and-thunder dime novels about the West that awaited so near in history's wings. As it happened, he was writing them about the East and calling them reports from the mission field. Notice, too, King's enlisting Muslim men to affirm his own daring, from the marauders who launched their "gallant" attack, to the member of the caravan who enforced his order not to fire, to the man whom he claimed to have "brothered" into ending the assault. Somehow it all makes sense, coming from a man who so prided himself on the trappings of Islamic masculinity that he risked a horseback ride through the gates at Damascus. A man who, knowingly or not, modeled his own persona on the fighting martyrs of Islam. And a man, too, who held in his mind's eye the image of Henry Martyn making himself over to meet the Persian giants of Shiraz. Those emblematic moments tell the ironic truth that evangelicals endowed Muslim men, a fraternity as choice as the Brethren, with the power to authenticate their manhood and their kind of Christianity. There are consequences for that kind of thinking, and they continue to play out in the present not as farce but as tragedy.

The two men boarded a vessel lying off Beirut in late September 1825. Pliny Fisk lingered for some time before returning to shore, taking leave of the man who had shared his life over the last three years. As for Jonas King, he was impatient to shake off the sand of Ottoman Syria. He would spend nearly a year in Smyrna studying Greek before making a leisurely progress to Constantinople, the coast of Spain, the South of France, Paris, and London. After that grand tour, he returned to the United States late in 1827 and starred on the lecture circuit for several months, talking his way up and down the East Coast and drumming up money for missions. Not everyone was glad to see him, including one liberal stalwart who fumed in the pages of a Unitarian magazine that King had learned Arabic "at the expense of others" and wandered "from place to place as a gentleman traveler, to be regarded as a suffering saint, while absent, and to be caressed as an apostle on his return." Evangelicals were far more welcoming of their "apostle," including the aspiring missionaries at Princeton Theological Seminary, whom he urged "to go forward and occupy" the Ottoman Empire.

Practiced as he was, King won plenty of admirers among the well-to-do. At one Gotham gathering, his eloquence netted pledges of about $5 million in today's money. Sampson Wilder pitched in, throwing parties to fete his protégé and lodging him with moneyed hosts during his speaking tours. When one donor forked over more than $100,000, King boasted to Jeremiah Evarts that "the same gentleman who gave me this will probably introduce me in two or three days to some of his wealthy friends," from whom he hoped to get "even more." That professorship of Oriental languages so long awaiting King at rustic Amherst— the prospect of teaching young clodhoppers to wrap their thick tongues around slippery new syllables—grew ever less beckoning. Besides, as Evarts assured him, it was the "common opinion of well-informed men, that there is no occasion to teach the Arabic in our colleges."[30]

For his part, Pliny Fisk had no plans to return home. Evarts and the American Board were now more eager than ever to enlist their most seasoned Palestine missionary for a fund-raising tour, but he put them off. It was impossible for him to leave, Fisk insisted, because, as the mission's only unmarried man, he now bore the sole responsibility for "itinerating." In fact, nothing could have suited him better. So as King's vessel sank from sight, Fisk strolled back to his lodgings in Beirut filled with his own pleasurable anticipation for what the future would bring. There was George English's book about his expedition to the Sudan, which Fisk had long coveted and King had promised to send. Then there was the project on Fisk's desk—an Arabic-English dictionary that had consumed most of his time since the summer. "We have good Arabic Latin Dictionaries, with which we can read Arabic," he explained in a rare letter to Evarts, who managed to contain his enthusiasm, "but have nothing that deserves to be named, to assist us in comparing or translating into this language." Fisk was still studying, putting in two hours each day with a tutor, but by now he felt confident enough to conduct religious services in Arabic—and to compile his dictionary.

That endeavor marked the last stage of preparations that had begun with Fisk's boning up on lithography at Aleppo before poring over the Qur'an and studying with Sheikh Khaleel at Jaffa. It seems likely that the future "itinerating" in the Middle East he had in mind—travels too far-flung and dangerous for the Palestine mission's married men—would include preaching to Muslims. But only a few weeks after he parted from King, another journey called Fisk even farther away. A fever, one that had already claimed many lives in Beirut, felled him. He prayed to recover or at least to "die in possession of my reason and not dishonor God by my dying behavior." The prayer went unanswered: Fisk drifted in and out of delirium for days before breathing his last at the end of October.

Tributes—and lengthy accounts of his final agonies and edifying farewells—followed in the religious press. If Catholics fetishized the corpses of their dead saints by taking relics of bone and teeth, hair and flesh, nineteenth-century Protestants embalmed in pious print every excruciating detail of the deaths that claimed their holy men and women, compiling over the decades a vast literary catacomb. The most prestigious of print reliquaries was the posthumous memoir, and Alvan Bond produced one in 1828 for his brother-in-law and former Andover classmate. It opened with praise for the "martyr-like devotion" of both Fisk and Parsons but ended with the telling disclaimer of any "effort to *canonize* him [Fisk] as a saint." Far be it from evangelicals to flirt with so popish a practice.[31]

Would it have made any difference if he had lived longer? The foreign missions movement created in Fisk a knowledgeable observer of Muslim beliefs and practices. A rigorous, honest cultural broker, he struggled to see Islam clearly, not through a glass darkened by the rivalries within Christendom or the striving of American evangelicals for broader appeal. His reports from the Middle East over many years might have carried forward the work of Henry Martyn's memoir, challenging caricatures of Islam as a religion of ignorance and intolerance. There might have been more missionaries who followed Fisk's lead, and the evangelical movement might have become a great resource for imparting accurate information about Islam and the ground shared by all the world's great monotheisms to a vast audience. Is it far-fetched to imagine that such a future could have unfolded? Maybe so: listen closely to Fisk's silences.

They grew deeper and more frequent as he chose to withhold more and more of what he heard and read, discovered and suspected, hoped and feared about Islam. His fellow evangelicals accepted, even celebrated, Martyn's portrayal of Muslims because it encouraged optimism about the missionary enterprise. But would they entertain provocative discoveries about the varied Western inventions of Islam, the affinities of Muhammad's faith with every stripe of Protestantism, and the permeable bounds of religious frontiers in a shrinking world?

No, they would not, Fisk feared, and for good reason. Even as he preached his farewell sermon to the crowd thronging the Old South Church, he had realized to tell all of what little he knew then about Islam would have robbed him of any chance to challenge that faith. From the start of his life in the Levant, he censored his official journals, glossing over or omitting altogether in those pages his widening circle of Muslim acquaintances and his entanglement with George English. During his last years in the field, he registered his resignation by communicating as little as possible with the American Board and refusing to return to the United States. Then there was his final, most eloquent silence: the book that he never wrote about his conversations with Sheikh Khaleel. The longer he spent in the Middle East, the more his encounters with Islam fled into Fisk's secret life. That retreat might have reflected his growing recognition of how little he understood Islam; more surely, it signaled how well he understood the expectations of most other evangelicals. What Fisk did not know, nor could he have known, was that his silences—more accurately, his being silenced by the same foreign missions movement that enabled his entry to a wider world—would amount to so many lost opportunities for evangelicals to play a much different role in the American encounter with Islam.

As Pliny Fisk's voice faded out, that of Jonas King filled the void. His invented Muslims attested to—and answered loudly—the pressing needs of nineteenth-century evangelicalism. Those inventions reveal, too, that King and others like him were endowing their old slogan about "the conversion of the world" with a new and even more sweeping significance. Evangelicals of his stripe envisioned that their spiritual empire arising at home and abroad would attain the power to create its own reality—not merely to turn people everywhere into proper Protestants, but also to dominate the ways in which Americans viewed the rest of the world, its inhabitants, and its religions. It is an ambition that still drives many in the present, including both religious and secular leaders in the United States, who make no secret of their outsized, nearly surreal confidence in the transformative sway of American imperium.[32]

# EPILOGUE

Evangelical ambitions in the Middle East took an unexpected turn at the end of the 1820s. As William Jowett and Pliny Fisk passed from the scene, Americans and Britons alike quietly abandoned their plans to evangelize among Muslims in the Ottoman Empire. Discouraged by official opposition, missionary organizations opted to focus almost exclusively on Eastern Christians. For the rest of the nineteenth century, the Greek Orthodox in the newly independent Greek republic, the Maronites of Syria, the Armenians of Turkey, and the Nestorians of Persia made up the vast majority of those who received tracts and Bibles, enrolled in mission schools, or visited mission clinics. The goal of keeping or retrieving those Eastern Christians from the clutches of Rome dominated the missionary strategy and drew strength from developments in the United States. It also prospered from Jonas King's next campaign abroad, one that modeled the crusading spirit of the foreign missions movement for the rest of the nineteenth century.[1]

King announced his future course with a blistering attack on Roman Catholicism written during his final months in Syria. Translated into Arabic and widely circulated among Eastern Christians, this "Farewell Letter" opened with a statement of his own Calvinist beliefs and then rehearsed the standard litany of objections to Catholic beliefs and practices. The complaints that Jowett had confined to the pages of his private diary, King pounded out in print, beaming his "Farewell Letter" as much at Protestants in the United States as at Christians in the Levant. Every New Yorker who picked up the Morse brothers' *Observer* at the end of 1825 could read King's assurances that "the Beast [Roman

Catholicism], and the False Prophet [Islam], are uniting their armies; but the 'Lamb shall overcome them.'"

By evangelical lights, of course, King was simply opening another front in the war against the Antichrist, because its twin horns, Islam and Catholicism, were allied in the apocalyptic struggle against Protestantism. Looked at another way, the foreign missions movement, with King in the lead, was reversing the direction in which—only a few years earlier—Levi Parsons had been traveling. Replacing Parsons's more accommodating approach with the hostility toward Catholics abroad promoted by King and other missionaries would have grave consequences back in the United States. It would help to spark the holy war that Protestants waged against Catholics a decade later, and it would sustain their estrangement for more than a century thereafter.[2]

Even before composing his "Farewell Letter," King had plenty of practice skewering Catholics. There were those French priests who slithered across his path from Paris to Malta. A year later in the spring of 1823, a long stay at Mount Lebanon provided him with another opportunity to let out shaft, because Catholics of every sort—Roman and Greek, Syrian and Maronite—abounded in the hamlets and convents that clung to its steep hills and nestled in its valleys. Once settled in the village of Dayr el-Qamar, King filled his reports to the board with the harangues that he inflicted on his hosts, the family of Yusef Doumani, a Greek Catholic silk manufacturer, as well as on the local sheikhs and priests. Whenever opportunity offered, King wrote to Isaac and Ann Bird, "I have been into the Market place, and in families, arguing, disputing, preaching." Not that he needed to sally forth: King could stir up controversy merely by staying at the Doumanis. While under their roof, he denied the infallibility of the pope, ridiculed the practice of making the sign of the cross, and mortified a visiting priest by insisting "that Joseph knew Mary after the birth of Jesus." Asked by another guest if he believed in the Virgin Birth, King shot back, "Should a single angel dare in heaven to sing glory to the Virgin Mary, he would instantly be thrust down to hell." At that, the company "all stared at me with a kind of wonder, and the conversation ceased."

King's attacks met with a much warmer reception by his evangelical audience, especially those passages guaranteed to flatter any proud American democrat. "Whom do you choose to obey—God or man?" he demanded of a Maronite layman. "What is your Patriarch? What is the Pope himself? A bit of clay!" Editors of the religious press ran King's reports from Mount Lebanon in full.[3]

Other members of the Palestine mission followed King's lead. They repeated among themselves like a mantra his remark that "when the angels fell from heaven, half of them fell upon *Mecca* and the other half at *Rome*." And in their reports to Boston, they portrayed the Levant's Catholic clergy as villains stepped from the pages of a gothic novel. Isaac Bird breathlessly informed the board that some thirty Spanish Franciscans had arrived at their missionary headquarters in the Levant "prepared for every work of violence and intrigue." Or so he believed, based on a rumor that they had poisoned their order's superior and then had arrested a man who overheard them plotting the murder. And after an angry Catholic mob in Malta stoned the dwelling of a Methodist missionary there, Daniel Temple wished "from the bottom of my heart that all the follies and abominations of the Romish church were painted in the most vivid and undying colors and spread before the eye of the universe." Even Fisk shed the more conciliatory views of his youth and joined in the fray.

Delighted by reports that doubled as a pep rally against the pope and a primer on the evils of Catholicism, the American Board encouraged its missionaries to keep piling on. The man who would succeed Evarts as the director of foreign missions, Rufus Anderson, wrote to Bird warning that American Catholics formed "a powerful hierarchy in this land of light and freedom and yet carry on their operations so quietly and slyly and civilly that our churches all feel secure." What a pity that "the *liberals* seem heartily to bid them Godspeed," which made it all the more important for missionaries in Syria to keep exposing "the policy and wickedness of that church, as you see in Palestine."[4]

So they did, providing the tinder that would explode into a firestorm of violence in the United States only a decade later when others lit the torches. There was Lyman Beecher, the nation's leading evangelical preacher, whose *Plea for the West* warned of papal schemes to plant a despotic Catholicism between the Appalachians and the Mississippi. There was Samuel F. B. Morse, an apple that did not fall far from Jedidiah's paternal tree, who made Catholics the featured villains in his *Foreign Conspiracy Against the Liberties of the United States*. And there was "Maria Monk," a group of evangelical ministers who concocted a salacious memoir of convent life that would outsell every book published before the Civil War except *Uncle Tom's Cabin*. In the incendiary climate of the 1830s, riots erupted in Boston and Philadelphia, with mobs burning down homes, a convent, and two churches. An influx of impoverished Irish immigrants and a succession of reactionary popes helped to fuel antebellum American Protestants' fear and loathing of their fellow Christians. But what did even more to stoke their animus and to keep it seething well into the twentieth century was the contempt for Catholicism so relentlessly committed to print by evangelical missionaries.[5]

That kept Jonas King in steady work over many decades. He had resumed his connection with the American Board in the 1830s and spent the rest of his long life teaching and preaching in Athens. Ever since Jowett's first visit to Greece, evangelicals' alliance with the Greek Orthodox—a liturgical tradition similar in most respects to Catholicism—had been an uneasy one, and the board's determination to turn Greece into a mission field brought those tensions to the surface. By the 1840s, King was openly attacking Greek Orthodoxy as Catholicism's evil twin and fending off assaults from mobs, once by wielding a large American flag. But sulfurous polemics against both faiths—a staple of his published missionary reports and a number of books—ensured King's stature in evangelical circles and beyond. When a Greek court sentenced him to a second exile in 1852, special agents sent by the State Department had to negotiate with the Greek government on three separate occasions—twice accompanied by naval warships—to allow King, by then the American consul, to remain in Athens, where he stayed until his death in 1869. It was a career that exemplified how evangelicals' support for missions and their hatred of Catholicism came to feed off each other's intensity. Their presses served up anti-Catholic invective that in turn fueled backing for missionaries in the Mediterranean, the Ottoman Empire, and anywhere else evangelicals vied for souls with Rome. That was nearly everywhere by the middle of the nineteenth century, as the competition for converts between Catholics and Protestants came to encircle the globe.[6]

It was no coincidence, then, that zeal for foreign missions and opposition to Catholics gathered momentum during the nineteenth century. Twinned dynamos, together they came to define evangelical identity, instilling unity in a movement fractured by denominational differences, slavery, race, and class and temporarily ruptured by the Civil War and Reconstruction. Nor could it have been a coincidence that the fiercest attacks on Catholics in the United States followed so closely on the defeat of evangelicals' confident expectations of converting the Muslim world. It would not be the first or last time in the West that a debacle abroad brought on campaigns to purge the homeland of perceived religious impurity and dissent. Just as the defeat of the original crusaders in the Levant led to the persecution of Jews and Christian heretics in medieval France and Germany, Islam's confounding of evangelical expectations fed the fires of bigotry against Catholics in the antebellum United States. That historical habit of failed crusades abroad replaying at home might now, more than ever, be worth bearing in mind.[7]

If the foreign missions movement was complicit in keeping prejudice against Catholics alive for many decades, not all the Protestants who followed King into the Middle East harbored the same crusading spirit against Islam. Well into the twentieth century, the play of more cosmopolitan and even ecumenical impulses surfaced in missionary ranks, at least with respect to Muslims. As their operations expanded throughout the Middle East, some Protestant missionaries acknowledged Islam's strengths, its similarities with Christian belief and practice, and even some of its truth claims. After the turn of the century, those of more irenic spirit also strove to include young Muslims in the schools and colleges established under evangelical auspices—most notably, what became the American University of Beirut and Robert College in Istanbul. As individuals and usually with little support from their sponsoring organizations in the United States, they carried forward the legacies of the first missionaries who challenged the earliest evangelical invention of Islam. Their work would echo Henry Martyn's admiration of the intellectual rigor of Islam's elite believers and Pliny Fisk's appreciation of its affinities with Christianity. Those evangelical Congregationalist and Presbyterian missionaries were the forebears of what became, by the mid-twentieth century, the liberal Protestant "mainstream." Embracing more relativistic views of religion, once the outlook only of some deists and Unitarians, these ecumenicist Christians have abandoned the ambition to convert the world and retreated from proselytizing abroad.

As a result, conservative evangelicals, many of whom hold the most adversarial views of Islam, now command the entire overseas mission field. They present the most visible face of American Christianity abroad. Organizations such as Franklin Graham's Samaritan's Purse conduct impressive relief work in some of the poorest countries in the world, places scourged by war and natural disasters, famine and disease. But proselytizing invariably accompanies that aid, causing some critics to charge that evangelicals exploit the neediest and most desperate people in the world to gain a hearing for their message. What's certain is that, like their nineteenth-century progenitors, today's foreign missions command the latest technology to focus their resources. The result is their systematically targeting a region of twenty-seven thousand square miles and 2.7 billion people that combines the highest levels of poverty with the lowest numbers of Christians—the "10/40 Window," as it is known. The most outspoken protests against the evangelicals' strategy to dispense material aid while promoting their faith across this great swath of the globe have come from Muslims.[8]

Among the American supporters of this undiminished evangelical drive to convert the world are some who see an opportunity in the Islamophobia that has come to haunt the West since 2001. Just as Jonas King and his allies encouraged the antipathy to Muslims aroused by the Greek Revolution, their descendants today have seized on terrorist attacks by extremists to endorse starkly negative images of Islam. Like King before them, such evangelical leaders have excelled at gaining public notice for their opinions, and like their counterparts of two hundred years ago, they wield their inventions to gain an advantage over their liberal opponents. They would do well to recall the curiosity about and the diverse views of Islam entertained by evangelicals in the Middle East in the not-so-distant past. They might consider, too, that a religious movement cannot be too careful when conjuring villains, because they are as likely as heroes to define its future course and character.

# NOTES

## ABBREVIATIONS

ABCFM      American Board of Commissioners for Foreign Missions Archives, Houghton Library, Harvard University (Microfilm Edition)

ABCFM HU      American Board of Commissioners for Foreign Missions Archives, Houghton Library, Harvard University

AMDC      American Missionaries in the Near East and Malta, 1825–65, Rauner Library, Dartmouth College

ANTS      Andover Newton Theological School, Special Collections, Trask Library

CMSC      Church Missionary Society Collections, University of Birmingham

JE      *Jewish Expositor* (London)

MAYU      Manuscripts and Archives, Sterling Library, Yale University

MH      *Missionary Herald* (Boston)

MJ I      Journal of Pliny Fisk, May 20, 1821, to February 5, 1823, vol. 1

MJ II      Journal of Pliny Fisk, February 6, 1823, to May 15, 1824, vol. 2
     Both volumes in Special Collections, Middlebury College

MR      *Missionary Register* (London)

SCAWC      Special Collections and Archives, Williams College

SCMC      Special Collections, Middlebury College

UTS I      Personal Journal of Pliny Fisk, November 3, 1819, to May 19, 1821

UTS II      Journal of Pliny Fisk, June 22, 1824, to October 1825

UTS III      The Reverend Pliny Fisk's Book of Extracts, Records, and so on
     All three volumes in Special Collections, Burke Library, Union Theological Seminary

WMMSA      Wesleyan Methodist Missionary Society Archive (London)

## INTRODUCTION

1. Reports from the Palestine mission, *MH*, July 1821, Nov. 1823, Feb., April, May, July, Sept. 1824, and March 1825. I refer to cities and regions with the place-names used by early nineteenth-century Westerners.

2. James A. Field, Jr., *From Gibraltar to the Middle East: Americans in the Mediterranean World, 1776–1882* (1969; Chicago: Imprint Publications, 1991); David H. Finnie, *Pioneers East: The Early American Experience in the Middle East* (Cambridge, Mass.: Harvard University Press, 1967); Michael B. Oren, *Power, Faith, and Fantasy: America in the Middle East, 1776 to the Present* (New York: W. W. Norton, 2007), 17–121; Robert J. Allison, *The Crescent Observed: The United States and the Muslim World, 1776–1815* (1995; Chicago: University of Chicago Press, 2000); Frank Lambert, *The Barbary Wars: American Independence in the Atlantic World* (New York: Hill and Wang, 2005).

3. The term "evangelical" does not imply that this movement was (or is) monolithic. Scholars refer to the Congregationalists and the Presbyterians who play a prominent role in this study as "formalists" to distinguish them from the "antiformalist" Methodists and Baptists. The author of that distinction is Curtis D. Johnson, *Redeeming America: Evangelicals and the Road to the Civil War* (Chicago: Ivan R. Dee, 1993), 18–54. For the earliest British missionary societies, see Elizabeth Elbourne, *Blood Ground: Colonialism, Missions, and the Contest for Christianity in the Cape Colony and Britain, 1799–1853* (Montreal: McGill-Queen's University Press, 2002), 59–70, and Alison Twells, *The Civilizing Mission and the English Middle Class, 1792–1850: The "Heathen" at Home and Overseas* (Basingstoke: Palgrave Macmillan, 2009), 25–51; for Continental influences, see Andrew F. Walls, "The Eighteenth-Century Protestant Missionary Awakening in Its European Context," in *Christian Missions and the Enlightenment*, ed. Brian Stanley (Grand Rapids, Mich.: Eerdmans, 2001), 24–44.

4. Adams to Jefferson, July 13, 1813, in *The Adams-Jefferson Letters*, ed. Lester J. Cappon (1959; Chapel Hill: University of North Carolina Press, 1987), 355; Jefferson to Dr. Benjamin Waterhouse, June 26, 1822, in *Thomas Jefferson: Writings*, ed. Merrill D. Peterson (New York: Library of America, 1984), 1458–59; Jefferson to Robert B. Taylor, May 16, 1820, www.miguel.servet/org/popups/jefferson2.htm. For Athanasius, see Elaine Pagels, *Revelations: Visions, Prophecy, and Politics in the Book of Revelation* (New York: Viking, 2012), 133–70.

5. Asa McFarland, *An Historical View of Heresies, and Vindication of the Primitive Faith* (Concord, N.H., 1806), 239–40. I am indebted to my colleague Anne Boylan for this perspective on evangelicals, especially her observation that they sought "to capture and define republicanism." (Anne M. Boylan, *The Origins of Women's Activism: New York and Boston, 1797–1840* [Chapel Hill: University of North Carolina Press, 2001], 8.) The classic studies of evangelicalism's ascent in early nineteenth-century America include Robert H. Abzug, *Cosmos Crumbling: American Reform and the Religious Imagination* (New York: Oxford University Press, 1994), 5–6, 32–56; Jon Butler, *Awash in a Sea of Faith: Christianizing the American People* (Cambridge, Mass.: Harvard University Press, 1990), 225–88; E. Brooks Holifield, *Theology in America: Christian Thought from the Age of the Puritans to the Civil War* (New Haven, Conn.: Yale University Press, 2003), 127–394; Mark A. Noll, *America's God: From Jonathan Edwards to Abraham Lincoln* (New York: Oxford University Press, 2002), 187–208; Amanda Porterfield, *Conceived in Doubt:*

*Religion and Politics in the New American Nation* (Chicago: University of Chicago Press, 2012), 1–47; Jonathan Sassi, *A Republic of Righteousness: The Public Christianity of the Post-Revolutionary New England Clergy* (New York: Oxford University Press, 2001), 130, 178; David Sehat, *The Myth of American Religious Freedom* (New York: Oxford University Press, 2011), 1–96; John G. West, Jr., *The Politics of Revelation and Reason: Religion and Civic Life in the New Nation* (Lawrence: University of Kansas Press, 1996), 79–136.

6. Jeremiah Evarts, "Evangelical Exertions in Asia," *Panoplist*, April 1812; for book prices, see the review of James Justinian Morier's account of his first journey through Persia in the *Christian Observer*, June 1819. By the early 1820s, according to one future member of the Palestine mission, "common newspapers seem to have become of late, useful vehicles of missionary information." (Isaac Bird to Pliny Fisk, Nov. 13, 1822, Isaac Bird Papers, box 1, Correspondence, MAYU.) On the influence of missionary reports, see also William R. Hutchison, *Errand to the World: American Protestant Thought and Foreign Missions* (Chicago: University of Chicago Press, 1987), 1; Susan Thorne, *Congregational Missions and the Making of Imperial Culture in Nineteenth-Century England* (Stanford, Calif.: Stanford University Press, 1999), 6–7. Seth Cotlar has coined the term "popular cosmopolitanism" to describe an outlook that he finds among a politically engaged, democratic constituency in the 1790s, an attitude that combined a sympathetic interest in the world with universalist views of human nature. While he concludes that this perspective retreated to the margins of American life after 1800, the emergence of the foreign missions movement suggests that a popular cosmopolitanism shorn of its earlier associations with political radicalism migrated to evangelical ranks. (Seth Cotlar, *Tom Paine's America: The Rise and Fall of Transatlantic Radicalism in the Early Republic* [Charlottesville: University of Virginia Press, 2011], 50–85, 111.) Though conceived in cosmopolitanism, the foreign missions movement came, ironically, to prepare the ground for American imperialism; see Emily Conroy-Krutz, *Converting the World in the Early Republic: Christian Imperialism and American Foreign Missions* (Ithaca: Cornell University Press, 2015).

7. For important work on civil society and the public sphere in this era, see John Brooke, *Columbia Rising: Civil Life on the Upper Hudson from the Revolution to the Age of Jackson* (Chapel Hill: University of North Carolina Press, 2010), esp. 1–8, and Cotlar, *Tom Paine's America*, 13–114. For nineteenth-century Concord, see Nathaniel Bouton, *The History of Concord* (Concord, N.H., 1856), 320–87; James Otis Lyford, *A History of Concord, New Hampshire*, 2 vols. (Concord, N.H., 1896), 1:45, 295–372; Asa McFarland, *An Outline of Biography and Recollection* (Concord, N.H., 1880), 16, 41. The estimate of newspapers comes from the "Prospectus" of the *New-York Observer*, May 17, 1823. The editors of this religious weekly, Richard and Sidney Morse, believed that "in no part of the world does the newspaper possess as extensive an influence as in our own country . . . With a large class of our citizens, the newspaper is the only publication that is regularly perused. From it they derive their opinions on almost every important subject." For print

culture, see David Paul Nord, "Benevolent Books: Printing, Religion, and Reform, 1790–1840," and Richard R. John, "Expanding the Realm of Communications," in *An Extensive Republic: Print, Culture, and the New Nation, 1790–1840*, ed. Robert A. Gross and Mary Kelley, vol. 2 of *A History of the Book in America* (Chapel Hill: University of North Carolina Press, 2010), 211–46; David Paul Nord, *Faith in Reading* (New York: Oxford University Press, 2004), esp. 22–23, 28, 30, 133; Candy Gunther Brown, *The Word in the World: Evangelical Writing, Publishing, and Reading in America, 1789–1880* (Chapel Hill: University of North Carolina Press, 2004), esp. 51, 155; Anne M. Boylan, *Sunday School: The Formation of an American Institution, 1790–1880* (New Haven, Conn.: Yale University Press, 1988), 6–77; Mark S. Schantz, "Religious Tracts, Evangelical Reform, and the Market Revolution in Antebellum America," *Journal of the Early Republic* 17, no. 3 (1997): 425–66; Ronald Zboray, *A Fictive People: Antebellum Economic Development and the American Reading Public* (New York: Oxford University Press, 1993), 89–92; Nathan O. Hatch, *The Democratization of American Christianity* (New Haven, Conn.: Yale University Press, 1989), 125–46; Ashley Moreshead, " 'The Seed of the Missionary Spirit': Foreign Missions, Print Culture, and Evangelical Identity in the Early Republic" (Ph.D. diss., University of Delaware, 2015.)

8. The emphasis on the complexity and heterogeneity of Western conceptions of Eastern cultures has emerged as an important theme in the work of many scholars who have both challenged and extended the arguments of Edward Said's *Orientalism* (New York: Vintage, 1978). Among the most astute commentaries are David Cannadine, *Ornamentalism: How the British Saw Their Empire* (Oxford: Oxford University Press, 2003); Linda Colley, *Captives* (New York: Pantheon, 2002); Dane Kennedy, *The Highly Civilized Man: Richard Burton and the Victorian World* (Cambridge, Mass.: Harvard University Press, 2005); Dane Kennedy, "Imperial History and Post-colonial Theory," *Journal of Imperial and Commonwealth History* 24, no. 3 (Sept. 1996): 345–63; Dane Kennedy, ed., *Reinterpreting Exploration: The West in the World* (New York: Oxford University Press, 2014); Zachary Lockman, *Contending Visions of the Middle East: The History and Politics of Orientalism*, 2nd ed. (Cambridge, U.K.: Cambridge University Press, 2010), 183–215; Lisa Lowe, *Critical Terrains: French and British Orientalisms* (Ithaca, N.Y.: Cornell University Press, 1991); John M. MacKenzie, *Orientalism: History, Theory, and the Arts* (Manchester: Manchester University Press, 1995), 209–15; Melani McAlister, *Epic Encounters: Culture, Media, and U.S. Interests in the Middle East Since 1945* (2001; Berkeley: University of California Press, 2005); Billie Melman, *Women's Orients: English Women and the Middle East, 1718–1918* (Ann Arbor: University of Michigan Press, 1992), preface to 2nd ed., introduction; Bernard Porter, *The Absent-Minded Imperialists: Empire, Society, and Culture in Britain* (2004; New York: Oxford University Press, 2006); Daniel Martin Varisco, *Reading Orientalism: Said and the Unsaid* (Seattle: University of Washington Press, 2007). R. W. Southern's *Western Views of Islam in the Middle Ages* (Cambridge, Mass.: Harvard University Press, 1962) prompted my thinking about Western conceptions of Islam as inventions. Scholars continue to dispute the character, coherence, and

timing of the Enlightenment, and this study confirms its thinkers' diverse opinions about Islam. For changing interpretations of the movement as a whole, see Keith Thomas, "The Great Fight over the Enlightenment," *New York Review of Books*, April 3, 2014, 68–72. For images of Islam circulating in British North America and the United States before 1800, see Timothy Marr, *The Cultural Roots of American Islamicism* (Cambridge, U.K.: Cambridge University Press, 2006), 2–33; Thomas S. Kidd, *American Christians and Islam: Evangelical Culture and Muslims from the Colonial Period to the Age of Terrorism* (Princeton, N.J.: Princeton University Press, 2009), 1–18; Denise A. Spellberg, *Jefferson's Qur'an: Islam and the Founders* (New York: Knopf, 2013), 13–40.

9. Pagels, *Revelations*, 116. His parents might have taken an interest in classical learning, despite their lack of formal education, and editions of Pliny the Younger's writings turn up in the holdings of some libraries in the early republic. The Fisk family valued books: his father Ebenezer's will specified the division of his library among his surviving children; see Will of Ebenezer Fisk, probated 1831, Registry of Probate, Franklin County Courthouse, Greenfield, Mass.

10. A descendant of later missionaries in the Ottoman Empire came into possession of Fisk's papers and sold them for small sums to Middlebury College and Union Theological Seminary in the mid-twentieth century. Portions of both collections were lost in the stacks for years, until tracked down, one as late as 2013, by resourceful archivists in these libraries.

11. Earlier accounts of the first Palestine missionaries rely on their published reports; see Samir Khalaf, *Protestant Missionaries in the Levant: Ungodly Puritans, 1820–1860* (London: Routledge, 2012), 146–58, 173–77, 186–88, 190; Lester I. Vogel, *To See a Promised Land: Americans and the Holy Land in the Nineteenth Century* (University Park: Pennsylvania State University Press, 1993), 95–106; and the works by Field, Finnie, and Oren cited above. The impact of missions on the Middle East falls outside the scope of this study, but the best books on that subject include Ussama Makdisi, *Artillery of Heaven: American Missionaries and the Failed Conversion of the Middle East* (Ithaca, N.Y.: Cornell University Press, 2008), and Heather J. Sharkey, *American Evangelicals in Egypt: Missionary Encounters in an Age of Empire* (Princeton, N.J.: Princeton University Press, 2008).

12. An extensive secondary literature treats the "feminization" of American Protestantism in general. On that phenomenon among evangelicals in the early republic, see especially David W. Kling, *A Field of Divine Wonders: The New Divinity and Village Revivals in Northwestern Connecticut, 1792–1822* (University Park: Pennsylvania State University Press, 1993), 178–79, 190, 205–6, 210, 215–27, 230–31; Nancy Cott, *The Bonds of Womanhood: "Women's Sphere" in New England, 1780–1835* (New Haven, Conn.: Yale University Press, 1977), 126–59; Curtis D. Johnson, *Islands of Holiness: Rural Religion in Upstate New York, 1790–1860* (Ithaca, N.Y.: Cornell University Press, 1989), 53–66.

13. For Said's influence on exploring ways in which images of the East defined "the West," see his *Culture and Imperialism* (New York: Vintage, 1993); Lockman, *Contending Visions*, 200–201; James Clifford, *The Predicament of Culture:*

*Twentieth-Century Ethnography, Literature, and Art* (Cambridge, Mass.: Harvard University Press, 1988), 271–72. Among the many studies of empire's impact on the colonizers' societies, the best treatment for antebellum America is Amy S. Greenberg, *Manifest Manhood and the Antebellum American Empire* (Cambridge, Mass.: Harvard University Press, 2005). For Britain, see especially Elbourne, *Blood Ground*; Catherine Hall, *Civilizing Subjects: Metropole and Colony in the English Imagination, 1830–1867* (Chicago: University of Chicago Press, 2001); Catherine Hall and Sonya Rose, eds., *At Home with the Empire: Metropolitan Culture and the Imperial World* (Cambridge, U.K.: Cambridge University Press, 2006); Anna Johnston, *Missionary Writing and Empire, 1800–1860* (Cambridge, U.K.: Cambridge University Press, 2003); Richard Price, "One Big Thing: Britain, Its Empire, and Their Imperial Culture," *JBS* 45 (July 2006): 602–27; Thorne, *Congregational Missions and the Making of Imperial Culture in Nineteenth-Century England*; Twells, *Civilizing Mission and the English Middle Class*; Kathleen Wilson, ed., *A New Imperial History: Culture, Identity, and Modernity in Britain and the Empire, 1660–1840* (Cambridge, U.K.: Cambridge University Press, 2004). For the influence of missions in shaping American views of the Middle East in the late nineteenth and the twentieth centuries, see Sharkey's work cited above.

## 1. THE AGE OF WONDERS

1. All citations of the Qur'an are from the translation of M.A.S. Abdel Haleem (2004; New York: Oxford University Press, 2010). On the Brethren, see "Introduction" and Pliny Fisk, "Historical Sketch of the Society," both in the Papers of the Brethren, ANTS; see also John H. Hewitt, *Williams College and Foreign Missions* (Boston: Pilgrim Press, 1914), 27–31, 35–56, 75; Arthur Latham Perry, *Williamstown and Williams College* (1899; Norwood, Mass: Norwood Press, 1904), 354, 367; Leverett Wilson Spring, *A History of Williams College* (Boston: Houghton Mifflin, 1917), 76–80, 92. For secret societies, see William Bentley, *Diary*, 4 vols. (Salem, Mass., 1905–14), 3:133; Steven C. Bullock, *Revolutionary Brotherhood: Freemasonry and the Transformation of the American Social Order, 1730–1840* (Chapel Hill: University of North Carolina Press, 1996); David S. Shields, *Civil Tongues and Polite Letters in British America* (Chapel Hill: University of North Carolina Press, 1997), 175–208, 313–14; Margaret C. Jacob, *Strangers Nowhere in the World: The Rise of Cosmopolitanism in Early Modern Europe* (Philadelphia: University of Pennsylvania Press, 2006), 98–99.

2. Pliny Fisk, "Historical Sketch of the Society," Ezra Fisk to Elijah Bridgman, June 24, 1829, Bridgman to Ezra Fisk, April 25, 1829, and H.G.O. Dwight to William Schauffler, Jan. 27, 1829, all in Papers of the Brethren. Yale College had a similar secret organization, described by one member as a "society for the promotion of religion." Its members discussed making celibacy a condition of membership; they also gathered information about non-Christian cultures. (Bird journal, April 10, 1813, Jan. 11, 1814, Bird Papers.)

3. Thomas C. Richards, *Samuel J. Mills: Missionary Pathfinder, Pioneer, and Promoter* (Boston: Pilgrim Press, 1906), 5–39, 60. Harriet Beecher Stowe memorialized the senior Mills as Father Morris in her first novel, *The Mayflower* (1843).

4. Mills also urged the Brethren to "be more cautious" in admitting new members to their ranks "than even [were] the Illuminati." (Mills to John Seward, March 20, 1810, SCAWC.) In the 1790s, books by Augustin Barruel and John Robison alleged that the Illuminati had swelled into an international conspiracy and brought on the French Revolution. Those ideas gained ground in the United States, particularly in New England, during the years around 1800; see Cotlar, *Tom Paine's America*, 105–7; James West Davidson, *The Logic of Millennial Thought: The Eighteenth Century* (New Haven, Conn.: Yale University Press, 1977), 288–93; Kling, *Field of Divine Wonders*, 49; Richard J. Moss, *The Life of Jedidiah Morse: A Station of Peculiar Exposure* (Knoxville: University of Tennessee Press, 1995), 68–81, 84; Joseph W. Phillips, *Jedidiah Morse and New England Congregationalism* (New Brunswick, N.J.: Rutgers University Press, 1983), 73–101, 170–71; Vernon Stauffer, *New England and the Bavarian Illuminati* (New York: Columbia University Press, 1918).

5. Pliny Fisk, "What Is My Duty Respecting Missions?," entries for Feb. 3 and 29, 1817, in a journal sent to the Brethren from Smyrna, Feb. 15, 1820, Papers of the Brethren; Alvan Bond, *Memoir of the Rev. Pliny Fisk, A.M., Late Missionary to Palestine* (Boston, 1828), 13–26; J. Ritchie Garrison, *Landscape and Material Life in Franklin County, Massachusetts, 1770–1860* (Knoxville: University of Tennessee Press, 1991), 13–64, 94–114; Nathaniel Hawthorne, *American Notebooks*, ed. Randall Stewart (New Haven, Conn.: Yale University Press, 1932), 50; David F. Allmendinger, Jr., *Paupers and Scholars: The Transformation of Student Life in Nineteenth-Century New England* (New York: St. Martin's Press, 1975).

6. William R. Hutchison, "New England's Further Errand: Millennial Belief and the Beginnings of the Foreign Missions," *Proceedings of the Massachusetts Historical Society*, 3rd ser., 94 (1982): 49–64. For the influence of the New Divinity in organizing the American Board, see David W. Kling, "The New Divinity and the Origins of the ABCFM," *Church History* 72 (2003): 791–819, and Joseph Conforti, *Samuel Hopkins and the New Divinity Movement: Calvinism, the Congregationalist Ministry, and Reform in New England Between the Great Awakenings* (Grand Rapids, Mich.: Eerdmans, 1981), 156–57. For the founding of the board and its first mission to India, see Joseph Tracy, *History of American Missions to the Heathen, from Their Commencement to the Present Time* (Worcester, Mass., 1840), 29–41, and John A. Andrew III, *Rebuilding the Christian Commonwealth: New England Congregationalism and Foreign Missions, 1800–1830* (Lexington: University of Kentucky Press, 1976), 70–96. From the outset, British missionary societies prompted the emulation of New Englanders; see Ruth Bloch, *Visionary Republic: Millennial Themes in American Thought, 1756–1800* (Cambridge, U.K.: Cambridge University Press, 1985), 202–31.

7. Adherents of the New Divinity at first called themselves Calvinists or Consistent Calvinists. More moderate believers were known as Old Calvinists, and they

labeled these theological archconservatives the New Divinity or Hopkinsians. For this religious subculture, see Timothy Woodbridge, *The Autobiography of a Blind Minister* (Boston, 1856), 32–41; Cyrus Yale, *The Godly Pastor: Life of the Rev. Jeremiah Hallock, of Canton* . . . (Boston, 1854); Thomas Robbins, *The Diary of Thomas Robbins, D.D., 1796–1854*, ed. Increase N. Tarbox (Boston, 1886). The most discerning secondary sources on the New Divinity are Kling, *Field of Divine Wonders*; William Breitenbach, "Unregenerate Doings: Selflessness and Selfishness in New Divinity Theology," *American Quarterly* 34, no. 5 (1982): 479–502; William Breitenbach, "The Consistent Calvinism of the New Divinity Movement," *William and Mary Quarterly*, 3rd ser., 41 (1984): 241–64. For an important discussion of the complicated relationship between the Enlightenment and evangelicalism, see Catherine A. Brekus, *Sarah Osborn's World: The Rise of Evangelical Christianity in Early America* (New Haven, Conn.: Yale University Press, 2013), 8–12, 100–101.

8. Daniel O. Morton, *Memoir of Levi Parsons, First Missionary to Palestine from the United States*, 2nd ed. (Burlington, Vt., 1830), 8, 15, 24; John Chester, *A Sermon Delivered Before the Berkshire and Columbia Missionary Society* . . . (Hudson, N.Y., 1813), 30; Levi Parsons to Electa Parsons, 1811, and Levi Parsons to Joshua Bates, Nov. 22, 1811, both in Levi Parsons Letters, SCMC. The Reverend Justin Parsons's brother Silas was married to an aunt of Pliny Fisk's; see Henry Parsons, *Descendants of Cornet Joseph Parsons* (New York: Frank Allaben Genealogical Company, 1912), 85–86, 115–18. Three of Justin's brothers were also ministers, one of them a Yale graduate. Probate records are suggestive of the greater wealth of the Parsons family; see those for Lieutenant Benjamin Parsons of Chesterfield (Justin's father), d. 1778, and Solomon Parsons (Justin's brother), d. 1815, both at Hampshire County Hall of Records, Probate Registry, Northampton, Mass. For the New Divinity's role in domestic missions, see James R. Rohrer, *Keepers of the Covenant: Frontier Missions and the Decline of Congregationalism, 1774–1818* (New York: Oxford University Press, 1995), 3–69.

9. Levi Parsons to Lucretia Parsons, March 17, 1814, Levi Parsons to Electa May Parsons, April 21, 1814, and Levi Parsons to Daniel and Lucretia (Parsons) Morton, June 24, 1814, Parsons Letters; Morton, *Memoir of Parsons*, 28; Levi Parsons, "Address to the Society of Inquiry," delivered Sept. 23, 1817, Papers for the Society of Inquiry Respecting Missions, Dissertations, vol. 9, ANTS.

10. Fisk entered Andover briefly right after graduating from Middlebury but to study for a year with Shelburne's pastor, Theophilus Packard. (Levi Parsons to Pliny Fisk, Dec. 30, 1814, ABCFM, reel 502.) Fisk also itinerated and taught school in Vermont for part of that year; he returned to Andover in 1815. Parsons was the president of the Society of Inquiry in 1817 and Fisk in the year following.

11. Old Calvinist Congregationalists, Presbyterians, and Baptists also offered this view of history; for a sampling of sermons on the "age of wonders" theme, see Abiel Abbot, *A Discourse Delivered Before the Missionary Society of Salem and Vicinity* . . . (Salem, Mass., 1816), 7–8; James Bradford, *The Presence of the Lord*

*Sufficient Ground for Encouragement and Exertion* . . . (Stockbridge, Mass., 1816); Francis Brown, *A Sermon, Delivered Before the Maine Missionary Society* . . . (Hallowell, Maine, 1814), 9; Timothy Mather Cooley, *The Universal Spread of the Gospel* . . . (Northampton, Mass., 1808); Joseph Harvey, *A Sermon Preached at Litchfield* . . . (New Haven, Conn., 1815); Joseph Lyman, *A Sermon, Preached at Boston, Before the ABCFM* . . . (Boston, 1819); Asa Lyon, *The Depravity and Misery of Man* . . . (Middlebury, Vt., 1815), 20; Asa McFarland, *A Sermon, Delivered Before the New-Hampshire Missionary Society* (Concord, N.H., 1812); Levi Nelson, *The Enlargement of the Church of Christ* . . . (Norwich, Conn., 1813); Elijah Parish, *A Sermon Preached Before the Massachusetts Missionary Society* . . . (Northampton, Mass., 1807); Alexander Proudfit, *An Address, Delivered at the Formation of a Society of Foreign Missions, in the City of New York* . . . (appended to his *Extent of the Missionary Field* . . . ) (Middlebury, Vt., 1817); Samuel Taggart, *Knowledge Increased by Travelling to and from, to Preach the Gospel* . . . (Northampton, Mass., 1807); Chester Wright, *A Sermon Preached Before the Female Foreign Missionary Society* . . . (Montpelier, Vt., 1817).

12. Oliver W. Elsbree, *The Rise of the Missionary Spirit in America, 1790–1815* (Williamsport, Pa.: Williamsport Printing and Binding Company, 1928); R. Pierce Beaver, "Missionary Motivation Through Three Centuries," in *Reinterpretation in American Church History*, ed. Jerald Brauer (Chicago: University of Chicago Press, 1968), 121–26; Richard Lee Rogers, "'A Bright and New Constellation': Millennial Narratives and the Origins of American Foreign Missions," in *North American Foreign Missions, 1810–1914: Theology, Theory, and Policy*, ed. Wilber R. Shenk (Grand Rapids, Mich.: Eerdmans, 2004), 39–59; Andrew Porter, "Evangelicalism, Islam, and Millennial Expectation in the Nineteenth Century," in Stanley, *Christian Missions and the Enlightenment*, 64–65; Phillips, *Jedidiah Morse*, 124–25; Bloch, *Visionary Republic*, 215–18; Davidson, *Logic of Millennial Thought*, 261–80; Kling, *Field of Divine Wonders*, 61–62; James H. Moorhead, "Between Progress and Apocalypse: A Reassessment of Millennialism in American Religious Thought, 1800–1880," *Journal of American History* 71, no. 3 (Dec. 1984): 524–42. Several scholars have emphasized the influence of prophecies about events preceding the Second Coming on Anglo-American evangelicals' understanding of the Islamic world; see John Demos, *The Heathen School: A Story of Hope and Betrayal in the Age of the Early Republic* (New York: Knopf, 2014), 57–65; Marr, *Cultural Roots of American Islamicism*, 82–133; Kidd, *American Christians and Islam*, 26–36; Makdisi, *Artillery of Heaven*, 61–67; Hans Lukas-Kieser, *Nearest East: American Millennialism and Mission to the Middle East* (Philadelphia: Temple University Press, 2010), 39–44.

13. Woodbridge, *Autobiography of a Blind Minister*, 32–33; John Fitch, *The Kingdom of Christ* (Middlebury, Vt., 1813), 11; Harvey, *Sermon*, 8–9, 12; Abbot, *Discourse Delivered Before the Missionary Society of Salem and Vicinity*, 13–14; Cooley, *Universal Spread of the Gospel*, 12–17; *Panoplist, and Missionary Magazine*, Nov. 1814; *MR*, Aug. 1819, 363; Brown, *Sermon*, 14; Joseph Lathrop, *A Sermon Preached*

*in Springfield Before the Bible Society and the Foreign Mission Society . . .* (Springfield, Mass., 1814), 12.

14. Ian Copland, "Christianity as an Arm of Empire: The Ambiguous Case of India Under the Company, c. 1813–1858," *Historical Journal* 49, no. 4 (2006): 1025–54; Andrew Porter, *Religion Versus Empire? British Protestant Missionaries and Overseas Expansion, 1700–1914* (Manchester: Manchester University Press, 2004), 70–75; Elizabeth Elbourne, "The Foundation of the Church Missionary Society: The Anglican Missionary Impulse," in *The Church of England, c. 1689–c. 1833: From Toleration to Tractarianism*, ed. John Walsh, Colin Haydon, and Stephen Taylor (Cambridge, U.K.: Cambridge University Press, 1993), 262–64; Jeffrey Cox, *The British Missionary Enterprise Since 1700* (New York: Routledge, 2008), 124–32; Rowan Strong, *Anglicanism and the British Empire, 1700–1850* (Oxford: Oxford University Press, 2007), 118–97; Penelope Carson, "An Imperial Dilemma: The Propagation of Christianity in Early Colonial India," *Journal of Imperial and Commonwealth History* 18, no. 2 (1990): 169–90.

15. Claudius Buchanan, *Christian Researches in Asia with Notices of the Translation of the Scriptures into the Oriental Languages* (Boston, 1811).

16. Claudius Buchanan, *The Star in the East: A Sermon Preached in the Parish-Church of St. James, Bristol, on Sunday, Feb. 26, 1809,* 8th ed. (New York, 1809), 17–21; Jacob Drake, *Truth Victorious; or, The Combat Between Christianity and Mahometanism* (Columbus, Ohio, 1816). By 1809, the story of Sabat and Abdallah was circulating in American evangelical magazines from New York to Georgia—even in a German-language newspaper in Pennsylvania. For other biographies published in the United States, see the *Panoplist, and Missionary Magazine,* Sept., Nov., and Dec. 1812. Fluent in Arabic and Persian, Sabat also claimed to have written treatises on logic and religion as well as poetry and fiction. He boasted, too, of his career as a soldier, fighting "in Syria, Tartary, Persia and India, been many times wounded and taken prisoner," making three pilgrimages to Mecca, and serving as "secretary to the kings of Bokkara and Cabul [Bukhara and Kabul]." (Henry Martyn to his cousin Mrs. T. M. Hitchens, Dec. 1807, in "Two Sets of Unpublished Letters of the Rev. Henry Martyn, B.D., of Truro," ed. H. M. Jeffrey, *Journal of the Royal Institution of Cornwall* 8 [1881–82]: 47–48; *Massachusetts Baptist Missionary Magazine,* May 1808.)

17. Mills to James Ripley, Esq., Nov. 17, 1813, SCAWC.

18. For this perspective on Puritanism, see Stephen Foster, "The Godly in Transit: English Popular Protestantism and the Creation of a Puritan Establishment in America," in *Seventeenth-Century New England*, ed. David Grayson Allen and David D. Hall (Charlottesville, N.C.: University of Virginia Press, 1984), 185–238.

19. For splendid studies of these themes, see Mary Kelley, *Learning to Stand and Speak: Women, Education, and Public Life in America's Republic* (Chapel Hill: University of North Carolina Press, 2006), 16–111, and Brekus, *Sarah Osborn's World,* 183–90. For the importance of women in the early missions movement, see Amanda Porterfield, *Mary Lyon and the Mount Holyoke Missionaries* (New York: Oxford University Press, 1997), 48–67; Lisa Joy Pruitt, *A Looking-Glass for*

*Ladies: American Protestant Women and the Orient in the Nineteenth Century* (Macon, Ga.: Mercer University Press, 2005), 12–23, 25–42. "Ignorance instead of being considered the necessary qualification of a good wife, or a dutiful daughter" was now a "mark of disgrace," Levi Parsons lectured his sister Lucretia. And when it came to religion, "females undoubtedly take the most interesting and feeling part," contributing to social progress and "the spread of scriptures" throughout the world. (Levi Parsons to Lucretia Parsons, May 1, 1814, Levi Parsons Letters.) His remarks illustrate the influences that Rosemarie Zagarri singles out as promoting the view that women were the intellectual equals of men; see Rosemarie Zagarri, *Revolutionary Backlash: Women and Politics in the Early Republic* (Philadelphia: University of Pennsylvania Press, 2007), 12–19.

20. Leonard Woods, *A Sermon Preached at Haverhill (Mass.) in Remembrance of Mrs. Harriet Newell . . . to Which Are Added Memoirs of Her Life,* 3rd ed. (Boston, 1814); Mary Kupiec Cayton, "Canonizing Harriet Newell: Women, the Evangelical Press, and the Foreign Mission Movement in New England, 1800–1840," in *Competing Kingdoms: Women, Mission, Nation, and the American Protestant Empire, 1812–1960,* ed. Barbara Reeves-Ellington, Kathryn Kish Sklar, and Connie A. Shemo (Durham, N.C.: Duke University Press, 2010), 69–93; Mary Kelley, " 'Pen and Ink Communion': Evangelical Reading and Writing in Antebellum America," *New England Quarterly* 84 (Dec. 2011): 564–69; Joseph Conforti, *Jonathan Edwards: Religious Tradition and American Culture* (Chapel Hill: University of North Carolina Press, 1995), 87–107; Joanna Bowen Gillespie, " 'The Clear Leadings of Providence': Pious Memoirs and the Problems of Self-Realization for Women in the Early Nineteenth Century," *Journal of the Early Republic* 5, no. 2 (1985): 197–221.

21. Daniel Morton, *Religious Exercises of Miss Laura Chipman* (Middlebury, Vt., 1818), 9; Rufus Anderson journal, ABC 30, vol. 4, Aug. 5, 1815, and vol. 5, Jan. 30, Feb. 2, 1816, ABCFM HU; Fanny Woodbury, *Writings of Miss Fanny Woodbury . . . ,* ed. Joseph Emerson (Boston, 1815), 26–27, 33, 48–49, 63, 64, 70–71, 131–32, 164–69.

22. Justus W. French to Samuel Worcester, n.d. [ca. 1817–19], ABC 6, Candidate Department, vol. 1, ABCFM HU, reel 60; Bond, *Memoir of Fisk,* 76; E.D.G. Prime, *Forty Years in the Turkish Empire: Memoirs of William Goodell, D.D.* (New York, 1876), 48–49. Jason Opal has written eloquently about the transformation of ambition from a "subversive wish" into a "public good"; see Jason Opal, *Beyond the Farm: National Ambitions in Rural New England* (Philadelphia: University of Pennsylvania Press, 2008); see also Brenda Wineapple's analysis in *Hawthorne: A Life* (New York: Knopf, 2003), 67, 85.

23. Anderson journal, vol. 4, Dec. 31, 1815; vol. 5, Feb. 11, April 12, 1816; vol. 6, Nov. 6, 1816, May 18, 1817; vol. 8, Aug. 16, 1818, ABC 30, vol. 1, ABCFM HU.

24. Leonard Woods, *A Sermon Delivered at the Tabernacle in Salem* (Boston, 1812), 11–13; Jesse Appleton, *A Sermon Delivered at Northampton* (Charlestown, Mass., 1817), 24; Bates, *Sermon Preached at Boston,* 6; Fitch, *Kingdom of Christ,* 16; Lyon, *Depravity and Misery of Man,* 6; Harvey, *Sermon,* 25; Nelson, *Enlargement of the Church of Christ,* 28.

25. Fisk, "What Is My Duty Respecting Missions?," entries for Feb. 3 and Aug. 10, 1817, Papers of the Brethren. That empathy with distant peoples might have come more easily to arch-Calvinists like the members of the New Divinity, who, convinced of their own powerlessness to win salvation, felt as much the helpless victims of depravity as the objects of their missions. For the influence of enlightened humanitarianism on the missionary movement, see Thomas L. Haskell, "Capitalism and the Origins of the Humanitarian Sensibility," pts. 1 and 2, *American Historical Review* 90, nos. 2 and 3 (April and June 1985), 339–61, 547–66; Cotlar, *Tom Paine's America*, 50–85, 111; Jason Opal, "The Labor of Liberality: Christian Benevolence and National Prejudice in the American Founding," *Journal of American History* 94 (March 2008): 1082–107.

26. *The Life of David Brainerd*, in *The Works of Jonathan Edwards*, vol. 7, ed. Norman Petit (New Haven, Conn.: Yale University Press, 1985), 526.

27. Woods, *Sermon Delivered at the Tabernacle in Salem*, 18.

28. Brown, *Sermon Delivered Before the Maine Missionary Society*, 6, 8; William Lyman, *A Missionary Sermon Delivered at Hartford* . . . (Hartford, 1811), 11; Taggart, *Knowledge Increased by Travelling*, 21; Edward Dorr Griffin, *Foreign Missions* (New York, 1819), 15; Wright, *Sermon Preached Before the Female Foreign Missionary Society*, 8–9. Estimates of the world's Protestant population stood at 50 million; estimates of Muslims ranged widely from a high of 210 million to a low of 73 million; most calculations pegged pagans at about half the population of the human race.

29. Jacob Norton, *Faith on the Son of God Necessary to Everlasting Life* . . . (Boston, 1810), 17; Joshua Bates, *A Sermon Preached at Boston* (Dedham, Mass. 1816), 11, 14; Asa Rand, *A Sermon Delivered in Buckstown* . . . *Before the Maine Missionary Society* . . . (Hallowell, Maine, 1815), 9; Henry Lord, *The Annual Report of the Committee to the Foreign Missionary Society of Northampton and Neighboring Towns* (Northampton, Mass., 1818), 3; William Lyman, *Missionary Sermon Delivered at Hartford* (Hartford, 1811), 12; Horatio Bardwell, *The Duty and Reward of Evangelizing the Heathen* (Newburyport, Mass., 1815), 7; *Christian Mirror* (Charleston, S.C.), Feb. 5, 1814; *Christian Spectator*, Oct. 1, 1819. New Divinity accounts of Islam's success echoed those of Jonathan Edwards; see Gerald R. McDermott, *Jonathan Edwards Confronts the Gods: Christian Theology, Enlightenment Religion, and Non-Christian Faiths* (New York: Oxford University Press, 2000), 166–75.

30. Donald M. Scott, *From Office to Profession: The New England Ministry, 1750–1850* (Philadelphia: University of Pennsylvania Press, 1978), 52–75; Peter S. Field, *The Crisis of the Standing Order: Clerical Intellectual and Cultural Authority in Massachusetts, 1780 to 1833* (Amherst: University of Massachusetts Press, 1998), 162–170; Sassi, *Republic of Righteousness*, 138; James W. Fraser, *Schooling the Preachers: The Development of Protestant Theological Education in the United States, 1740–1875* (Lanham, Md.: University Press of America, 1988), 33–42; J. Earl Thompson, "Church History Comes to Andover: The Persecution of James Mur-

dock," *Andover Newton Quarterly* 15 (March 1975), 213–27; Margaret Lamberts Bendroth, *A School of the Church: Andover Newton Across Two Centuries* (Grand Rapids, Mich.: Eerdmans, 2008), 11–24; Leonard Woods, *History of Andover Theological Seminary* (Boston, 1885), 63–158; Makdisi, *Artillery of Heaven*, 58–59.

31. Richards, *Samuel J. Mills*, 60; Alvan Bond, "The Present State of Mahomedanism," Dec. 17, 1816, 7, and Jacob Scales, "View of the Doctrines of Mohammedism and Their Influence on the Moral Character," July 27, 1819, 12, 21, Papers for the Society of Inquiry Respecting Missions, Dissertations, vol. 5 (Bond) and vol. 9 (Scales).

32. For a provocative exploration of the influences informing Sale's work, see Ziad Elmarsafy, *The Enlightenment Qur'an: The Politics of Translation and the Construction of Islam* (Oxford: Oxford University Press, 2009), esp. 21–25, 30–36, 41–47, 62–69, 80; see also Arnoud Vrolijk's entry in the online *Oxford Dictionary of National Biography*; Robert Irwin, *Dangerous Knowledge: Orientalism and Its Discontents* (Woodstock, N.Y.: Overlook Press, 2006), 100, 118, 120–21; Ibn Warraq, *Defending the West: A Critique of Edward Said's "Orientalism"* (Amherst, N.Y.: Prometheus Books, 2007), 35, 165; P. M. Holt, "The Treatment of Arab History by Prideaux, Ockley, and Sale," in *Historians of the Middle East*, ed. Bernard Lewis and P. M. Holt (London: Oxford University Press, 1962), 290–302; Norman Daniel, *Islam and the West: The Making of an Image* (1960, Oxford: Oneworld, 1993), 322–23. The term "Orientalist" denotes a scholar specializing in Eastern languages and literature.

Andover's library owned the most learned Protestant polemic against Islam, authored by an Anglican clergyman and Oxford don, Joseph White (1745–1814), *Sermons Preached Before the University of Oxford, in the Year 1784, at the Lecture Founded by the Rev. John Bampton* (Oxford, 1784), 66–71, 88–89, 93, 97, 165, 181, 354–56, as well as the work of Humphrey Prideaux, the best-known seventeenth-century British Protestant critic of Islam. (Humphrey Prideaux, *The True Nature of Imposture, Fully Displayed in the Life of Mahomet* [Fairhaven, Vt., 1798], 10, 19, 25, 61, 91, 98; see also Albert Hourani, *Islam in European Thought* [Cambridge, U.K.: Cambridge University Press, 1991], 12; David A. Pailin, *Attitudes to Other Religions: Comparative Religion in Seventeenth- and Eighteenth-Century Britain* [Manchester: Manchester University Press, 1984], 81–104; Ahmad Gunny, *Perceptions of Islam in European Writings* [Leicester: Islamic Foundation, 2004], 181–82.) The Andover library also held the Italian Catholic Lewis Maracci's Latin refutation of the Qur'an (1689), Theodoricus Hackspan's *Faith and Laws of Muhammad* (1646), some Arabic lexicons, and a number of extracts translated into German from medieval Arab scholars collected in German anthologies. I am indebted to my colleague James Brophy for identifying these German-language holdings in Andover's library.

33. George Sale, *Koran*, 2 vols. (London, 1801), 1:iii, iv, 51–54, 63–65, 93, 129, 133–37, 174, 176–78, 182, 188–91. Christian commentators often pointed up the affinities between Islam and other faiths to argue that Muhammad offered only a hodge-

podge of other religious traditions, but Sale drew attention to those similarities as a strategy to vindicate Islam. He noted that while the Qur'an sanctioned polygamy, it was a practice common throughout the East and that Muhammad had merely borrowed his teachings on divorce and inheritance laws from the Jews. Sale also justified Muhammad's promises of an immediate entry to paradise for martyrs fallen in the defense of Islam on the grounds that "the Jews and Christians, how much soever they detest such principles in others," had not "omitted to spirit up their respective partisans with like arguments and promises." For contemporary debates about the spread of Islam and Christianity, see John Renard, *Islam and Christianity: Theological Themes in Comparative Perspective* (Berkeley: University of California Press, 2011), 55–61, 90–92.

34. Scales, "View of the Doctrines of Mohammedism," 1, 19–20. The belief that Christians and Muslims do not worship the same God abides among the overwhelming majority of evangelicals—some 79 percent as measured by a poll taken in 2002. (McAlister, *Epic Encounters*, 285–86.)

35. Fisk, "What Is My Duty Respecting Missions?," entries for March 10, July 19, Aug. 10, 17, 31, 1817, Papers of the Brethren; Bond, *Memoir of Fisk*, 32, 36, 38, 41–42, 72–73, 77, 81, 83, 85–87; Alvan Bond to Jeremiah Evarts, Aug. 29, 1827, ABC 10, vol. 5, ABCFM HU; Parsons to Fisk, Oct. 23, 1817, ABCFM, reel 502.

36. *MR*, Nov. 1814, 432–33, May 1815, 257–60, and March 1816, 102–4; *Panoplist, and Missionary Magazine*, May 1815 and Nov. 1817; Bond, "Present State of Mahomedanism," 1, 4, 13–19; Pliny Fisk, "A Comparative View of the Claims of the Eastern and Western Missions upon the American Churches," delivered Feb. 25, 1817, Papers for the Society of Inquiry Respecting Missions, Dissertations, vol. 5, n.p. Extracts from another of Samuel Newell's letters, this one dated December 20, 1813, that appeared in *Panoplist, and Missionary Magazine* of November 1814 suggest a growing awareness if imperfect grasp among evangelicals of the different groups within Islam. He wrote that Persian Muslims (the Shia) were tolerant toward the Christians and that they "profess so lax a system of Mahometanism, that they are considered by some other mussulmans [the Sunnis in the Ottoman Empire and Arabia] as a kind of heretics." Then there were the Sufis, estimated in the missionary press as numbering eighty thousand Persians, whom many evangelicals made out to be to the Shia what the Wahhabis were to the Sunnis—a schismatic group whose presence proved the weakening of Islam. In fact, the Sufis represented a mystical tradition of long standing within Islam, but in Newell's hopeful view those in Persia had "openly renounced Mahomedanism."

37. Parsons to Fisk, Jan. 20 and May 26, 1818, ABCFM, reel 502.

38. Gardiner Spring, *Memoirs of the Rev. Samuel Mills . . .* (New York, 1820), 117, 134, 197–98; John F. Schermerhorn and Samuel J. Mills, *A Correct View of the Part of the United States Which Lies West of the Allegany Mountains, with Respect to Religion and Morals* (Hartford, 1814), 21, 33–34, 47–52; Samuel J. Mills and Daniel Smith, *Report of a Missionary Tour Through That Part of the United States Which Lies West of the Allegany Mountains* (Andover, Mass., 1815), 29, 37. For discussions of martyrdom in the Christian and Muslim traditions, see David Cook, *Martyr-*

*dom in Islam* (Cambridge, U.K.: Cambridge University Press, 2007), 20–23, 166; Asma Afsaruddin, *Striving in the Path of God: Jihad and Martyrdom in Islamic Thought* (New York: Oxford University Press, 2013), 1, 5–7; Keith Lewinstein, "The Reevaluation of Martyrdom in Early Islam," in *Sacrificing the Self: Perspectives on Martyrdom and Religion*, ed. Margaret McCormack (New York: Oxford University Press, 2001), 79–80; Dominic Janes and Alex Houen, eds., *Martyrdom and Terrorism: Pre-modern to Contemporary Perspectives* (New York: Oxford University Press, 2014), 13–15; Adrian Chastain Weimer, *Martyr's Mirror: Persecution and Holiness in Early New England* (New York: Oxford University Press, 2011), 144–45; Candida R. Moss, "The Discourse of Voluntary Martyrdom: Ancient and Modern," *Church History* 81, no. 3 (Sept. 2012), 531–51. By one count, of the 134 Andover graduates who served in foreign missions between 1812 and 1858, 34 died in the field; their average length of service was eleven years. Mortality among missionary wives and children ran higher still. (Rufus Anderson, *Memorial Volume of the First Fifty Years of the American Board of Commissioners for Foreign Missions* [Boston, 1861], 275.)

39. Fisk, "Historical Sketch of the Society," and Ezra Fisk to Elijah Bridgman, June 24, 1829, Papers of the Brethren. The Brethren remained a secret organization long after Fisk transcribed the minutes of their meetings. As late as 1829, Bridgman felt confident that "the existence of our Soc. [the Brethren] is not *known*, nor even *suspected* by any members of the Seminary except ourselves." (Bridgman to Ezra Fisk, April 25, 1829, Papers of the Brethren.) William Goodell recalled that the Brethren were like "a wheel within a wheel," which, though unseen, was not unfelt, for it moved and controlled all missionary societies and missionary operations in a way which, to the churches and even to the secretaries themselves, seemed perfectly unaccountable." (Prime, *Forty Years in the Turkish Empire*, 48–52.)


## 2. "BY THE BEARD OF MAHOMET!"

1. Bentley, *Diary*, 2:88, 321, 362, 382, 3:68, 132, 144, 194, 203, 321, 414, and 4:373, 377–78, 403, 444, 476, 491, 596, 598. See also Pringle to Bentley, Aug. 13, 1804, and Feb. 24, 1806, and his manuscript diary entry for April 9, 1818, both in William Bentley Papers, 1666–1819, American Antiquarian Society. The British geographer George Annesley also searched for Arabic books for Bentley and promised to send him an account of his voyages in the Red Sea; see Annesley to Bentley, Oct. 9, 1805. For Bentley's biography and thought, see J. Rixey Ruffin, *A Paradise of Reason: William Bentley and Enlightenment Christianity in the Early Republic* (New York: Oxford University Press, 2008).

2. Bentley, *Diary*, 3:226, 298, 409, 431, 527, 529, 4:81, 157–58, 356.

3. Ibid., 4:138, 143, 144–47, 149, 160–61, 377–78, 427, 543. American ships faced a mounting risk of being seized by the British as both countries moved closer to declaring war. For that reason, only one member of the board at first favored sending out the missionary party. The American Board missionaries had only

vague plans of what they would do after landing in India, but they hoped to establish a mission in Burma, evidently unaware that a civil war raging there had already prompted British evangelicals to abandon their missions in that country. (Samuel M. Worcester, *Memoir of the Life of the Rev. Samuel Worcester, D.D.*, 2 vols. [Boston, 1862], 2:121–22; *MR*, March 1815, 137–55; Emily L. Conroy-Krutz, "'Engaged in the Same Glorious Cause': Anglo-American Connections in the American Missionary Entrance into India, 1790–1815," *Journal of the Early Republic* 34, no. 1 [2014]: 21–44; Michael A. Verney, "An Eye for Prices, an Eye for Souls: Americans in the Indian Subcontinent, 1784–1838," *Journal of the Early Republic* 33, no. 3 [2013], 397–431.) Even their British evangelical supporters in Britain disapproved of the American Board's poorly timed plunge into foreign missions; see William Wilberforce to Jedidiah Morse, Aug. 19, 1814, Jedidiah Morse Papers, New York Public Library. Bentley marshaled considerable evidence to prove that the hasty decision was part of the board's efforts to secure a large and contested legacy; see Bentley, *Diary*, 4:12–15, 24, 66, 82, 98–99, 102, 138, 297–98.

4. Bentley, *Diary*, esp. 3:67, 130, 237, 273–74, 294, 296, 301, 309, 319, 321, 420, 437, 453, 456, 490, 500, 510, 4:16, 227, 263, 361–62, 382–83, 435–36, 456–57, 582, 621. There is a full inventory of his library in Bentley Papers, octavo vol. 12; see especially the page headed "Oriental Manuscripts—All for the Antiquarian Society." Fisk might also have received encouragement to visit Bentley from Moses Stuart, an Andover professor who aspired to become an accomplished Orientalist—much to Bentley's scorn; see Stuart to Bentley, Feb. 4, 1817, and n.d., 1815, Bentley Papers. For Fisk's work among Salem's free blacks, see his "Copy of a Report of Labors in Salem Performed in the Spring Vacation, 1818," ANTS.

5. Bentley's views on Muhammad appear in the unsigned news summary that he regularly contributed to the *Salem Register* (later the *Essex Register*); see esp. May 1, 1811. The director of the Salem Athenaeum, Jean Marie Procious, informed me in a December 22, 2011, e-mail that there were ninety-seven shareholders in that institution by 1823; a share granted use of the reading room and borrowing privileges to the holder and his family.

6. Michael Curtis, *Orientalism and Islam: European Thinkers on Oriental Despotism in the Middle East and India* (Cambridge, U.K.: Cambridge University Press, 2009), 57–100; Spellberg, *Thomas Jefferson's Qur'an*, 81–123; Kevin J. Hayes, "How Thomas Jefferson Read the Qur'an," *Early American Literature* 39, no. 2 (2004): 247–61. For the views of British liberals, see Joseph Priestley, *Lectures on History and General Policy*, 3rd ed. (Dublin, 1791), 365, 371, 374–75. For the mixed responses to Islam among major figures in the French Enlightenment, see David Allen Harvey, *The French Enlightenment and Its Others: The Mandarin, the Savage, and the Invention of the Human Sciences* (New York: Palgrave-Macmillan, 2012), 11–40.

7. Elmarsafy, *Enlightenment Qur'an*, 9–36; Irwin, *Dangerous Knowledge*, 113–22; Lynn Hunt, Margaret C. Jacob, and Wijnand Mijnhardt, *The Book That Changed Europe: Picart and Bernard's "Religious Ceremonies of the World"* (Cambridge, Mass.: Harvard University Press, 2010); Albert Hourani, *Europe and the Middle*

*East* (Berkeley: University of California Press, 1980), 27–31; Bernard Lewis, "Gibbon on Muhammad," *Daedalus* 105, no. 3 (1976): 89–101. For Reland, see his *Four Treatises Concerning the Doctrine, Discipline, and Worship of the Mahometans* (London, 1712), 5–6, and Alastair Hamilton, "From a 'Closet at Utrecht': Adriaan Reland and Islam," *Nederlandsch archief voor kerkgeschiedenis* 78 (1998): 243–50; for Boulainvilliers, see his *Life of Mahomet* (1730; London, 1752), 2–3, 97, 115, 120, 122–29, 148–49, 176–77. Among English historians, the most notable early figure was the Cambridge Arabist Simon Ockley, who wrote his *History of the Saracens* at nearly the same time that Sale was translating the Qur'an. Ockley portrayed the Prophet's first followers as heroic warriors and men of great learning, and his book was a staple of American libraries in the early nineteenth century.

8. Bernd Krysmanski, "We See a Ghost: Hogarth's Satire on Methodists and Connoisseurs," *Art Bulletin* 80, no. 2 (June 1998), 297; John Wesley, *Journal of John Wesley*, ed. Nehemiah Curnock, 8 vols. (London: Epworth Press, 1938), 5:242–43. Recent scholarship on views of Islam in the Middle Ages and the Renaissance emphasizes the diversity of Western opinion and the emergence of more nuanced appraisals, particularly among elites. Among the most helpful studies are David R. Blank and Michael Frassetto, eds., *Western Views of Islam in Medieval and Early Modern Europe* (New York: St. Martin's Press, 1999); Nancy Bisaha, *Creating East and West: Renaissance Humanists and Ottoman Turks* (Philadelphia: University of Pennsylvania Press, 2006); see also Samuel C. Chew, *The Crescent and the Rose: Islam and England During the Renaissance* (New York: Octagon Books, 1937), 388, 395–97, and Daniel, *Islam and the West*, 100–130.

9. Kenneth E. Carpenter, "Libraries," in Gross and Kelley, *Extensive Republic*, 273–86. Most libraries in the early republic did not keep printed catalogs of their holdings; my generalizations derive from a sample of twenty-two institutions that did.

10. Edward Gibbon, *The Life of Mahomet* . . . in *The Decline and Fall of the Roman Empire* (Leominster, Mass., 1805), 4, 8–9, 11, 14, 27–28, 34–35, 38, 48–49, 73, 82–84; Lewis, "Gibbon on Muhammad," 89; Hourani, *Europe and the Middle East*, 30–31. Like Bentley after him, Gibbon was fascinated with the Qur'an as a body of law; see Gibbon, *Life of Mahomet*, 11, 112–16. He also saw nothing amiss in the Qur'an's "image of a carnal paradise" because "useless would be the resurrection, of the body, unless it were restored to the possession and exercise of its worthiest faculties."

11. John Bigland, *A Geographical and Historical View of the World*, 5 vols. (Boston, 1811), 4:171, 173, 177–82; for his biography, see the entry in the *Oxford Dictionary of National Biography* and *Memoir of the Life of John Bigland, Written by Himself* (Doncaster, U.K., 1830).

12. Hannah Adams, *Dictionary of All Religions and Religious Denominations*, 4th ed. (Boston, 1817), 157, 316–23; see also Bentley, *Diary*, 3:215, 4:241–42; Gary D. Schmidt, *A Passionate Usefulness: The Life and Literary Labors of Hannah Adams* (Charlottesville: University of Virginia Press, 2004); Thomas A. Tweed, "An

American Pioneer in the Study of Religion: Hannah Adams (1755–1831) and Her *Dictionary of All Religions," Journal of the American Academy of Religion* 60, no. 3 (1992): 437–64; James Turner, *Religion Enters the Academy: The Origins of the Scholarly Study of Religion in America* (Athens: University of Georgia Press, 2011), 24–31.

13. *Life of Mahomet* (London, 1799), esp. 22, 26–27, 58, 76, 78, 86–88, 95–109, 115, 173, 183.

14. Much of the information in this section comes from the digital database America's Historical Newspapers; my search targeted the years 1807–8 and 1813–19. In many cases, articles appeared in multiple newspapers, but included here is one reference for each cited in the text: *The Witness* (Litchfield, Conn.), April 8, 1807; *Analectic Magazine* (Philadelphia), May 1813; *The Town* (New York), Jan. 3, 1807; *Polyanthos* (Boston), Jan. 1, 1807; *Freeman's Friend* (Salem, Maine), March 21, 1807; *Observer* (Baltimore), Sept. 19, 1807; *Republican Spy* (Northampton, Mass.), Dec. 23, 1807; *Salmagundi* (New York), Sept. 19, 1807; *New York Weekly Museum*, Jan. 23, 1813; *Baltimore Patriot*, Sept. 6, 1816; *Dedham Gazette*, Feb. 9, 1816; *Delaware Gazette* (Wilmington), May 27, 1816; *Portland Gazette*, June 18, 1816; *Connecticut Courant* (Hartford), Feb. 10, 1818; *Carolina Gazette* (Charleston), Sept. 5, 1818; *Alexandria Gazette and Daily*, Sept. 9, 1819.

15. Among the secular newspapers that offered the most coverage informed by Orientalist scholarship are the *Philadelphia Magazine and Weekly Repertory*, June 20, 1818, and the *Daily National Intelligencer* (Washington, D.C.), Oct. 26, 1816. For other references, see *United States Gazette* (Philadelphia), Jan. 21, 1807; *Literary Cabinet* (New Haven, Conn.), March 7, 1807; *Monthly Anthology and Boston Review*, Sept. 1, 1807; *North Star* (Danville, Vt.), April 8, 1807; *Hampshire Gazette* (Northampton, Mass.), Oct. 7, 1807; *Republican Star or Eastern Shore General Advertiser*, Oct. 20, 1807; Poulson's *American Daily Advertiser* (Philadelphia), March 9, 1808; *Evening Post* (New York), May 2, 1816; *Franklin Herald* (Greenfield, Mass.), Jan. 28, 1817; *Albany Daily Advertiser*, Jan. 23, 1816; *Boston Patriot*, Sept. 27, 1817; *New-York Columbian*, Feb. 19, 1818; *National Advocate* (New York), July 13, 1819; *Salmagundi* (New York), June 2, 1807. For some secular newspapers that shared the evangelical version of Muhammad's life and Islam, see *Franklin Monitor and Charlestown General Advertiser* (Charlestown, Mass.), Sept. 25, 1819; *City of Washington Gazette*, Feb. 6, 1818; *New-Hampshire Gazette* (Portsmouth), March 24, 1818; *Providence Gazette* (reprint of a *Scioto Gazette* essay), Feb. 21, 1818; *Northern Post* (Salem, N.Y.), Sept. 19, 1816.

16. For the influence of Napoleon, see esp. Elmarsafy, *Enlightenment Qur'an*, 143–57.

17. Lawrence A. Peskin, *Captives and Countrymen: Barbary Slavery and the American Public, 1785–1816* (Baltimore: Johns Hopkins University Press, 2009), 76–85, 173–84, 204; Hester Blum, "Pirated Tars, Piratical Texts: Barbary Captivity and American Sea Narratives," *Early American Studies* 1, no. 2 (2003): 133–58; James R. Lewis, "Savages of the Seas: Barbary Captivity Tales and Images of Muslims in the Early Republic," *Journal of American Culture* 13, no. 2 (1990): 75–84; Robert Battistini, "Glimpses of the Other Before Orientalism: The Muslim World in

Early American Periodicals, 1785–1800," *Early American Studies* 8, no. 2 (2010): 446–74; Kidd, *American Christians and Islam*, 19–26; Marr, *Cultural Roots of American Islamicism*, 30–54, 62–71; Jennifer Margulis, "Swarthy Pirates and White Slaves: Barbary Captivity in the American Literary Imagination" (Ph.D. diss., Emory University, 1999), 33.

18. Bird journal for 1813, entry for Sept. 17, Bird Papers. For Galland's translation, see Robert Irwin, *The Arabian Nights: A Companion* (New York: Penguin, 1994), 7, 14–19, and Madeleine Dobie, "Translation in the Contact Zone: Antoine Galland's *Mille et une nuits: Conte arabes*," in *"The Arabian Nights" in Historical Context*, ed. Saree Makdisi and Felicity Nussbaum (New York: Oxford University Press, 2008); Susan Nance, *How "The Arabian Nights" Inspired the American Dream, 1790–1935* (Chapel Hill: University of North Carolina Press, 2009), 19–23.

19. Geoffrey Wheatcroft, *Infidels: A History of the Conflict Between Christendom and Islam* (New York: Random House, 2003), 236–37; Benita Eisler, *Byron: Child of Passion, Fool of Fame* (New York: Knopf, 1999), 390–93; David S. Reynolds, *Faith in Fiction: The Emergence of Religious Literature in America* (Cambridge, Mass.: Harvard University Press, 1981), 16–20; *New York Courier*, June 19, 1816; *Commercial Advertiser* (New York), Sept. 27, 1816; *New-Bedford (Mass.) Mercury*, Nov. 20, 1818; for some reviews of *Ali Bey*, see *Analectic*, Oct. 1816, and *Portico*, Dec. 1, 1816.

20. Michael A. Gomez, *Exchanging Our Country Marks: The Transformation of African Identities in the Colonial and Antebellum South* (Chapel Hill: University of North Carolina Press, 1998), 59–87; Sylviane A. Diouf, *Servants of Allah: African Muslims Enslaved in the Americas* (New York: New York University Press, 1998); Allan D. Austin, ed., *African Muslims in Antebellum America: Transatlantic Stories and Spiritual Struggles* (New York: Routledge, 1997); Kambiz GhaneaBassiri, *A History of Islam in America* (Cambridge, U.K.: Cambridge University Press, 2010), 59–94.

21. Bentley, *Diary*, 3:409, 431, 4:2, 23–24, 34, 38, 80, 134–35, 261, 327, 342; Ruffin, *Paradise of Reason*, 166. Much as the New Divinity's defenders might assert that their Calvinist beliefs passed muster at the bar of reason, Bentley believed that they remained strangers to the true spirit of the Enlightenment.

22. Ruffin, *Paradise of Reason*, 4, 63–77, 184; Daniel Walker Howe, *The Unitarian Conscience: Harvard Moral Philosophy, 1805–1861* (Cambridge, Mass.: Harvard University Press, 1970); Porterfield, *Conceived in Doubt*, 1–47. Bentley believed in the redemptive mission of Jesus Christ, and he believed that Jesus had performed miracles, aided by God's power. The Socinian Jefferson rejected belief in biblical miracles.

23. John Adams to Jedidiah Morse, May 15, 1815, Morse Papers; Sydney E. Ahlstrom, *A Religious History of the American People* (New Haven, Conn.: Yale University Press, 1972), 388–402; J. D. Bowers, *Joseph Priestley and English Unitarianism in America* (University Park: Pennsylvania State University Press, 2007), 46–65, 167–204, 245–51; Elsbree, *Rise of the Missionary Spirit in America*, 84–101; Sassi, *Republic of Righteousness*, 116–19; Field, *Crisis of the Standing Order*, 180–207;

Mary Kupiec Cayton, "Who Were the Evangelicals? Conservative and Liberal Identity in the Unitarian Controversy in Boston, 1804–1833," *Journal of Social History* 31, no. 1 (1997): 86–108; David Robinson, *The Unitarians and the Universalists* (Westport, Conn.: Greenwood Press, 1985).

24. Bird journal for 1813, April 5, May 21; Bird diary and journal, 1814–15, Jan. 13 and 18, May 15, Sept. 16, 1814, Sept. 23 and Oct. 25, 1815, Bird Papers; Parsons, *Descendants of Cornet Joseph Parsons*, 85–86, 115–18.

25. Bird diary and journal, 1814–15, Jan. 13, 1814, Bird Papers.

26. Alexander McLeod, *Lectures upon the Principal Prophecies of the Revelation* (New York, 1814), 173–78; Samuel Worcester, "Third Letter," *Panoplist, and Missionary Magazine*, May 1816, 13–14, 28–29; Nabil Matar, *Islam in Britain, 1558–1685* (Cambridge, U.K.: Cambridge University Press, 1998), 48; Pailin, *Attitudes to Other Religions*, 81–102, 129–32, 149; Spellberg, *Jefferson's Qur'an*, 47–48, 79–80, 203, 228–30.

27. J. Christopher Herold, *Bonaparte in Egypt* (New York: Harper and Row, 1962), 68–71; *People's Friend and Daily Advertiser* (New York), Jan. 5, 1807; *Christian Observer* (Boston), Sept. 1807; *Farmer's Cabinet* (Amherst, N.H.), Feb. 24, 1807; *Weekly Inspector* (New York), May 23, 1807; *North American Review*, May 1816.

28. "We Can Do Nothing of Ourselves," *Christian Disciple* (Boston), June 2, 1814; Thomas Jefferson to Benjamin Waterhouse, June 20, 1822, in Peterson, *Thomas Jefferson: Writings*, 1458–59; William Ellery Channing, *Two Sermons on Infidelity, Delivered October 24, 1813* (Boston, 1813), 26–27; see also *Christian Disciple*, June 3 and Dec. 3, 1815.

29. Samuel L. Knapp, *Treasury of Knowledge and Library of Reference, Part VI, American Biography* (New York, 1833), 92–98; *Philanthropist*, July 30, 1822; Joseph Wolf[f], *Missionary Journal and Memoir of the Reverend Joseph Wolf[f], Missionary to the Jews . . .* (New York, 1824), 124; George Waddington and Barnard Hanbury, *Journal of a Visit to Some Parts of Ethiopia* (London, 1822), 114. English's father was a merchant who had moved from England to Boston; on his mother's side, he was descended from Huguenots, the Bethunes and the Faneuils. William Bentley described English's mother as "my favorite girl when I was Chaplain to her Grandfather"; see Bentley, *Diary*, 4:632–33; see also 2:243–44, 4:215, 226.

30. George Bethune English, *The Grounds of Christianity Examined* (Boston, 1813), esp. 66–69, 120–21, 152; Samuel Cary, *A Review of the Book Entitled "The Grounds of Christianity Examined, by Comparing the New Testament with the Old," by George B. English, A.M.* (Boston, 1813); George Bethune English, *A Letter to the Reverend Mr. Channing Relative to His Two Sermons on Infidelity* (Boston, 1813), esp. 4, 8; George Bethune English, *A Letter to the Reverend Mr. Cary, Containing Remarks on His Review* (Boston, 1813), esp. 76; Edward Everett, *A Defense of Christianity Against the Work of George B. English* (Cambridge, Mass., 1814), and the review in *Christian Disciple*, Dec. 2, 1814.

31. Bentley, *Diary*, 4:596; Zagarri, *Revolutionary Backlash* 46–147; Rosemarie Zagarri, "The Significance of the 'Global Turn' for the Early American Republic: Global-

ization in the Age of Nation-Building," *Journal of the Early Republic* 31, no. 1 (2011), 22–25.

32. *Lady's and Gentleman's Weekly Museum and Philadelphia Reporter,* Jan. 4, 1818; *Alexandria Gazette and Daily,* Jan. 30, 1818; *Weekly Visitor and Ladies Museum* (New York), Jan. 3, 1818; *City of Washington Gazette,* Feb. 6, 1818; *New-York Weekly Museum,* March 9, 1816; *Massachusetts Spy, or, Worcester Gazette,* Feb. 7, 1816; *Analectic,* Oct. 1816.

33. *Salmagundi,* Feb. 13, June 2, and Nov. 24, 1807.

34. *Connecticut Courant,* Feb. 6, 1818; see also *Athenaeum,* Sept. 1, 1817; on Montagu's life, see Lowe, *Critical Terrains,* 30–54.

35. *Salem Register,* Oct. 26, 1816 (also known by this date as the *Essex Register*); see also *Christian Observer,* Sept. 1816, and Christopher John Bartlett, *Great Britain and Sea Power, 1815–1853* (Oxford: Clarendon Press, 1963), 61–62.

36. *New-York Spectator,* Sept. 18, 1816; *Trenton Federalist,* Jan. 20, 1817; *Weekly Aurora* (Philadelphia), Feb. 24, 1817; Mordecai M. Noah, *Travels in England, France, Spain, and the Barbary States, in the Years 1813–14 and 15* (New York, 1819), 301, 314–17, 366–68; see also Bentley, *Diary,* 2:84, 105–6.

37. Maria Martin, *History of the Captivity and Sufferings of Maria Martin* (Brookfield, Mass., 1818), 16. The Saharan narratives include Judah Paddock, *A Narrative of the Shipwreck of the* Oswego . . . (London, 1818), esp. 112, 129, 144, 149, 170–71, 183–85, 197–99, 203–4, 263, 328; James Riley, *Sufferings in Africa: Captain Riley's Narrative,* ed. Gordon H. Evans (1817; New York: C.N. Potter, 1965), 82, 86, 140–41, 155, 245, 293, 304–5, 309; Archibald Robbins, *A Journal, Comprising an Account of the Loss of the Brig Commerce* . . . , 8th ed. (Hartford, 1818), esp. 69, 72–74, 87, 119–29, 195, 238, 254. See also *The Narrative of Robert Adams* (Boston, 1817), esp. 131, although its authenticity is questionable. (*North American Review,* July 1817; Ann Fabian, *The Unvarnished Truth: Personal Narratives in Nineteenth-Century America* [Berkeley: University of California Press, 2000], 10–11, 29–40.) For points of contrast, see the earlier Barbary narratives, including *Narrative of the Captivity of Joseph Pitts* . . . (Frederick-Town, Md., 1815); William Ray, *Horrors of Slavery* . . . , ed. Hester Blum (1808; New Brunswick, N.J.: Rutgers University Press, 2008); Thomas Nicholson, *An Affecting Narrative of the Captivity and Sufferings* (Boston, 1816); Jonathan Cowdery, *American Captives in Tripoli* . . . , 2nd ed., (Boston, 1806); John Foss, *A Journal of the Captivity and Sufferings* . . . (Newburyport, Mass., 1798).

38. Royall Tyler, *The Algerine Captive,* ed. Caleb Crain (New York: Modern Family, 2002), xxxii, 131–36, 175, 182–83; on Tyler's career, see Cathy N. Davidson, *The Revolution and the Word: The Rise of the Novel in America* (New York: Oxford University Press, 1986), 192–211; Marr, *Culture of American Islamicism,* 55–59; Reynolds, *Faith in Fiction,* 16–17.

39. *Daily National Intelligencer,* Nov. 12 and Dec. 3, 1816.

40. Bird journal and diary from Jan. 1, 1816, at Yale College to April 3, 1818, at Andover, March 5, 1818, Bird Papers.

41. Pliny Fisk, "On the Influence of Sectarian Zeal in Forming and Propagating Our Theological Opinions," Sept. 1817, in Andover Student Dissertations, 1810–49, vol. 1, n.p., ANTS; Bentley, *Diary*, 3:23, 51, 55, 298, 495, 501, 4:20, 162, 360–65, 502, 552–53, 566–67. Fisk presented his dissertation only weeks after his professors had recommended him for posting as a foreign missionary. With that secured, perhaps he felt able to speak his mind freely.

42. Both of Bird's journals covering his work in Boston are included in "Journal of a Vacation in Boston in 1819"; see esp. entries for Oct. 8 and 21, Nov. 2 and 6, 1820, Bird Papers. On anti-Catholicism, see John Wolffe, "A Transatlantic Perspective: Protestantism and National Identities in Mid-Nineteenth-Century Britain and the United States," in *Protestantism and National Identity: Britain and Ireland, c. 1650–c. 1850*, ed. Tony Claydon and Ian McBride (Cambridge, U.K.: Cambridge University Press, 1998), 291–309.

43. Joseph Tinker Buckingham, *Personal Memoirs and Recollections of Editorial Life* (Boston, 1852), 76; *New-England Galaxy and Masonic Magazine*, Jan. 9 and 23, 1818; Bullock, *Revolutionary Brotherhood*, 156–76, 196–97; Brooke, *Columbia Rising*, 82–83, 88–90; Jessica L. Harland-Jacobs, *Builders of Empire: Freemasons and British Imperialism, 1717–1927* (Chapel Hill: University of North Carolina Press, 2007), esp. 3, 64–77, 96–97. I am indebted to my uncle Owen Monfils for insight into the present-day Masonic Order. Parsons also appears to have joined the Masons before leaving the United States; see the communication from the Palestine Masonic Missionary Society of Louisville in the *Hampshire Gazette*, June 19, 1822.

## 3. "A PERFECT ROMANCE"

1. Morse identified as an Old Calvinist rather than with the New Divinity even as he worked to bring the two groups and all conservative Calvinists into the same movement. For his career, see Moss, *Life of Jedidiah Morse*, 54–112; Phillips, *Jedidiah Morse*, 70–71, 73–101, 129–60; Field, *Crisis of the Standing Order*, 141–79; Conrad Wright, "The Controversial Career of Jedidiah Morse," *Harvard Library Bulletin* 31 (1983): 64–87; George Burder to Morse, June 15, 1814, and John Adams to Morse, May 15, 1815, Morse Papers; Worcester, *Memoir*, 2:86, 117. As part of their campaign against Socinianism, the Brethren corresponded with sympathetic Presbyterian seminarians in New York to help identify those "enemies of the cross." (The Brethren to Robert McLeod and John M. Duncan [Theological School of the Associate Reformed Church], April 19, 1810, New York, Papers of the Brethren.)

2. Anne Baker, *Heartless Immensity: Literature, Culture, and Geography in Antebellum America* (Ann Arbor: University of Michigan Press, 2006), 122–26; Martin Brückner, *The Geographic Revolution in Early America: Maps, Literacy, and National Identity* (Chapel Hill: University of North Carolina Press, 2006), 146–72; Bruce A. Harvey, *American Geographics: U.S. National Narratives and the*

*Representation of the Non-European World, 1830–1865* (Stanford, Calif.: Stanford University Press, 2001), 28–33; Phillips, *Jedidiah Morse*, 32–35; Moss, *Life of Morse*, 25–26, 38–52, 58–60, 100, 107, 113. Virtually all other textbook writers lifted liberally from Morse, right down to his assessments of national character.

3. Jedidiah Morse, *The American Universal Geography*, 7th ed. (Charlestown, Mass., 1819), 1:806; 2:131, 209, 236, 491, 576, 581, 603, 611, 660, 713.

4. Morse, *American Universal Geography*, 2:421, 489, 530, 545, 577, 600, 603, 611, 612, 623, 660. For examples of Morse's close and continuing connection with the American Board, see Evarts to Worcester, Feb. 27, 1817, and April 12, 1819, ABC 11, vol. 1 (microfilm copy), ABCFM HU.

5. William J. Gilmore, *Reading Becomes a Necessity of Life: Material and Cultural Life in Rural New England, 1780–1835* (Knoxville: University of Tennessee Press, 1989), 64. The South offered the staunchest resistance to missions; see Bertram Wyatt-Brown, "The Antimission Movement in the Jacksonian South: A Study in Regional Folk Culture," *Journal of Southern History* 36, no. 4 (1970): 501–29.

6. "Popular missionary culture" is a term coined by Elbourne, "Foundation of the Church Missionary Society," 248–49.

7. This anecdote appears in Worcester, *Memoir*, 2:140–42. The unidentified author appears to have been about the age of Worcester's son and memoirist.

8. The *Panoplist*'s name changed to the *Panoplist, and Missionary Magazine* in 1808, and then to the *Panoplist, and Missionary Herald* in 1818; after 1820, it became the *Missionary Herald*. For its founding, see Moss, *Life of Jedidiah Morse*, 86–90, 92, 105; Phillips, *Jedidiah Morse*, 119–20, 136, 138; see also Felicity Jensz and Hanna Acke, "The Form and Function of Nineteenth-Century Missionary Periodicals: Introduction," *Church History* 82, no. 2 (June 2013): 368–73. For Evarts's career, see John Andrew III, *From Revivals to Removal: Jeremiah Evarts, the Cherokee Nation, and the Search for the Soul of America* (Athens: University of Georgia Press, 1992), 24–28, 53–84; Ebenezer C. Tracy, *Memoir of the Life of Jeremiah Evarts, Esq.* (Boston, 1845), esp. 1–98; Worcester, *Memoir*, 223–34. For Samuel Worcester's role, see Worcester to Evarts, Dec. 28 and 29, 1818, May 6, 1820, ABC 11, vol. 1 (microfilm copy), ABCFM HU. In their plans for the *Panoplist*, American evangelicals were reading straight from the British script. By demonizing Hinduism, British missionary societies not only gained access to the subcontinent but also grew immensely in membership, wealth, and influence—which enabled evangelicals to put an even deeper impress on popular attitudes toward the world in the future. See Elbourne, "Foundation of the Church Missionary Society," 262–64. On the ways in which print culture created communities of like-minded readers, see Benedict Anderson, *Imagined Communities: Reflections on the Origin and Spread of Nationalism* (New York: Verso, 1991). Applications of Anderson's ideas for understanding the early republic appear in Cotlar, *Tom Paine's America*, 16–17, and David Waldstreicher, *In the Midst of Perpetual Fetes: The Making of American Nationalism, 1776–1820* (Chapel Hill: University of North Carolina Press, 1997).

9. Evarts to Worcester, March 31, 1815, and April 25, 1816, ABC 11, vol. 1 (microfilm copy), ABCFM HU. The best guide to the early years of the American Board is Andrew, *Rebuilding the Christian Commonwealth*, esp. 70–96. For the ways in which other benevolent groups morphed into national nonprofit corporations, see Peter J. Wosh, *Spreading the Word: The Bible Business in Nineteenth-Century America* (Ithaca, N.Y.: Cornell University Press, 1994), 155–56.

10. Worcester to Mrs. Sarah Bonney, Feb. 15, 1817, Worcester to Miss Sarah Vaill, Dec. 2, 1818, Samuel Worcester letter books, ABC 1.01, vol. 2, ABCFM HU; Parsons to Fisk, Oct. 23, 1817, ABCFM, reel 502; Evarts to Battelle, Feb. 9, 1822, ABC 8.2.13, and Battelle to Evarts, ABC 10, vol. 3, Jan. 5 and 29, 1822, ABCFM HU.

11. Worcester to Gordon Hall and Samuel Newell, May 24, Oct. 1, and Dec. 7, 1817, ABC 1.01, vol. 2, ABCFM HU; Emily P. Kimball to Evarts, Nov. 28, 1827, ABC 10, vol. 9 (J–K), ABCFM HU; Anonymous to Evarts, Jan. 28, 1819, List of Contributions to the ABCFM, June 17, 1820, John Giles to Evarts, July 14, 1820, Evarts to Worcester, March 31, 1815, and March 4, 1818, all in ABC 11, vol. 1 (microfilm copy), ABCFM HU; Morton, *Memoir of Parsons*, 119; Spring, *Memoirs of Mills*, 58; Bentley, *Diary*, 4:358, 554, 556, 623, 625; Yale, *Godly Pastor*, 272. Andover's missionaries in the making typically spent vacations and their first year after graduation drumming up support for the American Board; ministers and laymen also acted as local or traveling agents. They raised money by passing the plate after addressing missionary societies, approaching wealthy individuals, and selling subscriptions to the *Panoplist*. All who gave could find their names listed in the magazine's back pages; even children came in for such recognition for donating pocket money earned by memorizing Bible verses, learning hymns, and "abstaining from sugar." In the 1810s the largest single group of contributors to the board and the most generous came from New England. Evarts also devised a number of small incentives, such as free subscriptions to the *Panoplist* for contributions of twelve dollars and honorary board memberships for gifts of over fifty dollars. Evarts even sold jewelry donated in the North to southerners to raise money. For the use of spectacle in the early nineteenth-century British missionary movement, see Thorne, *Congregational Missions and the Making of an Imperial Culture in Nineteenth-Century England*, 63–64.

12. Evarts to Fisk, March 4, 1819, ABC 1.01, vol. 2, ABCFM HU; Evarts to Worcester, Feb. 19, 1818 (entry for Feb. 12), March 4, April 6, and April 29, 1818, ABC 11, vol. 1 (microfilm copy), ABCFM HU. No evidence has turned up to indicate when or even if the board actually implemented a direct-mail campaign. Tellingly, Evarts's first step to extend the board's influence southward involved cultivating a network of Yankee women transplanted to the South.

13. Bentley, *Diary*, 3:173–74, 4:631; Worcester, *Memoir*, 2:124. John Adams and Thomas Jefferson shared Bentley's aversion. In reference to the American Bible Society, Adams joked about wishing that "societies were formed in India, China, and Turkey to send us gratis translations of their Sacred Books; one good turn deserves another." "What would they [evangelicals] say," Jefferson asked, "were

the Pope to send annually to this country colonies of Jesuit priests with cargoes of their Missal and translations of their Vulgate, to be put gratis into the hands of everyone who would accept them?" (Cappon, *Adams-Jefferson Letters*, 360, 493–94, 496; Bowers, *Joseph Priestley*, 84–85; Edwin Gaustad, *Without King, Without Prelate: Religion and the New Nation, 1776–1826* [Grand Rapids, Mich.: Eerdmans, 1993], 95.)

14. "Avarus Homunculus," *Boston Recorder*, Jan. 13, 1813; see also *Berkshire Star*, Aug. 29, 1816, *Athenaeum*, Oct. 1, 1817, and *The Reformer* (Philadelphia), Jan. 1, 1820. Agents in the field trying to raise money for missions met with similar criticisms; see Parsons to Fisk, Feb. 5, 1819, ABCFM, reel 502.

15. *New-England Galaxy and Masonic Magazine*, Jan. 16, 1818, and "Bereanus," Jan. 30 and Feb. 27, 1818; for Buckingham's contributions, see "Systematic Beggary," on Jan. 1, 1819, and also Feb. 12, 1819, and March 17, 1820. For his life, see Buckingham, *Personal Memoirs*, 78–79, 93–94; Gary J. Kornblith, "Becoming Joseph T. Buckingham: The Struggle for Artisanal Independence in Early Nineteenth-Century Boston," in *American Artisans: Crafting Social Identity, 1750–1850*, ed. Howard B. Rock, Paul Gilje, and Robert Asher (Baltimore: Johns Hopkins University Press, 1995), 123–35.

16. Samuel Knapp, *Extracts from a Journal of Travels in North America, Consisting of an Account of Boston and Its Vicinity. By Ali Bey* (Boston, 1818), 12–24, 59, 109–12, 119–20. For Knapp's career, see Ben Harris McClary, "Samuel Lorenzo Knapp and Early American Biography," *Proceedings of the American Antiquarian Society* 95 (April 1985): 39–67; see also Buckingham, *Personal Memoirs*, 73, 77. Knapp's American literary models include the letters in Washington Irving's *Salmagundi* and the letters of Mehemet in Peter Markoe's *Algerine Spy in Pennsylvania* (1787). Knapp might also have been riffing on Humphrey Prideaux, who argued that religious apathy among the English could expose them to being overrun by false religions and offered Muhammad's career as a cautionary tale.

17. Many American proto-Unitarians supported the early missions movement, at least publicly, as any issue of the *Christian Disciple* (Boston) before 1820 indicates. Privately, they appear to have been more critical. See Anderson to Henry Hill, Feb. 18, 1824, ABC 11, vol. 1 (microfilm copy), ABCFM HU; see also "Unitarian Defense of Foreign Missions," *New-York Observer*, Dec. 31, 1825, and "Correspondence Relative to Unitarian Christianity in India," *New-York Observer*, April 28 and Nov. 24, 1827; Johann N. Neem, *Creating a Nation of Joiners: Democracy and Civil Society in Early National Massachusetts* (Cambridge, Mass.: Harvard University Press, 2008), 115.

18. Moses Stuart, *A Sermon Preached in the Tabernacle Church, Salem, November 5, 1818* (Andover, Mass., 1818), 13, 14–16; appended in the same publication, Samuel Worcester, *Address to Missionaries*, 5. For similar British evangelical arguments, see David Bogue, *Objections Against a Mission to the Heathen, Stated and Considered* (1795; Cambridge, Mass., 1811), 22; Charles Grant, *Observations on the State of Society Among the Asiatic Subjects of Great Britain* (House of Commons

Parliamentary Papers Online, 2006), 89–90; Sydney Smith, "Indian Missions," *Edinburgh Review* 12 (April 1808): 151–81; see also David Kopf, *British Orientalism and the Bengal Renaissance: The Dynamics of Indian Modernization, 1773–1835* (Berkeley: University of California Press, 1969), 136–44.

19. Bentley, *Diary*, 3:529, 4:91, 98–99, 554, 631; Andrew, *Rebuilding the Christian Commonwealth*, 79; Matthew Bowman and Samuel Brown, "Reverend Buck's *Theological Dictionary* and the Struggle to Define American Evangelicalism, 1802–1851," *Journal of the Early Republic* 29, no. 3 (2009): 441–73. One measure of evangelicals' success was the strategy adopted by some Freemasons to vindicate their fraternity from charges of irreligion by making well-publicized donations to missions; see Communication from the Palestine Masonic Missionary Society of Louisville reprinted in the *Hampshire Gazette*, June 19, 1822.

20. Evarts to Worcester, Dec. 8, 1818, ABC 11, vol. 1 (microfilm copy), ABCFM HU; see also Andrew, *Rebuilding the Christian Commonwealth*, 82–96; Evarts to Colonel John Linklaen, Jan. 12, 1819, ABC 1.01, vol. 2, ABCFM HU.

21. *Panoplist, and Missionary Herald*, July 1817; *Christian Observer*, Nov. 1, 1817; *Religious Intelligencer* (New Haven), Nov. 1, 1817; *Boston Recorder*, Nov. 11, 1817; *Weekly Recorder* (Chillicothe, Ohio), Dec. 10, 1817 and Feb. 1818; *Boston Recorder*, May 26, 1818; *Evangelical Guardian and Review* (New York), June 1, 1818; *Panoplist, and Missionary Herald*, June 1818; *Religious Remembrancer* (Philadelphia), Dec. 10, 1817, and June 6, 1818; *Christian Herald* (New York), Nov. 22, 1817, and June 20, 1818; *Baptist Magazine* (Bennington, Vt.), July 11, 1818; *Christian Messenger* (Baltimore), Oct. 31, 1818.

22. Morton, *Memoir of Parsons*, 158–60; Parsons to Fisk, Oct. 23, 1817, Dec. 10, 1818, Feb. 5, 1819, ABCFM, reel 502. For romantic friendships, see Richard Godbeer, *The Overflowing of Friendship: Love Between Men and the Creation of the American Republic* (Baltimore: Johns Hopkins University Press, 2009); Carroll Smith-Rosenberg, "The Female World of Love and Ritual: Relations Between Women in Nineteenth-Century America," in *Disorderly Conduct: Visions of Gender in Victorian America* (New York: Knopf, 1985), 53–76; Anthony Rotundo, *American Manhood: Transformations in Masculinity from the Revolution to the Modern Era* (New York: Basic Books, 1993); Donald Yacovone, " 'Surpassing the Love of Women': Victorian Manhood and the Language of Fraternal Love," in *A Shared Experience: Men, Women, and the History of Gender*, ed. Laura McCall and Donald Yacovone (New York: New York University Press, 1998), 195–221; Caleb Crain, *American Sympathy: Men, Friendship, and Literature in the New Nation* (New Haven, Conn.: Yale University Press, 2001); Rachel Hope Cleves, *Charity and Sylvia: A Same-Sex Marriage in Early America* (New York: Oxford University Press, 2014). Some recent scholarship has yielded evidence suggesting that some romantic friends became sexual partners, but no evidence suggests an intimacy between Fisk and Parsons that was anything other than emotional and spiritual.

23. Fisk, "Historical Sketch of the Society"; Fisk, MJ I, Nov. 3 to 21, 1821; Parsons to Mary D. Brown, n.d. [1820], Parsons Letters. Mills's letter of December 22, 1807, appears to be addressed to Munis Kenney; see Richards, *Samuel Mills*, 62.

24. Harriet Atwood and Samuel Newell knew each other less than a year before they agreed to wed; he had never laid eyes on his second wife, a woman recruited by the board, until she stepped off the boat at Bombay (Mumbai). (Leonard Woods to Samuel Worcester, n.d. 1817, ABC 6, Candidate Department, vol. 1, ABCFM HU, reel 56; see also Evarts to Worcester, Aug. 14, 1815, June 18, 1816, ABC 11, vol. 1 [microfilm copy], ABCFM HU.) William Goodell included a long description in his autobiography of finding wives for two of the first missionaries bound for the Sandwich Islands after the mothers of the two young ladies to whom they were first engaged "interfered and refused to let their daughters go." See Prime, *Forty Years in the Turkish Empire*, 52–59.

25. Evarts to Worcester, Dec. 8, 1818, Feb. 16, 1819, ABC 11, vol. 1 (microfilm copy), ABCFM HU.

26. *New Hampshire Gazette*, Sept. 3, 1816; *Alexandria Gazette*, June 8, 1816; *Country Courier* (New York), Sept. 5, 1816; Morse, *American Universal Geography*, 2:421; see also David Brewer, *The Greek War of Independence: The Struggle for Freedom from Ottoman Oppression and the Birth of the Modern Greek Nation* (Woodstock, N.Y.: Overlook Press, 2001), 136.

27. George Barrell, *Letters from Asia* (New York, 1819), 10, 12, 18, 19, 20–21, 24–26, 35, 43, 44, 49–51. Excerpts appeared in many newspapers as far south as the Carolinas before the publication of the book itself. Barrell's father had made a fortune from privateering during the American Revolution and from more legitimate commerce thereafter. He spent it to indulge his exquisite taste, amassing a private library that fired William Bentley's lust and building a country house in Charlestown that Charles Bulfinch designed. (Harry F. Barrell, "Barrell Family and Connections . . ." [1897], and Joseph Barrell, "Genealogy of the Barrell Family" [1915], both in the library of the New England Historical and Genealogical Society, Boston.)

28. Jedidiah Morse, *The American Universal Geography*, 6th ed., 2 vols. (Boston, 1812), Special Collections, Millersville University, 2:419; William Eton, *Survey of the Turkish Empire*, 2nd ed. (London, 1799), 103–5, 115–22, 132–33, 200; *Travels of Ali Bey* (London, 1816), 355–60; see also Rhoads Murphey, "Bigots or Informed Observers? A Periodization of Pre-colonial English and European Writing on the Middle East," *Journal of the American Oriental Society* 110, no. 2 (April–June 1990): 291–303; Reinhold Schiffer, *Turkey Romanticized: Images of the Turks in Early Nineteenth-Century English Travel Literature with an Anthology of Texts* (Bochum: Studienverlag N. Brockmeyer, 1982), esp. 19–44; Ansli Çirakman, *From the "Terror of the World" to the "Sick Man of Europe": European Images of Ottoman Empire and Society from the Sixteenth Century to the Nineteenth* (New York: P. Lang, 2002), esp. 145, 151, 158–59; Norman Daniel, *Islam, Europe, and Empire* (Edinburgh: Edinburgh University Press, 1966), 103–4, 129, 219–20.

29. Thomas Thornton, *The Present State of Turkey* (London, 1807), esp. xi, 3–4, 17, 32, 44, 46–47, 249, 251–52, 280–88, 301–2, 312, 317, 335–81; Bigland, *Geographical and Historical View of the World*, 4:85–86, 90. For Thornton's background, see Gunny, *Perceptions of Islam in European Writings*, 195.

30. Fisk's private diary indicates that he bought Barrell's book sometime during the months before his departure and read it on arriving at Smyrna, perhaps not for the first time. (Fisk, UTS I, Dec. 11, 1819.)

31. Fisk to an unidentified correspondent in Marblehead [the Reverend Samuel Dana], Dec. 16, 1819, ABCFM, reel 513.

32. Julia Adams letter book, 1819–35, Oct. 26, 1819, Joseph Downs Collection of Manuscripts and Printed Ephemera, Winterthur Museum and Library.

33. Worcester to the Reverend Dr. Henry Kollock, Oct. 10 and Nov. 20, 1818, Evarts to Colonel John Linklaen, Jan. 19, 1819, Evarts to Levi Parsons, Jan. 12, Feb. 17, and March 5, 1819, Evarts to Fisk, March 4, 1819, and Evarts to Kollock, March 8, 1819, ABC 1.01, vol. 2, ABCFM HU; Worcester to Evarts, Oct. 14, 1818, Evarts to Worcester, July 7, 1817, Nov. 13 and 22, 1818, Feb. 16, 1819, ABC 11, vol. 1 (microfilm copy), ABCFM HU; Anderson to Henry Hill, May 20, 1824, ABC 11, vol. 1 (microfilm copy), ABCFM HU; Bond, *Memoir of Fisk*, 88–90, 93.

34. Julia Adams letter book, 1819–35, Nov. 12, 1819; *Panoplist, and Missionary Herald*, Dec. 1819. For background on the Sandwich Islands mission, see Clifford Putney, *Missionaries in Hawai'i: The Lives of Peter and Fanny Gulick, 1797–1883* (Amherst: University of Massachusetts Press, 2010), and Andrews, *Rebuilding the Christian Commonwealth*, 97–119.

35. Pliny Fisk, *The Holy Land an Interesting Field of Missionary Enterprise* (Boston, 1819); Stuart, *Sermon Preached at Tabernacle Church*, 13–16, 28–29; American Board of Commissioners for Foreign Missions, *Instructions from the Prudential Committee to the Rev. Levi Parsons and the Rev. Pliny Fisk* (Boston, 1819), 8. Fisk's sermon echoed Joseph White's view that Muslims were "lifted far above the ignorance of barbarians and the ferocity of savages" and that they were "neither involved in the impiety of atheism, nor the darkness of idolatry." See Joseph White, *A Sermon Preached Before the University of Oxford, July 4, 1784, on the Duty of Attempting Propagation of the Gospel Among Our Mahometan and Gentoo Subjects in India* (London, 1785), 31, 33.

36. "Systematic Beggary," Jan. 1, 1819; Fisk and Parsons to the ABCFM Prudential Committee, Sept. 21, 1819, ABC 6, Candidate Department, vol. 1, ABCFM HU; "List of Books for a Missionary Library at Smyrna," following the letter of Fisk and Parsons to Evarts, March 11, 1820, ABCFM, reel 513.

## 4. BRITISH CONNECTIONS

1. Parsons to Evarts, Jan. 3, 1820, Fisk and Parsons to Worcester, Jan. 6, 1820, and Fisk to Evarts, Jan. 7, 1820, ABCFM, reel 513; Parsons to Mary D. Brown, n.d., Parsons Letters, and Fisk to Isaac Bird, Dec. 27 and 28, 1819, Pliny Fisk Papers, SCMC; Fisk, UTS I, Dec. 24–27, 1819. Malta's early nineteenth-century lazaretto had rooms for meeting with visitors that used wooden railings or grilles to separate those in quarantine. Some meetings also took place outdoors; see Paul Cassar, *Medical History of Malta* (London: Wellcome Historical Medical Library, 1964), 292–96, 300–307.

2. Jowett to his mother, Dec. 11, 1815; Jowett to Eliza Pratt, March 26, 1816; Jowett journal, Feb. 16, April 27, 1816, April n.d., 1816, June 23, 1816, June n.d., 1817, Aug. 3 and Sept. 5, 1817, CMSC. (Most of Jowett's journals were addressed as letters to Josiah Pratt, but they are noted as diary entries.) For early nineteenth-century travelers' descriptions of Valletta, see Samuel Woodruff, *Journal of a Tour to Malta, Greece, Asia Minor, Carthage, Algiers, Port Mahon, and Spain in 1828* (Hartford, 1831), 32; John Galt, *Voyages and Travels in the Years 1809, 1810, 1811 . . .* (London, 1812), 116, 118; William Turner, *Tour in the Levant*, 3 vols. (London, 1820), 1:26–29; S. S. Wilson, *A Narrative of the Greek Mission; or, Sixteen Years in Malta and Greece* (London, 1839), esp. 27–30. Secondary accounts include Harry Luke, *Malta: An Account and an Appreciation* (London: G. G. Harrap, 1949), 39–49, and C. A. Bayly, *Imperial Meridian: The British Empire and the World, 1780–1830* (London: Longman, 1989), 197–202. On the sirocco wind, see Fisk, UTS I, April 24, 1820; James Emerson, *Letters from the Aegean* (New York, 1829), 25; Christian Müller, *Journey Through Greece and the Ionian Islands in June, July, and August, 1821* (London, 1822), 56.

3. According to Jowett, the Maltese outside Valletta spoke a dialect consisting of one-fifth Italian and four-fifths Arabic, while those in Valletta spoke "city-Maltese," a combination of four-fifths Italian with "Maltese declension and conjugation." (Jowett journal, July 23, 1817.) For Malta's strategic significance, see *American Register*, Jan. 2, 1807.

4. Jowett to Pratt, Dec. 9, 1815, and Jan. 27, 1816, and Pratt to Jowett, March 16, 1816, CMSC; *MR*, June 1816, 244. On Thomas Maitland's career, see C. W. Crawley, *The Question of Greek Independence: A Study of British Policy in the Near East, 1821–1833* (New York: H. Fertig, 1973), 20n11.

5. Eugene Stock, *The History of the Church Missionary Society: Its Environment, Its Men, and Its Work*, 3 vols. (London, 1899), 1:222, 226–27, 229; John Wolffe, *The Protestant Crusade in Great Britain, 1829–1860* (Oxford: Clarendon Press, 1991), 30–32; Jowett to Pratt, Dec. 21, 1816; Jowett journal, Nov. 9, 1816. For their part, Roman Catholic leaders hoped to bring Eastern Christians back into their orbit by establishing so-called Uniate churches that recognized the pope's authority. Among Eastern Christians, the Greek Catholics, Syrian Catholics, and Maronites acknowledged the Vatican. See Heleen Murre–van den Berg, "The Middle East: Western Missions and the Eastern Churches, Islam, and Judaism," in *World Christianities, c. 1815–c. 1914*, ed. Sheridan Gilley and Brian Stanley, vol. 8 of *Cambridge History of Christianity* (Cambridge, U.K.: Cambridge University Press, 2006), 458–72.

6. Stock, *History of the Church Missionary Society*, 1:224–25, 231; Elbourne, *Blood Ground*, 65–70; Elbourne, "Foundation of the Church Missionary Society," 247–64; Stephen Tomkins, *The Clapham Sect: How Wilberforce's Circle Changed Britain* (Oxford: Lion Hudson, 2010); Cox, *British Missionary Enterprise Since 1700*, 85–87; Boyd Hilton, *A Mad, Bad, and Dangerous People? England, 1783–1846* (Oxford: Oxford University Press, 2006), 174–84; Charles I. Foster, *An Errand of Mercy: The Evangelical United Front, 1790–1837* (Chapel Hill: University of

286 NOTES TO PAGES 102–104

North Carolina Press, 1960), esp. 32–144; Worcester to Fisk and Parsons, April 22, 1820, ABC 1.01, vol. 4, ABCFM HU; American Board of Commissioners for Foreign Missions, *Instructions from the Prudential Committee to the Rev. Levi Parsons and the Rev. Pliny Fisk*, 2, 6–7. The Church Missionary Society might have deliberately styled the genteel Jowett as its "literary representative" to set him apart from those specifically designated as missionaries, the majority of whom came from Britain's working class and lower-middle class during this period. See Lord Gambier (president of the Church Missionary Society) to Thomas Maitland, Aug. 16, 1815, CMSC; Stuart Piggin, *Making Evangelical Missionaries, 1789–1858: The Social Background, Motives, and Training of the British Protestant Missionaries to India* (Abingdon: Sutton Cortenay Press, 1984).

7. Jowett to his mother, Dec. 11, 1815, and Martha Jowett to her sister, Oct. 29, 1816, CMSC; Elnathan Gridley to Anderson, Dec. 28, 1826, ABCFM, reel 515; Parsons to Brown, n.d., Parsons Letters. Compared with Jowett's annual salary—three hundred pounds sterling, plus travel and expenses—Fisk sighed that his American Board pay amounted to "a mere pittance." (Fisk to Evarts, Feb. 4, 1822, ABCFM, reel 513.) Jowett did not regard the two American missionaries as his equals with respect to education or social standing, but he held them in greater regard than British Dissenters. He dismissed a Methodist or Baptist missionary who passed through Malta as "a plain man *of very few words*; so that one cannot exactly get into his mind: nor am I very prying." Jowett did not think "his education very complete," like that of most Dissenters. (Jowett to Eliza Jowett Pratt, Jan. 18, 1817, CMSC.) Jowett even urged Fisk and Parsons to spend some months at Malta studying Italian and modern Greek before heading into Ottoman dominions.

8. Martyn received notice in secular sources as well; see James Justinian Morier, *A Second Journey Through Persia, Armenia, and Asia Minor, to Constantinople . . .* (London, 1818), 223–24. For a shrewd discussion of evangelical memoirs like those of Martyn and Harriet Newell as a genre, see Kelley, "'Pen and Ink Communion,'" 563–64.

9. John Sargent, Jr., *Memoir of the Rev. Henry Martyn, B.D.*, 2nd ed. (Boston, 1820), 72–73, 85–86, 90–91, 118–19, 223–26, 295; George Smith, *Henry Martyn: Saint and Scholar* (New York, 1892), 6; William Carus, ed., *Memoir of Charles Simeon, M.A.* (London, 1847), 75–76. A later and fuller compilation of Martyn's letters and journals is Samuel Wilberforce, ed., *Journals and Letters of the Rev. Henry Martyn, B.D.* (1837; London, 1839), 55, 356, 512–17, 635. For background on the East India Company and British Protestant missions during the early nineteenth century, see Cox, *British Missionary Enterprise Since 1700*, 44–51, 70–75, 80–82, 86–92; Carson, "Imperial Dilemma"; Johnston, *Missionary Writing and Empire*, 16–17, 73–74.

10. Sargent, *Memoir*, 206–7, 224–25, 230–32, 250–55; see also Wilberforce, *Journals and Letters*, 523–24, 528. Martyn worked with two Muslim Indian munshis, Mirza Mahommed Ali and Moorad Ali; his Hindu pandit was Mirza Fitrut of Benares.

11. Sargent, *Memoir*, 276–79, 286–88, 325–27; Wilberforce, *Journals and Letters*, 476–77, 522–25, 528, 550, 574, 582, 588, 589, 594, 612, 615–16; Smith, *Henry Martyn*,

NOTES TO PAGES 104–105  287

228–32, 234, 268–70; *Memoirs of the Right Reverend Daniel Corrie, L.L.D.* (London, 1847), 160, 168, 172–74; Eli Daniel Potts, *British Baptist Missionaries in India* (London: Cambridge University Press, 1967), 55, 177–200; Karen Chancey, "The Star in the East: The Controversy over Christian Missions to India, 1805–1813," *Historian* 60, no. 3 (1998): 507–16. British missionaries also came under fire for publishing the "Persian pamphlet," which criticized Islam and, as some of their detractors alleged, ignited the Vellore mutiny; it was translated into Persian by a Muslim convert who was likely Sabat. See *Massachusetts Baptist Missionary Magazine*, May 1808.

12. The other man whose example put Martyn on the boat to Persia was Don Leopoldo Sebastiani, a missionary for the Propaganda Fide of the Roman Catholic Church who had spent three years at Isfahan before turning up at Calcutta in 1810. He arrived flashing a nearly completed translation of the New Testament into Persian, a rival to Martyn's work, and boasting about his disputes with Muslim religious leaders and near escapes from martyrdom at the hands of outraged crowds. Although Martyn occasionally socialized with Catholic missionaries, he privately referred to them as "formidable agents of the devil" and once declared, "Who would think that we should have to combat Antichrist again at this day?" Like most evangelicals, he regarded Catholics as nearly beyond the bounds of brotherhood. Now here was Sebastiani, snatching the laurels of translation from his grasp. See Sargent, *Memoir*, 294–95, 297, 299; Wilberforce, *Journals and Letters*, 594–95. On Roman Catholic missionaries in Persia, see Rudi Matthee, "The Politics of Protection: Iberian Missionaries in Safavid Iran Under Shah Abas I (1587–1629)," in *Contacts and Controversies Between Muslims, Jews, and Christians in the Ottoman Empire and Pre-modern Iran*, ed. Camilla Adang and Sabine Schmidtke (Würzburg: Istanbul Orient-Institut Würzburg Ergon-Verl, 2010), 245–71. For Sebastiani's career, see Thomas Simeon Rehill O'Flynn, "The Western Christian Presence in the Caucasus and Qajar Persia, 1802–1870" (Ph.D. diss., Oxford University, 2003), 20–38, 43. There was only one Roman Catholic missionary left at Isfahan when Martyn arrived in Persia. Martyn met him when he stopped briefly at Isfahan in May 1812. (Sargent, *Memoir*, 426; Morier, *Second Journey Through Persia*, 146–48.)

13. Sargent, *Memoir*, 347; Wilberforce, *Journals and Letters*, 723. The British and Foreign Bible Society (BFBS) provided the funds for Martyn's sojourn in Persia; the BFBS refused to reprint Sebastiani's Persian New Testament because of his Catholicism. For a description of Bushehr, see James Justinian Morier, *A Journey Through Persia, Armenia, and Asia Minor, to Constantinople, in the Years 1808 and 1809* (Philadelphia, 1816), 66–67.

14. Smith, *Henry Martyn*, 331; Sargent, *Memoir*, 360–61. For a description of Shiraz, see Morier, *Journey Through Persia*, 105–24, and Morier, *Second Journey Through Persia*, 111. I am indebted to my colleague Rudi Matthee for explaining the depopulation and ruin of major Persian cities such as Shiraz and Isfahan; see also his *Pursuit of Pleasure: Drugs and Stimulants in Iranian History, 1500–1900* (Princeton, N.J.: Princeton University Press, 2009), 241–45.

15. Sargent, *Memoir*, 355–62, 371–78, 420–22, 432–38, 488; Wilberforce, *Journals and Letters*, 731, 734, 736–38, 743–44, 747–48. Morier's account emphasizes the significance of seating precedence in Persian assemblies such as those attended by Martyn, while the historian Edward Ingram observes that "rulers of Islamic states treated ceremonies as a struggle for status." See Morier, *Second Journey Through Persia*, 143, 184; Edward Ingram, *Britain's Persian Connection, 1798–1828: Prelude to the Great Game in Asia* (Oxford: Clarendon Press, 1992), 162; Hamid Algar, *Religion and the State in Iran, 1785–1906* (Berkeley: University of California Press, 1969), 19; see also Willem Floor, "The Economic Role of the Ulama in Qajar Persia," in *The Most Learned of the Shi'a*, ed. Linda S. Walbridge (New York: Oxford University Press, 2001), 53–81. For an analysis of Martyn's influence on Iran's religious elite, see Abbas Amanat, "*Mujtahids* and Missionaries: Shi'i Responses to Christian Polemics in the Early Qajar Period," in *Religion and Society in Qajar Iran*, ed. Robert Gleave (London: Routledge Curzon, 2005), 247–69.

16. Sargent, *Memoir*, 207, 260, 264, 291–92, 382, 411–12; Wilberforce, *Journals and Letters*, 731, 759; Smith, *Henry Martyn*, 413, 438, 440. Sargent claimed that Martyn had converted "some Mahometans of consequence" before leaving Shiraz. (Sargent, *Memoir*, 488–89.) Whether he did in fact remains a matter of speculation. Charles Simeon arranged for the translations and publication of Martyn's polemics against Islam; see Samuel Lee, ed., *Controversial Tracts on Christianity and Mohammedanism by the Late Rev. Henry Martyn* (Cambridge, U.K., 1823).

17. Martyn to Simeon, July 18, 1811, Henry Martyn Papers, Henry Martyn Centre, Westminster College, Cambridge University (original at Duke University Library); Wilberforce, *Journals and Letters*, 725, 743–44. My discussion of Qajar Iran relies on Algar, *Religion and the State in Iran*, 5–72, 100–102; Ingram, *Britain's Persian Connection*, 153–83; Nikki R. Keddie, *Qajar Iran and the Rise of Reza Khan, 1796–1925* (Costa Mesa, Calif.: Mazda Publishers, 1999), 21–24; Vanessa Martin, *The Qajar Pact: Bargaining, Protest, and the State in Nineteenth-Century Persia* (New York: I. B. Tauris, 2005), 14–22; Rudi Matthee, "Suspicion, Fear, and Admiration: Pre-Nineteenth-Century Iranian Views of the English and the Russians," in *Iran and the Surrounding World*, ed. Nikki R. Keddie and Rudi Matthee (Seattle: University of Washington Press, 2002), 121–45; M. E. Yapp, *Strategies of British India: Britain, Iran, and Afghanistan, 1798–1850* (Oxford: Clarendon Press, 1980), 23–95. The discussion of early modern European views of Iran draws on Rudi Matthee, "The Imaginary Realm: Europe's Enlightenment Image of Early Modern Iran," *Comparative Studies of South Asia, Africa, and the Middle East* 30, no. 3 (2010): 449–62, and Rudi Matthee, "The Safavids Under Western Eyes: Seventeenth-Century European Travelers to Iran," *Journal of Early Modern History* 13 (2009): 137–71.

18. Jowett to Pratt, July 15, 1817, and Christopher Burckhardt to Cleardo Naudi, May 10, 1818, CMSC; Henry A. S. Dearborn, *Memoir on the Commerce and Navigation of the Black Sea, and the Trade and Maritime Geography of Turkey and Egypt*, 2 vols. (Boston, 1819), 2:346–47; Robert Adam, *The Religious World Dis-*

*played*, 3 vols. (Philadelphia, 1818), 2:312–13. The passages from Jonathan Edwards appear in Gerald R. McDermott, "The Deist Connection: Jonathan Edwards and Islam," in *Jonathan Edwards's Writings: Text, Context, Interpretation*, ed. Stephen J. Stein (Bloomington: Indiana University Press, 1996), 39–51; see also White, *Sermons Preached Before the University of Oxford, in the Year 1784*, and William Beveridge, *Private Thoughts upon Religion* (London, 1709), 16–17, 25–28. For this negative stereotype in travel books and geography texts, see Morier, *Journey Through Persia*, 168; see also *Travels of Ali Bey*, 358–59; John Hubbard, *The Rudiments of Geography*, 4th ed. (Walpole, N.H., 1808), 167; Susanna Rowson, *An Abridgment of Universal Geography* (Boston, n.d.), 103–4, 141. Among Enlightenment intellectuals, the French were particularly critical of Islam on the score of fostering ignorance. Condorcet, Volney, and Montesquieu emphasized that theme, but both Bayle and Voltaire believed that Islam itself was moving toward greater toleration. See Curtis, *Orientalism and Islam*, 35–36, 57, 60, 87–88; Rebecca Joubin, "Islam and Arabs Through the Eyes of the *Encyclopédie*: The 'Other' as a Case of French Cultural Self-Criticism," *International Journal of Middle East Studies* 32, no. 2 (2000): 197–217. Curiously, this negative assessment could coexist with the impression among both evangelicals and enlightened thinkers that medieval Islamic cultures, especially those in Arabia and Spain, had been notably learned. For the medieval origins of the view that Islam was opposed to intellectual inquiry and the reinforcement that early modern humanists provided for that view, see Bisaha, *Creating East and West*, 169–70, 178–84.

19. John Shore Teignmouth, *Memoirs of the Life, Writings, and Correspondence of Sir William Jones* (1804; Philadelphia, 1805), 65–67, 77–80, 85–86; Fisk, UTS I, April 12, 1820. For background on Jones and Shore, see their biographies in the online *Oxford Dictionary of National Biography* by Michael J. Franklin and Ainslie T. Embree, respectively; George D. Bearce, *British Attitudes Toward India, 1784–1858* (London: Oxford University Press, 1961), 20–26; Thomas R. Metcalf, *Ideologies of the Raj* (Cambridge, U.K.: Cambridge University Press, 1995), 12–15; Michael J. Franklin, *Orientalist Jones: Sir William Jones, Poet, Lawyer, and Linguist, 1746–1794* (New York: Oxford University Press, 2011). The emphasis on the rationality of Islam among some early modern Orientalists such as Sale inspired Jones's views, as did Ockley's praise for the first Muslim leaders as men of learning. His most important influence might have been Boulainvilliers, who contended that Arabians "have studied in every age, the most noble and exalted sciences," and that Muhammad himself aimed at "the reconcilement of the objects of religion with reason." (*Life of Mahomet*, 2–3, 25–26, 163.) For the controversy over Jones's legacy, see Said, *Orientalism*, 75–77; Kopf, *British Orientalism and the Bengal Renaissance*, 34–39; Varisco, *Reading Orientalism*, 127–30. Both Thomas Thornton and Giambattista Toderini, *De la littérature des Turcs* (1789), joined Jones in arguing against the view that Islam discouraged learning; see Gunny, *Perceptions of Islam in European Writings*, 186, 195.

20. Teignmouth, *Memoirs of Jones*, 82; William Jones, *The Letters of Sir William Jones*, ed. Garland Cannon, 2 vols. (Oxford Clarendon Press, 1970), 2:758, 766, cited in

290 NOTES TO PAGES 113–115

Garland Cannon, "Oriental Jones: Scholarship, Literature, Multiculturalism, and Humankind," in *Objects of Enquiry: The Life, Contributions, and Influences of Sir William Jones, 1746–1794*, ed. Garland Cannon and Kevin R. Brine (New York: New York University Press, 1995), 43; Wilberforce, *Journals and Letters*, 550; Carus, *Memoir of Simeon*, 35; Fisk and Parsons, "List of Books for a Missionary Library at Smyrna," marked received in Boston, July 4, 1820, ABCFM, reel 513. Jones was the dean of those Orientalists in British India who strove to minimize imperial interference in Indian culture and religion. Not only did they regard such intrusions as likely to provoke native protests, but many also, like Jones, harbored a deep admiration for Indian culture. Jones believed that in any case it would be difficult, if not impossible, to convert Hindus and Muslims. He pointed in particular to Muslims' "veneration for MOHAMMED and ALI, who were both extraordinary men, and the second, a man of unexceptionable morals." (*The Works of Sir William Jones*, 13 vols. [London, 1807], 3:395–96.) Most British evangelicals took the opposite view that wrongheaded Hindu and Muslim religious values lay at the root of India's disorder and that only Christianity could reform indigenous society. Martyn most likely agreed, but that did not prevent him from admiring some aspects of Islamic culture, much like William Carey, the first Baptist missionary to India, who combined Christian proselytizing with efforts to revitalize Hindu culture and preserve Indian languages. See Strong, *Anglicanism and the British Empire*, 118–97; Kopf, *British Orientalism and the Bengal Renaissance*, 77–80.

21. Sargent, *Memoir*, 434–35. For Martyn's expectation that learned Muslims would "ensure that Christianity percolated downward to their people," see Porter, "Evangelicalism, Islam, and Millennial Expectation in the Nineteenth Century," 65–66.

22. Pratt to Jowett, May 30 and Oct. 29, 1816, and Jowett journal, April 30 to July 7, 1818, CMSC; Carus, *Memoir of Simeon*, 365–66, 378–79, 408, 431, 435–36.

23. Jowett journal, Sept. 29, 1816, and May 30, 1818, Jowett to Pratt, Aug. 9 and Dec. 21, 1816, and May 26, 1817, CMSC; see also *MR*, March 1817, 90–94, Sept. 1817, 397, 401. Proselytizing by pointing up the affinities between Christianity and Islam was a popular tactic among evangelicals. Pratt asked Jowett to assist Sir Sydney Smith, who had sent an agent to Africa "with medals, on which are engraved some corresponding passages of the Bible and the Koran." (Pratt to Jowett, Oct. 29, 1816, CMSC.)

24. Jowett to Admiral Charles Penrose, July 15 and 25, 1818, and Jowett to Josiah Pratt, April 20, 1818, CMSC. Only months before Fisk and Parsons disembarked at Smyrna, a Greek servant who had converted from Christianity to Islam, perhaps under pressure from his master, recanted and paid the ultimate penalty of losing his head. But such executions for apostasy were rare. Charles Williamson, the British chaplain at Smyrna, told a British traveler that there had been three executions for apostasy from Islam there during the previous twenty years. (William Rae Wilson, *Travels in Egypt and the Holy Land* [London, 1823], 497–99.) The death penalty remained in force until 1844.

25. Robert Richardson, *Travels Along the Mediterranean, and Parts Adjacent; in Company with the Earl of Belmore, During the Years 1816-17-18*, 2 vols. (London, 1822), 1:87, 110–11, 2:464–65, 481–85; Richardson to Jowett, Aug. 18, 1818, and Martha Jowett to her sister, Oct. 29, 1816, both in CMSC. According to Richardson, "an absurd religion [Islam], or rather an absurd interpretation of that religion has produced a defective system of education," accounting for the ignorance of Muslim countries; see also Robert Walpole, *Memoirs Relating to European and Asiatic Turkey* (London, 1817), 24–25; William Jowett, *Christian Researches in the Mediterranean*, 2nd ed. (London, 1822), 119–20.

26. Jowett journal, Oct. 10 and 11, 1816, and Jowett to Pratt, Dec. 21, 1816, CMSC; see also *MR*, Aug. 1818, 339–40. The Greek Orthodox differed from Roman Catholics in that they practiced full-immersion baptism, rejected the belief in purgatory, and refused to recognize papal supremacy. They used pictures in their public and private worship but not statues. For missionary reports on "greagrea" or "gregree," see *MR*, March 1815, 164–66.

27. Jowett to his mother, Dec. 11, 1815, and Jowett journal, Sept. 2, 1816, CMSC.

28. Jowett, *Christian Researches in the Mediterranean*, 107–8.

29. Jowett journal, Sept. 5, 1817, Richardson to Jowett, Aug. 18, 1818, and Jowett to Pratt, in a letter titled "Substance of Dr. Richardson's Communications upon Egypt and Syria, August 18, 1818," CMSC. Richardson also considered "all Syria in effect as governed by Jews who get into power," while Jowett believed that "multitudes" of professing Christians in Spain were Jews, "known only to their own community by particular signs."

30. Jowett, *Christian Researches in the Mediterranean*, 249–50.

31. Sargent, *Memoir*, 347; Fisk, UTS I, Jan. 12, 14, 23, 30, 1820; Eli Smith to Benjamin Smith, March 26, 1827, Eli Smith Papers, Yale Divinity School Library. Eli Smith took copious notes on Martyn's memoir; see box 2, folder 11 of his papers at Yale. This intense concentration on a single text David Hall identifies as "traditional literacy," a reading pattern that typified the early modern period but lingered into the nineteenth century, especially among evangelicals. See David Hall, "The Uses of Literacy in New England, 1600–1850," in *Printing and Society in Early America*, ed. William L. Joyce et al. (Worcester, Mass.: American Antiquarian Society, 1983), 1–47.

32. Review of Sargent's memoir in the *Christian Observer*, May 1819; Smith, *Henry Martyn*, 329–31; John William Kaye, *Lives of Indian Officers*, 3 vols. (London, 1869), 2:16.

33. I have adapted the phrase "othering and brothering" from Jane Samson, who uses it to characterize "the constant tension between alterity and universalism" in missionary writing. She defines Christian universalism as the belief in equality before God. See Jane Samson, "Are You What You Believe? Some Thoughts on *Ornamentalism* and Religion," *Journal of Colonialism and Colonial History* 3, no. 1 (2002); see also Metcalf's *Ideologies of the Raj*, which emphasizes the interplay between images of differentness and images of similarity in efforts by the British to justify their imperialism in India.

292 NOTES TO PAGES 123–125

## 5. "OUR GREAT WEAPON"

1. Morton, *Memoir of Parsons*, 244, 248; Fisk's postscript in Parsons's letter to Daniel and Lucretia Morton, Jan. 18, 1820, Parsons Letters; Fisk and Parsons to Worcester, Feb. 8, 1820, and Fisk to Evarts, May 30, 1821, both in ABCFM, reel 513; Fisk, UTS I, Jan. 26, 1820; Jowett journal, Oct. 8, 1817, and "Fragments from My Smyrna Journal," April 30 to July 7, 1818, CMSC. For other early nineteenth-century accounts of Smyrna, see Barrell, *Letters from Asia*, 11, 26, 39–40; Woodruff, *Journal of a Tour to Malta*, 148–69; Richard Chandler, *Travels in Asia Minor and Greece*, 2 vols. (Oxford, 1825), 1:69–70, 349–50; Charles Thompson, *Travels Through Turkey in Asia, the Holy Land, Arabia, Egypt, and Other Parts of the World* (Carlisle, Pa., 1813), 20–21; Emerson, *Letters from the Aegean*, 38–64, 123–24; James Emerson, *A Picture of Greece in 1825*, 2 vols. (New York, 1826), 2:200–202. The best descriptions in the secondary literature include Richard Clogg, *I Kath'imas Anatoli: Studies in Ottoman Greek History* (Istanbul: Isis Press, 2004), 63–107; Elena Frangakis-Syrett, *The Commerce of Smyrna in the Eighteenth Century (1700–1820)* (Athens: Centre for Asia Minor Studies, 1992), esp. 1–74; Daniel Goffman, "Izmir: From Village to Colonial Port City," in *The Ottoman City Between East and West: Aleppo, Izmir, and Istanbul*, ed. Edhem Eldem, Daniel Goffman, and Bruce Masters (Cambridge, U.K.: Cambridge University Press, 1999), 85, 120–25, 129–30, 133; Philip Mansel, *Levant: Splendor and Catastrophe on the Mediterranean* (New Haven, Conn.: Yale University Press, 2011), 33–55. For overviews of the Ottoman Empire in the early nineteenth century, see Carter Vaughn Findley, *Turkey, Islam, Nationalism, and Modernity* (New Haven, Conn.: Yale University Press, 2010), 23–75, and Caroline Finkel, *Osman's Dream: The History of the Ottoman Empire* (New York: Basic Books, 2005), 413–46.
2. *Albany Gazette*, June 15, 1820; Fisk, UTS I, Jan. 17 and 26, 1820; *New-York Observer*, Aug. 16, 1823. Fisk might have sent similar criticisms of the Turks to Jedidiah Morse or his sons, but they did not appear in print until two of the Morse brothers began their newspaper. See "Character of the Turks," *New-York Observer*, Feb. 14, 1824.
3. Fisk, UTS I, Jan. 28, 1820; Elnathan Gridley to Anderson, Jan. 31, 1827, ABCFM, reel 515; Frangakis-Syrett, *Commerce of Smyrna*, 76–77.
4. Fisk to Evarts, May 30, 1821, ABCFM, reel 513; Finnie, *Pioneers East*, 20–35; James R. Fichter, *"So Great a Proffit": How the East Indies Trade Transformed Anglo-American Capitalism* (Cambridge, Mass.: Harvard University Press, 2010), 226–31; Frangakis-Syrett, *Commerce of Smyrna*, 185–86; Carl Seaburg and Stanley Paterson, *Merchant Prince of Boston: Col. T. H. Perkins, 1764–1854* (Cambridge, Mass.: Harvard University Press, 1971), 264–66, 296–99, 313–14; A. L. Tibawi, *American Interests in Syria: A Study of Educational, Literary, and Religious Work* (Oxford: Clarendon Press, 1966), 2.
5. Fisk, UTS I, Jan. 24, 1820; Fisk's postscript in Parsons to Mrs. Lucy P. Porter, Dec. 4, 1820, Parsons's Letters, SCMC; see also Fisk to John W. Langdon, Jan. 25, 1822, ABCFM, reel 513; Mansel, *Levant*, 44. Even Smyrna's two-hundred-odd

Protestants found Fisk and Parsons less than congenial, because their own religious views tended toward liberal Christianity.

6. Fisk to Evarts, Oct. 12, 1822 (entry for Aug. 23, 1822), and Fisk and Parsons to Worcester, Sept. 12, 1820, both in ABCFM, reel 513.

7. Williamson to Worcester, Feb. n.d., 1820, ABC 10, vol. 4 (1821–24); Jowett to his mother, May 31, 1817, and Jowett to Pratt, Aug. 8, 1818, CMSC; *MR*, April 1817, 170–73, and Aug. 1817, 351–52; Stock, *History of the Church Missionary Society*, 1:221–22; Galt, *Voyages and Travels*, 120–21. The British and Foreign Bible Society, founded in 1804, typified evangelical groups throughout Europe devoted to translating and circulating the Bible throughout the world. The BFBS viewed the difference between Protestant and Catholic Bibles as negligible, amounting to the fourteen books of the Apocrypha, which Roman Catholics and most Eastern Christians regarded as canonical parts of the Old Testament. Far more important from the evangelical perspective was the New Testament, which did not vary significantly from Catholic to Protestant editions. Jowett quickly became disillusioned with Drummond, in part as a result of learning about his radical religious views and also because he behaved "more like a man of fortune than like a man of business." See Pratt to Jowett, Aug. 2, 1817, and Jowett to Pratt, Aug. 29, 1818, CMSC. Drummond's goal of evangelizing Catholic Europe led to his formation of the Continental Society in 1819; for his career, see David Bebbington, *Evangelicalism in Modern Britain* (London: Routledge, 1989), 77–79, 82–83, 95, and Wolffe, *Protestant Crusade in Great Britain*, 30–32.

8. John Lewis Burckhardt, *Travels in Syria and the Holy Land* (London, 1822), 584–85; Katharine Sim, *Desert Traveller: The Life of Jean Louis Burckhardt* (London: Phoenix Press, 2000), 211–12, 288–90. For Christopher Burckhardt, see *MR*, Feb. 1818, 73, 77–80, Sept. 1820, 369–71, and a translation of his letters to Cleardo Naudi, May 10, 1818, sent by Jowett to Pratt, CMSC.

9. *MR*, Sept. 1818, 383–87, Aug. 1819, 365–69, Sept. 1819, 402–7, April 1820, 166–69, May 1820, 203–8, June 1820, 261–62, Sept. 1820, 384–98, May 1821, 208–9. See also George Browne, *The History of the British and Foreign Bible Society*, 2 vols. (London, 1859), 2:22–40, and Geoffrey Roper, "Arabic Printing in Malta, 1825–1845: Its History and Significance" (Ph.D. diss., School of Oriental Studies, University of Durham, 1988), 75–94.

10. *MR*, July 1818, 289, 292, Aug. 1818, 340, and Aug. 1819, 364. Jowett and Williamson's views on tracts jibed exactly with those of Jedidiah Morse, who organized the New England Tract Society in 1814. (Nord, *Faith in Reading*, 52–56, 119–20.)

11. "Extract of a Letter from the Rev. William Jowett to the Rev. James Connor, November 30, 1818," *Proceedings of the Church Missionary Society for Africa and the East* (1819): 261–62. The missionaries made no mention of any illustrations appearing in their tracts, although the practice of their incorporating engraved images, both to attract attention and to persuade, had become widespread among both British and American evangelical publications by the mid-1820s. (David Morgan, *Protestants and Pictures: Religion, Visual Culture, and the Age of American Mass Production* [New York: Oxford University Press, 1999], 50–52.)

12. Fisk, UTS I, Feb. 21 and 23, March 22, 23, and 31, April 7, May 25 and 28, 1820.

13. The newly founded Mediterranean Bible societies, the British and Foreign Bible Society, and the Massachusetts Bible Society provided Fisk and Parsons with Old and New Testaments and Psalters (selections from the book of Psalms). The Anglican Williamson believed that Eastern Christian bishops and patriarchs would not regard Congregationalists such as Fisk and Parsons as "regular clergymen." Nor was he inclined to do so: he refused to allow them to preach in his chapel at Smyrna. See Fisk and Parsons to Worcester, Feb. 8, 1820, ABCFM, reel 513; Williamson to Worcester, Feb. n.d., 1820, ABC 10, vol. 4, ABCFM HU; Worcester to Fisk and Parsons, June 16, 1820, ABC 1.01, vol. 5, ABCFM HU.

14. Fisk journal, Feb. 17 to May 18, 1821, entry for April 27, ABCFM, reel 513; Kyle Roberts, "Locating Popular Religion in the Evangelical Tract: The Roots and Routes of *The Dairyman's Daughter*," *Early American Studies* 4, no. 1 (2006): 233–70. Fisk and Parsons distributed as many tracts in English, mainly to British and American sailors at Smyrna, as they did to peoples native to the Mediterranean. In their first two years in the Mediterranean, they reported distributing ten thousand pages of tracts in English and at least another ten thousand pages in other languages. (Fisk and Parsons to Evarts, Dec. 31, 1821, ABCFM, reel 513.)

15. Fisk and Parsons journal, Aug. 1 to Sept. 1820, entries for Aug. 3, 4, and 25, Sept. 12, Fisk and Parsons journal on Scio, entries for Sept. 20 and Oct. 2, 1820, Fisk journal, Dec. 6, 1820, to Feb. 14, 1821, entries for Dec. 29, Jan. 24, and Feb. 6, Parsons to Worcester, Jan. 25 and Feb. 7, 1821, all in ABCFM, reel 513; William Goodell to Jowett, May 8, 1827, CMSC; *MR*, Sept. 1818, 387, and May 1821, 204.

16. Fisk journal, Dec. 6, 1820, to Feb. 14, 1821, entry for Dec. 27; Fisk to E. F. Ronneberg, June 17, 1822, British and Foreign Bible Society Archives, Cambridge University; "Extracts from Wolff's Journal," *JE* 7 (1822): 514; William St. Clair, *That Greece Might Still Be Free: The Philhellenes in the War of Independence* (London: Oxford University Press, 1972), 205; Roper, "Arabic Printing in Malta," 95, 107–8; Goffman, "Izmir," 128. A Dominican priest at Isfahan informed James Morier that some books had been stolen from the mission library there and "used as waste paper by the Persians." See Morier, *Second Journey Through Persia*, 148.

17. Richardson, *Travels Along the Mediterranean*, 1:468–69; William Jowett, *Christian Researches in Syria and the Holy Land in 1823 and 1824*, 2nd ed. (London, 1826), 120–22; James Silk Buckingham, *Travels in Palestine* (London, 1821), 459.

18. Nord, *Faith in Reading*, esp. 22–23, 28, 30, 133, 138; Brown, *Word in the World*, 1, 155; Boylan, *Sunday School*, 6–77; Gilmore, *Reading Becomes a Necessity of Life*, 5, 121; Zboray, *Fictive People*, 83, 89–92; Nord, "Benevolent Books"; John, "Expanding the Realm of Communications"; Schantz, "Religious Tracts, Evangelical Reform, and the Market Revolution in Antebellum America."

19. Fisk journal, Dec. 6, 1820, to Feb. 14, 1821, entry for Jan. 24, 1821, ABCFM, reel 513; Parsons to Mrs. Lucy Porter, Dec. 4, 1820, Parsons Letters. The Americans took careful stock of Greek schools—the number and gender of their pupils, the character of their teachers, the reading abilities of students, and the number of

books on hand. Those assessments revealed that literacy rates were low, female students scarce, teachers poorly trained, and reading material of any sort in short supply.

20. For similar views among British missionaries, see Copland, "Christianity as an Arm of Empire," 1026.

21. David Thurston, *A Sermon, Delivered in Saco, June 26, 1816, Before the Maine Missionary Society* (Hallowell, Maine, 1816), 9; Proudfit, *An Address Delivered at the Formation of a Society of Foreign Missions, in the City of New York*, 20. Parsons took the same view of his post-seminary work itinerating on the northern frontier: his letters referred to "our Vermont heathen." See Parsons to Fisk, May 26, 1818, ABCFM, reel 502. Susan Thorne finds a similar theme in British missionary literature during its first half century. "It seems to have been almost impossible," she writes, "for evangelicals to describe, and arguably even to think about, the laboring poor . . . without comparing them in some way to the empire's heathen races." (Thorne, *Congregational Missions and the Making of an Imperial Culture in Nineteenth-Century England*, 17, 82–83; see also Twells, *Civilizing Mission and the English Middle Class*, 12–16, 33–34, 40.)

22. *MR*, Feb. 1819, 77, and May 1820, 206; Parsons to Worcester, Jan. 25, 1821, and Fisk journal, July 24, 1823, ABCFM, reel 513.

23. *MR*, Sept. 1818, 389, and Feb. 1819, 80; Christopher Burckhardt to Dr. Cleardo Naudi, May 21, 1818, extract cited in Jowett to Pratt, Aug. 8, 1818, CMSC; see also Carsten Niebuhr, *Travels Through Arabia and Other Countries in the East*, trans. Robert Heron, 2 vols. (Edinburgh, 1792), 2: 92; Walpole, *Memoirs*, 25; Teignmouth, *Memoirs of Jones*, 79–80. Secondary treatments of print and Islamic cultures in the early nineteenth century include Jonathan Bloom and Sheila Blair, *Islam: A Thousand Years of Faith and Power* (New Haven, Conn.: Yale University Press, 2002), 192; Ian Proudfoot, "Mass Producing Houri's Moles, or Aesthetics and Choice of Technology in Early Muslim Book Printing," in *Islam: Essays on Scripture, Thought, and Society: A Festschrift in Honour of Anthony H. Johns*, ed. Peter J. Riddell and Tony Street (Leiden: Brill, 1997), 161–84; Wheatcroft, *Infidels*, 274–85; Nile Green, "Journeymen, Middlemen: Travel, Transculture, and Technology in the Origins of Muslim Printing," *International Journal of Middle East Studies* 41, no. 2 (2009): 203–43.

24. Burckhardt, *Travels in Syria and the Holy Land*, 585–86; Smith, *Henry Martyn*, 244. Similarly, Robert Walpole cited with approval the opinion of an Anglican minister that Islam would collapse among the Ottoman Turks if "the Koran was as common to them as the Bible to us, and that they might have free recourse to search and examine the flaws and follies of it." (Walpole, *Memoirs*, 26.)

25. Jowett, *Christian Researches in Syria and the Holy Land*, 320; Bird missionary journal, March 6, 1825, Bird Papers. The sources that have shaped my thinking on this subject include Jonathan Phillips, *Holy Warriors: A Modern History of the Crusades* (New York: Random House, 2009), 30–33, and Reza Aslan, *No god but God: The Origin, Evolution, and Future of Islam* (2005; New York: Delacorte Press, 2011), 80–86.

26. Fisk and Parsons to Evarts, March 4, 1820, and Fisk and Parsons to Worcester, Sept. 12, 1820, both in ABCFM, reel 513; Parsons to Mrs. Lucy Porter, Dec. 4, 1820, Parsons Letters. For an example of evangelical expectations, see the essay on Asia Minor in the *Concord Observer*, April 3 and 10, 1820; on the popularity of Martyn's memoir among American readers, see Bird to Pliny Fisk, Nov. 13, 1822, Bird Papers.

27. Parsons's journal covering his travels to and from Jerusalem appeared in installments from December 5, 1820, through December 4, 1821, all in ABCFM, reel 513. One *Missionary Herald* reader wrote to the board requesting that the Palestine missionaries make "little sketches or views of interesting places or ruins, particularly those mentioned in Scripture or any little pictures illustrating the present state of Palestine or its inhabitants." He believed that such visuals would be ideal for children's books to give them "some idea of the moral condition of the dark places of the earth." (Harlan Page to Evarts, May 27, 1823, ABC 10, vol. 4, ABCFM HU.)

28. Fisk, UTS I, Feb. 22 and 23, March 2, April 5 and 28, 1821; Fisk journal, Dec. 6, 1820, to Feb. 14, 1821, entries for Jan. 9, Feb. 10 and 20, and Fisk journal, Feb. 17, 1821, to May 18, 1821, entries for Feb. 22, March 2, April 5 and 28, both in ABCFM, reel 513; Fisk, MJ I, Oct. 15, 1821. Fisk also kept up visits to Greek schools. What interested him most was the dearth of female pupils: he looked in on every Greek school in Smyrna, a total of thirty with more than a thousand students, only sixty-six of whom were girls. He found none at Turkish and Armenian schools. So it surprised him to encounter two Greek schoolmistresses, one of whom, Despinoula, explained to Fisk that parents feared that if their daughters "learn to read and write they will be writing letters to their sweethearts." He promised to pay her a small sum every month if she could recruit "four or five poor girls" as new pupils, or even poor boys "in case the girls could not be obtained." (Fisk, UTS I, Jan. 23 and 26, Feb. 9 and 14, March 12 and 23, 1821.)

29. Fisk, UTS I, April 13, 1821; Fisk journal, Feb. 17, 1821, to May 18, 1821, entry for April 13, ABCFM, reel 513; Fisk, MJ I, May 28 and June 1, 1821; Finkel, *Osman's Dream*, 430–31. For self-censorship on the part of British missionaries, see Natasha Erlank, "'Civilizing the African': The Scottish Mission to the Xhosa, 1821–1864," in Stanley, *Christian Missions and the Enlightenment*, 141–68.

30. Fisk, UTS I, April 12 and 30, May 5 and 8, 1821; Parsons to Worcester, May n.d., 1821, Fisk to Parsons, April 14, May 11 and 23, 1821, all in ABCFM, reel 502; Fisk journal, Feb. 17, 1821, to May 18, 1821, entries for April 12, 13, 26, 27, May 18, Fisk journal, May 5, June 2–4, 16–20, July 2, 1821, Parsons journal, May 20, June 18 and 20, 1821, and Fisk to Evarts, July 6, 1821, all in ABCFM, reel 513; Fisk, MJ I, June 2, 4, 8, 16–18, 21, 27, 30, July 4, 15, 16, 19, 20, 24, 30, 31, and Aug. 4, 1821. For overviews of the Greek struggle, see Brewer, *Greek War of Independence*; Douglas Dakin, *The Greek Struggle for Independence, 1821–1833* (Berkeley: University of California Press, 1973); Finkel, *Osman's Dream*, 428–32; Mansel, *Levant*, 46–51; Mark Mazower, *Salonica, City of Ghosts: Christians, Muslims, and Jews, 1430–1950* (London: HarperCollins, 2004), 125–32; John Julius Norwich, *The*

*Middle Sea: A History of the Mediterranean* (London: Chatto and Windus, 2006), 462–92; St. Clair, *That Greece Might Still Be Free*, 1–12; Wheatcroft, *Infidels*, 222–40; Angelo Repousis, *Greek-American Relations from Monroe to Truman* (Kent, Ohio: Kent State University Press, 2013), 10–56.

31. Parsons cited Werry's letter in his correspondence with Worcester, July 17, 1821, ABCFM, reel 513; for other evidence of Werry's sympathies, see Clogg, *I Kath'imas Anatoli*, 224, 231, 233. Because the fighting disrupted trade in the Levant, most merchants and consuls were pro-Turkish. (Crawley, *Question of Greek Independence*, 29n26.) For the missionaries' views, see Parsons to Fisk, June 30, 1821, ABCFM, reel 502; Fisk, MJ I, May 21, 1821, Fisk to Evarts, July 6, 1821, ABCFM, reel 513. For his fullest assessment of the Greek Revolution, see the entry at the end of Fisk's journal, Oct. 3, 1821, ABCFM, reel 513. It includes an extract of a letter from an English gentleman dated June 30, 1821, followed by Fisk's comments.

32. Fisk journal, June 16, 1821, ABCFM, reel 513.

## 6. TURNING TURK

1. Fisk, MJ I, Aug. 4, 6, 8, 23, 26, 31, Sept. 7, 9, 15, 16, 19, 25, 28, 30, Oct. 1, 3, 5, 7, 9, 1821; Fisk to Parsons, May 11, 1821, entries for May 21 and June 3, ABCFM, reel 502. For Hamilton's career, see William R. O'Byrne, *A Naval Biographical Dictionary . . .* (London, 1849), 449; on the seige of Istanbul, see Finkel, *Osman's Dream*, 413–14.

2. Fisk, MJ I, Aug. 4, Sept. 3, 4, 6–9, 11, 14, 15, 1821. For Bradish's career, see Stephen Larrabee, *Hellas Observed: The American Experience of Greece, 1775–1865* (New York: New York University Press, 1957), 49–51; W. L. Wright, "American Relations with Turkey to 1831" (Ph.D. diss., Princeton University, 1928), 81; Field, *From Gibraltar to the Middle East*, 51–52. Writing from Constantinople to John Quincy Adams about the Ottomans, Bradish described them as "a very Singular People," at once "extremely uncivilized" but also "capable of the most elevated and refined sentiments." (Dec. 20, 1820, Luther Bradish Papers, 1783–1863, New-York Historical Society.)

3. Fisk's variant spelling of English's Muslim name include "Mehemmet Vebbi" and "Mehemmet Vehbit." (Fisk, MJ I, Feb. 9 and Mar. 6, 1822.) Fisk had earlier spoken about English with Francis Werry, who reported his stopping in Smyrna en route to Egypt, where "he is employed in trifling business but not esteemed." (Fisk, UTS I, Jan. 21, 1820.) William Bentley might have played a part in securing English's military commission, given his friendship with his mother and his close connections with Benjamin Crowninshield, who only a month after becoming the secretary of the navy made English a first lieutenant in the marines. Bentley's correspondence includes letters from other young men seeking naval appointments. (Henry E. Dix to Bentley, Sept. 29 and Nov. 7, 1817, Bentley Papers; notice of English's commission appears in the *New-York Daily Advertiser*, May 3, 1817.) After leaving the marines, English might have first offered his services to the Ottoman sultan at Constantinople; the earliest American reports of

his turning Turk appeared in the *Christian Messenger* (Middlebury, Vt.), Feb. 10, 1819, the *Newburyport Herald*, Feb. 19, 1819, the *Connecticut Gazette* (New London), Feb. 17, 1819, the *Baltimore Patriot and Mercantile Advertiser*, Feb. 5, 1819, the *Alexandria Herald* (Va.), Feb. 5, 1819, the *Palladium of Liberty* (Warrenton, Va.), Feb. 19, 1819, the *Pendleton Messenger* (Pendleton, S.C.), Feb. 24, 1819, the *Winyaw Intelligencer* (Georgetown, S.C.), Feb. 24, 1819, the *Camden Gazette* (Camden, S.C.), Feb. 25, 1819, and the *Weekly Recorder* (Chillicothe, Ohio), Feb. 19, 1819. For the denial of his conversion, see the *Franklin Monitor and Charlestown General Advertiser* (Charlestown, Mass.), Feb. 20, 1819; for William Bentley's comment, see his *Diary*, 4:632–33. Bentley also took note of English's conversion to Islam in the Salem newspaper but not in his regular column: "The lesson we should learn, may be, that we should give less temptation to these conversions from the fame or interest which may accompany them. Some men will force themselves into notice." (*Essex Register*, Feb. 6, 1819.) Secondary accounts of English's career in Egypt include Finnie, *Pioneers East*, 53–55, 143–49; Field, *From Gibraltar to the Middle East*, 133–34; and Oren, *Power, Faith, and Fantasy*, 101–5, 111–13.

4. Waddington and Hanbury, *Journal of a Visit to Some Parts of Ethiopia*, 114–18. Egypt under Mehmet Ali became a magnet for Europeans with military or technical skills looking for work and new lives. The pasha recruited officers, particularly French and Italians, to drill his army, and a condition of their command was embracing Islam. English exceeded that obligation by writing his defense of Islam. See Maya Jasanoff, *Edge of Empire: Lives, Culture, and Conquest in the East, 1750–1830* (New York: Vintage, 2006), 242–43; John Dunn, "Napoleonic Veterans and the Modernization of the Egyptian Army, 1817–1840," *Consortium on Revolutionary Europe, Proceedings, 1992* (1993): 468–75; Samuel Gridley Howe, *An Historical Sketch of the Greek Revolution* (New York, 1828), 165–66.

5. Porl's surname also appears as Poll or Paul; see *Essex Register*, Sept. 25, 1819; *New York Commercial Advertiser*, Sept. 20, 1819; Fisk, UTS I, Jan. 21, April 12, May 18, 1820, Fisk, MJ I, Oct. 3, 1821; Morton, *Memoir of Parsons*, 271–72. In the early nineteenth-century Ottoman Empire, there were still a number of young Christian women who, sold as slaves, became wives or concubines of Muslims; there were also men who, as children, had been forced into military service as janissaries. In the summer of 1821, Fisk noted meeting such a man, Swiss by birth, who "was on board a vessel when quite young which was taken by the Turks, and he then became a Turk." (Fisk, MJ I, June 4, 1821.)

6. *Christian Spectator*, Oct. 1, 1819. The evangelical sensitivity to renegades also registered in their short pieces beamed at a popular audience describing Muslim conversions to Christianity. The classic of this genre is John Edwards, *The Conversion of a Mahometan to the Christian Religion*, which was widely reprinted in eighteenth-century Britain before first appearing in the United States in the 1780s; presses reissued it until 1817. A similar story for juveniles is *An Entertaining History of Two Pious Children Who Were Stolen from Their Christian Parents by a Jew and Sold to the Turks as Slaves* (Newmarket, Va., 1816).

7. For the phrase "turning Turk," see Chew, *The Crescent and the Rose*, 144–45, 373–78; Matar, *Islam in Britain*, 21–49; Warner G. Rice, " 'To Turn Turk,' " *Modern Language Notes* 46 (March 1931): 153–54. The most careful study of the early modern Mediterranean slave trade is Robert C. Davis, *Christian Slaves, Muslim Masters, 1500–1800* (New York: Palgrave Macmillan, 2003); see also his "Counting European Slaves on the Barbary Coast," *Past and Present* 172, no. 1 (2001): 87–124. For a splendid analysis of early modern England's encounters with Islam in North Africa, see Colley, *Captives*, 43–134; see also Fernand Braudel, *The Mediterranean and the Mediterranean World in the Age of Philip II*, 2 vols. (New York: Harper & Row, 1972), 1:871, 886–87; Nabil Matar, " 'Turning Turk': Conversion to Islam in English Renaissance Thought," *Durham University Journal* 86 (1994): 33–42; Nabil Matar, *Turks, Moors, and Englishmen in the Age of Discovery* (New York: Columbia University Press, 2000); Daniel Goffman, *The Ottoman Empire and Early Modern Europe* (Cambridge, U.K.: Cambridge University Press, 2002); Daniel Goffman, *Britons in the Ottoman Empire, 1642–1660* (Seattle: University of Washington Press, 1998); Stuart B. Schwartz, *All Can Be Saved: Religious Tolerance and Salvation in the Iberian Atlantic World* (New Haven, Conn.: Yale University Press, 2008), 71–74. Literary studies offer an imaginative treatment of renegades and their cultural significance; see esp. Daniel Vitkus, *Turning Turk: English Theater and the Multicultural Mediterranean, 1570–1630* (New York: Palgrave Macmillan, 2003); Nabil Matar, "The Renegade in English Seventeenth-Century Imagination," *Studies in English Literature* 33 (1993): 489–505; Jonathan Burton, *Traffic and Turning: Islam and English Drama, 1579–1624* (Newark: University of Delaware Press, 2005); Emily M. N. Kugler, *Sway of the Ottoman Identity in the Long Eighteenth Century* (Leiden: Brill, 2012), 17–33.

8. Between 1680 and 1780, Christian slave populations in North Africa stood at a fifth of their size in the century before; see Davis, "Counting European Slaves on the Barbary Coast," 93, 106–7; Godfrey Fisher, *Barbary Legend: War, Trade, and Piracy in North Africa, 1415–1830* (Oxford: Clarendon Press, 1957), 303; John Wolf, *The Barbary Coast: Algiers Under the Turks, 1500 to 1830* (New York: W. W. Norton, 1969), 330–38; Gary E. Wilson, "American Hostages in Moslem Nations, 1784–1796: The Public Response," *Journal of the Early Republic* 2, no. 2 (1982): 123–41.

9. Adams, *Narrative*, 32–33, 74, 77–78, 133; Cowdery, *American Captives in Tripoli*, 12, 26, 28; Ray, *Horrors of Slavery*, 59, 65–67, 94, 102, 106–7; *American Advocate and Kennebec Advertiser* (Hallowell, Maine), Feb. 13, 1819; see also "Anecdotes of the Late Sultan Valide," extracted in *The Weekly Visitor and Ladies' Museum* (New York), Sept. 5, 1818. Judah Paddock's account is singular in implying that a Westerner could regard Islam as a faith superior to Christianity. Other authors—even in those Saharan narratives offering more positive and nuanced treatments of Islam—insisted that captives turned Turk only because of compulsion or calculation. Opinions varied more widely on whether Muslims pressed Christian captives to embrace Islam. Robert Adams believed that self-interest prompted most masters to discourage such conversions, because they would be

obliged to free those slaves who took the turban. But Christians fending off threats or blandishments made for a better story. (Adams, *Narrative*, 131–32; Robbins, *Journal*, 115, 174–75, 183, 230–31.) Islamic law prohibits believers from enslaving co-religionists, prompting some Muslim masters to free their slaves who converted, but the law does not promise freedom to an alien slave who embraces Islam. See Chew, *The Crescent and the Rose*, 376–77.

10. Robbins, *Journal*, 115, 166, 210, 230–31; see also Adams, *Narrative*, 131.

11. Paddock, *Narrative*, 108, 334–37. Similarly, a printer in tiny Fredericktown, Maryland, produced a tellingly revamped version of the English renegade Joseph Pitts's century-old Algerine captivity narrative in 1815. In its original 1704 version, Pitts briefly recounted being sold into slavery as a teenager and then described at great length the ways and customs of the Algerians before ending with a briefer account of how his master bastinadoed him into "turning Turk." By contrast, what dominated the much-revised Fredericktown edition was Pitts's tale of forced conversion. (Pitts, *Narrative of the Captivity*, 1–15.)

12. For a typical report on Athanasius, see *Columbian Centiniel* (Boston), March 26, 1817; on stage productions, see *Boston Intelligencer and Evening Gazette*, Nov. 21, 1818, and Frederick Reynolds, *The Life and Times of Frederick Reynolds*, 2nd ed. (London, 1827), 2: 391. For "renegade" coming into vogue as a proverb and a synonym for a man switching parties, see, for example, *The Columbian* (New York), June 17, 1820.

13. Ray, *Horrors of Slavery*, 67. For fears of Muslims holding office, see Jonathan Elliot, ed., *The Debates in the Several State Conventions on the Adoption of the Federal Constitution . . .* , 5 vols., 2nd ed. (New York, 1888), 4: 191–200; Spellberg, *Jefferson's Qur'an*, 158–86.

14. After Sabat's defection, American evangelicals found a replacement in an East Indian Muslim convert known as "Abdool Mensee," whose doings received extensive coverage in the *Missionary Herald*.

15. Jowett, *Christian Researches in the Mediterranean*, 264–73; Jowett journal, June 5, 1818, included in letter to Josiah Pratt, Aug. 8, 1818, CMSC; *MR*, Dec. 1818, 516–18. He shared this story with Fisk and Parsons during their stop at Valletta in early 1820; see the letter from Parsons, Jan. 31, 1820, printed in *Concord Observer*, Sept. 4, 1820. This early nineteenth-century ritual described by Jowett includes none of the humiliating features described by Western Christians who claimed to have witnessed such ceremonies in the sixteenth and seventeenth centuries; see Chew, *The Crescent and the Rose*, 376–77.

16. Jowett, "Fragments from My Smyrna Journal," at the end of Jowett's journal, April 30–July 7, 1818, Jowett journal, June 5, 6, and 20, 1818, and Jowett to Pratt, Aug. 8, 1818, CMSC; Jowett, *Christian Researches in the Mediterranean*, 271. Jowett also suspected that Muslim authorities isolated and intimidated renegades. Shortly after leaving Smyrna, he dined with a British ship captain in the Greek archipelago who confided that four of his sailors had lately turned Turk and that "they were kept some days by the Turks, before it was made known where they were." Such secrecy was typical, according to Jowett, "so close is the watch kept by the

Mahomedans over Renegadoes, when they are once in their power." But he also knew that pressure from Islamic authorities did not always push or keep renegades in the Muslim fold. During a visit to Egypt in 1819, he encountered an Englishman in his late thirties who had turned up with his camels and his young Abyssinian wife at the gate of the British consulate in Cairo. Many years earlier, Nathaniel Pearce, then an unhappy sailor in the British navy, had deserted at a port on the Red Sea, briefly avowed Islam, and went unpunished by Muslim authorities after returning to Christianity. Pearce lived in Abyssinia (Ethiopia) for the next fourteen years; he became acquainted with the British consul in Egypt, Henry Salt, and remained in his employ thereafter. He also assisted Jowett in translating a portion of the New Testament into one of Ethiopia's languages. (Nathaniel Pearce, *The Life and Adventures of Nathaniel Pearce*, ed. J. J. Halls, 2 vols. [London, 1831], 1:37–39, 52–53.) The evidence is mixed on the role of Muslim intimidation in Western conversions. Jowett consistently emphasized it: according to him, John Werry had witnessed two boys turning Turk, one of whom "said, rather emphatically, I'll stay here *now*—as had he been reasoned with sooner, he might have been persuaded not to turn. He seemed ready to cry ... The young one now heartily cried—they are constantly watched—they cannot go without a guard." By contrast, Fisk and Parsons reported that Thomas Pewett, despite repenting his apostasy, insisted that "the Turks did not urge or even invite him to the measure." See Fisk and Parsons journal, March through Aug. 1820, May 18 and July 7, ABCFM, reel 513.

17. Jowett, *Christian Researches in the Mediterranean*, 271–73; Jowett, "Fragments from My Smyrna Journal"; Jasanoff, *Edge of Empire*, 144–46; *MR*, Aug. 1819, 366–67; Jason Thompson, "Osman Effendi: A Scottish Convert to Islam in Early Nineteenth-Century Egypt," *Journal of World History* 5, no. 1 (1994): 112. Westerners believed that Muslims by birth held renegades in contempt. (Jowett journal, June 4, 1818; Fisk and Parsons journal, March through Aug. 1820, May 18, ABCFM, reel 513.) Westerners also observed that non-Muslim religious groups in the Mediterranean disdained apostates. James Emerson, an Irish traveler who toured the Aegean in the 1820s, reported that a Greek Christian, allegedly a forced apostate to Islam, became the source of a vampire legend on the island of Santorini. (Emerson, *Letters from the Aegean*, 67–68, 104–6, 171–80.) Men of African descent might have been drawn to Islam by ancestral ties, real or fictive.

18. Fisk, UTS I, Feb. 18 and 28, March 1 and 2, April 19, 1820; Parsons and Fisk to Worcester, March 5, 1820, ABCFM, reel 513. A description of Sediqui appears in Dearborn, *Memoir*, 2:64; for Fisk's stay there, see his MJ I entries between October 19 and November 21, 1821. Fisk might have first read White's work at Andover, where the library held a copy; his farewell sermon suggests that White had strongly influenced his thinking about Islam by then.

19. Ignatius Mouradgea d'Ohsson, *Tableau général de l'empire Ottoman*, 5 vols. (Istanbul: Les Éditions Isis, 2001), 1:7–9; for Fisk's notes, see UTS III, 8–41. D'Ohsson's work appeared in Paris, beginning in 1787 with his first volume on the Islamic religious code; his final volumes on the civil, judicial, and military codes

were published in 1821. Fisk might first have heard about d'Ohsson back in the United States when he was entertained by Philadelphia's Freemasons, who had published a portion of d'Ohsson's work in 1788 under the title *Oriental Antiquities, and General View of the Othoman Customs, Laws, and Ceremonies* (Philadelphia, 1788). What Fisk read in Smyrna could only have been an early French edition in four volumes, because there are notes in his "Book of Extracts" that cover parts of d'Ohsson's work not included in the Philadelphia edition. By then, Fisk was fluent in French but knew no German, the only other translation available in the 1820s. His notes indicate that he read d'Ohsson's section on Ottoman religious belief and practice in its entirety; he might have read the other books of *Tableau* without taking notes. A thoughtful account of d'Ohsson's career is Carter V. Findley, "A Quixotic Author and His Great Taxonomy: Mouradgea d'Ohsson and His *Tableau General de L'Empire Othoman*" (Oct. 25, 1999), www.oslo2000.uio.no/program/papers/m1b/m1b-findley.pdf; see also Wheatcroft, *Infidels*, 270–73, and Finkel, *Osman's Dream*, 493.

20. D'Ohsson, *Tableau*, 1:15–16, 77, 79, 84, 88–89, 134, 137–38, 164, and 2:6, 38–39, 68. His praise for the Ottoman legal and religious code reads, "Il verra dans les différents Codes qui composent la Législation universelle de cet l'Empire, ce qu'il y a de grand dans plusiers de ses dogmes, de sublime dans la plus grande partie de sa morale, d'imposant dans son culte, de sage dans ses lois, de simple, de naturel dans ses usages et dans ses moeurs." Curiously, nowhere in Fisk's notes is any reference to d'Ohsson's main thesis—his defense of Islam against the charge that it had fostered despotism, ignorance, and fatalism among the Ottomans. No reader could have missed the point: d'Ohsson announced that argument in his opening pages and rehearsed it throughout the book. Perhaps Fisk wished to avoid any reckoning on paper, with the evidence piling up from his readings that what he had been taught to believe about the baleful influence of Islam was wrong.

21. D'Ohsson, *Tableau*, 1:49, 68, 70–71, 79–80, 84–85, 90, 165, 2:97, 131–39; Lockman, *Contending Visions*, 63. Some evangelicals, including Joseph White, acknowledged but did not dwell on the beliefs that Protestants shared with Muslims; see White, *Sermons Preached Before the University of Oxford, in the Year 1784*, 33.

22. D'Ohsson, *Tableau*, 2:59–61, 63, 81, 128–29; Fisk, UTS I, April 22, 1820.

23. Their placement on the page indicates that Fisk entered his lists in this private journal after he had made his final entries therein, which date from May 1821, and probably before he left Smyrna at the end of that year. He flipped the filled journal upside down and jotted his lists on the blank space of what would be the bottom of the page if the journal were right side up. (UTS I, 5–10 upside down, 160–67 right-side up.) My thinking on what Fisk made of his reading owes a great deal to Michel de Certeau's view that readers are active in their approach to texts, modifying what they find and assembling meanings to suit their own purposes. See Michel de Certeau, *The Practice of Everyday Life* (Berkeley: University of California Press, 1984), 169, 174; see also Wolfgang Iser, *The Implied Reader: Patterns of Communication in Prose Fiction from Bunyan to Beckett* (Baltimore:

Johns Hopkins University Press, 1974), and Wolfgang Iser, "Interaction Between Text and Reader," in *The Reader in the Text: Essays on Audience and Interpretation*, ed. Susan R. Suleiman and Inge Crosman (Princeton, N.J.: Princeton University Press, 1980), 106–19.

24. Morier, *Journey Through Persia*, 42–43. Fisk's notes on Morier directly follow his notes on d'Ohsson in his "Book of Extracts." (Fisk, UTS III, 52.)

25. Fisk, MJ I, Nov. 20–22, Dec. 5, 1821; Fisk and Parsons to Worcester, Feb. 8, 1820, Fisk to Evarts, May 18 and Nov. 22, 1821, ABCFM, reel 513; Fisk, UTS III, 62–67; Howe, *Historical Sketch of the Greek Revolution*, 82–83. Before the outbreak of the conflict, some Greek Christians seeking political advancement in the Ottoman Empire had voluntarily embraced Islam. Partisans on both sides during the war might well have concocted or exaggerated stories of forced conversion among adults, but both Turks and Greeks circumcised or baptized some of the boys seized as slaves. See St. Clair, *That Greece Might Still Be Free*, 9, 39; see also Emerson, *Letters from the Aegean*, 67–68, 142, 171–80. For the Qur'an's prohibition of forced conversion, see 2:256; a good recent account of Islam's early expansion is Fred M. Donner, *Muhammad and the Believers at the Origins of Islam* (Cambridge, Mass.: Harvard University Press, 2010).

26. Fisk, MJ I, Dec. 3 and 24, 1821, Jan. 5 and 8, 1822.

## 7. AN AMERICAN MUSLIM

1. Fisk, MJ I, Jan. 15–17 and 24, Feb. 4, 1822; Fisk to Evarts, Jan. 16, 1822, ABCFM, reel 513. English published his account of the Sudan campaign, led by Mehmet Ali's son Ismail Pasha, under the title *A Narrative of the Expedition to Dongola and Sennaar* (London, 1822); for a summary of his role in that campaign, see Finnie, *Pioneers East*, 143–49.

2. Morton, *Memoir of Parsons*, 365. For descriptions of Alexandria, see Dearborn, *Memoir*, 2:344–54; *Travels of Ali Bey*, 353–71; Henry Light, *Travels in Egypt, Nubia, Holy Land, Mount Libanon, and Cyprus, in the Year 1814* (London, 1818), 7–12; Turner, *Tour in the Levant*, 2:315–28, 487–88; Edward de Montulé, *Travels in Egypt During 1818 and 1819* (London, 1821), 4; Richardson, *Travels Along the Mediterranean*, 1:22–23. The best description in a secondary account is Mansel, *Levant*, 59–60, 67–74.

3. Parsons to Fisk, Jan. 23, 1822, ABCFM, reel 502; Parsons to Joshua Bates, Nov. 22, 1811, and to Elizabeth Hooker, Dec. 25, 1821, Parsons Letters. For their earliest weeks in Alexandria, see Fisk, MJ I, Jan. 15, 1822.

4. Parsons's letters written during his voyage to Jerusalem appeared in *Hampshire Gazette*, June 6, 1821, and *New-York Spectator*, June 22, 1821; the letters themselves are dated Dec. 9 and 18, 1820. A suggestive example of the missionaries' self-censorship appears in the contrast between Parsons's description of the three Muslim passengers in his private correspondence and his report to Worcester, which deleted entirely his positive response to their piety. (Parsons to Worcester, Jan. 25, 1821, ABCFM, reel 513.)

5. Parsons journal, Dec. 5, 1820, to Feb. 17, 1821, and Feb. 17 to May 8, 1821, 21, 39, 48–49, ABCFM, reel 513.

6. Parsons to Daniel and Lucretia Morton, Dec. 28, 1821, Parsons Letters. For his time on Syra, see his journal entries from July 2 to Nov. 22, 1821, ABCFM, reel 513, esp. the entry for Aug. 18, and Morton, *Memoir of Parsons*, 350.

7. Parsons dared do no more than hint at his more tolerant views to the board with the passing remark in his journal that "if a missionary can reside here [Jerusalem] with no other employment than to read the scriptures with pilgrims without uttering a word against Catholics, Greeks, or Turks, a great work might be accomplished." (Parsons journal, March 22, 1821, ABCFM, reel 513; that entry appeared in *MH*, Feb. 1822.) At least thirteen religious and secular newspapers in New England and upstate New York carried excerpts from Parsons's Jerusalem journal; some twenty Christian magazines published primarily along the Eastern Seaboard also gave coverage to his mission there.

8. Fisk, MJ I, Dec. 1 and 3, 1821, and Feb. 10 and 14, 1822.

9. Fisk, MJ I, Jan. 23, 25–27, Feb. 1, 2, 4, 5, 7, 13, 20, 21, 28, 1822; Fisk to Evarts, Feb. 28, 1822, ABCFM, reel 513; Wolff, *Missionary Journal*, 103, 108, 110–12, 115; Turner, *Tour in the Levant*, 2:487–88. Marpurgo told Fisk, "Within three years if God will I shall be in America," but when he moved his practice, it was to Beirut. (Isaac Bird to William Goodell, Oct. 3, 1835, ABCFM, reel 503.) In contrast to Jowett, Fisk and Parsons betrayed neither any hint of anti-Semitism nor racialized thinking of any sort about the peoples of the Levant.

10. Fisk, UTS III, 78–97; C. F. Volney, *Travels Through Egypt and Syria, in the Years 1783, 1784, and 1785 . . .* , 2nd ed., 2 vols. (New York, 1801), 2:235; Irwin, *Dangerous Knowledge*, 133–36; Hourani, *Europe and the Middle East*, 81–86.

11. Fisk, UTS I, Dec. 11, 1819; Fisk, UTS III, 98–103. An English translation of Niebuhr's work did not appear until 1792, yet even in the 1820s some Westerners in the Levant, including Henry Salt and Joseph Wolff, still regarded it as the best book about the region. ("Extracts from Wolff's Journal," *JE* 7 [1822]: 86.) Niebuhr was much more favorable to the Arabians than to the Turks or the Egyptians, and he believed that the Sunnis had corrupted Muhammad's message and that the Wahhabis were trying to restore it and to reform Islam. He also praised how openly Muslim men displayed their religious devotion, their refraining from public drunkenness, and their kindness to slaves. Niebuhr was critical of many elements of the region's culture—its tyrannical governments, high taxes, ignorance, lack of libraries—but he did not ascribe those evils to Islam. See Niebuhr, *Travels Through Arabia*, 1:29–30, 37, 78–79, 122, 196–97, 227, 229, 248, 256, 258, 272, 2:5, 20, 32–33, 130–36, 184–90, 192–93, 212–16, 262, 272; for his career, see Irwin, *Dangerous Knowledge*, 130–32.

12. Fisk, MJ I, Jan. 18 and 29 and Feb. 7 and 23, 1822; Khaled Fahmy, *All the Pasha's Men: Mehmet Ali, His Army, and the Making of Modern Egypt* (Cambridge, U.K.: Cambridge University Press, 1997), 9, 11–12; Mansel, *Levant*, 56–67. During his weeks in Alexandria, Fisk also read accounts of Egypt written by other Westerners, not all of whom sided with Volney. Both the explorer Giovanni Belzoni, who

excavated many ancient tombs and temples, and the diplomat William Hamilton, who had brought the "Elgin Marbles" to England, dismissed Islam as a rank "superstition," but the artist and archaeologist Vivant Denon defended Islam as a "religion of precept" that promoted "a reasonable morality." See Giovanni Belzoni, *Narrative of the Operations and Recent Discoveries Within the Pyramids, Temples, Tombs, and Excavations in Egypt and Nubia* . . . 2nd ed. (London, 1821), 15; William Hamilton, *Remarks on Several Parts of Turkey, Part I: Aegyptiaca, or, Some Account of the Antient and Modern State of Egypt, as Obtained in the Years 1801, 1802* (London, 1809); Dominique Vivant Denon, *Travels in Upper and Lower Egypt, in Company with Several Divisions of the French Army, During the Campaigns of General Bonaparte in That Country*, 3 vols. (London, 1803), 1:323–27. For Fisk's notes on these authors, see UTS III, 68–77.

13. Turner, *Tour in the Levant*, 2:358–70; Dearborn, *Memoir*, 2:366, 368.
14. Fisk, MJ I, March 6–11, 13, 21, 1822. Fisk referred to him as "Osman Hakeem" and gave his Christian name as William Thompson; other sources have identified it as William Taylor. For his biography, see Thompson, "Osman Effendi," 99–123; Jasanoff, *Edge of Empire*, 229–30, 290. Thompson argues persuasively for the authenticity of Osman's conversion to Islam. Dr. Robert Richardson recommended Osman to Jowett as a contact who might help him to discover "the hidden man of Islamism": "He [Osman] could introduce you and by mingling in their families and coteries, you might discover both their strength and its vulnerable part." (Richardson to Jowett, Aug. 18, 1818, CMSC.)
15. Fisk, MJ I, March 7, 11, 14, 1822; Fisk to Evarts, May 9, 1822, ABCFM, reel 513; Roper, "Arabic Printing in Malta," 101–2; see also Naudi to Josiah Pratt, Feb. 20, 1817, CMSC, and "Extracts from the Journal of Mr. Wolff," *JE* 8 (1823), 78–79, 108. For Nureddin's career, see Wolff to Henry Drummond, Dec. 7, 1821, *JE*, 7 (1822): 214–15, and Fahmy, *All the Pasha's Men*, 81–82, 163. Missionary schools in late eighteenth-century India pioneered the Lancastrian system, which quickly spread to both Britain and the United States, especially in schools for the children of the poor. More advanced students taught beginners in small groups, allowing teachers to supervise the schooling of large numbers of children.
16. Fisk, MJ I, March 2, 22, 25, 1822.
17. Ibid., March 21, 27, 28, 1822.
18. It is possible that Lee arranged for Fisk and English to sail on another vessel, the *Despatch*, because the captain of the *Sicily* would have known that Fisk did not have a servant. Less than a year after English's escape to Malta, Wolff made note of a French Jewish renegade in a similar fix: one Ibrahim Effendi failed to fashion a hydraulic machine for Mehmet Ali and ended up fleeing "under the shape of a Domestique for an Italian gentleman." See Joseph Wolff journal, from the year 1823, entry for March 25, General Theological Seminary (Episcopal Church), New York City.
19. The reasons for returning to Malta that Fisk included in his private journal made no mention of English; most likely, he wished to keep his complicity in the escape a secret. Smuggling a renegade out of the Ottoman Empire was imprudent, even

reckless—enough to make Jeremiah Evarts blanch—and if it went wrong, Fisk's effects would have ended up either in the hands of Muslim authorities or back at the mission rooms in Boston, where his private journal would be private no longer.

20. Waddington and Hanbury, *Journal of a Visit to Some Parts of Ethiopia*, 114–15, 117–18; for Khalil Aga's journal, see the Papers from the Collections of Henry Salt, folio 2, 46–76, #54195, entries for Dec. 25 and 26, 1820, Jan. 16, Feb. 12, 14, 28, May 11, June 28, July 14, 15, 20, 21, 1821, Manuscripts Room of the British Library. The catalog entry mistakenly lists the author as anonymous and possibly a British traveler, but he is clearly Khalil Aga and identified by English as his companion on the return trip to Cairo in his *Narrative of the Expedition*, 53, 93–94, 203–4, 211–29. For Khalil's later career in Egypt, see James DeKay, *Sketches of Turkey in 1831 and 1832* (New York, 1833), 488.

21. Wolff, *Missionary Journal*, 5–51. For Wolff's background, see also Joseph Wolff, *Travels and Adventures of the Reverend Joseph Wolff . . .* (London, 1860), 16–139. Marpurgo described Wolff as "a sensible, clever, sociable, learned man"; see Fisk, MJ I, Jan. 23 and Feb. 2, 1822.

22. Wolff, *Missionary Journal*, 124–30, 150–53, 164–65, 171, 173, 175–76; Wolff, "Extracts from the Journal of Wolff," *JE* 7 (1822): 243–45. According to Wolff, English drew a sharp distinction between the movement within Judaism founded by Peter and James that would later become Christianity and the doctrines taught by Paul to the Gentiles. English believed that Peter and James accepted Jesus as the Messiah predicted in the Old Testament but otherwise added no new articles to the Jewish creed, whereas Paul preached many doctrines that Peter and James judged heretical. English would have found support for his views among Muslims, who also held that disagreements among the apostles had corrupted the New Testament. Many contemporary biblical scholars emphasize the sharp rivalry among early "Christian" leaders; see, for an example, Pagels, *Revelations*, 37–72. I am indebted to Anne Heyrman-Hart for enlightening me on this point.

23. Khalil Aga journal, July 14, 1820, folio 2, 46–76, #54195; Fisk, MJ I, March 6, 1822. Fahmy, *All the Pasha's Men*, 40, 86–89, 92. English's published account repeatedly justified the brutality of the Sudan campaign, perhaps to keep Henry Salt in the pasha's good graces. (English, *Narrative of the Expedition*, xi–xii, 58, 138–39, 178.)

24. Wolff, *Missionary Journal*, 127, 143, 153, 164–65, 171, 173; "Extracts from Wolff's Journal," *JE* 7 (1822): 250, 290–93. In turn, Lee passed Wolff's news on to Fisk when he arrived in Alexandria at the beginning of 1822; see Fisk, MJ I, Jan. 15, 1822.

25. Wolff, *Missionary Journal*, 175–76; English, *Narrative of the Expedition*, 93–94, 203–4; J. J. Halls, *The Life and Correspondence of Henry Salt* (London, 1834), 2:212–13; Jasanoff, *Edge of Empire*, 233–81.

26. Fisk to Mrs. L. P. Porter, April 22, 1822, cited in Bond, *Memoir of Fisk*, 205. Some members of the Malta Bible Society were aware that Fisk had arrived with English, but no evidence suggests that they knew of Fisk's role in the escape. ("Let-

ter from Dr. Naudi," *JE* 9 [1824]: 73.) While he waited in quarantine, Fisk disclosed to the newly arrived Daniel Temple that he and English were debating biblical prophecies pertaining to the return of the Messiah. The two men were close friends, so Fisk might also have confided in Temple about his role in English's exit from Egypt. (Fisk to Temple, April 22 and 24, 1822, ABCFM, reel 502.)

27. Fisk to English, May 12, 1822, ABCFM, reel 502. Fisk was so demoralized that he might not have sent English this parting letter. Fisk affixed no address on the back of the last page, which bears the inscription "To Mr. English" and served as the cover. Nor is it likely that the extant letter is a copy of one actually sent: Fisk indented his script on both sides on the middle of the last page, a common practice among correspondents in the Levant to keep their writing from being defaced by postal officials who slit the covers of letters to allow fumigation to penetrate the pages. That Fisk kept the letter suggests the significance of this episode to him; its order of placement in the American Board's archives indicates that the letter did not arrive in Boston until after Fisk's death. For this original, see Fisk to English, May 12, 1822, ABC 16.5, vol. 1, ABCFM HU.

28. Sargent, *Memoir*, 240; Smith, *Henry Martyn*, 223; Sim, *Desert Traveller*, 211–12, 288–90. English's career calls out for comparison with that of the English explorer and ethnographer Richard Burton, who entered Mecca dressed as a Muslim pilgrim in 1853. Elusive characters who gloried in the freedom that they gained by assuming Muslim dress and manners, both men deployed Islam to criticize the Christianity of their day. But while Burton was a freethinker and an agnostic, English was a believer in his own brand of radical monotheism who accepted the Pentateuch and the Qur'an as divine revelation. For a superb analysis of Burton's stance toward Islam, see Kennedy, *Highly Civilized Man*, 58–92.

29. John Brooke, "Joining Natural Philosophy to Christianity: The Case of Joseph Priestley," in *Heterodoxy in Early Modern Science and Religion*, ed. John Brooke and Ian MacLean (New York: Oxford University Press, 2005), 328; John Macgowan, *Socinianism Brought to the Test; or, Jesus Christ Proved to Be Either the Adorable God or a Notorious Imposter, in Twenty Letters to the Reverend Doctor Priestley*, 3rd ed. (London, 1805), 125; Daniel Merrill, *Jesus Christ Magnified, and Mahomedan Christians Exposed and Warned* (Portland, Maine, 1825); Knapp, *Extracts from a Journal of Travels in North America*, 114; Jowett journal, Sept. 4, 1816. The Web site www.hymnary.org/text/sun_of_unclouded_righteousness gives the full text of Charles Wesley's hymn and indicates that it enjoyed peak popularity between about 1815 and 1830. Shortly after Martyn proclaimed that he rejected the Qur'an, he fortified his resolve by reading arguments against those who denied the doctrine of the Trinity; see Smith, *Henry Martyn*, 213–14; Sargent, *Memoir*, 264.

30. R. W. Southern first brought to light the way in which Western Christendom's interests and religious preoccupations inflected its conception of Islam. Southern, *Western Views of Islam in the Middle Ages*, 13.

31. White, *A Sermon Preached Before the University of Oxford, July 4, 1784, on the Duty of Attempting the Propagation of the Gospel Among Our Mahometan and*

*Gentoo Subjects in India,* 31–32; *Panoplist, and Missionary Herald,* Nov. 1814; Smith, *Henry Martyn,* 383.

32. There were historical precedents for the nineteenth-century evangelical strategy. Nicholas of Cusa, the fifteenth-century historian and philosopher, hoped to advance the cause of rapprochement with the Muslim world by arguing that the Qur'an's teachings were drawn from Nestorian Christian heresies. See Southern, *Western Views of Islam in the Middle Ages,* 38, 81, 94; see also Chew, *The Crescent and the Rose,* 397; Hourani, *Europe and the Middle East,* 8–9, 24–25; Irwin, *Dangerous Knowledge,* 22–23; Matthew Dimmock, *New Turkes: Dramatizing Islam and the Ottomans in Early Modern England* (Burlington, Vt.: Ashgate, 2005), 59–60; Said, *Orientalism,* 75.

33. Ziad Elmarsafy refers to the perspective that shaped English's thinking as "the equivalence of religious belief across Abrahamic monotheisms," a view that he attributes to Sale and regards as "rapidly acquiring axiomatic status" among enlightened thinkers by the turn of the eighteenth century. (Elmarsafy, *Enlightenment Qur'an,* 64–67.) If, as William Bentley believed, English was a deist at the time he broke into print in Boston, he had changed his views substantially by the time he left Egypt.

34. Fisk to Evarts, April 18, 1822, ABCFM, reel 513; Fisk to Isaac Bird, May 7, 1822, SCMC.

35. English, *Narrative of the Expedition,* 60–61. In 1824, English published *Five Pebbles from the Brook: A Reply to "A Defence of Christianity" Written by Edward Everett . . .* (Philadelphia, 1824), a piece he professed to have written in the summer of 1820. He declared himself to be neither a Christian nor an infidel, and he defended religious beliefs consonant with Islam but without identifying himself as a Muslim. All that he had seen during his travels, English wrote, "while it has confirmed my reasons for rejecting the New Testament has rooted in my mind the conviction that the ancient Bible does contain a revelation from the God of Nature" and that "this world was made and is governed by just such a Being as the Jehovah of the Old Testament" (7, 203).

36. For the flurry of generally positive newspaper accounts about English, see *New Bedford Mercury,* July 5, 1822; *Baltimore Patriot,* July 10, 1822; *Essex Register,* July 6, 1822; *Columbian Star* (Washington, D.C.), Aug. 24, 1822; *Providence Patriot,* July 31, 1822; *The Christian Philanthropist* (New Bedford), July 30 and Aug. 27, 1822; *Portsmouth Journal of Literature and Politics,* July 20, 1822; *Independent Chronicle and Boston Patriot,* July 24, 1822; *Richmond Enquirer,* Aug. 2, 1822; *Village Register and Norfolk County Advertiser,* Aug. 2, 1822; *Boston Recorder,* Aug. 3, 1822; *Portsmouth Oracle,* July 30, 1822; *New Hampshire Sentinel,* Aug. 17, 1822.

37. John Quincy Adams, *Memoirs . . . Comprising Portions of His Diary from 1795 to 1848,* ed. Charles Francis Adams, 12 vols. (Boston, 1874–77), 6:320–21, 414, 442, 447–48, 8:60, 62; Field, *From Gibraltar to the Middle East,* 133–34; Oren, *Power, Faith, and Fantasy,* 111–14. His friend and biographer Samuel Knapp insisted that English denied ever becoming a Muslim, but allowed that "he had often joined in prayer, both with the Turks and with the Jews, as they addressed the Supreme

Being alone." Knapp, *Treasury of Knowledge and Library of Reference, Part VI,*
*American Biography,* 96.

## 8. EPIPHANIES

1. "Letter from Mr. King," Sept. 24, 1822, Paris, in *Evangelical and Literary Maga-*
   *zine,* Dec. 1822; the account of the journey from Paris to Valletta appears in his
   journal entries from Sept. 30 to Nov. 12, 1822, ABCFM, reel 513; King to the
   American Board, Aug. 12, 1822, King to William Hendrick Nolthenius, July 22,
   1822, King to Claude Crommelin, Aug. 7, 1822, and King to Evarts, Sept. 21, 1822,
   all in ABCFM, reel 513. For Wilder's background, see Anon., *Records from the*
   *Life of S. V. S. Wilder* (New York, 1865), esp. 29–128. Wilder's home served as a
   gathering place for devout Protestants throughout Europe; at its height, his weekly
   Sabbath prayer meeting drew three hundred people. (*New Hampshire Repository,*
   Feb. 23, 1824.)
2. Gwynne Lewis, *The Second Vendée: The Continuity of Counter-revolution in the*
   *Department of the Gard* (Oxford: Clarendon Press, 1978), 113–231; Gwynne Lewis,
   "The White Terror of 1815 in the Department of the Gard: Counter-revolution,
   Continuity, and the Individual," *Past and Present* 58 (Feb. 1973): 108–35; Daniel
   P. Resnick, *The White Terror and Political Reaction After Waterloo* (Cambridge,
   Mass.: Harvard University Press, 1966), 41–62; see also Walter Markov, *Grand*
   *Empire: Virtue and Vice in the Napoleonic Era* (New York: Hippocrene Books,
   1990), 105–6, and Robert Tombs, *France, 1814–1914* (London: Longman, 1996),
   241–42.
3. For King's background, see Mrs. F[rancina] E[lecta] Haines, *Jonas King, Mis-*
   *sionary to Syria and Greece* (New York, 1879), esp. 11–48; Haines was one of
   Sampson Wilder's daughters. King belonged to Andover's less select Society of
   Inquiry Respecting Missions, which suggests he had held back from the commitment required by the Brethren. His interests were also more scholarly than
   those of the first missionaries in the Levant: his Andover dissertations included
   an essay on the importance of biblical exegesis and a review of an eighteenth-
   century German theologian, philologist, and biblical critic. (Papers for the Society of Inquiry Respecting Missions and Andover Student Dissertations, 1810–49,
   vol. 1.) While at Smyrna, both Fisk and Parsons had some correspondence with
   King, possibly in reference to the latter's interest in learning Arabic; see Fisk,
   UTS I, Feb. 19, 1820, and p. 96, n.d. (ca. early 1821).
4. "Narrative of the Voyage of the Rev. Lewis Way," *JE* 9 (1824): 48.
5. King journal, Nov. 28, 1822, ABCFM, reel 513; King to Drummond, Dec. 25, 1822,
   *JE* 8 (1823): 157; "Extracts from Wolff's Journal," *JE* 7 (1822): 113, 154.
6. Jowett, *Christian Researches in the Mediterranean,* 247–64, 356–57. Jowett still
   advocated for evangelizing Muslims in 1825 as "an enterprise which demands to
   be taken up systematically and fully; perhaps, in order to give it greater advantage, for a time, at least, exclusively." (Jowett, *Christian Researches in Syria and the*
   *Holy Land,* 369–71.)

7. Fisk to Bird, May 1820, SCMC; Haines, *Jonas King*, 90–91. Both Wolff and King agreed with Fisk's assessment of the mood among Muslims; see King journal, Oct. 16, 1822, ABCFM, reel 513, and "Extracts from Wolff's Journal," *JE* 7 (1822): 86.

8. Benjamin Barker to E. R. Ronneberg, March 10, 1823, British and Foreign Bible Society Archives, Cambridge University; Fisk to Temple, May 2, 1823, ABCFM, reel 502; Fisk, MJ I, Jan. 21–23, 1823, and MJ II, March 10, 1823; Wolff journal from the year 1823, Jan. 22–24 and Feb. 7, 1823, General Theological Seminary, New York City; "Extracts from Wolff's Journal," *JE* 7 (1822): 154, and 8 (1823): 273–75. For contemporary descriptions of Rosetta, see Richardson, *Travels Along the Mediterranean*, 1:36; Dearborn, *Memoir*, 2:354–60; Turner, *Tour in the Levant*, 2:344; Montulé, *Travels in Egypt*, 5:5–6; Edward Daniel Clarke, *Travels in Various Countries of Europe, Asia, and Africa*, 2 vols., 2nd ed. (New York, 1818), 2:180.

9. Wolff journal from the year 1823, Feb. 20 and March 4, 1823; extract from a "Letter of a Gentleman Traveling in Palestine," and Wolff to Drummond, Dec. 7, 1821, *JE* 7 (1822): 149–50, 214–15; "Extracts from Wolff's Journal," *JE* 7 (1822): 215, and 8 (1823): 279–80; Fisk and King journal, Feb. 6, 1823 (entries by Fisk), and Salt to King, Fisk, and Wolff, Feb. 9, 1823, ABCFM, reel 513; Fisk, MJ II, March 23, 1823. Like Nureddin, Gibraltar had traveled in Europe and spoke English, French, and Italian.

10. "Extracts from Wolff's Journal," *JE* 8 (1823): 359–66; Fisk and King journal, March 12, 14, 23, 1823, ABCFM, reel 513; Fisk to Daniel Temple, March 29, 1823, ABCFM, reel 502; King to the Reverend Ebenezer Porter, March 30, 1823, in *Boston Recorder*, Dec. 13, 1823; see also King's letter to his sister in *Hampshire Gazette*, Jan. 28, 1824.

11. Fisk, MJ II, April 11 and 19, May 1, 4, and 5, 1823; Wolff journal from the year 1823, April 16 and 17, May 4, 1823; "Extracts from Wolff's Journal," *JE* 9 (1824): 36–37, 63–64, 107–8; King and Fisk journal, May 4, 1823, ABCFM, reel 513. According to Francis Werry, there was a Masonic lodge in Smyrna, and the caravan's Turks claimed that there were others in Persia, Damascus, and Mount Lebanon. In their letters to Evarts, the missionaries defended their identifying as English; see Fisk to Evarts, Feb. 28, 1824, ABCFM, reel 513. For the Jerusalem officeholders, see Yehoshua Ben-Arieh, *Jerusalem in the 19th Century: The Old City* (New York: Palgrave Macmillan, 1985), 104–7.

12. Donna Robinson Divine, *Politics and Society in Ottoman Palestine: The Arab Struggle for Survival and Power* (Boulder, Colo.: Lynne Rienner Publishers, 1994), 13–45; Thomas Philipp, *Acre: The Rise and Fall of a Palestinian City, 1730–1831* (New York: Columbia University Press, 2001), 83, 90–93, 183–84; Ruth Kark, *Jaffa: A City in Evolution, 1799–1917* (Jerusalem: Yad Izhak Ben-Zvi Press, 1990), 14–16; Dick Douwes, *The Ottomans in Syria: A History of Justice and Oppression* (London: I. B. Tauris, 2000), 109, 120–21; Gudrun Krämer, *A History of Palestine: From the Ottoman Conquest to the Founding of the State of Israel*, trans. Graham Harman and Gudrun Krämer (2002; Princeton, N.J.: Princeton University Press, 2008), 37–63; A. L. Tibawi, *A Modern History of Syria Including Lebanon and Palestine* (London:

Macmillan, 1969), 40–62. For a firsthand account of the sharpening of Muslim-Christian tensions as a result of the Greek war, see S. N. Spyridon, ed., "Annals of Palestine, 1821–1841," *Journal of the Palestine Oriental Society* 18, nos. 1–2 (1938): 63–132; see also Jowett, *Christian Researches in Syria*, 242–43, 312, 315.

13. King diary of 1823, April 7, 14, 18, and July 4, MS, American Antiquarian Society (hereafter King, AAS diary), and King to Electa Wilder, May 8, 1823 (copy in diary). For biblical references, see Mark 14:48 and Psalm 92:10.

14. Bertram Wyatt-Brown, *Southern Honor: Ethics and Behavior in the Old South* (New York: Oxford University Press, 1982); Craig Thompson Friend and Lorri Glover, *Southern Manhood: Perspectives on Masculinity in the Old South* (Athens: University of Georgia Press, 2004); Steven M. Stowe, *Intimacy and Power in the Old South: Ritual in the Lives of the Planters* (Baltimore: Johns Hopkins University Press, 1987); Kenneth S. Greenberg, *Masters and Statesmen: The Political Culture of American Slavery* (Baltimore: Johns Hopkins University Press, 1985); Kenneth S. Greenberg, *Honor and Slavery* (Princeton, N.J.: Princeton University Press, 1996); Christine Leigh Heyrman, *Southern Cross: The Beginnings of the Bible Belt* (New York: Knopf, 1997), 206–52. Amy Greenberg draws an apt distinction between the "restrained manhood" typical of many middle-class northerners, who internalized moral self-discipline, and the ideal of "martial manhood" embraced by many in the northern working class and by most southern whites. (Greenberg, *Manifest Manhood and the Antebellum American Empire*, 10–13, 139–52.) Efforts to associate Christianity with masculine virtues date to antiquity and the martyr narratives of early Christian communities; see E. Stephanie Cobb, *Dying to Be Men: Gender and Language in Early Christian Martyr Texts* (New York: Columbia University Press, 2008).

15. At a missionary ordination in 1818, Bentley cackled, "The number of females I observed to be very great. Of men comparatively few." (Bentley, *Diary*, 4:351, 359; see also citations in the introduction, note 12.) That gender disparity heralded changes in the composition of American missions abroad: by the end of the nineteenth century, women would outnumber men in the field. For another response to the feminization of Christianity, see Paul E. Johnson and Sean Wilentz, *The Kingdom of Matthias: A Story of Sex and Salvation in 19th-Century America* (New York: Oxford University Press, 1994). For its relationship to financial concerns about missions, see Evarts to Anderson, Dec. 5, 1826, ABC 11, vol. 2 (microfilm copy), ABCFM HU.

16. Evarts to Henry Hill, Feb. 20 and 21, 1824, ABC 11, vol. 1 (microfilm copy), ABCFM HU; Evarts to Hill, Feb. 16, 1826, Evarts to Anderson, Nov. 27 and Dec. 5, 1826, March 18, 19, 22, and 31, 1827, Evarts to Hill, Feb. 25, 1826, and March 27, 1827, all in ABC 11, vol. 2 (microfilm copy), ABCFM HU.

17. Fisk, UTS I, Feb. 10, 1820, July 5, 1821. Levant women were most likely to appear in the journals of both Fisk and King in discussions of the dearth of opportunities for girls to acquire even basic reading skills; see Fisk, UTS I, Jan. 23 and 26, Feb. 9 and 14, March 12 and 23, April 1, 1821; Fisk, MJ II, Jan. 13, 1824.

18. King, AAS diary, April 18, June 26 and 28, 1823; King journal for the Paris Missionary Society, May 26 and June 23, 1823, ABCFM, reel 513; Lockman, *Contending Visions*, 217-18.

19. King to Cook, May 29, 1823, Jerusalem, WMMSA. King and Cook had met in the South of France. For descriptions of Jerusalem, see *MR*, Nov. 1824, 503; Ben-Arieh, *Jerusalem in the 19th Century*, 24-27; Buckingham, *Travels to Palestine*, 186-287; Wilson, *Travels in Egypt and the Holy Land*, 192-289; Richardson, *Travels Along the Mediterranean*, 2:254-403.

20. Fisk journal, Oct. 28 to Nov. 1823, entry for Nov. 13, ABCFM, reel 513; Fisk, MJ II, Nov. 3 and 17, 1823; Fisk to Temple, July 5, 1825, ABCFM, reel 502. For all of Fisk's official reports during this period, see his journal, July 14 to Oct. 26, 1823, and Oct. 28 to Nov. 23, 1823, both addressed to Evarts, ABCFM, reel 513.

21. Fisk to Temple, Dec. 12, 1823, ABCFM, reel 502; Douwes, *Ottomans in Syria*, 125-51; Divine, *Politics and Society in Ottoman Palestine*, 19-20. For Fisk's account of the hostilities between the government of Jerusalem and Bethlehem, see Fisk, MJ II, Dec. 30, 1823, and Fisk to Evarts, May 24, 1824, 37-39, ABCFM, reel 502; for his accounting of sums paid by convents, see Fisk, MJ II, May 23 and Nov. 25, 1823, as well as one of the unpaginated back leaves of that volume.

22. Fisk, MJ II, Nov. 3, 1823; Jowett, *Christian Researches in Syria*, 149-53. For descriptions of Acre and al-Jazzar's career, see Divine, *Politics and Society in Ottoman Palestine*, 26-28; Philipp, *Acre*, 48-78, 131, 157-64; Ruth Kark, "The Rise and Decline of Coastal Towns in Palestine," in *Ottoman Palestine, 1800-1914*, ed. Gad G. Gilbar (Leiden: Brill, 1990), 69-89; Buckingham, *Travels in Palestine*, 66-80; Douwes, *Ottomans in Syria*, 52-59, 87-99.

23. Fisk to Temple, Jan. 12, 1823, ABCFM, reel 502; Fisk, MJ I, Feb. 3, 1823, and MJ II, March 26 and April 3, 1823. Note the contrast with King, who also attended the gathering at Ismael Gibraltar's. He presented Gibraltar with a New Testament in Turkish and a Bible in Italian and gave Nureddin a book on the "evidences" of Christianity. The latter fixed King with "a look which evidently showed he was not so well pleased with it as I could have wished," while the former, whenever "we approached the subject of religion, he turned the conversation, or else said, he knew nothing about it." (King, AAS diary, April 3, 1823.)

24. Fisk to Evarts, Nov. 9 and Dec. 22, 1823, ABCFM, reel 513; Fisk's postscript in Wolff's letter to Temple, Sept. 15, 1823, and Fisk to Temple, Oct. 25, 1823, ABCFM, reel 502; Henry Hill to Evarts, May 17, 1824, ABC 11, vol. 1 (microfilm copy), ABCFM HU. Fisk's intimacy with Temple might have begun at Andover, and if so it had only deepened during the spring of 1822, when Fisk finally left quarantine at Valletta—and the company of George English—and fled to Temple's familiar company. The correspondent to whom Fisk confided his thoughts on patriotism is almost certainly the Reverend Samuel Dana of Marblehead; the letter originally appeared in the *Boston Recorder* under the title "Mr. Fisk's Letter to a Clerical Friend in the Vicinity of Boston," and it was reprinted in both Washington, D.C.'s *Columbian Star* and the *New York Religious Chronicle* for July 24, 1824. Fisk added that the United States should "be distinguished, not by a national

religious establishment, enforced by law, but by a national religious character."
For thoughtful discussions of cosmopolitanism, see Harland-Jacobs, *Builders of
Empire*, 67–69, and Jacob, *Strangers Nowhere in the World*.

25. Compare Fisk, MJ II, Nov. 3, 1823, with his official journal entry for the same date,
ABCFM, reel 513. In case he had spoken too highly of Islam, he self-censored his
official journal, adding a phrase that dismissed those Muslim "doctors" for being "so wise in their own conceits." A man who lived between two worlds had to
choose his words carefully.

26. Fisk, MJ II, March 9 and April 5, 1824, and Fisk to Evarts, May 25, 1824, 14–19,
ABCFM, reel 502; for other exchanges on millennialism, see Fisk, UTS II, July 10
and 18, 1824, and March 10, 1825; King journal, Jan. 21–May 4, 1824, entry for
March 9, ABCFM, reel 515; see also Aslan, *No god but God*, 12, and Renard, *Islam
and Christianity*, 62–65. Fisk would also soon discover that Muslims and evangelicals dreaded the same Satan. "Lucifer" to Christians was "Iblis" to his fellow
believers in Islam, a Muslim sheikh explained, but all agreed that pride had
caused the devil's fall from heaven and that he took his revenge by tempting
humankind to sin. (Fisk, UTS II, Feb. 9, 1825.)

27. Fisk to Evarts, May 25, 1824, ABCFM, reel 502, 20; Bird missionary diary from
Jan. 1824, entry for Feb. 2, and Bird to Fisk, Nov. 13, 1822, Bird Papers.

28. For Fisk's reports of the arrest to the board, see Fisk to Evarts, Feb. 28, 1824,
ABCFM, reel 513; Fisk to Evarts, May 25, 1824, ABCFM, reel 502. The account in
Fisk's private journal appears in MJ II, Feb. 12, 17, March 2, 5; for others, see Bird
missionary journal from Jan. 1824, entries for Feb. 10, 11, 17, Bird Papers; Charles
Cook journal, March 23, 1824, WMMSA; *MR*, July 1825, 320–24; Fisk to the Secretary of the British and Foreign Bible Society, April 1824, BFBS Archives, Cambridge University Library.

29. Fisk, MJ I, Aug. 21, 1822, and MJ II, Feb. 17 and March 3, 1824; Fisk to Temple,
June 11, July 12, Dec. 12, 1823, and Feb. 3, 1824, Fisk to Evarts, May 25, 1824, 1–9,
ABCFM, reel 502; Bird missionary journal from Jan. 1824, entry for Feb. 17, Bird
Papers; King to the Committee of the Bible Society at Malta, Oct. 31, 1823, BFBS
Archives; King journal, Dec. 11, 18, and 19, 1823, ABCFM, reel 513; Cook journal,
April 14, 1823, WMMSA. For the antagonisms among Christians in Syria, see
Burckhardt, *Travels in Syria and the Holy Land*, 28–29, 182. The missionaries
believed that Muslims were as reluctant to share the Qur'an with Christians as
they were to read their translations of the Old Testament; see Bird and Goodell
journal, Dec. 18 and 19, 1823, ABCFM, reel 513.

30. *MH*, Feb. 1825, 33–39; see also *Christian Advocate* (Boston), Sept. 1, 1824; *Circu-
lar* (Wilmington, Del.), Sept. 10, 1824; *Washington Theological Repository*, Feb. 1,
1825; *New York Religious Chronicle*, Feb. 19, 1825; *Religious Intelligencer* (New
Haven), Feb. 26, 1825; *Western Recorder* (Utica), March 1, 1825; *Latter-Day Luminary* (Philadelphia), March 1, 1825; *Philadelphia Recorder*, March 5, 1825; Cook
to Taylor, May 11, 1824, WMMSA; Goodell to Temple, March 16, 1824, ABCFM, reel
503. For the tradition that Jesus had been sentenced in Pilate's palace, see Ben-
Arieh, *Jerusalem in the 19th Century*, 158–59.

31. Fisk, MJ II, Feb. 23, 1824; Cook to the Reverend Joseph Taylor, March 27, 1824, WMMSA; Jowett, *Christian Researches in Syria*, 160. The Catholics might have been hoping for just such a misstep: a few months earlier, an Italian Catholic missionary had baited Fisk by declaring that "the object of the English in distributing so many books" was "the forming of a party in these countries." (Fisk, MJ II, Nov. 16, 1823.)

32. Fisk journal, Oct. 28 to Nov. 23, 1823, entry for Nov. 3, ABCFM, reel 513; Fisk to Temple, Feb. 3, 1824, ABCFM, reel 502; *MR*, Nov. 1824, 501, and Oct. 1825, 473–74; Anderson to Bird, April 5, 1825, Worcester letter books, ABC 1.01, vol. 5, ABCFM HU. Several scholars have drawn the important distinction between martyrs of this stripe and present-day suicide terrorists who seek support for their cause through mass murder. For discussions of martyrdom as a strategy for marking the boundaries of religious community, see Thomas Sizgorich, *Violence and Belief in Late Antiquity: Militant Devotion in Christianity and Islam* (Philadelphia: University of Pennsylvania Press, 2009); see also Cook, *Martyrdom in Islam*, 2; Kate Cooper, "Martyrdom, Memory, and the 'Media Event': Visionary Writing and Christian Apology in Second-Century Christianity," in ed. Janes and Houen, *Martyrdom and Terrorism*, 30–39.

33. Bird missionary journal from Jan. 1824, entries for April 22 and Nov. 15, Bird Papers; Fisk to Evarts, Dec. 22, 1823, ABCFM, reel 513; Fisk to Evarts, May 27, 1824, ABCFM, reel 514; Henry Hill to Evarts, May 17, 1824, ABC 11, vol. 1 (microfilm copy), ABCFM HU; Evarts to Fisk, Aug. 14 and 17, 1824, Worcester letter books, ABC 1.01, vol. 5, ABCFM HU. The missionaries had agreed to be frank in their journals about the government in Ottoman Syria; see Minutes of a Meeting at Beirut, May 8, 1824, in Pliny Fisk, "Missionary Questions and Discussions," Sept. 20, 1823, Antoura, to May 1824, Beyroot, Congregational Library, Boston.

34. The best source for King's published record of his time in Ottoman Syria is *MH*, 1825, 1827. His official journals survive for the entire period except for his months in Aleppo with Fisk during the latter half of 1824.

35. Richard C. Morse to Bird, June 2, 1823, Bird Papers. Within a few years, Evarts was complaining about the *Missionary Herald*'s being scooped by the *New-York Observer*: "Something must be done to prevent the Herald being so often supplanted by letters from the missionaries to Mr. Morse." (Evarts to Anderson, March 22, 1827, ABC 11, vol. 2 [microfilm copy], ABCFM HU.) There is some question about the name of the Jaffa sheikh who tutored King and later Fisk in Arabic. King made no mention of it, and Fisk, after noting in his journal that he would not identify the sheikh by name, referred to him in one entry as "Sheyk Khaleel." (Fisk, UTS II, Feb. 2 and 9, 1825.) For descriptions of Jaffa, see Richardson, *Travels Along the Mediterranean*, 2:215–16; Buckingham, *Travels in Palestine*, 146–59; François-René Chateaubriand, *Travels in Greece, Palestine, and Barbary During the Years 1806 and 1807* (Philadelphia, 1813), 362–78; George Robinson, *Three Years in the East* (London, 1837), 19–21; Wilson, *Travels in Egypt and the Holy Land*, 140; Kark, *Jaffa*, 16–20, 53–61, 146.

36. Haines, *Jonas King*, 161; Jonas King journal, Jan. 21–May 4, 1824, Feb. 7, 10, 18, 19, 21, 23, 25, March 9, 12, 18, 20, 29, April 17 and 23, ABCFM, reel 515; Cook journal, April 24, 1824, WMMSA; *MH*, April 1825. For extant copies of King's letter to Sidney Morse, March 7, 1824, see the reprints from the *Observer* in *Boston Weekly Messenger*, July 15, 1824, *Hampshire Gazette*, July 14, 1824, *Salem Gazette*, July 16, 1824, *Hallowell Gazette*, July 21, 1824, and *Farmer's Cabinet*, July 31, 1824. The *New Hampshire Gazette*, July 7, 1824, subsequently reported on the sheikh's efforts to induce King to "give up the divinity of Jesus" under the heading "Unitarian Mussulman." For Muslim ideals of martyrdom, see Cook, *Martyrdom in Islam*, 20–23, 166, and Lewinstein, "Reevaluation of Martyrdom in Early Islam," 79–80.

## 9. AT THE GATES OF DAMASCUS

1. *MH*, Nov. 1825, 341–42; King journal, Jan. 21–May 4, 1824, June 26 and July 10, ABCFM, reel 515; Fisk, UTS II, June 26, 1824; Cook to the Reverend Joseph Taylor, July 13, 1824, WMMSA; Goodell to Daniel Temple, Nov. 4, 1822, entry for Nov. 22, ABCFM, reel 503; Haines, *Jonas King*, 149, 165; "Letter from Dr. Naudi" and "Extracts from Wolff's Journal," *JE* 9 (1824): 108–9, 355–58; "Persecution of the Jews by the Turks," *Hampshire Gazette*, May 5, 1824; Burckhardt, *Travels in Syria and the Holy Land*, 322–23; Hamilton, *Remarks on Several Parts of Turkey*, 330–31; Chateaubriand, *Travels*, 261–62; *Travels of Ali Bey*, 353–71; Light, *Travels in Egypt*, 2:265, 273; Robinson, *Three Years in the East*, 135–40. For descriptions of late eighteenth- and early nineteenth-century Damascus, see Thompson, *Travels Through Turkey in Asia*, 133–41; Wilson, *Travels in Egypt and the Holy Land*, 442–57; Richardson, *Travels Along the Mediterranean*, 2:461–97.
2. Fisk to Temple, Sept. 11, 1824, ABCFM, reel 502; see UTS III, from the sixth page at the back of the book for Fisk's notes on the lithography manual.
3. Fisk, UTS II, entries from Feb. 9 to March 28, 1825. Fisk's "Book of Extracts" indicates that he did a little reading in the Talmud and borrowed a book from a rabbi that included "History of the New World," which related the discovery of the Americas by a Jewish counselor to the king of Spain. (Fisk, UTS III, 154–71.)
4. "Extract of a Letter from Messrs. Goodell and Bird, Dated at Beyroot," *Hampshire Gazette*, July 14, 1824. The *New-York Observer* was establishing itself as a leading religious periodical, and Wilder, after returning to the United States in the summer of 1823, assumed the presidency of the American Tract Society, a key organization in the evangelicals' interlocking institutional empire. The Morse brothers' and Wilder's correspondence has disappeared, but King's side makes it clear that they exchanged letters frequently. The missionaries also received regular issues of the *New-York Observer* and the *Missionary Herald*.
5. *New-York Observer*, Nov. 26, 1825. King received extensive coverage in the *Missionary Herald* during April, October, November, and December 1825; for his reports in the *New-York Observer*, see especially the issue above and those for

July 31, 1824, and December 24, 1825. At least forty other newspapers and magazines offered some coverage of the Palestine mission between 1823 and 1825; perhaps one-third of those periodicals were secular rather than religious. Most were concentrated in New England, but they were published as far west as Lexington, Kentucky, and as far south as Augusta, Georgia. When King left Beirut for Smyrna in the fall of 1825, pirates seized the ship carrying his private papers and official journals; he recovered some of them, and the *Herald* printed portions in February and March 1827, a few months before King returned to the United States.

6. King journal, July 5, 19, 20, 21, Nov. 3, 1824, ABCFM, reel 515; *MH*, Nov. and Dec. 1825. Fisk mentioned the opposition to their entering the shaded tomb, but he made no mention of King's challenge to the Muslim Turks; see Fisk, UTS II, July 19, 1824. At least by his own account, King often engaged with Muslims about theology. Besides his journal entries, see Jonas King, *Extraits d'un ouvrage écrit vers la fin de l'année 1826 and au commencement de 1827, sous le titre de Coup d'oeil sur la Palestine et la Syrie, accompagné de quelques réflexions sur les missions évangéliques* (Athens, 1859), 101–3, 142. King did not disclose to his American readers that he had adapted the story about the mouse from his Muslim tutor at Jaffa, who had told him, "Ah, you are like a sparrow which has seen a drop of water—an ocean remains to be seen!" (King journal, July 10, 1824.)

7. Niebuhr, *Travels Through Arabia*, 1:81, 144–46, 213, 221, 226, 228, 316–17, 360, 2:240–44; see also Richardson, *Travels Along the Mediterranean*, 1:469; John Griffith, *Travels in Asia Minor and Arabia* (London, 1805), 154–55; Wilson, *Travels in Egypt and the Holy Land*, 17–18; a letter from Isaac Bird to "Mrs. B." reprinted in the *Newburyport Herald*, Aug. 27, 1824. The notion that Islam encouraged a sense of superiority among its adherents now serves as the basis for the arguments of Bernard Lewis and other scholars that being outstripped by the West has produced "Muslim rage" and an implacable "clash of civilizations." (Lockman, *Contending Visions*, 216–20.)

8. King, AAS diary, March 27, 1823; Jowett journal, May 28, 1818; Abigail Goodell to Elizabeth Dodd, Nov. 14, 1823, William Goodell Papers, Library of Congress. On homosexuality in Islamic cultures and the Western association of the Middle East with sexual deviance, see Stephen O. Murray and Will Roscoe, eds., *Islamic Homosexualities* (New York: New York University Press, 1997); Marjorie Garber, "The Chic of Araby: Transvestism and the Erotics of Cultural Appropriation," in *Vested Interests: Cross-Dressing and Cultural Anxiety*, ed. Marjorie Garber (New York: Routledge, 1992), 304–52. The Scots renegade Osman favored Fisk with "a most horrible account of the lewdness and sodomy which are practiced at Mecca—Parents even bring their children to the Pilgrims for this purpose." "Sodomy" was "notoriously common" among the Turks, too, he added. (Fisk, MJ I, March 8, 1822.) King seems to have believed that both Muslim women and Muslim men engaged in same-sex intimacies; see King to the Reverend Ebenezer Porter, March 30, 1823, in *Boston Recorder*, Dec. 13, 1823. The concern about manliness might have been particularly intense for the Palestine mission's bach-

elors, Fisk and King. Fisk alluded often to his single status and once described himself as "a poor monk"; see Fisk to Bird, March 18, 1825, AMDC.

9. Volney, *Travels Through Egypt and Syria*, 1:252–55; Boulainvilliers, *Life of Mahomet*, 5, 25–27; Niebuhr, *Travels Through Arabia*, 2:20; *Travels of Ali Bey*, 353–71; Light, *Travels*, 2:359; Walpole, *Memoirs*, 28; Jedidiah Morse and Sidney Edwards Morse, *A New System of Geography*, 24th ed. (Boston, 1824), 229; Burckhardt, *Travels in Syria and the Holy Land*, 290–91; Chateaubriand, *Travels in Greece, Palestine, Egypt, and Barbary*, 212–13, 350; Isaac Bird, *Bible Work in Bible Lands* (Philadelphia, 1872), 91; Emerson, *Letters from the Aegean*, 61–62; see also Cook journal, April 1, 1824, WMMSA; Chandler, *Travels in Asia Minor and Greece*, 1:14.

10. Goodell to Daniel Temple, Dec. 27, 1823, ABCFM, reel 503; Light, *Travels*, 2:182, 228–29; Fisk to Clarissa in S[helburne], July 15, 1825, Beirut, cited in Bond, *Memoir of Fisk*, 406–7. For adopting native dress, see Niebuhr, *Travels in Arabia*, 1:24, 296–97; Burckhardt, *Travels in Nubia*, xxvii; Wilson, *Travels in Egypt and the Holy Land*, 122, 185–86; Thompson, "Osman Effendi," 109; Marr, *Cultural Roots of American Islamicism*, 265–68; Willard J. Peterson, "What to Wear? Observation and Participation by Jesuit Missionaries in Late Ming Society," in *Implicit Understandings: Observing, Reporting, and Reflecting on the Encounters Between Europeans and Other Peoples in the Early Modern Era*, ed. Stuart B. Schwartz (Cambridge, U.K.: Cambridge University Press, 1994), 403–21.

11. On gendering the East as feminine, see Said, *Orientalism*, 40, 44, 137–38.

12. Fisk, UTS II, entry for Jan. 10, 1825; "Mr. Fisk's Letter to a Clerical Friend in the Vicinity of Boston." For ideals of evangelical manliness on both sides of the Atlantic, see Greenberg, *Manifest Manhood and the Antebellum American Empire*, 10–13, 139–52; Leonore Davidoff and Catherine Hall, *Family Fortunes: Men and Women of the English Middle Class, 1780–1850* (Chicago: University of Chicago Press, 1987), 108–14; Anne S. Lombard, *Making Manhood: Growing Up Male in Colonial New England* (Cambridge, Mass.: Harvard University Press, 2003); John Tosh, *A Man's Place: Masculinity and the Middle-Class Home in Victorian England* (New Haven, Conn.: Yale University Press, 1999); Twells, *Civilizing Mission and the English Middle Class*, 53; William C. Barnhart, "Evangelicalism, Masculinity, and the Making of Imperial Missionaries in Late Georgian Britain, 1795–1820," *Historian* 67, no. 4 (2005): 712–32.

13. Eliza Griswold offers a superb account of Graham's ministries and the conservative evangelical influence on foreign policy in the Sudan and elsewhere during the George W. Bush administration; see Eliza Griswold, *The Tenth Parallel: Dispatches from the Fault Line Between Christianity and Islam* (New York: Farrar, Straus and Giroux, 2010), esp. 83–87. On muscular Christianity, see Clifford Putney, *Muscular Christianity: Manhood and Sports in Protestant America, 1880–1920* (Cambridge, Mass.: Harvard University Press, 2001); Gail Bederman, *Manliness and Civilization: A Cultural History of Gender and Race in the United States, 1880–1917* (Chicago: University of Chicago Press, 1995); and Clare Pettit, *Dr. Livingstone, I Presume? Missionaries, Journalists, Explorers, and Empire* (Cambridge,

Mass.: Harvard University Press, 2007). For background on neoconservative foreign policy in the Middle East, see McAlister, *Epic Encounters*, 288-90, 302.

14. Sereno Edwards Dwight, "The Greek Revolution: An Address," in *Select Dis-
courses of Sereno Edwards Dwight, D.D., Pastor of the Park Street Church*, by
William T. Dwight (Boston, 1851), 370, 374-76; *Christian Watchman*, Feb. 8,
1823; *New-Bedford Mercury*, Dec. 26, 1823; "Mr. Baylie's Speech," *New-Bedford
Mercury*, Feb. 6, 1824; *Newburyport Herald*, Dec. 16, 1823 (reprint from *Boston
Evening Gazette*); Address of the Committee for the Relief of the Greeks in Bos-
ton, Dec. 19, 1823, *Independent Chronicle and Boston Patriot*, Jan. 14, 1824; *North
American Review* 17, no. 41 (Oct. 1823): 420; William Channing Woodbridge, *A
System of Universal Geography* (Hartford, 1824), 178-79, 211; *Connecticut Herald*
(New Haven), Dec. 23, 1823; *National Gazette and Literary Register*, Feb. 5, 1824.
See also "Address of the Committee of the Greek Fund in the City of New York,
to the People of the United States," *Connecticut Herald* (New Haven), Dec. 23,
1823; Gregory Townsend Bedell, *The Cause of the Greeks* (Philadelphia, 1824);
*Salem Gazette*, Feb. 6, 1824; Ezekiel G. Gear, *A Sermon, Delivered at the Taking
Up of a Collection for the Benefit of the Greeks* (Ithaca, N.Y., 1824); *Norwich Courier*, Dec. 24, 1823. Secondary accounts include David Mayers, *Dissenting Voices
in America's Rise to Power* (Cambridge, U.K.: Cambridge University Press,
2007), 56-79; Edward Mead Earle, "American Interest in the Greek Cause, 1821-
1827," *American Historical Review* 33, no. 1 (Oct. 1927), 44-63; Myrtle A. Cline,
*American Attitude Toward the Greek War of Independence, 1821-1828* (Ph.D.
diss., Columbia University, 1930); Wheatcroft, *Infidels*, 237-40; Larrabee, *Hellas
Observed*, 29-30; Justin McCarthy, *The Turk in America: The Creation of an Enduring Prejudice* (Salt Lake City: University of Utah Press, 2010), 19-31. Even
before their struggle for independence began, Greek immigrants to the United
States reinforced this image of the Turks; see Bird, "Journal of a Vacation in
Boston in 1819," entry for Sept. 27, 1819, Bird Papers.

15. *Baltimore Patriot and Mercantile Advertiser*, Sept. 20, 1823; *Times, and Hartford
Advertiser*, Aug. 26, 1823, and Jan. 20, 1824; *Salem Gazette*, Jan. 30, 1824; *Museum
of Foreign Literature, Science, and Art*, Jan.-June 1823.

16. Fisk's private views of the Greek conflict remained complicated. His journal includes a conversation with a Greek refugee from Scio who "was there when the
Turks destroyed the place but he was saved by a Turkish judge who concealed
him and afterwards sent him away privately." More outspoken was the missionary printer Daniel Temple, after he met a man from Vermont who stopped at
Malta en route to join Greek forces; he advised him to "go about a better business than redressing the wrongs sword in hand of other nations" and "rather to
take up arms with the oppressed slaves of the west Indies and our own country
against their cruel masters." See Fisk, MJ II, May 17, 1823; Temple to Bird and
Goodell, Oct. 24, 1824, AMDC; see also Anderson to Temple, April 13, 1825,
ABC 1.01, vol. 5, ABCFM HU.

17. *Guardian, or Youth's Religious Instructor*, June 1, 1823; excerpt from a work titled
*All Religions and Religious Ceremonies* in the *Hampshire Gazette*, June 2, 1824;

*Newburyport Herald* (reprint from *Boston Gazette*), Dec. 16, 1823; *Providence Gazette*, Jan. 1, 1823; *New-England Galaxy and United States Literary Adviser,* May 9, 1823; biography of Muhammad from the *New Edinburgh Encyclopedia,* reproduced in *Hampshire Gazette*, Dec. 10, 1823; *New-Hampshire Patriot and State Gazette*, Sept. 29, 1823; *Alexandria Herald*, May 14, 1823; *Portland Advertiser*, Jan. 14, 1824; Woodbridge, *System of Universal Geography*, 178–79. For examples of American coverage of the Pera fire, see *New-Hampshire Patriot and State Gazette*, June 2, 1823; *Vermont Journal* (Windsor, Vt.) and *American Federalist Columbian Centinel* (Boston), Sept. 6, 1823; *Spectator* (New York), June 13, 1823; *Boston Recorder*, May 31, 1823.

18. King to Moses Stuart, March 19, 1823, ABCFM, reel 513; King journal, Jan. 21–May 4, 1824, entry for April 17, and King journal, July 10 and 21, 1824, ABCFM, reel 515; Bird missionary journal from Jan. 1824, entry for Nov. 23, 1824, Bird Papers; Fisk, UTS II, July 10, 1824, Jan. 29, Feb. 9, 10, 24, and March 21, 1825; *MH*, Nov. and Dec. 1825; see also "Extracts from Wolff's Journal," *JE* 8 (1824): 280, 368. D'Ohsson described at length the popularity of divination, magic, and prodigies among Ottoman Muslims, but he did not attribute these beliefs to the influence of Islam. (D'Ohsson, *Tableau général de l'empire Ottoman*, 1:134–64.)

19. Holifield, *Theology in America*, 173–307; see also Mark A. Noll, "The Rise and Long Life of the Protestant Enlightenment in America," in *Knowledge and Belief in America: Enlightenment Traditions and Modern Religious Thought*, ed. William M. Shea and Peter A. Huff (Washington, D.C.: Woodrow Wilson Center Press, 1995), 88–124; Bebbington, *Evangelicalism in Modern Britain*, 74; Brian Stanley, "Christian Missions and the Enlightenment: A Reevaluation," in Stanley, *Christian Missions and the Enlightenment*, 2–4. Kenneth Cracknell traces the identification of all non-Christian religions as idolatry or superstition directly to the premium placed on enlightened reason by evangelical Protestants. (Kenneth Cracknell, *Justice, Courtesy, and Love: Theologians and Missionaries Encountering World Religions, 1846–1914* [London: Epworth Press, 1995], 14–20.) Jonathan Boyarin's work has shaped my thinking about the ways in which imagining Muslims helped to create evangelical identity; see esp. Jonathan Boyarin, *The Unconverted Self: Jews, Indians, and the Identity of Christian Europe* (Chicago: University of Chicago Press, 2009), 52–53.

20. King journal, Jan. 21–May 4, entry for April 23, ABCFM, reel 515; Fisk, UTS II, March 28, 1825.

21. Fisk, MJ II, Feb. 12 and March 9, 1824, Fisk, UTS II, Feb. 24, 1825; Bird missionary journal from Jan. 1824, Feb. 10, 1824, Bird Papers; Fisk to Evarts, May 25, 1824, ABCFM, reel 502. Here was a point of no small import to Fisk, because praying to Muhammad would make Muslims less than monotheists and more like pagans. Other difficulties would also have complicated Fisk's exchanges with Muslims about religion: inexact translations could have lost or confused precise meanings, and some native informants might have deliberately misinformed Fisk.

22. *MR*, Jan. 1825, 38–39; the author was almost certainly William Jowett. For Fisk's exchanges with Khaleel, see UTS II: the descent of the Qur'an from heaven over

twenty-three years (Feb. 15); fasting during Ramadan (Feb. 16); the soul's fate immediately after death (Feb. 16); the five duties of Islam and the description of a pilgrimage to Mecca (Feb. 17); the penalty for apostasy (Feb. 18); rules about charging interest for loans (Feb. 23); the primacy of Muhammad's soul in the order of creation and the miraculous events surrounding Muhammad's birth (Feb. 28); Muhammad's treatment of idolaters contrasted with his treatment of Christians and Jews (March 1); millennialism (March 2); sinless prophets, Mary's status, and the character of a true martyr (March 3); the belief that humans cannot sin merely by bad intentions, only by actions (March 9); Muhammad's miracles, conversion of Jews to Islam, and the crucifixion of Judas in place of Jesus (March 10); modes of prayer (March 21). For debates between Fisk and the sheikh, see the following entries: whether Islam spread through force (Feb. 22); whether Jesus is the son of God (Feb. 24); whether the prophets were without sin (March 3); the nature of paradise (March 4); whether eclipses were a sign of God's displeasure (March 8); their method of reading the Qur'an (March 28). King was in Jaffa at this time, and he appears to have attended Fisk's first session with Khaleel, but no mention of King appears thereafter. UTS II, Feb. 2, 1825.

23. Fisk, UTS II, July 10, 1824, and for 1825: light from Mecca (Jan. 29); the jinn and divination (Feb. 9, 10, 24, March 21); tree in paradise (Feb. 26); Muslim cosmology, exchange over the nature of paradise (March 4, 21); "Island of the Girls" (March 9); bridge of the Mohammedans (March 21). In time, too, the poetic grandeur of Islamic cosmology came to capture Fisk's imagination. His notes dwelled on the sheikh's account of how "under our earth there are seven earths each of the same size as ours, with inhabitants, beasts, sun, moon and stars," and that the "arch of heaven comes down to the circumference of the earth so that the 7 earths and 7 heavens together form a globe."

24. King to the Paris Missionary Society, April 18, 1825, entries for Jan. 22 and March 25, 1825, ABCFM, reel 515; King to Mr. and Mrs. Wilder, Oct. 27, 1824, Antioch, Jonas King Papers, SCAWC; Cook journal, April 14, 1824, WMMSA; *MH*, Feb. 1827; Light, *Travels*, 2:132, 198, 204–5, 228, 246; Burckhardt, *Travels in Syria and the Holy Land*, 40, 351, 460–62, 517–21; Waddington and Hanbury, *Journal of a Visit to Some Parts of Ethiopia*, 42.

25. Fisk, UTS II, all entries for 1825: contracting marriage, divorce, and remarriage of divorced and widowed women (Feb. 18, 21); veiling (Feb. 23); women in paradise (Feb. 9 and 24, March 4); polygamy, penalties for adultery, wife beating (March 5). For a contrasting view of Muhammad's teachings with respect to women, see Aslan, *No god but God*, 61–66.

26. Fisk, UTS II, March 12 and 28, 1825; Evarts to Fisk, Aug. 14, 1824, June 24, 1825, Evarts to Temple, Nov. 6, 1824, and Anderson to Bird, April 5, 1825, ABC 1.01, vol. 5, ABCFM HU; Temple to Evarts, Dec. 10, 1824, ABCFM, reel 514.

27. Fisk, UTS II, April 21–May 9, 1825; Buckingham, *Travels in Palestine*, 172; see also Fisk, UTS I, Oct. 12, 1820.

28. King journal to the Paris Missionary Society, April 18, 1825, entries for Feb. 23 to May 9, ABCFM, reel 515, reprinted in full, *MH*, Feb. 1827.

29. Fisk to Temple, July 5, 1825, Beirut, ABCFM, reel 502; Fisk, UTS II, May 12, 1825; King journal to the Paris Missionary Society, April 18, 1825, entries for May 10 and 12, ABCFM, reel 515, reprinted in full, *MH*, March 1827.

30. Evarts to King, June 24, 1826, ABC 1.01, vol. 6, ABCFM HU; King to Evarts, Oct. 18, 22, 27, Nov. 27, and Dec. 14, 1827, ABCFM, reel 502; Evarts to Henry Hill, April 29, 1825, Savannah, and Feb. 2, 1826, ABC 11, vol. 2 (microfilm copy) ABCFM, HU; *Christian Register*, Oct. 27, 1827; *New-York Spectator*, Oct. 19, 1827; *Farmer's Cabinet*, Oct. 27, 1827; *Western Luminary*, Jan. 30, 1828; *Christian Watchman*, Feb. 8, 1828; "Extract of a Letter from a Student in the Theological Seminary at Princeton," *Western Luminary*, Jan. 30, 1828; *Hampshire Gazette*, Nov. 7, 1827.

31. Bond, *Memoir of Fisk*, 435; Fisk to Evarts, June 21, 1825, and Fisk to Temple, Sept. 19, 1825, ABCFM, reel 502; Goodell to Temple, Sept. 5, 1825, ABCFM, reel 503; Bird and Goodell to Evarts, Oct. 25, 1825, ABCFM, reel 515; Goodell to Temple, Oct. 18, 1825, Goodell Papers. Fisk's request for English's book is on the back of the front cover of Fisk, UTS II, headed "September 20 1825 by Mr. King." Rufus Anderson advised Bond on the best publishing strategy for maximizing profits from the sale of his memoir of Fisk; see Anderson to Bond, March 25, 1826, ABC, 1.01, vol. 6, ABCFM HU.

32. Perhaps best known is the remark of an unnamed aide to President George Bush, widely believed to be Karl Rove, in the course of an interview in 2004 with the journalist Ronald Suskind: "We're an empire now, and when we act, we create our own reality. And while you're studying that reality—judiciously, as you will—we'll act again, creating other new realities, which you can study too, and that's how things will sort out." Cited in Mark Danner, "Rumsfeld: Why We Live in His Ruins," *New York Review of Books*, Feb. 6, 2014, 36–40.

EPILOGUE

1. *MR*, Jan. 1826, 51; Oren, *Power, Faith, and Fantasy*, 120–48, 210–27, 283–92; Field, *From Gibraltar to the Middle East*, 153–65, 176–86, 199–205, 266–74, 285–97, 345–59; Sharkey, *American Evangelicals in Egypt*, 50–51, 63–71, 90–95. Missionaries made few converts even among Eastern Christians, but one of that number became a bona fide martyr to their faith. He was Asaad Shidiak, a teacher, poet, and scribe who helped King to translate and circulate his "Farewell Letter"; he died five years later after a long imprisonment in a Maronite convent for refusing to abjure his Protestant beliefs. (King journal, May 18, 1825, ABCFM, reel 515; Makdisi, *Artillery of Heaven*, 75–79, 93, 103–37.)

2. A copy of King's "Farewell Letter," Sept. 5, 1826, translated from the Arabic, appears in ABCFM, reel 502 and also in Jonas King, *The Oriental Church and the Latin* (New York, 1865); King to Wilder, Aug. 13, 1824, King Papers; *New-York Observer*, Dec. 24, 1825; Goodell to Temple, Feb. 23, March 16, and April 28, 1824, ABCFM, reel 503. King's militant anti-Catholicism, his frequent references to the prophetic writings of the Bible in connection with both Catholics and

Muslims, and his close ties to Wilder and Drummond, both key players in the Continental Society, suggest that his own religious beliefs hewed closely to those of the proto-Fundamentalist strain emerging in British evangelicalism. John Wolffe has shown that by the 1820s the evangelical movement on both sides of the Atlantic had begun "to acquire a more dogmatic and more explicitly anti-Catholic temper." See Wolffe, *Protestant Crusade in Great Britain*, 1–64; Wolffe, "Transatlantic Perspective," 293–94.

3. King journal, July 28, 1823–Sept. 22, 1823, ABCFM, reel 513; Burckhardt, *Travels in Syria and the Holy Land*, 184, 189, 193; Jowett, *Christian Researches in Syria*, 16, 79; *MR*, Dec. 1824, 542; Makdisi, *Artillery of Heaven*, 72–95. To read King's journals from his time at Dayr el-Qamar is to marvel at its inhabitants' restraint in the face of his provocations. They could not have been surprised, because many Syrian Christians had long since concluded that the "English" were heretics. A few years earlier and a little farther south, James Silk Buckingham had encouraged some Catholic laymen to air their views about the religion—or lack thereof—among Britons. Some insisted that none of the English believed in the existence of God, while others regarded it as even more shocking that they "did not bow to the Pope" or "hold the Virgin Mary in esteem" or wear the crucifix. King's presence thus presented Dayr el-Qamar's people with the chance to find out how outrageous "English" beliefs really were. Then, too, Mount Lebanon's overlord, Emir Bashir, had maintained friendly relations with British naval officers and consuls since Napoleon's attacks on the Syrian coast twenty years earlier. To Dayr el-Qamar's residents, suffering King seemed a small price for cultivating the emir's continued goodwill along with that of the British, who, as the company of Syrian Catholics had assured Buckingham, "always paid twice as much as the people of any other nation for any service rendered to them." Besides, they added, what with "their wealth, their wisdom, and proficiency in the black art," nothing was more certain than the British "being the greatest in this world whatever fate they might be doomed to in the next." The emir's ties to the British may also account for his tolerating Lady Hester Stanhope, the eccentric niece of William Pitt the Younger and a longtime resident of Mount Lebanon. King parlayed Wilder's connections into a meeting with her, and his patented charm overcame her distaste for missionaries long enough for Lady Hester to arrange for his lodgings with the Doumani family. (Buckingham, *Travels to Palestine*, 460–62; King journal, July 7 and 17, 1823, King to Evarts, Sept. 21, 1822, and Bird to Anderson, Oct. 20, 1823, ABCFM, reel 513; Haines, *Jonas King*, 129–30; Fisk, MJ II, July 7 and 8, 1823; Cook journal, June 5, 1824, WMMSA.)

4. Goodell to Temple, March 16, 1824, ABCFM, reel 503; Temple to Anderson, Dec. 11, 1823, Daniel Temple's journal kept at Malta, Feb. to Sept. 1822, entry for March 17, and Bird to Evarts, Oct. 14, 1823, ABCFM, reel 513; Bird to Anderson, March 27, 1824, and March 14, 1826, ABCFM, reel 514; Goodell and Bird to Evarts, Sept. 6, 1824, ABCFM, reel 515; Anderson to Bird, Oct. 4, 1825, ABC 1.01,

vol. 6, ABCFM HU; Bird missionary journal, May 13 and 28, 1824, Bird Papers; *MH*, Sept. 25, 1825; Bird to a friend in New Haven, April 9, 1824, Jerusalem, in *Christian Watchman*, Oct. 16, 1824; Cook to Taylor, Aug. 13, 1824, WMMSA; Temple to Bird, March 27, 1825, AMDC; see also King's reports of his trip back to the United States in *MH*, April, Nov., Dec. 1826 and March, Nov. 1827. Fisk shared with the readers of the Morse brothers' newspaper his exchange with a priest from Philadelphia touring Palestine who ventured that those put to death by the Inquisition "generally deserved it." "I believe many Protestants begin to think that Popery has of late assumed a more mild form . . . and in the United States if anywhere," Fisk concluded. "But Protestants ought to remember that it is Papal policy to be mild until they have power to be severe." (Fisk to Richard or Sidney Morse, May 20, 1824, *New-York Observer*, Nov. 13, 1824; Fisk, MJ II, April 10, 1824.)

5. Important sources on antebellum anti-Catholicism include Ryan K. Smith, *Gothic Arches, Latin Crosses: Anti-Catholicism and American Church Designs in the Nineteenth Century* (Chapel Hill: University of North Carolina Press, 2006); Jon Gjerde, *Catholicism and the Shaping of Nineteenth-Century America*, ed. S. Deborah Kang (New York: Cambridge University Press, 2012), 1–60; Ray Allen Billington, *The Protestant Crusade, 1800–1860* (New York: Macmillan, 1938); John Davis, "Catholic Envy: The Visual Culture of Protestant Desire," in *The Visual Culture of American Religions*, ed. David Morgan and Sally M. Promey (Berkeley: University of California Press, 2001), 105–28; Jenny Franchot, *Roads to Rome: The Antebellum Protestant Encounter with Catholicism* (Berkeley: University of California Press, 1994); John Wolffe, "Anti-Catholicism and Evangelical Identity in Britain and the United States, 1830–1860," in *Evangelicalism: Comparative Studies of Popular Protestantism in North America, the British Isles, and Beyond, 1700–1990*, ed. Mark A. Noll, David W. Bebbington, and George A. Rawlyk (New York: Oxford University Press, 1994), 179–97.

6. Despite their many commonalities with Roman Catholic belief and liturgy, the Greek Orthodox did not recognize the spiritual leadership of the pope and maintained frosty relations with Rome generally. On King's career in Greece, see Angelo Repousis, "'The Devil's Apostle': Jonas King's Trial Against the Greek Hierarchy in 1852 and the Pressure to Extend U.S. Protection for Missionaries Overseas," *Diplomatic History* 33, no. 5 (Nov. 2009): 807–37; Repousis, *Greek-American Relations from Monroe to Truman*, 71–91; Hewitt, *Williams College and Foreign Missions*, 83–93; Larrabee, *Hellas Observed*, 182, 194–205; Field, *From Gibraltar to the Middle East*, 204–6, 290–92. Throughout his years in Greece, King's reports were a staple of the American religious press, and he published a summary of his embattled relations with and attacks on Greek Orthodoxy in *The Oriental Church and the Latin*, 34–127. By contrast, King's memoir of the Palestine mission, published in 1859, appeared only in French.

7. Jonathan Riley-Smith, review of *God of Battles: Holy Wars of Christianity and Islam*, by Peter Partner, *Speculum* 75, no. 3 (July 2000): 719–21.

8. Griswold, *Tenth Parallel*, 83–92; Hutchison, *Errand to the World*, 91–209; Kidd, *American Christians and Islam*, 120–64; Sarah H. Ruble, *The Gospel of Freedom and Power: Protestant Missionaries and Culture After World War II* (Chapel Hill: University of North Carolina Press, 2012), 117–33; Sharkey, *American Evangelicals in Egypt*, 90–178.

# ACKNOWLEDGMENTS

It feels like flying with one wing, writing without being able to ask advice from my mentor, Edmund Morgan. Fortunately, two other trusted critics, Richard Godbeer and Ryan Smith, stand at the ready, unsparing as only former students can be. I owe another large intellectual debt to several learned colleagues at the University of Delaware who have brought me up to speed on countless subjects: Anne Boylan, James Brophy, Peter Kolchin, Rudi Matthee, Patricia Sloane-White, and Owen White. Others who have seen me through this project with their expertise and encouragement include Joe Califano, Mary Kupiec Cayton, Catherine Clinton, Emily Conroy-Krutz, James West Davidson, Jerrold Epstein, Ernie Freeburg, Angie Hoseth, Mary Kelley, Timothy Marr, Louisa Bond Moffitt, and Danielle Rougeau. Librarians throughout New England and New York have also made invaluable contributions, even if some might have wanted to hide in the stacks when they saw me coming yet again. Most notable is the longtime (and now emeritus) head of special collections at Middlebury College, Andrew Wentink—every scholar's dream archivist—who introduced me to the single most important source for this study. After swearing never to get an agent, now I can't imagine publishing a book without the help of Dan Green, who set me up with two extraordinary editors. Dan Gerstle helped me to develop the possibilities that he glimpsed in an early draft, and Alex Star favored successive versions with his sharp eye and this author with his unstinting intellectual generosity. Alex's assistant, Laird Gallagher, who answered my e-mails even on weekends, shepherded the manuscript through the press, ably supported by its production editor, Elizabeth Gordon, and production manager, Peter Richardson. Thanks also to the designer, Abby Kagan, and to Debra Helfand.

The blame for making me feel equal to anything—this book included—belongs to my fast friends. For decades of inspiration, I am indebted to Emily Grosholz, poet and philosopher; Lisa Keamy, physician and gardener; my niece, Rachel Speer, neuroscientist and Sacred Harp singer; and my sister, Anne Heyrman-Hart, scholar of world religions and culinary deity.

That leaves the best friend of all, my husband, Tom Carter, who was until his retirement a logistics specialist in the Office of the Secretary of Defense. As we followed the path of the first Palestine missionaries through the Levant over the last several years, he developed other remarkable skills—haggling with shopkeepers in Egyptian bazaars, finding the most splendid mosques in Turkey, and saying exactly the right things to guards at the border between Syria and Lebanon. I feel so lucky, having a boon companion. And never luckier than on that September day in 2001 when he called from the Pentagon, told me not to worry, and then came safely home.

# INDEX

and, 85–86, 208, 215, 216, 282n22; in
Jerusalem, 138, 145, 170, 296n27,
303n4, 304n7; Jowett and, 97, 101, 113,
125–26, 286n7, 300n15, 304n9; King as
replacement in Palestine mission for,
192, 252; martyr-like devotion of, 43,
248; at Middlebury College, 24–25,
72, 85; New Divinity conversion of,
25, 34; privileged family background
of, 24, 59, 79, 93; in Smyrna, 122–26,
130–32, 161, 162, 292n5–93n, 294nn13,
14, 309n3; in Vermont, 78, 85, 295n21;
voyage to Smyrna of, 94, 97, 98, 111,
119
Parsons, Lucretia, 267n19
Parsons, Silas, 264n8
Pearce, Nathaniel, 301n16
Persia, 4, 73, 84–85, 161–63, 251, 266n16,
310n11; Fisk's and Parsons's mission
to, 40–41, 46, 84; Martyn in, 112–13,
119–20, 172, 197, 203, 208, 287n13;
Wahhabi influence in, 114, 270n36; see
also Shiraz
Persian language, 103, 107, 109, 110, 131,
137, 184, 194, 198, 266n16, 287nn11, 12
Peru, 73
Peter, St., 306n22
Pewett, Thomas, 149, 155, 301n16
Philadelphia, 52, 54, 78, 109, 254, 302n19
Philistines, 246
Pitt, Joseph, 300n11
Pitt, William, 146
Pitt, William, the Younger, 322n3
Plea for the West (Beecher), 253
Pliny the Elder, 13
Pliny the Younger, 13, 261n9
Polymenos, Emmanuel, 116–19
Polymenos, Spiridion, 116, 119
Porl, John, 148–49
Pratt, Josiah, 115–17, 127, 285n2, 290n23
Presbyterians, 7, 23, 58, 60, 68, 75, 202,
237, 255, 258n3, 264n11, 278n1
Present State of Turkey (Thornton), 89, 94
Prideaux, Humphrey, 269n32

Priestley, Joseph, 58, 182, 183
Princeton Theological Seminary, 247
Procopius, 166
Protestant Reformation, 26, 53, 100, 126,
132, 150, 158
Prussia, 87
Ptolemies, 110
Puritans, 30, 72, 159

Qajar Persia, 108, 109
Quakers, 7
Qur'an (Koran), 45, 61, 62, 90, 107, 177,
269n32, 273n10, 295n24, 308n32,
313n29; commonalities of Bible and,
15, 29, 114, 212–13, 290n23; denigration
of, 234–35; divine revelation of, 11, 52,
74, 175, 185, 307n28, 319n22–20n;
Fisk's studies of, 14–15, 160, 162, 169,
195, 223, 238, 241–42, 248; King's
tutoring in, 217, 223, 237; Martyn on,
109–10, 112, 136, 157, 181, 219, 307n28;
Orientalists on, 51–52, 67, 110–11, 157;
Sale's translation of, 37, 39, 47, 50, 156,
187, 273n7; verses of, 19, 44, 71, 97, 122,
145, 164, 191, 196, 221, 238, 242; Wolff's
reading of, 177, 198

Ramadan, 3, 52, 152, 320n22
Rangoon, 74
Reland, Adriaan, 48–50
Renaissance, 273n8
Renegade, The (Reynolds), 152–53
renegades (renegadoes), 150–56, 161, 162,
171, 298n6, 299n7, 300nn11, 12,
300n16–301n, 301n17, 305n18, 316n8;
see also English, George
Republican Party, 70
Reynolds, Frederick, 152–53
Richardson, Robert, 115–16, 118, 133,
291nn25, 29, 305n14
Robbins, Archibald, 151–52
Robison, John, 263n4

## A Note About the Author

Christine Leigh Heyrman is the Robert W. and Shirley P. Grimble Professor of American History at the University of Delaware. She is the author of *Commerce and Culture: The Maritime Communities of Colonial Massachusetts, 1690–1750* and *Southern Cross: The Beginnings of the Bible Belt*, winner of the 1998 Bancroft Prize.